THE MESSENGERS

Clelland, Mike. *The Messengers: Owls, Synchronicity and the UFO Abductee*
Second edition, September 2020.
The text has been updated for clarity and typos. Some accounts have had additional information added to reflect new developments. Some names in the book are pseudonyms, and some minor details have been purposely altered to protect the anonymity of persons involved.

ISBN 978-1733980814
Audiobook and ebook available
Cover design and illustrations by Mike Clelland
Edited by Suzanne Chancellor
Publisher's website: www.mikeclelland.com

First edition published in the United States by Richard Dolan Press, Dec. 3, 2015

THE MESSENGERS
Owls, Synchronicity and the UFO Abductee

by Mike Clelland

Table of Contents

Acknowledgments

This book is dedicated to everyone who has reached out to me with their stories. Without their sincerity, this book would not have been possible. So many wonderful individuals have helped me with this book, yet some have asked for anonymity. These are difficult issues, so I understand why anyone would want to remain unknown. A number of accounts are told using a pseudonym, or just their first name. There are a very few places where unimportant details were purposely changed to better hide the identity of the witness. This book is very much a product of the digital age, and a lot of the quoted correspondence is cited from email. There are points throughout where these passages are revised very slightly for clarity and grammar.

I owe a debt of gratitude to all these comrades, and so many more:

Aaron, Colin Andrews, Annalie, Kim Arnold, Ashlee, Tracie Austin, Kenneth Bakerman, Brigitte Barclay, Kevin Bartell, Anthony and Rachel Beckett, Ben, David Biedny, Joan Bird, Christopher Bledsoe, Sr., Hakan Blomqvist, Brendan, Anya Briggs, Charis Melina Brown, Will Bueche, Grant Cameron, Kristen Lee Cardinal, Kim Carlsberg, James Carman, John Carpenter, Alan Caviness, Suzanne Chancellor, Will Christie, Carol Cleveland, Heather Clewett-Jachowski, Joseph-Mark Cohen, Steve Colbern, Janet Elizabeth Colli, Peter Collori, Lorin Cutts, Cynthia, Megan Dafoe, Miriam Delicado, Derek, Richard Dolan, Shelly Dove, Adrianne Dumas, Stephen and Lisa Dyer, Erika Earles, Peter Faust, Tom Fieger, Lorraine Flaherty, Marla Frees, Lonn Friend, Jill G., Suzanne Gordon, Ph.D., Robbie Graham, Alan Green, Alan Green, Kim Greenfield, Melanie Griffin, Rosemary Ellen Guiley, Gypsy Woman, Cam Hale, Micah Hanks, Lucretia Heart, Lauren Heeren, Sesh Heri, Rey Hernandez, Dr. Bob Hieronimus, Race Hobbs, Chris Holly, Cathy Hohmeyer, Budd Hopkins, Michael M. Hughes, Niara Terela Isley, Bert Janssen, Natascha Jatzeck, Jack Jawczak, Joe, Ron Johnson, JT, Kelly, Christina Knowles, Christopher Knowles, William Konkolesky, Susan Kornaki, Melissa

1

Kriger, Jujuolui Kuita, Barbara Lamb, Kewaunee Lapseritis, Lisette Larkins, Regan Lee, Eve Lorgen, Joe Lewels, Rob and Trish MacGregor, Susan MacLeod, Jordan Maxwell, Laurie McDonald, Ben McGuire, Bonnie Jean Mitchel, Joe Montaldo, Meghan Moriarty, Nigel and Helen Mortimer, Pamela Necerato-Loffred, John Norris, Christopher O'Brien, Sebastian Penraeth, Tom Phillips, Jaymie Phipps, Stephanie Quick, Elizabeth Randall, Raquel, Nick Redfern, Peter Robbins, Alejandro Rojas, Red Pill Junkie, Colin Reid, Mary Rodwell, Corina Saebels, Derek Savory, Phil Schneider, Susana Carvalho Vidigal Silbermann, Peter Maxwell Slattery, Janet Slottje, Jacquelin Smith, Aimee Sparrow, Ryan Sprague, Leo Sprinkle, Audrey Starborn, Brad Steiger, Jeanne Stimson, Denise Stoner, Whitley and Anne Strieber, Nancy Talbot, Lindy Tucker, Jacques Vallee, John W, David Weatherly, Stacey J. Warner, Paul Weston, Maria Wheatley, Gibbs A Williams, Rebecca Hardcastle Wright, PhD, Anthony Ziehut...

After all my years of compulsively reading UFO literature, I was keenly aware of owls as a *screen memory* within the experiences reported by abductees, and felt this might be a possibility. I was hyper-focused on these three owls as they swooped low over us, watched us from trees, and landed on the ground right up close to us. I feel confident in declaring those were, in fact, real owls.

...and a great big heartfelt thank you to Andrea Lisette Villiere.

Foreword

by Richard M. Dolan

You are about to read one of the most original books ever written on UFOs, one that will make any thoughtful person ask fundamental questions about the nature of reality itself. More than any work in recent memory, it successfully ties the UFO phenomenon not simply to possible extraterrestrial intelligences, but to synchronicities, ancient archetypes, dreams, shamanistic experiences, magic, personal transformation, and death.

And owls. Because Mike Clelland has gathered together compelling and persuasive accounts from innumerable people who have had UFO sightings and apparent abduction experiences in conjunction with absolutely bizarre experiences with owls. Yes, real owls, not owls as screen memories (although as anyone familiar with abduction research knows, this has often been reported).

The accounts of these people—including those of Mike himself—suggest undeniable synchronicities at work. That is, coincidences that are highly meaningful to the persons involved. So meaningful in some cases that they seem staged for that person, and usually in a manner that only that person could decipher.

This is heady stuff for those of us raised in the standard western-based materialistic rendition of reality, one with a comprehensible cause and effect, and one in which there are no unseen intelligences playing us like characters in a video game. And yet, as one goes through account after account of meticulously documented experiences, it becomes hard to avoid thinking along these lines.

Some of the synchronicities in this book defy common sense. Mike writes about two women living only 43 miles apart from each other in Massachusetts with experiences so parallel, with such similarity in detail, that they seem like bookends. Both had a kind of mystical experience after a focused intention that had a profound effect on their lives. Both of them had this experience while lying on their outdoor hammock. For both of them, their event started while they were alone, and both were soon joined by their child and husband. They were even friends on Facebook, alt-

3

hough unaware of each other's hammock experience. They even look remarkably alike. For one of the women, the mystical encounter involved two owls; for the other, it was the sighting of a UFO. As Mike wrote, "it feels like the owl and UFO are, in many ways, playing the same metaphysical role in each story." Even stranger perhaps, Mike happened to interview these two women one day apart from each other.

Other stories included here suggest that owls play a role in a number of alien or UFO encounters. One witness stated that his contact experiences "were often preceded or followed by the sound of owls on top of my house hooting." Others seem to have been directed to see UFOs because of actions by owls. In one case, a husband and wife were relaxing together on a dock when the hooting of an owl led directly to the couple seeing an inexplicable UFO high in the sky.

Mike Clelland has made several contributions toward understanding UFOs and the phenomenon of encounters with apparent alien beings. One of these is his notion of "the maybe people." The idea of UFO abduction is fraught with preconceptions and baggage, and a very specific idea has emerged of what it is supposed to involve. There are certainly accounts that play out with all the harrowing details of getting plucked from a lonely road or a bedroom at night. But there is a more subtle gray zone, where large numbers of people have described many of the strange aspects relating to this mystery, yet without any UFO contact. Mike's concept of "the maybe people" underscores the complexity of this phenomenon.

But this is more than a UFO book. In these accounts, the presence of owls signify important personal and transformative events in a person's life. Certainly, this can include a UFO encounter, but these owls are also serving as harbingers of other forms of spiritual awakening. And they are connected to death—the ultimate transformation. What's interesting is that this is precisely how ancient people understood owls. It is in fact a restatement of their ancient archetype: the ability to peer into the darkness representing an ability to penetrate the dark mysteries of existence.

One of these stories concerns a woman who saw a large white owl outside her window as she was jolted out of a sound sleep. It sat on a bare branch, positioned perfectly for her to see it. The next morning, she again woke with a start. Just as she sat up in bed, the phone rang, informing her of the death of a family member. This woman also had multiple UFO sightings, a near-death experience, possessed psychic abilities, and had other strange events occur in her life. As Mike wrote, "it's as if her lifetime of unusual experiences created an opening that morning for an owl to land on that bare branch. It could be that this owl was delivering a message, sad though it may have been, to someone with the life experiences that would allow her to receive it."

Another account described here concerns a man who was literally touched on the forehead by the wing of an owl that flew alongside his car as he drove. The owl and the man locked eyes in "some sort of hypnotic trance" before it glided off. Of course, this itself is practically unheard of, but several other elements make this event mysterious and profound. As Mike takes us into its progressively deeper layers, we see it intimately connecting to the man's medical history, his psychic flashes, a close up UFO sighting from his front door, his long lost sibling, and much more. We discern the pattern of a transcendent intelligence.

Among the most poignant stories in this book concerns a woman who's suicide surely seems to have been prevented by the appearance of an owl at exactly the right moment. The manner in which this happened is, like so many stories in this book, uncanny. The encounter with the owl stunned her, and it triggered a deep realization to face her fears and recognize that life would get better. In this story, like all the others in this book, there are layers of meaning that are made clear as we go deeper into the experience.

Something very odd is going on in our world. It is not simply the manifestation into our physical reality of things that western culture merely considers symbolic or archetypal. It is also that these manifestations appear in a bizarrely synchronistic manner. It is as if someone or some intelligence is pulling the strings of our reality, and doing so in order to tell us something. To teach us.

So, what are these owls doing? Mike believes they are best seen as messengers, hence the title of this book. And what is the message? Somehow, it has to do with transformation, and the need to wake up and pay attention. Pay attention to what is going on in your life, and to the true nature of reality. As he puts it, "When someone is deeply asleep, whispering won't wake them. Sometimes you have to really shake them. If that doesn't work, send in the owls."

Although this book includes intriguing stories from so many people, the main journey here is that of the author himself. Mike Clelland has examined his life with a rare commitment to the truth. It isn't that he planned to undertake this project. Rather, as he said, something triggered it. That something, as strange as it would seem, was owls. When he began exploring his own past with bravery and honesty, he found much more than he had ever imagined. During this process, he went through moments of great duress and even questioned his own sanity. He has now come to terms with his own alien encounters, which he describes here with great detail and power. Indeed, the event he aptly calls his "confirmation event," is nothing short of mind-blowing. It's refreshing, too, that he writes about all this not as a victim, nor as some sort of new age prophet. In telling his story, Mike simply strips away all pretense and dedicates himself to exposing the truth as best he can. As a result, his deeply personal journey is one that we can all relate to.

His research itself was filled with oddities. During the writing of this book, he related to me how the stories themselves would arrive to his email in a synchronistic flurry. And while it is obvious that he has done a great deal of research in creating this wonderful book, he strongly believes that the core of it happened "magically." One might well wonder if a guiding intelligence has simply used him as the conduit for making it happen. Mike seems to feel that way.

Like all works of great originality, *The Messengers* can be hard to describe because there are no clean and neat categories within which to place it. Perhaps the book that feels the most like this one is Whitley Strieber's classic, *Communion*, another profound and personal journey that explores the high strangeness of alien encounters. Even so, *The Messengers* is something new.

I believe Mike Clelland is taking the study of UFOs and what we loosely call the paranormal into a new and fresh direction. It is as if he has opened up a new vision of exploring our reality, a new vein in which to explore and dig further. Answers will be hard to come by. But the questions make it all worthwhile.

Richard M. Dolan
Rochester, New York

Introduction

Owls, whether real or symbolic, are somehow intertwined with the UFO abduction phenomenon. I am firmly convinced of this connection. Why they are connected and what it might mean is another matter.

Seeing an owl in the wild can feel unnerving, they project something intense, almost sinister. Their mere presence has a power. People are in awe of owls, and it's very common for folks to describe an owl sighting as *an honor* or *a blessing.* Throughout the ages the owl has held a place as both wise and evil, and when seeing an owl yourself, it's easy to understand how that mythology has emerged. Those big eyes seem to have the power to pierce the soul.

Owls can navigate the darkness, and this is a metaphor for passing beyond the veil and into the unknown. Ancient sages saw the role of the owl as traveling to and from the hidden places we can't perceive, and bringing back messages from the great beyond.

The owl isn't just a bird with big eyes. *It is a symbol.*

It's easy to project supernatural characteristics onto the owl, something I do more than I should. The owl is an expression of all things mysterious, so when we confront an owl we are confronting a mystery, perhaps *the ultimate mystery.* The same can be said for confronting a UFO.

I love stories. At this point, I have read or heard thousands of amazing owl stories, and I continue to be swept away by the power of what I am hearing. The sheer volume of what I've found, or what has found me, has changed the simplistic way I once looked at the world. There is a sense— a knowing—that a troupe of arcane forces, both physical and mystical, has intersected with our reality.

On one level, this book is merely a set of stories about owls, UFOs and all the emotions that come along with these two overlapping subjects. What is emerging is that real owls are showing up for real people. These mythic birds are still performing their ancient role, messages are still being delivered.

Beyond just a collection of stories, this book is a personal odyssey, an account of my own journey. Both owls and UFOs have somehow invaded my life. I have been confronted with a mystery that is both seductive and scary, and the challenge has been not to shy away from the paranoia and uncertainty that comes with looking inward. My task as an author has been to find meaning in a set of ideas that are, on some level, unknowable.

I haven't given anyone a lie detector test, or performed background checks on the people who have brought me their stories. I am not an academic, and I have no training in investigative techniques. There are only a few stories in this book with multiple witnesses, and in those cases I've made an effort to talk with each person involved. What I want to see is some grand pattern in all these experiences, but what I'm finding won't fit into a clean spreadsheet of data. Instead, it's much more of a mood, or a vibe. Even though each narrative is different, they all evoke a similar feeling, and I am trusting that. It is this ethereal mood I hope to convey, much more than any attempts at conclusions. There are no one-offs in this book, any story here is part of a bigger pattern. What you are reading is a small part of a much larger pool of similar reports.

Some of these stories have the quality of an ancient fable shared around the campfire. My concern is that overly scrutinizing each account might sabotage their deeper meaning. Yes, examining the details and the patterns is required, but I try to keep it to a minimum. I feel these stories should be felt at a heart level, where their true power emerges. One woman described what I am doing as creating a sacred space where these ideas are allowed.

There is a heartfelt depth and power in these owl and UFO accounts, and that includes the ones you aren't hearing. It feels terrible that I can't share more of these remarkable stories here, but this book would have been far too long to include all of them. Just know, that behind each and every anecdote you are about to read is a grand novel that has yet to be written.

I feel a bond and a closeness to the people who have shared so much with me. Their life events are emotional, challenging, and complex—each with their own deeper message. Every person who has shared their experiences with me deserves their own long chapter, if not their own entire biography. Because of that, there is a set of these longer stories in a companion book titled *Stories from The Messengers*.

I am deeply indebted and grateful to every single person who has helped me with this very personal obsession. I appreciate you, from my heart, more than I can ever say.

—Mike Clelland, 2015

PART I

PERCEIVING OWLS

Chapter 1:

Owls at Sunset

Any path is only a path, and there is no affront, to
one-self or to others, in dropping it if that is what your
heart tells you to do. Look at every path closely and
deliberately. Then ask yourself, and yourself alone,
one question, does this path have a heart? If it does,
the path is good; if it doesn't, it is of no use.

—Carlos Castaneda, *The Teachings of Don Juan*

Owls started manifesting in my life with a flurry of weirdness in the autumn of 2006. It happened while camping with a young woman I hardly
knew. Her name is Kristen and we went out for one night in the mountains
near my home.

We had hiked several miles to a beautiful spot, and were sitting together on a big flat rock in the middle of an open meadow. The sun was
setting and it was warm and calm. We talked as I prepared dinner on a
small camp stove. It was that magic moment of twilight time when the
first stars were starting to dot the sky. Our conversation reached a point
where we were opening up about our spiritual beliefs and insights. Listening to Kristen, I recognized something truly impressive about her.
There came a point in our conversation when I felt a really strong and
delightful connection. It was hugely life-affirming.

Right at that moment an owl swooped over us, just a few feet above our heads. This was a beautiful sighting and we were both delighted. Then there was another owl. And then a third.

All three were circling and swooping silently above us. It lasted for over an hour. During this time, we set out our sleeping bags to sleep under the stars. As we lay there looking up at the night sky, the owls would swoop right above our faces, blotting out the stars for a brief instant. Owls have specialized feathers so they are amazingly quiet, and this eerie silence made the entire experience all the more strange.

It was absolutely *magical.*

It was almost three years later when I recognized the synchronistic intensity of the arrival of those owls and the mood of our conversation. I called Kristen and asked if she remembered what we were talking about when that first owl flew above us. This was the moment I realized we were both on exactly the same spiritual wavelength.

Without hesitating, she said, "Oh yeah, I remember exactly what I was saying. *I was trying to articulate my deepest beliefs about God.* It was right at that moment that the owls appeared."

I was shocked at the magnitude of what she said. Whatever was going on, that one detail added a depth to the overall experience that tipped it into the realm of the transcendent.

The morning after Kristen and I saw the owls dawned calm and clear. We hiked a series of beautiful trails, taking a different route back to the car. We talked excitedly, marveling about the owls from the night before. In the final mile of the hike, we met an old girlfriend of mine on the trail. I'll call her Carol (a pseudonym), she was now married, and was walking with her young daughter and son. In the years since we split up, there had been an awkward tension between us. We lived in the same small town, and even though we saw each other often, we never spoke beyond just a cautious hello.

I picked up her boy and carried him while Kristen walked a little bit ahead of us on the trail with her daughter, both of them holding hands. Carol and I had the conversation I'd been waiting to have for over five years. It was calm and hugely reassuring. A short time later, Kristen and I said goodbye to Carol and her kids in the dusty parking lot. After we parted, Kristen excitedly told me that talking with that little girl was the most important thing that had ever happened in her life. I couldn't quite grasp what she said, but there was something about the little girl that reminded Kristen of herself when she was that age.

I should add that four years later, in 2010, I had another chance meeting with Carol, her kids, and a close-up sighting of a great horned owl in full daylight. This shared experience, told later in the book, plays out within a web of heartwarming synchronicities.

Less than a week later, Kristen and I went out camping again. We were in a completely different area of the mountains. Once again, it was only a single night of camping. In the evening, as the sun was setting, we both felt a little bit cold. I suggested we walk up to a nearby hilltop to see the view, this would warm us up a little before going to sleep.

We did the short hike, maybe ten minutes, up to the gently rounded hill. Within seconds of getting to the top, we had the exact same experience. *Three owls appeared and flew around us!* They swooped in close and perched on nearby branches. They eventually landed on the ground, within a few yards of where we stood and stared at us—this is highly unusual behavior, owls standing so close to us. The whole thing lasted about half an hour. Kristen and I just stood there the entire time in a tingly state of astonishment. I think these were short-eared owls, a common species in these mountains. Now this may seem funny, but I'm pretty sure these were the *same* three owls from earlier in the week.

Like before, the experience was absolutely *magical!*

Seeing three owls once was pretty neat, but having the same experience just a few days later was positively bizarre. In the time after this second event, Kristen and I were searching the internet for anything on spirit animals and mystical insights surrounding owls, and the results were curious. One thing kept coming up, the owl is a sign to face your fears, and Kristen felt this was an important message for her.

For me, the intensity of our owl experiences created a weird emotional urgency. I saw the whole thing as terribly important, but couldn't figure out any meaning. I was swallowed up in a kind of fanatical madness, and that made much of our time together really awkward. I'm 18 years older, and this created a lot of weirdness, but at the same time we were seeing each other almost every day. We were constantly emailing and phoning, much of this in an attempt to decipher any deeper meaning to those owls.

Despite the tensions we had a real connection, and our time together was a swirling cloud of cryptic synchronicities. Kristen calls me a "kindred spirit," and that feels like an understatement. She left town about a month after we saw those owls, moving back to her hometown in Michigan.

I posted this story about Kristen and the owls on my blog on March 4th, 2009, and this was only the second day of the blog's incarnation. The very first comment came from none other than Whitley Strieber. He authored what is probably the single most important book on the alien contact experience, *Communion* (1987). I suspect he read the essay and just zipped out a rapid fire reply. That said, I'm impressed at the outright divinity of his comment. He wrote:

> The grays come in threes. They often appear as owls. Contrary to popular belief, they are profoundly surrendered to God. We find this frightening, because we are not. An experience like that is mostly outside of space and time. You need not look back on it. It is always happening for you both and all who know of it, forever. So, thank you!

I was shocked to see his comment at a point when pretty much nobody could have known about my blog. I found out later that my friend Mac Tonnies had sent him a Twitter link to the story. His references to God came before I realized that Kristen had been talking about God at the exact moment of our initial sighting.

I asked Kristen about her feelings on what our shared owl experience meant to her. Below is an excerpt from an email. In it she is responding to my question, as well as Strieber's comment. Here's her thoughtful reply:

> I am all about the divine aspect of this whole thing. Obviously. I like that Whitley said that, about being connected to God. Because that night I saw the owls and whenever I dream of them, that is the benevolent sort of "spirit guide" feeling I get. Not that they are otherworldly, but that they are in-worldly.
>
> Because there's no way that I could explain any of this outside of the context of God. And, you know, not "God" in the "because

the Bible tells me so" sense, but God in the real, eternal, "I know this much is true" sense. And by God I mean the all-that-is.

That's what I felt and that's what I feel...that if anything happened that night, it was definitely some sort of communion with the all-that-is. (As I was just writing that sentence, I remembered that Whitley Strieber's book was called Communion, right?)

Kristen sums up what I feel in my gut, that UFOs are in communion with each other. This book is my attempt to explore one tiny fragment of the overall UFO phenomenon. I know owls are insignificant within such a gargantuan subject, yet on a purely intuitive level, they seem to be reflecting back the *all-that-is*.

Northville Michigan, 1974

Memories that haunted me

I have a set of memories from my youth that paint a disturbing picture—three events that have always haunted me. In 1974, as a twelve-year-old boy, I had a very clear UFO sighting at night. I was with a friend, and we both watched a coffee can-shaped craft out his bedroom window. It was slowly descending and rotating in an eerily smooth motion. It's hard to say how big it was, but it seemed about the size of a van, and it felt close to his home. We watched it gliding downward for maybe less than a minute, and then it disappeared. It didn't fly away—it *vanished*.

A few months later I saw a weird orange flash in the sky. It happened with a friend while walking home from a high school football game on a Friday night. For barely a second, everything above us turned deep orange, then "clicked" back to normal, and we both said, "What just happened?" This was a block away from my house, and when I got home, my parents were angry at me for being out so late. It should have been about 9:30, but it was nearly 11:30. It seems I had about two hours of missing time. The next Monday at school, my friend told me he saw, "A UFO with lights and everything."

I was 30 years old in the winter of 1993, and living alone in a small house in Maine. I woke up in the middle of the night because a bright light was shining into the room. I sat up in bed, looked out my bedroom window, and saw five spindly aliens walking towards the house. These were the typical gray beings, with oversized bald heads and huge black eyes. This should have been terrifying, but I felt absolutely nothing. I was oddly sucked dry of any emotion. After a few moments of looking at these beings, I heard a voice in my head say: "*Oh yes, they're here. Now is the time to put your head on the pillow and black out.*" And that's exactly what I did. The next morning I dismissed the entire thing as a wildly vivid dream, and never bothered to look for footprints in the snow (this event is revisited later in this chapter).

These three events define my more overt experiences. I've also had plenty of less obvious episodes like psychic impressions, hyper-vivid predictive dreams, an obsession with UFOs, and profound synchronicities. Yet, I had spent my life actively denying that there was anything unusual about these heavy-handed memories. But at the same time, the pressure was building. I recognized what it all pointed to, but I was working hard to ignore the implications. The time was rapidly approaching when I would need to look into what I suspected might be at play in my life.

The owl sightings with Kristen came in September of 2006 when I was 44 years old. I had arrived at the point in my life where all these confusing experiences and their UFO implications were refusing to stay buried.

These memories were in the forefront of my mind during both those weird owl episodes in the mountains with Kristen. Right in the moment, as I was looking at those owls, there was an alarm in my head blaring, "This is real! This has something to do with the UFOs!" I was seeing

15

owls, but my mind was screaming UFOs. The message I heard was clear—You are a UFO abductee! This connection might seem illogical, but all I can say is right then I felt a strong sense of knowing. It took great strength to put the lid on that voice in my head and hide it away. The problem was that the owl sightings continued and the pressure kept building.

It was easy to ignore all my UFO experiences, I mean, those just seemed absurd. But I couldn't ignore what was happening with all the owls. When someone is deeply asleep, whispering won't wake them. Sometimes you have to really shake them. If that doesn't work, send in the owls.

The owls came in tandem with a set of insanely powerful synchronicities, and it scared me. Synchronicity is the term for a coincidence that is meaningful to the observer. These experiences have been so vital—and so magical—that the word synchronicity is in the title of this book. For me, there's a blurry line between synchronicity and owls, so much so that they seem like the same thing. I don't think a mere mortal could untangle these arcane threads, so I won't even try. When I saw those owls in the mountains with Kristen, I was stuck in a place of denial. The person I once was is gone, and it's a newer person that's writing this book. It was the owls that changed me.

Seeing those owls with Kristen was the initial awakening event for me, and I'll refer back to those two evenings throughout this book. That experience stands as a sort of baseline, and everything to come will get piled onto that foundation.

Owl in the desert

What follows is a good example of an owl showing up in relation to a UFO sighting; it was told to me by a guy named Derek. There is a lot to the story, implying a depth that goes well beyond the initial event. Derek was camping in the Arizona desert in the summer of 1995 with three friends. Here's what he wrote:

> We had set up our tents in a long canyon with steep walls on either side of us. Two of my friends had gone into a tent to retire early, and I stayed up to talk and star gaze with the other guy. The

night sky was incredible, and we were lying on the desert floor in line with the canyon.

In mid-conversation, I noticed an extremely large owl sitting on top of a cactus maybe 20 feet from where we were lying. I could see it really clearly and I had not seen it land there, nor did I know how long it had been sitting there, but it was staring directly at us. I clearly remember not only feeling really excited at spotting it, but also a little uneasy at how intently it seemed to be watching us. I felt very exposed. I think the scale and openness of the desert kind of struck me in that moment. As soon as I pointed it out to my friend, it took off in flight.

We resumed our conversation and a bit more time passed, maybe 15 minutes or so. As we were talking, a large black triangular craft came from behind us and flew along the top canyon wall to our left. It was wedge shaped, a very dark matte black, and had a row of red lights with smaller white lights between each red light along its side. It flew silently, extremely quickly and completely mirrored, or hugged, the topography of the top of the canyon wall as it flew. It went from entering my peripheral vision towards the horizon in the direction of our feet and out of view in approximately five seconds. That said, I feel like I got a pretty clear look at it. It was really close, maybe 75 yards away. It was large, about two-thirds the size of a commercial airliner. It was completely silent and really fast.

We both immediately sat up and I turned to my friend and asked, "Did you see that?" To which he responded, "Yes." I asked, "What did you see?" His response matched exactly what I described above. I asked him if he thought it could have been an airplane. He didn't think so.

A few days later, Derek saw another unidentified flying object with one of his fellow campers who had been sleeping through his first sighting. They were driving together in Scottsdale, Arizona at about 11 p.m.

My car at the time had a sunroof and we were driving on a long, perfectly straight road that reached to the horizon. As we were chatting, we saw a very brightly lit sphere come over the sunroof and proceed to the horizon centered directly above the road. It was fast, significantly faster than any plane I have ever witnessed, but it stayed visible in the sky far too long to be a meteor. I have no way to know the altitude of the object, but it appeared slightly smaller than a golf ball held at arms' length.

This witness described two strange UFO sightings that were preceded by an owl sighting. The owl was looking directly at him and his friend, and he felt uneasy under its intense gaze. From everything I've heard, the details of his story are curiously *normal*, this includes the owl right before seeing a silent craft. In our follow-up emails, Derek shared some more experiences, including this memory from when he was about seven years old.

One evening I was playing a replica of the arcade version of Pac-man. I was alone in a room in our house with all the lights off. That's a little unusual because I've been scared of the dark for most of my life, and was especially so as a child. I remember as I was playing the game, something very unusual happened. In an instant, it felt like time slowed to a crawl, and then I snapped out of that sensation and my nose was absolutely flowing with blood. This was not a typical nosebleed, it was really running. I calmly walked into another room to tell my mother, and she was beside herself at the sight of my bloody face.

For anyone with even a little bit of awareness of the abduction lore, this experience should cause some alarms to go off. There are no UFOs involved, but the slowing of time and the bloody nose are both commonly reported by abductees. These clues aren't enough to declare that Derek has had some sort of direct contact, but they certainly imply *something* is going on, and that it's very strange. He also admitted he had an obsession with UFOs as a child, and that's continued to this day.

Derek also wrote to me about something that happened in the last year. His girlfriend, who has zero interest in the UFO subject, saw "an alien" in their bedroom. She is quite certain she was awake and it wasn't a dream. She described it as somehow shape-shifting, she was panicked and squeezed her eyes shut. She resisted trying to wake him because she thought by waking him in its presence that maybe, "They wouldn't be able to return him to his body" (her words). That's quite a striking statement from someone without any interest in UFOs.

His memories continue, this time in the form of what might have been a dream. He writes:

> I have had some very "real" feeling dreams that are not at all vague. One included being levitated out of my bed by six beings, three on each side of me. I was floating at their shoulder height, and I left my apartment building through the wall. I was very scared. I cannot recall what happened outside of my home, but I do recall being returned to my bed and placed on my stomach.

The implications of that dream are transparent. In the same email Derek talked about his personal evolution. He described what has been unfolding presently in his life.

> In the last few years something very interesting, unexpected, and wonderful has happened to me. I've found myself opening up, learning, knowing, and growing in ways I never would've considered just a few years back. It feels very much like what one would describe as a spiritual awakening. I spend little to no time thinking about the nuts and bolts type speculation in the UFO community. I have become much more interested in issues like consciousness, enlightenment, purpose, knowing, and growing. I've slowly started to meditate. I find myself open to things I would have scoffed at in the past, they almost make very clear sense to me now!

His spiritual awakening seems intertwined with his UFO experiences. I can't help but recognize myself in this part of his personal account. Like me, Derek is someone with multiple UFO sightings, odd childhood memories, an expanded consciousness—and, for some reason, an owl shows up as a pivotal player in the overall narrative. Also, he is cautious and unsure of the source of the experience. I can't help but think that the owl is playing the role of an alarm clock, trying to wake up the experiencer. Something is happening, and it implies that there is a lot more to reality than what we've been taught.

The birth of the blog

In March of 2009, I started an online blog called *Hidden Experience*. I felt a need, or perhaps a compulsion, to document my life events in this very public forum. The initial posts were about my personal synchronicities and owl sightings, and there have been a lot of both of these. I've also been writing about my struggles with the UFO abduction phenomenon, and how it seems somehow connected to my life—and also connected to owls.

I've also been hosting a series of podcasts, and at this point I have well over 200 hours of audio interviews posted on my site. The focus of most of these interviews is UFO abduction; I'm either talking to researchers or people who have had the direct experience. I should say that these audio interviews, like the blog itself, has been a form of personal therapy.

I've been seeing a parallel within the alien abduction lore and people seeing owls, and I'm fascinated by any story that reveals this improbable relationship. There is an almost mystical *knowing* inside me that sees a connection between these two arcane elements.

I've written a lot on this owl stuff over the years, and in July of 2013, I posted a long format essay titled *Owls and the UFO Abductee*. That essay is the foundation for the book you are reading now.

I'm the owl guy

If you Google *UFOs* and *owls*, my name is the first thing that comes up. So, if someone out there has had an experience that involves both UFOs and owls, and they want to research it, they're going to find me. At this point there are also a handful of presentations that I've given at conferences, and some are posted online. These videos are me at a podium talking about my owl research.

Because of all this, I'm now known as *the owl guy*. I've used the blog to put out a request for people to contact me with their experiences, and I'm getting a steady flow of amazing owl stories.

This all traces back to the events in the mountains with Kristen. Since then, I've simply made it a point that anyone I talk with, whether it's a researcher or an experiencer, I'll ask this one question: *Have you ever had any odd owl experiences?* It's not one hundred percent of the people, but a surprising number will have an unusual story to tell. I've been publicly asking that same question on my site, during interviews, and at conferences.

A lot of remarkable owl stories have been arriving in my email inbox. Presently, it's about one a day. I've made the effort to get back to every one, but it can be hard to keep up. Before I can reply in any meaningful way, there are new owl stories accumulating. These are from sincere people who are confused and uneasy about what has happened to them. I've been collecting, documenting, and archiving these owl and UFO accounts. I feel less like a researcher, and more like a folklorist. I deeply appreciate that people are reaching out to me with their stories, and I take this responsibility seriously.

I didn't choose to study owls. They chose me. When I turned my attention to this research I figured I would collect some interesting anecdotes, type up an article and be done with it. That was the genesis of the online essay from the summer of 2013. I had no idea that the next few years of my life would be consumed by this focused avenue of inquiry.

Friedrich Nietzsche wrote that, "...if you gaze long into an abyss, the abyss also gazes into you."

Owls are an almost insignificant part of the UFO enigma, but within that tiny fractal is an allegory for the overall phenomenon. I am staggered by the volume of fascinating stories I've heard involving owls. It's far beyond anything I expected. What is presenting itself to me is so powerful that I can't help but wonder if I was somehow chosen to archive these reports and turn them into a book. Yes, that sounds presumptuous, *but that's how it feels.*

The "maybe" people

This research means talking with a lot of people who've had UFO experiences. On one end of the continuum are people who absolutely *know* they've had face to face contact with the UFO occupants. On the other end are people who will deny any kind of direct involvement with UFOs or aliens, *but they still have odd stories to tell*. When digging just a little deeper into their experiences, I'll often hear things that send up red flags. They'll list off odd experiences and dismiss it as nothing, but these will fit a pattern of what abductees are reporting.

People will tell odd stories of having had unaccountable blocks of time, from minutes to hours, and sometimes days. These missing time accounts are a primary clue in what might be a hidden experience. We are dealing with something that can erase memories and alter perceptions, so it becomes terribly difficult to truly know the extent of a person's experiences. Someone might have had nothing more than a chance sighting of an odd little dot in the sky, yet this could be just the tip of the iceberg, with the core of their experience buried in their subconscious. It's these kind of uncertainties that make any firm conclusion nearly impossible.

Some will tell of dramatic UFO sightings, but reject any notion that they might have been abducted. Yet these same people will often tell of psychic experiences, vivid dreams, intense synchronicities, healing abilities, spiritual awakenings, and a laundry list of other paranormal oddities.

The folks with clear memories of having direct interactions with the aliens while aboard a craft are, fairly or unfairly, easy to categorize. But a lot end up in a more elusive category. These are people who might be abductees, yet very little is definite, all they are left with is a fuzzy maybe.

These, to me, are *the maybe people*, the folks who've *maybe* been abducted by aliens. Curiously, it's these maybe people who seem to be seeing a lot of owls.

Doing the kind of research I do, I receive a lot of interesting UFO accounts, as well as odd owl stories, mostly through email. I try to check in with all these folks and when I do, I make sure to ask each of them the big question: *Do you think you are a UFO abductee?* When I asked Derek that question, even though he's had a lot of weird experiences, he answered with a very firm no. I understood his response, recognizing how deeply challenging this material can be. I feel a kinship with these folks, these *maybe people*, because in a lot of ways, they are me—or more correctly, the person I was.

Digging into these stories, I am less interested in what we would call UFO Abduction and more interested in the blurry netherworld of the maybe experience. Even without the overt memories of abduction, it seems these maybe people have had a subtle intrusion into their psyche. On the simplest level, it's as if these folks are granted a kind of insight into reality; they know there is a lot more going on that what we've been taught in high school physics class.

Imperfect though it might be, I'll be using the term *maybe people* throughout this book. I'm also using a few other imperfect terms: *abductee*, *experiencer*, and *contactee*. Each of these words might seem interchangeable, but they all imply something different, and each has its own conflicting baggage. *Abductee* would imply something negative—individuals being taken against their will by the UFO occupants. *Contactee* would imply something positive. Such people might see themselves as asked to take part in a grand cosmic fellowship. *Experiencer*, in the middle, is a little more neutral. Sometimes I'll use the phrase *direct UFO contact* instead of abduction—it's essentially the same thing, just a bit more understated.

The word *alien* is used throughout this book, and some object to this because it implies a being from another planet. Others prefer visitors, ETs, UFO occupants, or star beings. I know one woman who refers to them only as creatures. The dictionary has several definitions for alien, one of them is: "Differing in nature or character typically to the point of incompatibility." For me, this seems entirely acceptable. Yet all these words fall short because none of this is straightforward. I sense a lot of overlap and blurring, a disparate gray zone where easy answers seem impossible.

I struggle because this stuff can be terribly complex, there's no simple way to sum up the conflicting experiences that get reported by real people. Some will tell hellish nightmare stories at the hands of their alien kidnappers. Others will tell blissful stories, as if they are communing with angels. I try my best not to weight one side more than the other, because these opposing experiences both fit within a pattern of very similar accounts.

There is both deep trauma and mystical transcendence woven into this phenomenon, and these opposite extremes need to be acknowledged. Ignoring one divergent aspect means deliberately denying part of the mystery. Something is happening, and I sense it's far more complex, and far more bizarre, than simply metal spaceships filled with little scientists. Trying to understand the overall subject means wrestling with assumptions and speculation, and this kind of scrutiny can distract from the heartfelt stories at the core of my research.

Kim's unease

I've spoken on the phone with a woman named Kim. Like so many others, she told of odd experiences, like weird synchronicities and seeing odd lights in the sky. She was cautious to say it, but she was very worried she might have had some sort of alien contact events in her life. During our very first phone conversation I asked, "Have you ever had any odd experiences with owls?"

I could tell she didn't quite get my question, and she replied hesitantly, "Do you mean like lots of owl dreams, seeing owls at weird times, and having them answer when I hoot?"

I laughed and told her yes, that's exactly what I meant. Kim described a dream of opening her closet and seeing a bunch of owls all lined up on a shelf. "I knew how tall they were because they all fit so well on that shelf." As we talked further and she told me more, I realized that she was one more of these *maybe people*. She'd had plenty of experiences that certainly pointed to UFO abduction, but connecting those dots was a bigger leap than she was prepared to take.

It isn't my place to call someone a UFO abductee if they aren't saying it themselves. I know all too well because other people have said as much to me, and it's damned unsettling.

This research into owls and UFOs is essentially therapy. There are people with similar experiences that I first spoke with in the early stages of my struggles, and over the years we've become friends and talk often. Some of these would be maybe people, or at least they started off that way. I've watched as they wrestle with their own disturbing memories, and more than a few have come to a point where they accept their abduction experiences. This conversion comes grudgingly, and I fully understand that I've played a role in their self-awareness. I clearly see myself, and my own transition, in their metamorphosis from maybe to certainty, and I take this responsibility very seriously.

Kim and I had our first conversation when she was initially struggling with these challenging issues. In the interim years, I've followed her evolution, and I recently asked Kim the big question, "What is your sense of your own involvement with this weirdness?" And by this weirdness, I meant the UFO contact experience.

Her reply was that if the weirdness in her life is actually true, then it explains what has happened. She told me, "In other words, it takes it all out of the speculation box and puts it in the *oh shit* category."

Like myself, Kim was born in 1962, and also like myself she started looking into her own experiences in 2006. Although we've never met, we grew up only a few miles from each other in the suburbs of Detroit. I am not sure what to make of these kinds of coincidences, all I can do is take note and pay attention.

It would be wrong to assume that all these *maybe people* are in fact abductees, but I sense that a great many of them have had hidden experiences at the hands of the UFO occupants.

I'm also finding there's a wider range of experiences than just people being plucked from their bedrooms, or along lonely roads at night, by little aliens that erase their memories. That certainly plays a part in what gets reported, but there is a more elusive aspect. Some experiences are much more mystical, as if they're interacting with spirit guides or energy beings. These might not be *beings* in the way we imagine them to be, but a form of arcane consciousness that interacts at the level of the soul. The *maybe people* might not fit the UFO abduction model, but the life changes do. They've endured the same kind of psychic events, emotional challenges, and spiritual awakenings that have shaped the lives of so many abductees.

Chapter 2:

Owls as Screen Memory

I sat in on an abductee support group while at a UFO conference in Laughlin, Nevada. This was like any other support meeting, like Alcoholics Anonymous, where people talk about their issues. There were about twenty of us in the room, all sitting in a circle. There was one guy who sat silently for almost the entire two-hour session, but near the end he raised his hand and cautiously asked, "Has anyone here had any experiences with owls?" He nearly jolted out of his chair when pretty much *everybody* in the room, including me, raised their hand.

After he got his wits back, he told a story of being alone in his car and driving at night down a lonely country road. Along the edge of the pavement was a giant owl, standing about four feet tall. He slowed the car, rolled the window down, and stopped directly alongside the owl. It didn't fly away. It just stood there. He said he got a weird vibe, like the owl was angry and wanted him to leave. He drove off feeling confused and frightened.

This guy was a professional photographer, and not long after this event, he went to take pictures of an owl nest in a wooded area near his home. When he saw the real owls in their nest, he immediately thought, *"I don't think that was an owl I saw that night."* He eventually used hypnosis to try to retrieve a more detailed memory, but all he came up with was that the giant owl on the side of the road was wearing boots!

The implication is what he saw wasn't an owl. Instead, it was an illusory projection that was somehow beamed into his mind, making him think that what he saw on the side of the road was an owl. Within the small pool of abduction researchers, this kind of deception is called a *screen memory*. Instead of what it appeared to be, most researchers would conclude it was a small gray alien with oversized black eyes. It's these penetrating eyes that seem to mimic the giant eyes of an owl, making it a less frightening stand-in than an alien. A four-foot-tall owl wearing boots is a tidy example of a screen memory.

This guy's story is part of a commonly reported pattern within the UFO abduction literature. Beyond owls, these deceptive memories can take the form of deer, cats, raccoons, dead relatives, clowns, and even Jesus. These and more are all commonly reported. It's impossible to know exactly what's at play, but some sort of powerful mind control seems to be influencing the consciousness of the witness.

Sigmund Freud first used the term *screen memory* in 1899. He described it as a psychological reaction, where an earlier memory is used as an overlay to hide a later event. So, in Freud's explanation, the screen is something generated internally. In the present-day UFO literature, the term screen memory implies something generated externally. It's a form of hypnotic or telepathic projection coming from the mind (or technologies) of the UFO occupants.

Dolores Cannon and a new path

The late author, hypnotherapist, and researcher Dolores Cannon wrote about an unusual owl sighting in her 1999 book *The Custodians*. This happened in the winter of 1988 after a meeting with colleagues where they'd been discussing metaphysical matters, including UFO abductions—something she hadn't yet investigated. She was confronted with a choice, should she change the direction of her practice and follow this less traveled path? It was well after midnight when she began driving home from the meeting. She was a little over a mile away from her home in an isolated part of the Ozark Mountains of Arkansas when she saw a huge owl standing in the middle of the road. She wrote:

> I drove right up to it, and it wouldn't move. It just kept standing there, apparently mesmerized by my headlights. Its head was even with the top of the fender, so I could see its huge unblinking eyes quite clearly. I honked and came closer to it. I didn't want to hurt it, just to make it move out of the road. It then turned and flew very low to the ground with a large wingspan, and alighted just out of

the range of my headlights. Once again I approached it and it wouldn't move until I got right up to it. Then it would fly a short distance again, alight and turn to face the car.

This continued all the way to my gate. It would stop at various places in front of my car, and just stare unblinking at me. Each time it took several seconds to make it move. I laughed because it seemed very peculiar... Finally the last time it flew to the other side of the entrance to my driveway and just stood there while I turned in.

Once home, she thought the owl seemed unusually large. She wondered if this could have been some sort of screen memory, and she checked the clocks, but there didn't seem to be any missing time.

Years later, in 1996, the strangeness of this event came rushing back with a tinge of apprehension. While on a lecture tour in England, Ms. Cannon went to the Natural History Museum in London. She entered a room where all kinds of birds were presented in glass cases, and she was caught off guard by what she saw. She wrote:

In one case, all the species of owls were displayed. What shocked me and sent chills down my spine, was that none of them were as large as the one I saw on the deserted road years before. None of these could have been seen over the fender of my car.

As I stared at them in wonder and perplexity questions flooded into my mind. What did I really see that night in the road? Did I have a similar experience to the ones I was investigating? Did something else happen that night? If something did occur it was a gentle and easy preparation for the work I do, and it was definitely not to be feared. I am not saying this was an example of contact with alien beings. I am just saying that it bears an uncanny resemblance to the cases I have since investigated. [1]

This story marked a change in the direction of Ms. Cannon's research. It was shortly after her owl event on the lonely road that she began working with people who sought help for their UFO memories. She used hypnosis to explore the deepest parts of the subconscious, and this eventually lead to a form of channeled communication with alien beings. She is keenly aware that her 1988 owl sighting plays out as preparation for her work as an abduction researcher.

Ms. Cannon's description of an owl being tall enough to look over the hood of her car is impossible, yet giant owls are common within UFO abduction reports. These are usually described at around four feet tall (122 cm). This is problematic because the tallest owl in the world, with a maximum height of 33 inches (84 cm), is the great gray (yes, a gray!). This bird is found in northern latitudes in a wide stripe around the globe. It inhabits North America from Alaska to Canada, and dipping down into the northern United States. The great gray also ranges across Northern Europe through Russia and Mongolia.

The Eurasian eagle-owl is considered the largest owl by overall size, with a wingspan of up to 74 inches (188 cm). The largest owl by weight is the Blakiston's fish owl, tipping the scales at a little over 10 pounds (4.6Kg). This owl is only found in the old growth forests of Siberia and the Far-East. Although impressively large, none of these owls come close to the four-foot height consistently reported by abductees. It's worth noting that the spindly gray aliens reported by abductees are usually described as being about four feet tall.

Aaron's story

The report below is from a man named Aaron (a pseudonym). He's had a lot of extremely strange experiences, but none of his memories actually involve UFOs. What follows is what I can only conclude to be a screen memory, again, involving an owl:

> I made plans for Saturday night with my best friend. I was going to meet him at his house and then we'd go downtown. I spoke with him at about 8:00 p.m., and told him that I was walking out the door and would be at his place in about 20 minutes. He told me to make it quick, because he was ready to leave.
>
> I remember leaving the house and pulling out of the driveway. It was just starting to get a little dark outside. I drove about a half

a mile down the road before I saw a huge whitish-gray owl standing in the middle of the road. It was about three feet tall. I don't remember hitting it or anything like that—just seeing it standing there in front of the car.

The next thing I remember was pulling into the drive of my friend's house. It was dark out, and when I went in, my friend was furious. He said, "Where in the fuck have you been? You said you were leaving right away!"

I told him that I did leave right away, and he snapped back, "It's after ten!"

I started to tell him what happened, but as soon as the words three-foot owl came out, I felt like an idiot. I ended up apologizing for being late and we left. I was sober up until that point, then I drank to get rid of the uneasy feeling I had in the pit of my stomach.

Years later, I read a book that talked about UFOs and missing time. When I saw that it said that seeing owls, rabbit, and deer was normal, I almost threw up.

Aaron's story is a good example of the standard screen memory account. Seeing a huge owl in the middle of the road and then realizing there was missing time is all too common. I have heard this story, in one form or another, so many times that it now seems almost mundane. He described a three-foot-tall owl, and although still huge, is slightly smaller than the four-foot height that seems more commonly reported. For me, this variance doesn't change the significance of his story.

During an email exchange with Aaron, he told me that around the time of this event, his life had become a descending spiral of alcohol, drugs, and depression. He was clear that his self-destructive behavior nearly killed him. It's hard not to wonder if some hidden event from that missing time might be the source of his tortured anguish. If there were some kind of dark trauma buried in his subconscious, it might explain his conduct.

He is now a born-again Christian, and he shared a video of himself playing guitar and singing a soulful gospel song. I was moved by the heartfelt depth of his performance. I liked him immediately, and was relieved to hear his life is presently much more stable.

The first reference of an owl as a screen memory

Alien abduction burst into the public awareness in 1987 with Whitley Strieber's book *Communion*. There had been other abduction accounts leading up to this, but none can compare to the phenomenal impact of this bestselling book. It ushered in an explosion of people coming forward and discussing their own contact experiences. It also introduced the idea that the owl was somehow a part of the overall mystery.

The central event in Strieber's book is a harrowing first-person account of an abduction that took place in his rural cabin on the winter's night of December 26th, 1985. This is not a simple story, it's challenging in almost every aspect. Strieber begins his tale with a nighttime intrusion into his bedroom, and from there the narrative spirals to the point where the very fabric of reality comes into question. His initial impression after that transcendent night was of seeing an owl:

> I awoke the morning of the twenty-seventh very much as usual, but grappling with a distinct sense of unease and a very improbable but intense memory of seeing a barn owl staring at me through the window sometime during the night.
>
> I remember how I felt in the gathering evening of the twenty-seventh, when I looked out onto the roof and saw that there were no owl tracks in the snow. I knew I had not seen an owl. I shuddered, suddenly cold, and drew back from the window, withdrawing from the night that was falling so swiftly in the woods beyond.
>
> But I wanted desperately to believe in that owl. I told my wife about it. She was polite, but commented about the absence of tracks. I really very much wanted to convince her of it, though. Even more, I wanted to convince myself.

If it wasn't an owl, then it was something else entirely. Later in the book, Strieber describes an event from the early 1960s involving his sister and an owl. She was driving alone on the highways of rural Texas, and shortly after midnight, "She was terrified to see a huge light sail down and cross the road ahead of her. A few minutes later an owl flew in front of the car. I have to wonder if that is not a screen memory, but my sister has no sense of it." [2]

I contacted Strieber via email to ask about owls and their role within this mystery, he replied with memories of his childhood.

> There was a white owl that stood in our back yard and watched the windows of my bedroom when I was a child. It made my folks very nervous. This was during the time that they nailed the screens shut.

That he would have seen a white owl in his yard came as no surprise. Then I asked if this owl from his youth could have been some sort of screen memory.

> I don't have any way to tell if it was a screen memory. I remember an owl, and certainly nobody said that it was anything different. My parents never said why they nailed the screens shut, but I assume that it was either because they feared that somebody might be coming in, or I might be going out at night.

It could be my own mind grasping at nothing, but I can't help but see window screens being nailed shut out of fear as a metaphor. The word *screen* is just too perfect, and the term *window* is sometimes used by researchers to describe the gateway that UFOs might use to enter into our reality.

Researchers of the alien abduction phenomenon will point out that owls have an eerie likeness to the commonly reported gray alien. Both have penetrating oversized eyes, and some have suggested this is why UFO occupants are choosing the owl as one of their screen memories.

Abduction researcher John Carpenter discussed what he had found with his work using hypnosis with abductees. He was aware of what might be hidden behind the images of common animals like owls and squirrels. He considered the motive behind screen memories, saying: "I think the aliens do that to make it easier for us. We would much rather look at an owl or a squirrel than an alien. I actually think they do that on purpose, so we aren't so freaked out and are more cooperative."

Carpenter has a few cases where the small gray aliens telepathically told the abductee that: *You will remember us an an owl.*[3]

These memories were retrieved using hypnosis, a controversial tool for this kind of investigation, so it's difficult to truly know what might have taken place during these contact experiences. Nonetheless, memories emerged of an alien standing right in front of a person, informing them that they were putting the memory of an owl into their mind. This communication often takes place while these gray beings are staring directly into the eyes of the abductees, further implying a psychic influence.

Lucretia Heart's story

It's amazing that so many of these screen memories play out seamlessly, leaving the experiencer convinced they've seen a real owl, even if the size or context is absurd. Yet other times, the events are so weird that the abductee will recognize the utter strangeness. And sometimes the aliens screw up.

Blogger and abductee Lucretia Heart (her pen name) confronted the screen memory of an owl when she was 19 years old. It happened while she was working at a summer camp for girls in the Pacific Northwest. What follows is her (slightly edited) memory. She describes walking alone on a path through the forest:

> It was a beautiful, sunny day and I could hear the girls laughing and playing in the camp area behind me as I walked. As I rounded the final corner... something to my right caught my attention.
>
> There was a big white thing there. I kept walking as I turned my head to look and I just could not believe what I saw... It was an alien gray only it was almost perfectly stark white. Its head was as big as a football helmet and it had those wrap-around eyes. It was standing still [and it] didn't see me quietly padding up the pathway. This being was solid and physical. The sun shining on his head made it stand out like crazy. I was in such shock I didn't ever stop walking because my mind was still trying to process the moment.
>
> My mind insisted that they weren't supposed to exist during the day! Of course, in an isolated area with plenty of cover, that's nonsense, but since I almost only ever saw them at night, I apparently

developed a sort of belief system about it. All my panic attacks came at night. And now here I was seeing this thing out during the day, as plain as you please!

Another moment and I saw him turn his head to look in my direction and I caught the, "Oh shit!" sort of thought-wave (without the words, but you get the point) before he turned to run away.

It was in the very next instant that something very interesting happened. It was an important moment, because I was wide awake and paying very close attention, despite my shock. At the same time the gray scrambled to run away, dashing through the underbrush—a very powerful image of a big white owl came to my mind. Of course, I had just seen an alien gray. Not to mention there are no owls that stand four feet tall and lack feathers! So I wasn't fooled, but I wondered at the power of the image and idea that what I had actually seen had been a huge owl. Because it wasn't just that I suddenly had an image in my mind of a big owl, I also had the idea planted firmly there as well. A suggestion if you will...

I kept walking right by where the being had stood, and I could hear loud, clumsy crashing sounds as the being made its way through the foliage in an utter panic. I really felt the panic coming off of it, and owls don't project thought-waves! [4]

So here we have a vivid description of an abductee actually witnessing *the change from alien gray to owl*. Instead of seeing a flawless screen memory, she saw something frantic and sloppy. Integral to her description is the feeling of thought-waves being projected into her mind.

Some people think that the aliens are shape-shifting in a way where they physically *become* an owl. This might be how Native Americans would frame a spirit guides, but this isn't how the evidence plays out concerning screen memories. An experiencer might be able to untangle their owl memories while under regressive hypnosis. The hypnotist could take the relaxed subject to the event with the owl, and ask the subject to describe what they're seeing. What might unfold is a description of something with a big bald head, skinny body, and huge black eyes. Lucretia's story is an oddly comic example remembered without hypnosis.

I heard a similar story from researcher Alan Caviness. He told me about a woman who was woken up in the middle of the night by a bright flash of light. She got out of bed to investigate. She stepped out her front door and surprised three gray aliens standing right next to her, just off the porch. They stared at each other for about five seconds, then she watched these skinny beings morph into three deer and ease backwards, huddled awkwardly together, retreating into the darkness away from the house. This example was deer, not owls, but both these women saw the morphing from alien to animal.

Corina Saebels' story

Corina Saebels is an abductee from the Okanagan Valley of western Canada, and she recounts an odd owl event in her book *The Collectors*. She had been stargazing at night with her children and a friend named Rob. They were all at a lake together, enjoying the nighttime sky. There came a point when they all noticed an unusual stillness. The air was suddenly cooler, and there was an odd smell. Right at that moment the kids said they were feeling tired and wanted to sit in the car, so they all went to the car to rest. Then everybody fell asleep.

They all woke up about two hours later, feeling disoriented and nauseos. Two people had headaches, and one of the children had a bloody nose. Everyone felt awful, and they all agreed to head home. Corina was driving slowly, and at the first sharp bend, right in the beam of the headlights, they all saw what she describes as a typical gray alien standing on the side of the road.

> I slammed on the breaks in the middle of the road and screamed. The children and I began to shake uncontrollably, but oddly enough, Rob just calmly turned to me and said, "What are you guys so worried about? It's only a big owl!"
>
> "Are you kidding?" I screamed, "Have you lost your mind? Since when do we have four-foot-tall owls in the Okanagan Valley or anywhere for that matter?" [5]

We have a story where multiple people see a gray alien, but one person sees an owl. Why didn't they all see the same thing? Of note, it's not uncommon for a car full of people to come to a complete stop squarely in front of a hovering flying saucer, and some of them will see it, while others won't see anything at all.

Holding a tiny owl

There can be a fuzzy blurring between what might be a screen memory and what might be a real experience with an owl. A woman name Cynthia shared a story with me that happened years before she was consciously aware of her lifelong contacts with the UFO occupants.

She remembers driving at night with her husband and her two children, who were about nine and twelve years old. Her husband was driving on a quiet twisting rural road near their home. They turned a corner and there before them, in the middle of the road, was a tiny owl. They stopped the car and without knowing exactly why, she got out and ran up to the little owl. She assumed it was injured, and she reached down and picked it up in her hands. She noticed an eerie silence while standing alone on the road.

Cynthia carried the owl back to the car, and the family continued home. As they drove, she marveled that this little owl, maybe six inches tall, would sit so quietly in her cupped hands.

When they arrived home, everybody got out of the car and stood in the driveway. She raised her hands, opened them, and the small owl spread its wings, and with what seemed like a single flap rose up and silently disappeared into the night. She stated that the wingspan seemed far too large for such a tiny little bird.

> I remember the owl's dark silhouette against the unusually dark night. It was uncommonly dark for the entire event, and I could only see him as his wings flapped down, then he was gone. Totally silent. He vanished. This was a profound experience that affected me for years after. I knew it was an unusual event, and I felt fortunate to hold the beautiful owl. Even today, I remember how amazing I felt.

Cynthia also noted the same odd silence was there in the driveway, just as it had been when she picked up the owl. This strange vacuum-like silence seems to be another example of the *Oz Factor*. She recently asked her children if they remember that night, and both said no. This seems unusual, as one would think that driving around with a live owl in a car would be hard to forget.

Here we have a strange owl experience told by an abductee at a time when she was unaware of her history of contact. There are odd details in this story that don't seem to follow the pattern of a typical screen memory, nor that of a concealed abduction. I've spoken to her at length and she's confident she was holding a real owl, but she'll quickly flip-flop, as if the strangeness implies something unknown. That tiny owl certainly isn't the four-foot-tall variety from other reports, but her story has the flavor of a screen memory.

Drawing an owl

I heard from a young man who has been doing paranormal research, as well as collecting Bigfoot reports. He told me his mother has had a lifelong fascination with owls—she has owl paintings, knickknacks, and figurines all over the house. This is a curious detail, some of people with these experiences will have amassed a large collection of owl trinkets. It's also common that people will tell me their mother collects owls.

She told her son about seeing a big owl in the driveway. The sighting began when her dog was barking at something outside, she went out to investigate and saw something in the darkness at the end of their long gravel driveway. She walked towards the figure and stopped when she realized she was looking at a huge owl.

Her son asked how big it was, and she said it was about her own height, perhaps a bit smaller. His mother isn't very tall, so that puts the estimated size of this owl at around four-and-a-half to five feet. Again, this is impossibly large for any known owl.

He asked if she could draw it, so his mother sketched a typical owl figure with big eyes. The son sensed an unease and asked her, is this *really* what it looked like? She thought for a moment and said, not really. She then re-drew the face on the same paper, trying to capture her memory.

37

This time she drew what clearly looked like the face of a gray alien. With his interest in UFOs and the paranormal, the implication was immediately obvious to her son. He asked if she remembers anything unusual that night, any sense of missing time?

She asked why he wanted to know, and he told her that sometimes oversized owls get reported in connection with UFO abductions. Hearing that, all the color drained from her face. He could never follow up on what might have happened because she refused to talk about it.

The trigger memory

Joe Montaldo is both a contactee and abduction researcher, and this is a rather common combination. He runs an organization called ICAR (International Community for Alien Research), with a focus on the abduction phenomenon. I asked him if any unusual owl reports are showing up in his research. He said, "Absolutely, we regularly get reports of people seeing owls standing on the side of the road, and they're usually about four-foot-tall."

He was describing exactly what I've been finding, and I'm certain any other researcher looking into the abduction mystery is finding the same thing too.

Joe doesn't use the term screen memory, instead he calls them *trigger memories*. He feels they aren't there to hide anything; they're there as a trigger so you know that something happened. This means that if an abductee remembers seeing a four-foot-tall owl in the middle of the road, they'll always know that something wasn't quite right, and someday they'll need to look into these memories. It's a marker for an event.

He goes further, saying, "Almost all UFO sightings are meant to be trigger memories, they are designed to let you know something happened."

Joe declared, "ET never has to show himself to anybody." He's implying that their technology is so advanced, that making their craft invisible is effortless, so if anyone sees something, it's because *they want to be seen for a reason.*

He told me a story of a man in Louisiana, who while sitting on his porch at night noticed something big and white flittering around up in the trees at the edge of his yard. When he walked out to investigate, he saw about twenty big owls flying around together in the treetops.

This man drew a picture of the owl, and Joe tried to research it. He took the drawing to the local game warden and asked what kind of owls they might have been. The warden laughed, saying that there were no owls as big as what he was describing. This was in the Deep South, and what he remembered was so big it could only match a flock of oversized great gray owls, and that would have been impossible given the latitude. Later, under hypnotic regression, when he was trying to describe looking at these owls, he suddenly blurted out, "Oh fuck!" Joe asked him what he was seeing, and he nervously described standing in the dark surrounded by three gray aliens.

At this point, I've heard so many owl stories that play out as screen memories that I can barely keep them all straight in my head. These are told to me by real people who are shaky with emotion as they try to convey the utter strangeness of what they've seen.

The story of seeing an impossibly large owl, or multiple owls, standing on a lonely road is the most common. But they are also reported in backyards and front yards, standing in doorways, looking in windows and looking down from roofs. I've had two people who were both in the same room describe seeing a large owl sitting on a windowsill looking in at them, with its face against the glass. Later they realized that there was no sill, the window was flush against the outside wall, so there was no place for the owl to stand.

I've heard accounts where giant owls enter a bedroom by floating down through the ceiling. I've been told of skinny alien beings appearing in bedrooms at night, but with big owl heads. I've also had people describe waking up with a group of giant four-foot-tall owls standing around their beds. Parents will tell me their children are telling them about big owls that come into their bedrooms at night. Most of these giant owl stories are part of a larger narrative, one that includes UFO sightings or an outright abduction.

There are also stories of what seem to be *real owls*, but the context is so strange that it's hard to truly know. I heard a story from a woman who had a nighttime of bizarre experiences, including a compulsion to walk through her neighborhood in the middle of the night, only to meet a

strange man with a Scottish accent. This whole night plays out with distorted time and irrational fears. The next morning she woke to an owl
sitting on a branch outside the big sliding glass doors of her kitchen. She
described the owl as enormous, and the branch was dipping down low
from its weight. It stayed there most of the day, staring in at her. I asked
if she thought this was a real owl, or some sort of screen projection. She
answered in a shaky way, as if she wasn't sure, but she remembered it as
a real owl.

Peter Maxwell Slattery and owls

Peter Maxwell Slattery is a young, outspoken contactee from Australia. He's had a lifetime of powerful experiences, including UFO sightings, profound synchronicities, and odd owl sightings.

The first owl experience happened when Peter was working as a security guard; his job involved driving a route at night with a partner and
checking on a set of businesses. This was at a time before his more intense
UFO experiences had started. They were driving slowly through a dark
industrial area. Suddenly, a big white owl appeared out of nowhere—*but
it wasn't flying*—instead, it was moving toward the windshield in a weird
static pose. He hit the brakes and came to a complete stop.

Then it vanished, and they both exclaimed, "What the hell just happened?"

The owl weirdness continued a few years later. Peter was at home on
the night of June 9th, 2012, when a little after 10 p.m., a thought popped
into his head. He had an unusual urge to leave the house and go to a
nearby area with hiking trails.

While driving there, Peter fully realized that something wasn't right,
but nothing was going to stop him. When he arrived at the parking lot, he
asked himself, "What am I doing here?" Despite being plagued by an ominous feeling, he started hiking uphill into the darkness.

After about two kilometers, something told him to stop. He turned off
his flashlight and looked up into the sky. He saw a white light like a big
star that stopped directly above him. As he watched, the light shot off at
an unbelievable speed and disappeared. He writes about this in his fourth

book titled *Operation Starseed*. What follows is a short excerpt from the chapter, The Two Owls:

> While taking in what happened, and that I was basically in the middle of nowhere, I got a sudden feeling of not being alone (the air around me felt like static electricity).
>
> I turned around and what I saw shocked me. I saw two owls right in front of me, about three meters away. They were about three to four feet tall and about a foot wide.
>
> At this time I freaked out, turned the other direction and went to run out of shock, but as soon as I turned around, I couldn't run, I just froze, my heart was beating so fast, it caught me off guard, it was unexpected.
>
> Next the owls appeared overhead, like as if they jumped over me. At that moment I closed my eyes. A few seconds later the static feeling in the air around me disappeared, then I opened my eyes. Nothing was there. At this time I could move again.
>
> Straight away, I turned my torch on and headed back to the car. On the way down the hill I was just thinking, "I didn't know that owls could get that big."

It was over a month later when Peter described what he had seen to his brother, who laughed and told him owls aren't that big. From this point on, Peter was aware that he was probably at the receiving end of some sort of psychic deception.

Peter had a third unusual owl sighting. On this night, he was out sky watching with two women. One was his neighbor, who had seen a craft hovering above their neighborhood. The other was Carol, and Peter feels he's fathered hybrid children with her—yes, that's an odd detail, and he shared it with me in a nonchalant way. This should have been a surprise, but wasn't, I've heard claims like this enough times that it now seems ordinary.

They all drove a short distance to an isolated area with an amazing view of the nighttime sky. They meditated for a while, and even saw a few odd lights in the sky. When they drove home, Peter was behind the wheel, driving slowly on the bumpy rural road. At one point, Peter was struck with a wave of anxiety, and the same moment Carol said, "Something is about to happen."

Seconds later they came around a corner, and a huge owl was suddenly in front of the car at windshield height. It had a white belly and grayish wings. Peter was very clear that it didn't fly into his line of sight, but *manifested out of nothing.* Right before impact, it veered off and vanished into nothingness.

Peter stopped the car saying, "I don't feel right." The other two women felt the similar, each of them describing an odd sensation. They could all feel a weird energy. The woman in the back seat said that from her view, the owl seemed giant, filling the entire windshield.[6]

Sideways owl

A young man named Joe saw both a UFO and owls within minutes of each other, this happened in 2012 when he was 20 years old. These sightings took place at about three in the morning while he was driving with four friends in his car. Joe and his close friend Dave were in the front seats when they both saw a brilliant blue light descending in the sky.

Joe said, "It was bright as hell, so I couldn't make out the shape of the craft, but it was high enough to pass through the clouds." Both Joe and Dave were silent until after they'd lost sight of it beyond the trees.

After the shock wore off, they told the three people in the back seats what they'd just seen. They dropped off one of the passengers, and began the drive back to their friend's house. They were traveling about 55 miles per hour when a white owl flew right up alongside their car with its head turned, staring directly at the passengers.

This owl was flying right next to the passenger window, close enough that Dave could have reached out and touched it. Even though the car was moving fast, the owl "hovered" there for about five seconds before it flew off. Then, less than a mile down the road, another white owl did the exact same thing—again staring sideways while flying right up next to the car and staring in Dave's window. Suddenly everyone in the car began screaming, as if they all felt the same primal fear. Joe doesn't understand why, but he slammed on the brakes, and everyone yelled to keep driving.

Afterward, no one could explain why they were all screaming. The strange way the owl was flying right up next to the car triggered a feeling none of the passengers had ever felt before. Joe said, "The owls were almost sideways while staring directly into the window. It didn't make sense how they were doing it. It's hard to explain. The physics didn't add up."

Later, when he tried to bring it up to the other passengers, they all seemed to want to bury the memory. Joe said, "They acted like they would be punished if they talked about it."

Joe saw another white owl about a week after seeing the bright blue light in the sky. Curiously, he was again with Dave for this follow-up sighting. Joe had been living in that area for about ten years, and until that week he had never once seen an owl. He has since seen the same bright blue light several more times, one time with Dave.

The odd behavior of these owls, and the unsettling description of them *flying sideways* seems more like some sort of hologram than any real bird in flight. The typical screen memory implies a gray alien cloaking itself with the image of an owl. Usually these owls are seen standing still in the middle of a road, making this kind of deception easy to comprehend. But what of an owl flying sideways next to a speeding car? It seems doubtful that a gray alien could be zooming in the air at 55 miles per hour. So what did these people actually see?

Joe's account of a car full of people screaming in primal fear parallels my own experience from 2010 with my friend Natascha, where we both awoke while camped in a tent screaming without knowing why. This is described later in the book.

The paradox syndrome

Anne Strieber, the late wife of author Whitley Strieber, had a simple way of evaluating the truth of a UFO report. She said, "If it's not weird, I don't trust it."

Within these stories is a confusing collision of overlapping experiences—all of them weird. Things feel mixed up with threads running off everywhere in a tangled knot of implausibility, and synchronicity spills over the edges like an unattended sink. For me, this kind of chaos is a sign *to trust the event as legitimate.* The more complicated the interwoven details, the more valid it seems. This all becomes a shaky form of proof that something truly paranormal is unfolding.

Within these pages, I'll be referring to this frenetic pattern as the *paradox syndrome*. A paradox is an attempt at sound reasoning, but the conclusion appears unacceptable. A syndrome is a group of related or coinciding things, events, and actions. I don't understand how or why, but all the messy threads must tie into some core event, and the challenge is not to get lost in the mayhem. And when there is an owl tied to one of these threads, I pay very close attention.

This next story is an example of the paradox syndrome, it's a mess of twists and turns that baffle a set of players trapped in a storm of irrational events.

Alan Caviness is both a UFO investigator and experiencer (again, that combination), and he was at the center of a web of interconnected experiences. The initial event in a long string of weirdness took place in the evening along a quiet road in central North Carolina. Alan was driving near his home when he saw an owl in the beam of his headlights. It was standing perfectly still along the shoulder of the two-lane road. The owl was squarely facing Alan's car, and its penetrating black glossy eyes seemed to be looking straight at him. He slowed down to just a few miles per hour, and the owl didn't even flinch as he passed.[7]

He brought the car to a stop about 100 feet past the owl at the very bottom of the hill. Looking back, he saw the owl standing, still frozen like a statue. A few seconds later, he watched it eerily pivot around like a penguin, and then waddle into the woods at the edge of the road.

Alan immediately realized that seeing such an unusual owl might imply an abduction event, but if this was an illusion, it would've fooled anyone on earth. There was an odd sense the owl had been waiting for him on the side of the road. He had lived in the immediate area for over fifty years, and had never seen an owl anywhere in the region. This bird seemed big, but not unusually large.

Alan parked in the exact same spot the next night at about the same time, but something didn't make sense. Without any streetlights, it would have be impossible for him to have seen the owl from the rear window of his car. There was a problem—he clearly saw the owl from this location, yet it was far too dark for the memory to be real.

This is only the beginning of the story. A few days later, Alan was called to investigate a UFO in his small town. What followed was an overlapping collision of stories that both took place on that same night, within a few hours of Alan's owl sighting, and none of it is simple.

One of the events of that night involved a creepy deer that ran right next to a woman's car as she drove. She was going 55 miles per hour, and all the while this deer kept staring at her from the shoulder.

This deer sounds eerily similar to the owl from Joe's report. Both the owl and deer traveled alongside a car, and both were staring sideways, leaving the drivers astonished.

Another woman saw a UFO above her driveway. The sighting didn't last long, but the darting motions were strange enough to leave her astonished. Both women, the UFO witness and the one who drove alongside the deer, worked in the same building, but neither knew each other. Both events took place within minutes of each other, and when plotted out on a map, all three events were within four miles of each other. The synchronicities and clues continued to pile up, including other women seeing unusually large owls in the same area.

This small town in North Carolina was subjected to a cluster of extremely odd events, including a set of probable screen memories of and owl and a deer. What is remarkable is that Alan was first a witness and then the investigator of this weird flap. It's his impression (and my own) that these sightings, synchronicities, and screen memories were all carefully orchestrated, with each strange event playing a small part in some larger drama—all of it affecting Alan directly. The why of it is anyone's guess, but the knot of clues are tied too tightly to ignore. [8]

The screen memory aspect of the phenomenon can make it nearly impossible to truly know if someone is reporting a *real* owl or some form of telepathic projection. At the heart of this mystery is an influence so powerful that it can invade the consciousness of the witness, and convince them they are seeing something that isn't there. All of this leaves the experiencer, as well as the researcher, trying to guess the image on a jigsaw puzzle with pieces that won't fit together. Owl imagery keeps reoccurring as part of the witness accounts, from simple stories of seeing a dot in the night sky, to more dramatic events like beings walking through bedroom walls. I don't understand why, but the owl, both literal and symbolic, is playing some role in a larger drama.

Chapter 3:

Real Owls

Owls are remarkable not only for their place in the lore of mythology and UFO accounts, but also for what they are—creatures of astounding abilities. When a cartoonist draws an owl, something I know a little bit about, they'll depict them with enormous eyes. This caricature is quite accurate; an owl's eyes outweigh its brain. Unlike our round eyeballs, theirs are elongated tubes—a shape better suited for gathering light, even in near-complete darkness. These cylinders are locked in their skull, so owls can't roll their eyes like we do, they can only look straight ahead. It's this inability to move their eyes that gives an owl that eerie stare.

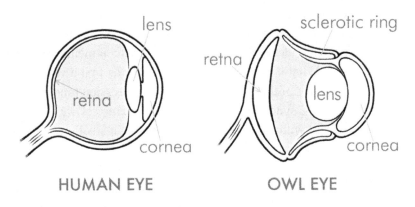

HUMAN EYE   OWL EYE

Their tubular eyes allow for a larger cornea, enabling the lens to collect more available light. This cylinder shape has a sort of mushroom-like bulge on the backside, boosting the surface of the retina. This interior surface is packed with an abundance of photoreceptor rod-shaped cells, yet very few cone-shaped cells.

This means heightened night vision and a very limited ability to see color. Tawny owls have the most developed night vision eyes of all the owls, and of all vertebrates. Their eyes are about 100 times more sensitive in low light than ours.

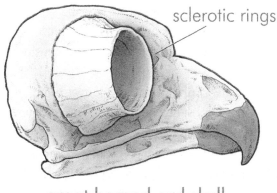

great horned owl skull

The owl's cylinder-shaped eyes are locked in place by bony structures in the skull called sclerotic rings. To compensate for their unmoving eyes, owls direct their sight by moving their heads with a highly flexible neck. We can only rotate our heads about 80 degrees, but owls can rotate theirs up to 270 degrees. Although, despite the folklore, owls cannot turn their heads all the way around. This robotic flexibility also allows their eyes and ears to stay precisely fixed on their prey—even while in flight. Owls rotate their heads with a weirdly smooth proficiency, unlike the nervous twitchiness of most other birds, and that calm demeanor creates the illusion of an owl's perceived wisdom.

A set of experiments were conducted in the early 1970s to increase our understanding of how owls catch their prey in almost total darkness. These were done with common barn owls in a large soundproof and light-proof room. When mice were released in the room with only a minimal amount of light, the owls would swoop down from their perch above and seize them with pretty much 100 percent consistency, even if the mouse was moving. When the same thing was attempted in absolute darkness, the owls 'ability to catch a mouse on the first strike was still close to 100%, but only if it was stationary. If the mouse was moving, the owls ' accuracy dropped to around 79%. This is still remarkable, given the total darkness of the room.

This variance is because of the owls' exceptional hearing. Initial tests were done with a thin layer of dried leaves and twigs on the floor, mimicking a forest environment. The scientists realized that owls were focusing on the faint rustling noises created by the mouse, and they used that audio signature to locate their prey in a three-dimensional space of complete darkness.

A grid was created on the floor of the test room, and tiny speakers were used to project very subtle noises in specific frequencies and ranges. One speaker was positioned within each square of the grid. The owls were rewarded if they struck the grid point at the source of the emanating sound. The scientists learned that the owls only needed a very minute portion of the overall frequency spectrum to hit their mark. This nano-sound is well beyond anything humans can perceive. [9]

Radar dish shaped depressions
in an owl's face focus sound to the ears

When we think of animals with excellent hearing, we picture rabbits or deer, both with oversized scoop-like ears. Owls don't have external ears. Instead, they collect sound with the actual shape of their face. Most owl species have very pronounced facial discs around each eye. These defined cup-shaped depressions act like a radar dish, reflecting sounds into the ear openings. The shape of the disc itself can be adjusted by facial muscles, sculpting the position of specialized feathers, further focusing minute sound waves. Even the owl's bill is shaped to reflect sound towards the ears.

An owl's ear openings are set close to the outside edges of their eyes. In many owls, if you gently part the feathers and look into the rather large opening of its ear, you can clearly see the backside of its eye!

Some owls have asymmetrically set ear openings, with one ear positioned slightly higher on their skull than the other. They can discern the minute time difference between their ears with more exactness than if these were positioned evenly, allowing them to pinpoint the precise source of even the slightest noise. Owls can detect a left/right time difference of 30 millionths of a second!

When proportioned to the size of its skull, the tiny saw whet-owl has what might be the largest ears in the animal kingdom. A great gray owl can hear a beetle moving along the forest floor 100 feet away, and a mouse squeaking at a distance of half a mile.

Owls have a distinctive thickset look, with their large heads and seeming absence of any neck, but this appearance is an illusion. Their bodies are deceptively small under their dense coating of feathers. Anyone who has held an owl will realize at once that they are much lighter than they appear.

It's these thick specialized feathers that produce the finest stealth technology of the avian kingdom. This near-silence also lets an owl use its locational hearing to stay focused on a mouse in motion while in flight. Owl feathers have a tattered fuzzy edge along one side. With any other bird in flight you'll hear a pronounced fluttering noise, but an owl's specialized feathers will dampen down any turbulence. The outcome is an eerily silent flight.

Owls have big wings for their size. It's common for someone to retell an owl sighting with dramatic adjectives like enormous and gigantic when excitedly describing those big wings. The Eurasian eagle-owl, one of the

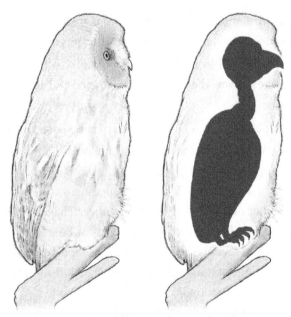

an owl's body under
its thick coating of feathers

world's largest owls, has a wingspan that can reach 79 inches (200 cm)—
that's six and a half feet wide, well over twice its height. These big wings
create a slow-motion buoyant look when it flies. An owl doesn't need to
do much flapping to stay aloft. It can glide smooth and slow for long
stretches. The slower the flight, the less noise created.

A falcon hunts using speed; its smaller wings are designed with a
knife-like shape. Falcons zoom in fast before their prey has a chance to
run. Owls, in contrast, float in slowly, and strike without being heard.

An owl can still hunt even if a mouse is hidden under a blanket of
snow, an excellent insulator of sound. There may be nothing to see on a
cold winter's night, but from its perch high in a tree, an owl can still accurately pinpoint the faint noises made by a mouse beneath the snow. The
owl uses its off-set ears in unison with those big night vision eyes creating
a mental image of this dark three-dimensional space. The owl targets the
exact location of the sound and locks onto it with its eyes, even from incredible distances. Against all this unified "technology," a little mouse
doesn't have much of a chance.

Once the owl determines the precise spot in a blank field of snow, it drops off its perch, opens its oversized wings, and glides smoothly toward the sound. Its body twists and turns while maneuvering around trees, but its head remains locked, eyes and ears zeroed-in on the source of the almost imperceptible noise. Flying low and slow, the owl hugs the terrain and avoids obstacles, all without flapping its wings.

If the prey moves beneath the snow, the owl will hear it, and make in-flight targeting corrections. When it gets to within two feet of its prey, it widens its wings and slows down. At the same moment, it brings its feet forward in a direct line between its eyes and the unseen mouse, its face never wavering from the sound under the snow. The talons strike, and the owl has food, all in near total darkness.

This is a book about owls, and their magnificent physical abilities are paralleled by their equally magnificent place in our folklore. We share the world with an amazing creature, highly adapted to travel in the shadow realm. Yet we rarely ever see an owl. This beautiful bird calmly performs its hunting rites in the darkness, night after night, beyond the watchful eyes of man. When you connect the UFO mystery to owls, a question arises: is there more to this masterful animal that we don't understand?

Fact-checker and a mournful call

The initial writing for the previous bit on owl physiology was completed late on a Sunday afternoon in October. There was still some sunlight, so I figured I could ride my bike to the little health food store on the main street. I usually listen to music on this three-mile ride from my house to town, and I was frustrated when I couldn't find my iPod.

I was feeling insecure as I peddled along the rural bike trail. It was a dreary evening, and I was unsure if my writing accurately captured the owls 'essence. I labored over that first draft, and worried it read like a biology textbook. About halfway to town, I heard a mournful harsh squawking. The calls were ringing out from a cluster of cottonwoods off in a horse pasture.

I got off my bike and saw the outline of an owl up in the branches. I shimmied under a barbed wire fence and walked towards the trees to get a better look. The previous few days were spent obsessively writing about owls and their heightened ability to see and hear, so I knew there was no way I could sneak up on it. I got close enough in the steely twilight to see a handsome great horned owl.

I stood in silence for about a minute, then watched the owl calmly drop from her perch. She opened impossibly large wings, given that she only looked to be about a foot tall in the tree. I watched her silently coast away, gliding slowly just above the sagebrush. I lost sight of her as she dipped low, but she reappeared to alight on a hay-barn about a quarter of a mile from where I stood.

Right then I recognized that this owl was playing the role of fact-checker, acting out some of the very things I had been writing about. Dropping from a tree branch, flying oddly slow, the silent flight, the over-sized wings, and hugging the ground in flight were right out of the text I had finalized less than an hour before.

When I got home, I found my iPod sitting in the middle of my desk, right where I should've seen it before riding to town. If I had been listening to music, I never would have heard those mournful squawks and never would have had the confirmation that my writing was pretty accurate.

Incidentally, I found an online audio excerpt titled great horned owl, female squawk. This exactly matched what I heard, which is why I referred to this owl as she.

Heightened senses

Homing pigeons will instinctively fly to their home nest, even if they are taken and released over 1,000 miles away. This remarkable ability was used to deliver the news of the Olympics in ancient Greece, over 3,000 years ago. A small message can be attached to their foot, so they are sometimes called messenger or carrier pigeons. Evidence strongly suggests that homing pigeons can see the lines of the Earth's magnetic field, and they use this ability to perform their namesake: homing in to an exact location. But what are they actually seeing?

Foxes hunt mice that are hidden under a deep blanket of snow. They wait and listen with their big ears, then pounce nose first into the snow. A fox needs an exact calculation of distance, depth, and alignment to catch a mouse under a meter of snow. Their success rate is low, that is, unless they are lined up and jumping 20 degrees east from magnetic north, then it vaults up to nearly 75% success. Researchers think that foxes align their pounces to the Earth's magnetic field, somehow using it to calculate their trajectory and target the mouse's position under the snow.

Other animals—sharks, turtles, ants, lobsters, beetles, bats, deer, cows, and mole rats—have the same ability to sense and use the Earth's magnetism. How they do this is not yet understood by science.

Bees see ultraviolet light. Hummingbirds see near ultraviolet light. Dogs hear ultra-high frequency sounds. Bats and dolphins navigate using ultrasounds and echolocation. A bear can smell carrion up to 20 miles away. My point here is that plenty of animals have extremely subtle and seemingly impossible sensory abilities.

The owl, however, could be the most gifted input receiver in the animal kingdom, so they might actually be sensing a UFO with that heightened aptitude. UFOs create some very weird effects, and owls might be able to detect their presence in ways we can barely comprehend, let alone test scientifically. The question is, are owls attracted to the site of UFO activity with enough consistency that it gets noticed by the abductees?

My cat Spazzy gets super focused when a piece of string is dragged across the floor. I'll skitter it along in front of her, trying to mimic the motions of a mouse. Doing this, her pupils dilate, turning almost entirely black, and her body conforms into that eager spring-loaded, pre-pounce pose. Her reactions are purely instinct, she simply can't help it, even though all she is seeing is a wiggly piece of string. Is there some unknown instinct that attracts owls to UFOs?

My cat is also attracted to the heater in my living room. This is a piece of technology that produces a measurable effect; warm air comes out of a vent. When it's turned on, she'll position herself in close proximity. There's no mystery here, the cat senses something and moves toward it. Are the owls simply sensing something and moving toward it? Maybe there is nothing more than curiosity that draws them to UFOs.

Owls are noted, in both mythology and firsthand accounts, to show up around highly charged locations and environments. Powerful emotions, synchronistic energies, sacred sites, and paranormal happenings like ghosts and hauntings; these are all environs where an owl might make an appearance. Maybe little kids draw owls next to a haunted house for a reason. Yes, this kind of speculation is pretty slippery, but it seems to address some of the more elusive aspects of the UFO experience, as well as the overlap with other highly charged events.

What about abductees who tell of owls hanging around their home? Do UFO abductees give off some sort of glow that owls can see? It might be something as simple as an aura around them that is slightly different than non-abductees. Perhaps people who have contact experiences are now tagged with some ethereal vibration that can be seen by owls. Maybe they've undergone some change not so much on a physical level, but there might be something heightened within their emotions, or their subconscious—or it might be happening at the level of their soul. I don't know what it might be; I'm just speculating that there could be something non-physical that an owl can see, and that attracts them. This distinct individuating vibe may fluctuate in relation to contact events, increasing or decreasing before or after an abduction.

I've asked people who might have had abduction experiences if they can wear a watch. Curiously, many say they can't. They'll say that it will simply stop, or the batteries will drain. The implication is that there is something about them that interferes with electronics (just so you know, I can wear a watch without any problems). Abductees will also report that streetlights will turn off above them when they are driving at night or walking under them—this has happened to me at prescient moments. What is happening? It seems abductees are influencing the reality around them in some very bizarre ways.

Will someone someday invent a highly sensitive camera that can pick up the subtle psychogenic emanations from a person in a way that might differentiate the abductees from the general population? This might not be all that far-fetched, I say that simply because there is evidence, albeit fleeting, that owls are seeing something in the abductee.

A gifted psychic might walk into a room and instantly pick someone out as being different. They might say they can see a white light around them, or they might get a deep instinctual knowing. I have spoken to more than one psychic who has looked to the empty spot next to where I was standing and they've told me they are seeing little aliens.

Do cats see invisible things? Any cat owner will tell you that their pet will sometimes look at nothing as if something were there.

My cat acts scared

There was a night a few years ago where I was alone in my cabin sitting on the couch watching a DVD, and as always, my cat Spazzy was sitting by my side. The whole scene was completely ordinary, but she was suddenly acting really scared. She got into a scrunched-up defensive pose and her tail poofed up huge. The hair along her back was sticking straight up. I tried to pet her to calm her down, but she didn't respond at all. I could feel her back was rigid and tight with tension, something I'd never felt before. I leaned over, looked at her face, and her eyes had dilated entirely black. She wasn't moving, she was totally focused on an empty spot in the center of the room just a few yards in front of the couch. I saw nothing, but my cat's overt display obviously meant *something*.

I got up and stood in front of the couch. I could see right where she was focused. She stayed frozen in that anxious pose with her dilated eyes fixed on an empty spot right in the center of the living room rug. At that point, my cat's intensity was so acute that I absolutely *knew* something must be there.

I stood in the middle of the room, and confronted the empty spot. I spoke out loud, "I can't see you, but if you have anything to say to me, I respond well when I receive messages in my dreams, so please communicate that way." That said, nothing happened in my dreams that night. This speaks to where I was at with all the weird stuff in my life—it felt absolutely normal to talk to an empty spot on the rug in my living room.

This went on for about ten minutes, and I was getting really paranoid. Eventually, Spazzy changed her posture, jumped down from the couch, and sat under the coffee table, still focused on that empty spot. I watched as she slowly eased her way closer to the center of the room, and cautiously sniffed around that empty spot on the rug.

This whole event was decidedly unusual. I should add that earlier in the day I had a 90-minute psychic session with a gifted clairvoyant, Anya Briggs. I was at a point in my life when a lot was happening, and I needed some answers. She wrote me an email when she heard about my cat and her intense reaction. Here's what she said:

I don't want to freak you out, but sometimes, beings open portals to check things out. That is all they come to do. I think that's what happened—actually, hold on—the beings are saying that's exactly what happened. I think I should explain because I am not surprised this happened at all and cats are naturally psychic...

What was Spazzy reacting to? Was there an open portal to another dimension in my living room? Or an alien specter peering into my reality? I don't have any good answer, all I know is that my cat was absolutely focused on something I couldn't see. What if an owl was in my living room that night, would it have stared at the same empty spot?

As a curious aside, the movie on the DVD was *The Hustler* (1961) starring Paul Newman and Jackie Gleason. It was well known that Gleason was quite the aficionado on the UFO subject, and there is a wonderful story that late one night he got a knock on his front door from his golfing pal Richard Nixon. This would have been during Nixon's presidency, and he drove Gleason, just the two of them alone in the car without any security, to nearby Homestead Air Force Base. As the story goes, they entered a tightly guarded building to view little alien bodies, supposedly from the Roswell, New Mexico UFO crash of 1947.

The Oz Factor

I sent an email to UFO investigator, Dr. Jacques Vallee, and asked if he'd come across any unusual owl reports in his research. He replied with an account of two people driving together at night, who were forced to stop because an owl made an awkward landing on the road in front of them. It was completely disoriented and unable to take off. Right at that moment, their attention was diverted from the owl to an unknown craft above them. This helpless owl was flopping around on the pavement at the same time a close encounter was in progress. It seemed as if the owl had somehow been affected by the hovering craft.

Owls are, if nothing else, extremely sensitive input receivers, the entirety of their physiology is a combination of very acute hearing and remarkable night vision. Could these finely tuned senses have been disrupted by the proximity of a UFO?

One of the questions an investigator will ask a UFO witness is if they noticed any odd animal reactions during their sighting event. Dogs might whine, cats might hide, horses might act jittery—this kind of odd behavior is commonly reported. What exactly are these animals reacting to? The witnesses, the human kind, might also have reactions. Hair rising on their heads or arms gets reported; this might mean there is a source of static electricity nearby. Car radio disturbances, electrical malfunctions, and streetlights shutting off are all repeated throughout the literature. Accounts of irrational fear, or irrational calm, both get reported. Some witnesses will describe a feeling of moving in slow motion, as if time itself has been distorted. What is creating these reactions?

If a craft has landed, there might be physical marks on the ground. The dirt and plants can show signs of high heat. Soil samples from landing sites might be incapable of absorbing water, and the affected area can remain chalky and dry for years. Conversely, sometimes the soil becomes more productive and the plants within the landing zone will grow unusually large and healthy. We don't know what energies might be creating these effects, but from so much witness testimony, it seems safe to say that something very unusual is happening. How we might perceive the strange physical effects of a close up UFO is hard to know, and trying to guess how an owl might react is speculation at its flimsiest.

Earlier in this chapter, I put forth a long list of specialized abilities that make the owl remarkably well suited for perceiving extremely subtle input. Could it be that UFOs are emanating some tone or vibration within a narrow band of sound waves, and these vibrations are unheard by humans, yet line up with an owl's hyper-attuned ability to hear? Basically, a UFO could be the equivalent of a giant dog whistle that can attract owls.

Owls and UFOs are both described as flying with an eerie silence. There are some odd consistencies in close-up UFO reports, and one of the most commonly noted effects is this unusual silence. It's not that the unknown object flies silently, it seems to turn off all the sound in the area. No bird noises, no crickets, no rustling of leaves—*nothing*. If there is any sound from a UFO it gets reported in odd ways. There might be a buzzing, like a hive of bees, or the witness might describe an ultra-low bass noise that is felt in the chest, like standing too close to the thumping amps at a rock concert; this might not be heard as a sound at all, but as a sensation within the body. Sometimes UFOs can sound like owls (reported later in this book). This is just a small part of a long list of bizarre details that get reported by close encounter witnesses.

Beyond the eerie silence, close encounter experiencers will often report a bizarre warping of reality, as if their consciousness was being altered or distorted.

The term *Oz Factor* was coined in 1983 by British UFO researcher Jenny Randles. She was trying to describe this strange, but commonly reported, effect that emerges in close proximity to these unknown craft. She noted that the witnesses consistently described a strange calmness, which was in contrast to the highly bizarre circumstances they were confronting. The Oz Factor was a way to describe "the sensation of being isolated, or transported from the real world into a different environmental framework... where reality is but slightly different." She went on to state that, "The Oz Factor certainly points to consciousness as the focal point of the UFO encounter." This is a bold statement given the nuts and bolts mindset of the research community at that time.

Randles wrote about these highly unusual sensations and how they are described by UFO witnesses:

> If someone saw a light in the sky or even had a mundane UFO encounter with a strange looking craft, then these things would rarely appear. But if they had a close encounter, then these symptoms were there more often than not.
>
> Witnesses would tell me that they felt a strange sensation prior to the encounter—a sort of mental tingling as if they were aware that something was about to happen. They would even tell me that they just had to look up and see what was there—as if it had called to them silently.
>
> Then I would be told that during the experience time seemed to disappear and lose all meaning. It was as if the encounter were happening in a timeless, magical void. Further clues kept popping up the more that I tabulated these cases. For instance, there were claims that at the onset of the episode all ambient sounds faded away—bird song, the wind in the trees, distant train noises, etc.

All these clues pointed towards an isolation factor at work, as if the witness were being singled out and put into a cocoon... this sense of isolation became very obvious.

The Oz Factor implies that the UFO close encounter has a visionary component. You might interpret that as meaning it is all in the imagination, but it really means there is a direct feed, if you like, from the source of the encounter to the consciousness of the witness. [10]

Randles paints a vivid picture of an elusive sensation, as if some weird effect is emanating from the UFO and distorting our ability to perceive reality. Could this be what attracts the owls? Could they see it, or sense it, in ways we simply don't understand? Maybe an owl can receive input in ways that stretch beyond the boundaries of the physical. Can it see our emotions, our auras, or maybe even our souls?

When an abductee describes their contact experience, they'll almost always paint the event with an odd dreamlike vibe. They'll struggle to articulate their memories because everything seems distorted—reality takes on a heightened clarity and an eerie silence. People might say their experience was *more real than real*. This same dreamlike quality might be present while under hypnosis, making it difficult for the hypnotized experiencer to truly trust their memories. A powerful vision could emerge in that vulnerable state, yet what they see and hear might never have happened.

Any abduction researcher will be familiar with these descriptions of hyper-vividness. They'll state that direct contact with the aliens seems to take place in some altered reality. But what does that actually mean?

One thought is that merely being in the presence of the alien entities is so traumatic to the experiencer, that their sanity would be in jeopardy. So, this altered state might be imposed as a protection for our benefit. I have talked to a few people who have seen aliens in what would be their normal waking consciousness. What they'll describe is a sledgehammer blow to the very fabric of reality, as if their soul might be shattered from the discordant shock. It goes way beyond simply seeing something scary, it's as if the actual proximity to these aliens is incompatible with existence itself. Some abductees will say the aliens vibrate in a different way, and we just can't handle it.

Some contact experiences seem to take place in an *out of body experience* (OBE), where an abductee can look down and see their physical body as they are floated away by the aliens in an etherial form. These altered experiences with reality might be tied into the Oz Factor, and it's these heightened or altered states that might be perceived by the owls.

Winter of 1993, near Standish Maine

I've had my own experiences with these subtle realms, and they've played out with a palpable exactness. The sensations have been unmistakable and distinct each time they have happened. This distorted feeling has permeated everything, and each time it has had an apparent connection to a UFO event.

I've experienced this sensation, or something similar, four separate times. The first was in 1993, which I discussed previously. I awoke from a sound sleep because a bright light was flooding my bedroom. I sat up in bed and looked out the window to see five spindly gray aliens walking towards my house.

They were on the lawn, very close to my bedroom window. They were back-lit by a singular round bright shape, and this light seemed oddly small. My response to this frightening image was to think to myself, "*Oh yes, they're here. Now is the time to put your head on the pillow and black out.*" After that, I nonchalantly laid my head on the pillow and promptly fell back asleep.

Shouldn't I have jumped out of bed screaming in terror? Instead, I felt absolutely empty, as if my emotions were switched off, and my reactions were somehow controlled. This whole event probably lasted less than 30 seconds. The next morning I dismissed it as a dream and, as noted earlier, I never bothered to check for footprints in the snow.

This happened over twenty years ago. I've written about it, drawn pictures, and wrestled with the implications. I wrote a long post on my blog where I tried to express the utter strangeness of this memory. At the core of this experience was a definite change in normal perceptions, a kind of distorted consciousness.

It felt dreamlike, but unlike any other dream I've ever had. I don't dream of myself being in bed, as I was at the moment. Here is an excerpt of what I initially wrote to describe this sensation:

> This memory is strangely vivid in a way that seems entirely different from a normal state of mind—weirdly quiet—sort of like being in a pressurized fish bowl—the deepest part of my psyche is displaced and moved to the forefront—the normal thought chatter in my head is turned off—maybe—kinda—sorta—a distinct warping of my psyche, whatever that means—because this strangely vivid state of mind was so weird, I do not fully trust this memory.[11]

In the years since writing that, I've had three other experiences with that same distinct sensation. It is unmistakable, feeling exactly the same each time. The power of these follow-up experiences are enough to confirm to me that what happened on that winter's night in 1993 wasn't a dream.

Attempting to describe this distorted feeling in words would only hint at the sensations. All I can say is that what I felt was completely unique. I have made a concerted effort to ask other UFO abductees if they've ever experienced this altered state of consciousness.

Brigitte Barclay has had a lifetime of UFO contact experiences, and even a few odd owl events (more on this in chapter five). I spoke with her in person in the summer of 2014, and she tried to articulate what it felt like to be in the presence of this unknown force. She held up both hands with her palms facing each other, and slowly moved them closer together, and then just as slowly backed off.

She described the sensation of holding two powerful magnets so they repel each other when you try to press them together. She said, "You know that weird warping energy? That's what it feels like, it's like my whole body is in between those magnets in that distorted zone."

When she said that, *I absolutely knew we had both experienced the same thing.* She was describing something physical, the energies produced by two magnets, and this was exactly what I'd felt. A junior high school student can see these waves of energy on a smooth surface using a magnet and iron shavings. A homing pigeon can see similar waves in the sky. Could it be that an owl can see these energies with its highly attuned vision?

In his 1992 book, *Visitors from Time*, the late Marc Davenport proposed that it might be a distortion of time that is creating the sensation of silence and altered consciousness. He speculates that the actual propulsion of the UFO might be some form of time disruption. Some close encounter witnesses will tell of feeling as if they are moving in slow motion, or as if they are in some other time dimension. I read one report where an abductee told of being taken from a crowded swimming pool in the summertime. She described time stopping. The UFO occupants stepped in, escorted her from the scene, and later returned her to the same moment. Time around her had stopped so completely that she could see water being splashed by children in the pool, and the droplets stood frozen in mid-air.

Marc Davenport died in 2008 after a long battle with cancer. It was well known within the small community of UFO researchers that he was an abductee. What I find so fascinating is that someone with direct contact experiences would write a book with such a compelling set of ideas. He made a strong argument that altering time could be *both* a form of propulsion *and* the source of the anomalous effects commonly reported in proximity to a UFO. This is daring stuff that almost nobody else has touched in this field.

It's not uncommon to hear abductees say that they knew an abduction would be taking place soon, and then it happens. For people with a history of UFO contact, these impressions might come as a psychic premonition or as a tangible physical feeling. They'll describe a vibration or buzzing sensation in their body. They might feel it within their gut or chest. Sometimes it's a sense of knowing. What are they feeling? Are they psychically predicting the future, tapping into something further along the timeline? Or is there some palpable energy that precedes an event like a UFO abduction? I've been told directly that there is an unmistakable vibration that can be recognized from previous abduction accounts. Does the craft itself send out some barely perceivable emanation that people can sense? Does reality itself somehow vibrate in advance of a cosmic doorway opening into another dimension?

I've collected quite a few reports where people will hear an owl hooting right before an abduction occurs. These folks don't need to feel a psychic vibration, the owl seems to announce the arrival of the UFO occupants. Maybe in some cases, this eerie call is an audio form of screen memory?

There are countless stories of mysterious unmarked vans parked in front of the homes of abductees, and after repeatedly hearing these accounts, a kind of paranoid narrative emerges. If these vans are there for some reason, are they hiding shadowy government technicians who are busily gathering information? They seem to be positioning themselves within close proximity to the abductees. Are these vans filled with advanced instrumentation that can monitor subtle changes in things as simple as heat, high-pitched noises, or radiation? Or, are they trying to monitor something more exotic like gamma-ray bursts, or maybe shifts in time itself? I am only guessing what might be at play, but the accounts of these cloak-and-dagger vans are so consistent that they must be there for a reason.

Something as profoundly strange as UFO contact would probably produce some profoundly strange effects. There must be *something* happening that can be sensed or even measured. It might be that owls can sense this unknown something.

The hospice cat

There is a rather famous cat named Oscar that lives in a nursing home in Providence, Rhode Island. This cat seems to have the mysterious ability to know when a patient is close to death. Most of the time he's aloof, shunning attention from the staff and patients, but he has a sense of *knowing* that has proven eerily accurate. Oscar spends his days pacing from room to room. He sniffs and looks at the patients but rarely spends much time with anyone, except when they have only hours to live. He's accurate enough that the staff understands that it's time to call family members when Oscar curls up beside their patients, most of whom are too ill to notice his presence. If he's kept outside the room of a dying patient, he'll scratch at the door trying to get in.

What is Oscar sensing? Is he simply attuned to some extremely subtle metabolic stresses that are part of the death process? Is he tapping into the subconscious emotional awareness of the patient? Or, is he somehow seeing the astral presence of long-dead loved ones who have come from beyond the veil to hold vigil at the bedside of their dying friend, waiting to usher them to the other side? Is he seeing into the future, somehow predicting the death? Is he sensing an aura, a vibration, a life force, or the presence of angels? I don't know, but he certainly seems to be sensing *something* that we cannot.

It appears possible to sense death approaching. Could it be that predators, like cats and owls, have developed some ability to detect the parting of the veil? Oscar might sense the door to the other side gently opening, welcoming a soul to the afterlife. If owls share this ability, this might be the source of the ever-present folklore that they are somehow connected to death.

Seeing through the eyes of the owls

The UFO abduction literature is awash in stories where the abductee is influenced to do things that are completely beyond their normal behavior. A recurring example would be someone waking in the middle of the night and feeling compelled to drive alone to some remote location. It might be a place they've never been to before, but they drive there as if

64

they know the route by heart. They'll do all this without ever questioning that it's in any way unusual. They will arrive at some secluded field at the end of a dirt road to find a UFO waiting for them. What follows would be an all-too-familiar abduction event. When it's all done, they'll calmly drive home without any sense of having done something out of the ordinary.

This kind of mind control, in one form or another, is consistently reported. Abductees are being controlled with absolute mastery by unknown entities from an unknown place. The UFO occupants might be controlling owls in a similar way.

Whitley Strieber has speculated that the gray aliens, using some sort of telepathy, might be able to *see* through the eyes of owls. The ability both to see and fly in almost total darkness would make owls an excellent choice for the role of *alien surveillance camera*. The implication is that these alien entities were looking at both Kristen and me, through great big eyes, on two separate nights in the mountains.

Using owls as a kind of flying camera seems quite practical, although pretty far-fetched. That said, the entirety of the UFO phenomenon is pretty far-fetched, but the consistency of what gets reported is impossible to ignore. Whatever the source of the contact experience, there are reliable reports of powerful psychic and telepathic abilities on the part of these unknown entities.

I spoke at length to a woman who had what seems to have been a UFO abduction experience, which involved a stretch of missing time while in her car. Soon after this event, she began to experience clear telepathic messages. She says that this communication was from her ancient ancestors, all of them shamans, and they said *they could see through her eyes*. Among other requests, they pleaded with her to go to the tea aisle in the grocery store. They told her to carefully inspect each and every box to indulge their curiosity. She described them as positively giddy when she obliged, carefully reading the ingredients on the back of each little box. This story paints a picture of tea drinkers from long ago who are now in some other realm where doing something so three-dimensional, like drinking tea, is now impossible.

The late Ida Kannenberg was an author, abductee, and psychic channel. She wrote that her alien guides were totally thrilled on the day she went to Sea World. They were excited to be able to watch the dolphins *through her eyes*. She also said these guides would get frustrated and scold her for skimming through books and not reading every word on every page. It seems that they were looking through her eyes and reading along with her.

Using the eyes of birds as a kind of avian-reconnaissance is part of Norse mythology. Odin created two Ravens, *Huginn* and *Muninn*, or thought and memory. They would fly around Midgard (Earth) each day and then return to Odin, transferring all they had perceived to him. Odin, the father of Thor, is a principal member the Norse pantheon of gods and is associated with death, wisdom, shamanism, magic, and prophecy.

Seeing through the eyes of an animal could be part of the shamanic mission. I have the image of the village elder dragged into the spirit realm after ceremonially drinking a brew of sacred psychedelic plants, and then racing through the jungle as if merged with his totem animal, like a puma, deer, or owl.

Heather Clewett-Jachowski is a shaman and researcher of ancient sacred sites. She has a powerful story from a summer's night in the crop circle country of southern England. She described an electric feel in the air as she approached a white owl perched on a fence post. It watched her, spread its wings, and flew off into the darkness. At that point, Heather had odd visual sensations. She saw the ground zipping below her, getting closer, and then farther away. It took a moment to realize what she was experiencing—she was *seeing through the eyes of the owl* as it flew over the undulating terrain.[12]

From stories like these, seeing through the big night vision eyes of an owl should be no big deal for the UFO occupants. I talked about these ideas with another abductee at a UFO conference, and he thought using an owl as an alien surveillance camera was perfectly pragmatic. There is no better animal in the world to play this role than the stealthy owl.

We speculated that the owls could be employed as an advance scout before any actual abduction. They are equipped with excellent onboard night-vision, and this could be used to send back real-time images of their intended landing spot and the exact location of an unsuspecting abductee. Owls could sit on window sills and eavesdrop on conversations with their powerful ears. They could patiently watch from trees so the monitoring aliens would know when an abductee had arrived at home. Plus, the owls could fly around in near-complete silence to ensure there weren't any other people nearby who might witness the alien's impending covert operations. The owls could also be on the lookout for any sneaky government intelligence agents spying on the abductee from a parked van or the neighbors' bushes. This transfer of sound and visuals could all be done with purely psychic means, a direct mind-to-mind connection between the owl and the UFO occupant.

It's also possible that this form of spying might require a physical device within the owl's body. I've had more than one abductee tell me that they have tiny implants in their body, and the aliens use these to see what we see, and hear what we hear. Others will say they are tracking devices, similar to what a biologist might put on a grizzly bear in Yellowstone. These curious implants are occasionally removed from these abductees by surgeons. What is then studied is usually very small, but with some extremely strange properties. These objects have been scrutinized in advanced laboratory settings, and they've found isotopic ratios incompatible with anything here on Earth, better likened to meteorite samples. Researchers and experiencers have put forth plenty of ideas as to the purpose of these implants, but there's no good answer what they actually do

If these tiny implants can be put into people, they could certainly be put into owls. So there might be a little technological gizmo that allows the aliens to watch the owl-cam using a big view screen and joy-stick from aboard their flying saucer, but that notion is probably far too simplistic.

I have no idea if any of this is true, but it seems reasonable. All I can say is that there is a tidy practicality for an owl to play such a sneaky covert role. Researchers who have really studied the perceived abilities of these aliens might scoff at any need for an owl to act as camera. They'd assert that these beings are so immeasurably advanced they could simply use their psychic skills to read every thought, and know the location of anyone of interest, including owls.

It's impossible to know precisely what is going on with the owls and their connection to the UFO lore. The screen memory aspect of owls requires we accept the psychic (or technological) powers of the aliens to influence the mind of the observer. Once we go down that path, it all gets thorny—perhaps the entirety of the phenomenon is some form of grand screen memory.

There is a reason to be in awe of owls. Even if you completely dismiss the paranormal aspects reported by abductees, they are still amazing creatures with near mystical abilities. Their presence alongside UFOs might be something purely physical, and they could be using their heightened senses to notice things we simply can't perceive. Or it might be something metaphysical; the owls could be tapping into the synchronistic ether like a winged mystic. These are muddy waters, yet there may come a day when we invent something that can sense the presence of a flying saucer. Until then, we may need to look to the owl as a silent oracle, the same role it has played throughout the ages.

PART II

EXPERIENCING OWLS

Chapter 4:

Owls and the UFO Abductee

Instead of looking at the screen, what I want to do is to
turn around and look the other way. When we look the
other way what we see is a little hole at the top of the
wall with some light coming out. That's where I want
to go. I want to steal the key to the projectionist's
booth, and then, when everybody has gone home, I
want to break in.

—Jacques Vallee

If you ask a UFO abduction researcher, "Have you had any odd experiences with owls show up in your reports?" They'll say yes, and then rattle
off some screen memory accounts with owls, much of it will sound like
the stuff you've just read.

If you follow up by asking, "Beyond screen memories, do you have
any unusual reports in your files involving *real owls?*" They'll most likely
answer, no, they haven't.

I've asked these questions of some of the elder statesmen in the field
of UFO abduction research, people like Budd Hopkins, Dr. David Jacobs,
Dr. Leo Sprinkle, Jerome Clark, Barbara Lamb, Joe Montaldo, John Carpenter, Yvonne Smith, and Mary Rodwell. These researchers must have
a century of research among them. Collectively, they have talked with
what I can only assume are tens of thousands of people who have had

direct UFO contact. But when I ask about *real owls*, I am continually surprised that there is almost nothing they can tell me.[13]

I searched through books and reports by the late Dr. John Mack wondering if I would find any reference to owls beyond the screen memory aspect, but never found anything. I then contacted someone at the Mack estate who ran a database search of his transcripts. I was allowed to review some redacted excerpts from a series of support meetings facilitated by Dr. Mack. Within these accounts were participants talking about odd experiences with what seemed to be real owls.

Dr. Mack commented on one of these stories. He said his initial thought was that the owl was some sort of screen memory, although what was described in the account seemed more like a real owl. Dr. Mack said: "I think there's some way in which it may be more symbolic." This clearly implies he was aware of something well beyond just the screen memories reported by experiencers.

Dr. Mack used the term *reified metaphor* to express that these experiences may be both literal and metaphorical. *Reify* means to make an abstract idea real. This idea of a *reified metaphor* presents itself as a paradox. Dr. Mack was clear that these experiences can be vividly and undeniably real "while at the same time it is deeply metaphoric or archetypal, including representations of death, birth, rebirth, transcendence, and enlightenment."[14]

Many experiencers have told me extremely bizarre accounts of real owls showing up in connection to their UFO encounters. It's certainly not one hundred percent of the abductees that will tell these stories, but it happens enough that I recognize a pattern. Something is going on.

I tried to explain my ideas about real owls showing up around the time of UFO contact during a phone conversation with abduction researcher Dr. David Jacobs. He was quick to challenge me, pointing out that he had done a lot of work with abductees, saying, "You need to be extremely careful—*extremely* careful."

He told me that every time he'd investigated this, it's turned out owls were actually a screen memory. I tried to hold my ground, detailing some of my own experiences as well as my research, but he was having none of it. He then asked if these were actually real owls, why aren't people getting pictures of them? I replied that I've received a lot of owl pictures from experiencers. He was unimpressed, and I wasn't up to arguing my point.

Why are so many researchers unaware (or dismissive) of the strange role real owls have played in the lives of some abductees? Maybe I've been seeing a pattern simply because I'm asking a question that the UFO abduction researchers aren't.

During this research, I've had owl stories arrive in my lap in wildly synchronistic ways. Obviously, I am asking for these kinds of owl experiences on my website, so that must be a big part of what I'm receiving. Yet, I can't help but wonder if there are magical forces at work that are making sure that any relevant story involving owls and UFOs somehow ends up in my files. It feels like I haven't done that much research—all I do is check my email each morning to find amazing stories. It feels like a weird aspect of synchronicity is somehow generating exactly what's needed for this book project. It has been absolutely bizarre how the perfect owl story will arrive at the perfect moment, as if some veiled influence outside myself has been creating this book project for me.

The UFO abduction researchers will point out that owls have great big eyes, and this is similar to the great big eyes of the aliens. As noted earlier, it's as if the UFO occupants are choosing the owl as a screen memory simply because they look like them. This explanation has been repeated so many times that it's considered to be a truth. It's instead an assumption; there's no answer as to *why* they're choosing the owl as one of their screen memory costumes.

The screen memory aspect of the contact experience is fascinating, and the mind control implications are staggering. But of more interest to me are the *real owls* that are showing up in connection with these sightings and experiences. The focus of this research has been people who tell of seeing real owls, and this traces back to my own experiences with owls, very often at highly charged or synchronistic moments. I feel strongly that the owls I've seen are *real owls*. They appeared normal in every way, in size, and behavior.

The question arises, why are real owls showing up in connection to UFOs?

I have amassed a wealth of reports where people describe what seem to be real owls right around the time of a UFO sighting. While reviewing these cases, I'm forced to ask two questions; one: Is the witness actually an abductee? And two: Is the sighting actually a hidden abduction experience? Neither are easy to answer. The initial problem is that it's hard to know if the witness is seeing a real owl, or some sort of psychic projection.

Stranger yet, I've talked to abductees, or people I suspect has had abduction experiences, and I'll ask the question: "Have you ever had any odd experiences with owls?" And every so often I'll get a reply like: "Oh yes, I had an experience with an owl that totally changed my life!"

It's as if the owl triggered a spiritual awakening. These are rare, but I've heard enough of these transcendent stories that it forces me to look at the overall mystery in a much deeper way. It's my sense—and this is impossible to know for sure—that *most* of the people coming to me with unusual owl stories have had direct contact with the UFO phenomenon, and by this I mean abduction.

I've seen a lot of owls, and I feel strongly that none of these sightings have been screen memories. These owls were normal sized, flying around, and doing things that real owls would do. But some of these sightings are clustered around such powerful moments in my life that they just feel important—as if owls are manifesting for some deeper purpose. I've been trying to come to terms with how the UFO reality has collided with my life, and it feels like owls have been signposts along this path.

I heard a nice analogy from a guy who has had an overwhelming amount of unusual activity in his life, both with UFOs and owls. He said: "Owls are like firemen. If you see a building on fire, you might see a bunch of guys running around with funny helmets, long rubber jackets, and hoses. *They didn't start the fire, they just seem to show up.*" He's as baffled as I am about the role of the owls in this mystery, and like myself, he's convinced they are somehow connected.

Ashlee's story

What follows is a short excerpt from an account written in October 2010, by a young woman named Ashlee. She begins by describing something unusual in the night sky, and in the wake of her sighting, weird things began to occur. She wrote:

> I had to pull over onto the side of the road. There was a large flying object hovering in the sky above me. It was making no sound whatsoever, and was flying very low (about a house and a half high) There weren't any flashing lights on it, only a red dangling string that was lit up. There were three cars pulled over behind me, and the guy from the first car was taking pictures. The pictures were unclear, you could only make out the red light.
>
> After seeing this UFO I started noticing some weird things… I started having encounters with owls. Why owls? I have no idea.

Ashlee asked the same question that has been plaguing me—*why owls?* She was seeing and hearing them with a heightened frequency that scared her. From what she described, these seem to be real owls and not screen memories. She also started having strange dreams with both owls and UFOs together. Along with all that, she wrote about an odd experience with her mobile phone.

> Two weeks ago I woke up to a text from my boyfriend that said, "What the hell are you talking about?" When I checked my outbox I noticed four strange texts that I don't remember sending. I saved them in my phone.
>
> **Message one:** It will identify all planes in the sky. Will detect unotherized flying objects and will warn them of aliens near by.
>
> **Message two:** Yes, destroy it. We must hold our ground.
>
> **Message three:** You will remain undetected.
>
> **Message four:** They threaten us but they are weak, report back to me.
>
> I don't know what these mean, they don't make very much sense. I know it's possible to sleep walk and sleep talk, *but sleep text?*

74

Ashlee ended her written account by asking, "If anyone has had any similar experiences, please let me know." So, she did the same thing I've been doing.

I have spoken to Ashlee and she shared enough that I see her as one more of the *maybe people*. She is a sensitive young woman dedicated to meditation and shamanistic practices with the goal of someday being a spiritual counselor. This kind of divine commitment has been a very clear pattern within this research. The people seeing UFOs and owls are, for the most part, seekers.

Bonnie Jean Mitchell's stories

Bonnie Jean Mitchell is very clear that she is a life long contactee. She has written about her extensive experiences with the star people (her term for who she's been in contact with) in her 2011 book, *Invitation To The Self*. She's also had experiences with owls, both as screen memories and with real owls. She sees owls as messengers, and as spiritual beings with a direct link to the star people.

During a time of heavy contact in her 20s, if Bonnie heard or saw an owl in the evening, she knew the star people would show up that night. Her descriptions and experiences match what a lot of others have hinted at, but she states it with a refreshing directness. She describes these owl sightings in her book:

> Owls have made a huge impact on my life, not just by appearing in screen memories, but by entering my waking world as well. I've come to find that when I hear an owl in the evening, there is a good probability I will have a visitation. I do not know what the connection is, but it's there. On more occasions than I can count, owls have "alerted" me to the possibility of visitation. In many ways, I consider the owl to be a helpful guide. Sometimes, however, I'm not pleased when all I remember from a night's experience is the vision of an owl… but this also alerts me and tells me to look deeper for hidden memories.
>
> For example, one evening I heard two owls hooting outside my bedroom window, somewhere very close by. I thought that I might look out the window to see the owls, but then I thought better of it,

75

not wanting to "bring on" a visitation; some nights I longed for regular sleep. So, I didn't look, but that did not prevent the event from occurring. The next morning, my left arm felt sore, like I had a bruise. I checked it out and found a brand new scar. I had no recollection of any dreams that night, which was quite abnormal for me. I realized there must have been something going on, but I never did figure it out. That was not always the case.[15]

Bonnie went on to explain about waking up on another morning without any memory of dreams. Then she recalled something strange from that night; she woke to the hooting of an owl. She wrote: "I looked out the window and saw a huge owl staring back at me. I am talking *big*, like three feet tall!" After that, she couldn't remember anything else. She was aware that this was a deceptive screen memory, and she was angry, feeling like she was being lied to by these visiting beings.

Nadine Lalich's story

Nadine Lalich has had a lifetime of UFO experiences. After decades of keeping these memories to herself, she came forward and openly shared her history of contact. She co-wrote a book with abduction researcher Barbara Lamb where she documents her own story. The book, *Alien Experiences*, was published in 2008. I spoke with Nadine in a recorded interview in 2012, and asked if she had any odd experiences with owls.

In her very clear way, she replied yes. She then went on to say:

2005 or 2006 was right at the point when I was making this turn, when I was stepping out and speaking my truth about this reality. It was at this time that owls started appearing around my apartment, great big owls. These weren't just owls that I would see in a dream, these were actually owls around my apartment, big owls. I would come home at night and there would be one on a branch near my door, or something similar. This was the first time I ever recall seeing owls in my life. It was strange that they would show up at that time in my life.

Nadine is well past the "maybe" point, and now accepts the reality of what she has endured. It's striking that these owls would make themselves known at the point she began sharing her experiences. Maybe the owls were somehow encouraging her to speak her truth.

Ron Johnson's stories

I have become friends with a soft-spoken man named Ron. I've met him over the years at a series of annual UFO conferences. His experiences are rich, detailed, and ongoing. In many ways, he reminds me a lot of myself. He has always been very cautious to avoid coming to any conclusions. All he will do is tell of his own direct experiences.

Ron is featured in an entire chapter in the book *Alien Encounters in the Western United States* by researcher Tracie Austin. She writes:

> Ron repeatedly witnessed numerous UFO sightings and encountered alien visitations at his home. He would also experience visitations from animals, an owl in particular, that would sit on the front porch of his mother's house, and remain there constantly day and night for over a week. Every morning, the owl would watch him walk down the steps to get into his truck to go to work, and then when Ron returned home, the owl would still be perched in the same spot, watching him get out of his truck, walk up the steps, and go into the house. Every day was the same.[16]

This sounds very much like a real owl showing up in an overt way in the life of an abductee. One more story of an owl (or owls) that are "staking out" the home during a time of heightened activity.

Ron also experienced something that sounds very much like a screen memory. I visited his home in May of 2013, and sat with him as he shared stories. He told me about waking up in the middle of the night and feeling a need to go outside. He walked out onto his front porch and saw a giant four-foot owl standing on his driveway. He described how they both stood there and stared at each other.

There was something about this experience that seemed so weird, and I asked him if this was a dream. He replied, "I'm pretty sure this was no dream. I remember feeling the cold porch under my bare feet. I think I was really out there."

There was an odd tone in the way he described standing on the porch and seeing that huge owl. There is a dreamlike quality that surrounds some of these experiences, and I sensed he was articulating this odd distorted reality. This ethereal sensation might imply the close proximity of the UFO occupants, and may be another example of the Oz Factor.

I received this note shortly after my time at his home, "After you left my house, there was an owl perched again in my garage watching me through the window into my living room."

Ron, along with plenty of other folks, has sent me photos of owls taken from his yard. Over the years, I've collected quite a few of these pictures, and some will be remarkably close up. I have a beautiful flash photo of a barred owl taken by a woman from her back porch. This image is captioned, "Took this from less than six feet away." Like Ron, she has sent me a lot of owl photos, and she's also an abductee.

Owl accounts from Sweden

In the summer of 1966, two young men were traveling by moped to Sörbo in the Swedish province of Dalarna, and the event took place while taking a short break in the countryside. This would have been around ten in the evening, still dusk at that northern latitude. While off their bikes, they noticed an owl sitting on a post beside the road.

Right after this, they noticed something else, a large silvery craft was hanging in the sky about 150 meters above the ground. The craft then moved slowly across the nearby fields as it emitted flashes of light. The boys hopped back on their mopeds and followed, watching it land in a nearby field. Once on the ground, it seemed to be surrounded by an unusual fog, and they saw what appeared to be humanoid figures. When the boys tried to get a closer look, the craft left the ground and accelerated away at a very high speed.

This 50-year-old case has witnesses seeing an owl right before seeing a UFO. This is a pattern found in a long list of other cases. There is no way to know if there is a buried abduction event connected to this sighting, but the details certainly send up a red flag. An owl sitting on a post sounds more like a *real* owl, and less like a screen memory.

This story came from the archives of Håkan Blomqvist, a UFO researcher from Sweden. He sought me out after learning of my investigation into owls and UFOs. What is even more curious (at least to me) is that Blomqvist, who has been actively researching UFOs for over 40 years, *also collects owls!* Here's what he wrote in his blog:

> For many years I have been collecting owl figurines of various types and material. I became fascinated by these unusual birds symbolizing both wisdom, magic and mysticism and my collection now comprises something like 60 plus owls. But it was not until the last couple of years that I became aware of the connection between UFO sightings and owls.[17]

Blomqvist has written three books on the paranormal (all in Swedish) with a focus on the connection between esoteric traditions and the UFO phenomenon. He's never had a UFO or contact experience, but he's had several mysterious experiences, including distant healing, precognition, and telepathy. So, a dedicated UFO researcher who has had psychic experiences is also collecting owls.

Blomqvist also shared another account, this one from August 8th, 1987, from the Swedish *Daily Post*, with the sensationalistic headline "I Saw The Devil." This event happened in the summer of 1980. No UFO in this account, but a weird owl-like apparition seems to proceed an even more bizarre monster sighting.

The article tells of Swedish-American Ingvar Oskar Johansson, who was traveling by car on a beautiful moonlit night from the eastern coast to Åseda. His eleven-year-old son was sleeping in the back seat. Not far from the town of Blomstermåla, the sky suddenly lit up with a blue light, and a large owl appeared in front of the car. He stopped, and the owl landed on the windshield. Ingvar could hear its cries. The owl's face seemed human, which frightened him—he felt as though the owl was looking right at him. After a few moments, it lifted and disappeared.

After traveling a few more miles, Ingvar had another experience with the unknown. While driving, he noticed what he first believed was an animal coming up from the side of the road. The next thing he realized was that this creature was floating up in the air in front of the car. He couldn't see its face, because it was covered with brown hair. It had two legs, a tail, two horns, and long ears. Ingvar's initial reaction was fear that it was an animal that had been hit by a car. He stopped, got out, and looked around, but found no trace of anything unusual. The rest of his journey was quiet.

Aimee Sparrow's stories

I've bumped into a woman a few times over the years at conferences. Her name is Aimee Sparrow, and I first saw her in the closed confines of a UFO support group, probably in 2008. I was rapt as she spoke with a curious confidence about her lifelong contact experiences. After the meeting, I went up to her and asked if she'd ever had any synchronicities. She responded without words, simply rolling her eyes in an expression of exasperation. It was the same pantomimed response you might get from a resident of Winnipeg if you ask them if it gets cold in the winter.

Some years later, she hinted to me that she'd had a few owl experiences. I contacted her by phone to ask about it, and we spoke late into the night, both of us sharing a long list of strange owl events. She's had a lifelong fascination with owls, and this seemed to play out alongside her abduction experiences. They've been showing up around her throughout her life, but it's only recently that she sensed they were somehow connected.

She had a powerful experience in the summer of 2010 at the ECETI Ranch (Enlightened Contact with ET Extraterrestrial Intelligence) near Mount Adams in Washington State. This is a gathering point for UFO watchers and new-age believers run by a fellow with his own contact experiences, James Gilliland. This place is an easy target for skeptics because of an almost cult-like lore, but pretty much *everyone* I've ever spoken with who has been there tells of having their own strange experiences.

Aimee describes standing in a field at night with a group of over 200 people. They were all collectively putting out the intention to see something in the sky. Suddenly they all saw some sort of orange glowing plasma pass over the entire group. Aimee was at a loss to describe what she saw and felt. It was as if time had stopped, the bright light was morphing in and out of reality—and she was awash in a feeling of unconditional love. It felt like she was being downloaded with highly charged emotions, and these were penetrating directly into her consciousness.

Aimee had a second UFO sighting the next night at the ranch. She was watching the sky along with at least 75 other witnesses when she saw a red rainbow-colored UFO morph into existence. This happened right after James did a "stargate opening" ceremony, and she had the same profound feeling of unconditional love.

When she got back home to California, she sat with her two kids and started telling them what she had seen and felt that night at the ECETI ranch. It was dark outside as they all sat together and she began to describe the event. Then she suddenly blurted out, "I gotta go upstairs!"

Without knowing why, she ran up to the second-floor balcony off her bedroom. As soon as she stepped outside, a large white owl swooped in slow motion close to her with its wings wide open. She was instantly flooded by the same emotional timelessness and love that she experienced in the presence of the orange light in that field in Washington.

Years later, Aimee woke in the middle of the night with the strange feeling of being called to go outside. She acted on this intuitive urge, and stepped out onto that same balcony off her bedroom; she clearly remembers it was 4:44 in the morning.

For reasons she doesn't understand, she thought to herself, "I'd like to see a spaceship, but I'd settle for a white barn owl." At that moment, she heard a loud screech and then saw a beautiful white owl in flight. It was huge and silent. Once again, she felt that same timeless sensation of unconditional love.

There was another event where she was with a handful of close friends. They were all out together at night in the Angeles National Forest. She and her companions saw a huge owl perched above them in a tree. They watched it for a little while before it flew off. At that instant, a giant triangular craft moved across the sky above them. This wasn't anything that could be described as metal, or even physical. Instead, they could see right through it, as if it was somehow *"beyond 3-D*, almost crystalline." It seemed as if its form was reflecting and distorting reality itself. This seems curiously similar to Derek's owl and UFO sighting, told earlier in this book. Although both crafts were triangular, the craft seen by Derek was described as decidedly physical.

The morning after seeing the triangular crystalline ship, Aimee saw a wobbly "Billy Meier" type of flying saucer floating along near her home. This happened in full daylight, and her house was high on a hillside, giving her an excellent vantage. She watched from above as this somewhat cartoonish craft slowly floated above a busy freeway in the canyon below. She was shocked that none of the drivers reacted. Her impression was that the traffic should've come to a screeching halt in the presence of something so bizarre. The implication is that only Aimee could see this craft, as if it were some sort of theatrical projection just for her.[18]

Aimee has had other equally strange owl experiences that leave me absolutely perplexed as to their purpose and source. The *vibe* of these owl events seems to match the overall weirdness of UFO sightings, even without any craft in the sky.

An owl and a flying orb

I received a long set of reports from a young man with the initials of JB, who had been documenting his many UFO sightings. When printed out, it was nine pages long, and each sighting was detailed and concise. He has been seeing a lot of unusual objects in the sky. Most of these are orbs that seem to have a circular glow around them appearing as orange, red, blue, and violet.

JB describes many of the orbs as silent and solid, flying beautifully smooth and fluid in a way that doesn't seem to conform with our reality. Many will materialize out of nothing and then disappear. He's also seen a bright metallic silvery ball that levitated in a stationary position, as well as a long silver, cigar-shaped object. Some of the sightings play out as if these craft are conscious of his thoughts, and many of these are seen (and confirmed) by other witnesses.

That one individual could see so many UFOs, and often photograph or video-record these sightings is rather common in this subject. It seems to play out as if these craft are manifesting specifically to be seen by these people. One set of sightings was particularly impressive.

> I saw something tonight... It was an orange/white orb coming from the south. It was quite small, and it seemed to be at a reasonable altitude. It moved rapidly and definitely faster and smoother than a plane. I do not think, feel, or believe this was a satellite, of any kind...
>
> What are the chances of seeing one whenever I go outside at night or think about them? This has happened nearly every night for the past few weeks. These aren't lies, nor do I think they are psychic fabrications... [This orange/white orb] was sighted at around 9:58 p.m. It was 10:05 p.m. as I finished writing this passage.

JB went inside to document what he had seen within minutes of his sighting. Most of his reporting was written in a very dry "just-the-facts" way. But that night he lamented about the *why of it*, and that so much of what has been happening to him goes beyond mere chance. What happens next, following his *questioning*, shouldn't surprise anyone who has gotten this far in the book.

> I went back outside, scanned the sky, saw a huge orange comet (?) that made a sizzling noise, and eventually saw another orb flying in the sky. It was possibly the same one as mentioned above, but this time it was coming down from the north.
>
> I kept hearing noises, and I started getting a little anxious. I turned my head to my right and I saw an owl on a power-line next to my house, it was staring at me and making noises. I was juggling between looking at the sky, the orb, and the owl in amazement. The owl was facing its head at me, and then redirecting its head towards the sky and moving its head around in a circular motion, or, circular like fashion. I kept going between the sky, and owl, searching for the orb again. The owl kept repeating this noise and

because of this I ended up losing the orb in the sky. The owl had flown away right before I could see the orb again.

I asked him if the owl actually looked at the orb, and he replied yes, the owl saw it too. I'm not sure if this qualifies as a multiple witness report, but this is the only account I have where an owl actually looks up at a UFO. It's also one of the very few accounts I have of an owl being seen right in the same moment with a UFO. In this case, both the owl and UFO flew off simultaneously. What is interesting is that it shows up right at the point that JB questions his numerous sightings.

Most UFO encounters have no connection with owls, but there are enough that I'm totally overwhelmed. Some of these owl accounts are so tightly intertwined with UFO contact that, to me, they've merged into one thing. I've collected such a wealth of these stories, and the similarities in tone are impossible to ignore. People are seeing or hearing owls before, during, and after seeing UFOs, as well as before, during, and after abduction events. I spoke with one young man about how he heard owls hooting out his window, waking him in the night, and then there were suddenly spindly gray aliens surrounding his bed. After that he blacked out.

I spoke with two women who were together when they saw an owl on a windowsill, staring in at them. What they described wasn't just seeing a bird out a window, it was emotional and dreamlike. Later they realized that the outside edge of the sill was far too small to allow a big bird like an owl to stand there and stare in at them. Based on separate conversations, I feel strongly that both these women are abductees.

This chapter is titled *Owls and the UFO Abductee*, and within these stories is the core mystery of the book. That people are actually having experiences that imply contact with some sort of non-human intelligence is strange enough, but adding owls into the mix makes it all the more bizarre. Like a performance on a stage, the owl is playing a small role in a grand drama, and the part it plays is a riddle begging to be solved.

Whatever is happening, it's real enough to see the patterns, yet elusive enough to remain a mystery. There is a mood to these stories, a gut feeling that goes far beyond just the nuts and bolts data collected by most UFO investigators. These are hunches and clues that lead nowhere, except perhaps *within*.

Chapter 5:

Owls and Windshields

A woman named Jan contacted me with an interesting owl experience. She lives in Australia and had recently become a member of a local UFO research group. She had no personal connection with any UFO events, but she has had a rich set of paranormal experiences with a form of intense spirit possession. For a time, she claimed to be sharing the consciousness with the spirit of William the Marshal, an English knight who died in the year 1219. This manifestation was so fierce that her home erupted in poltergeist activity, and electronic equipment either stopped working or outright exploded.

Jan recognized that these divergent phenomena, both UFOs and past lives, seemed somehow related. She also feels she has psychic abilities and has had prophetic dreams. She felt drawn to explore these subjects, and took part in a series of meditative programs with the intention of drawing in UFOs. These were night watch events, and used protocols created by Dr. Steven Greer.

A curious event took place in the follow up to her involvement with this UFO group. She was driving at night with her husband through a heavily forested area, and she was drifting off towards sleep. While in this half-awake state, she silently sent a question to the UFO occupants, "Are you real? I've spent years researching you and I haven't personally witnessed anything to suggest that you are real." She immediately received an answer. It came as a clear voice in her mind: "We don't want to startle you."

Having been at the receiving end of so much paranormal stuff, she laughed, "Startle me? As if anything could actually startle me!"

Right at that instant, an enormous owl smashed into the windshield. Both Jan and her husband were extremely alarmed and stopped the car. They got out and looked around, but there was no evidence of an injured owl, not even a feather on the road.

She described watching the owl lifting off from a low barrier between the forest and the road. It seemed to be flying in slow motion, and headed straight toward their car. Even though her husband put on the brakes, it hit the glass hard.

I am struck by the symbolism embedded in this story. She described the owl as perched on "a low barrier between the forest and the road." The road is symbolic of *the path*, or life journey. *The forest* represents the darkness that must be entered, a place of testing before reaching spiritual goals. The owl sat on *the barrier* between these two. This is the mythic role of the owl—the gatekeeper between the realms—and in this story it smashes violently against another barrier, the windshield, jolting her awake. The owl as alarm clock is another meaning, and it certainly played that role too.

Jan also pointed out that the road they were on winds its way through a beautiful area with a deep connection to Australia's indigenous people and their dreamtime mythologies.

I've collected a lot of stories where owls swoop in front of cars at night, but only a few where they actually hit the windshield. All these stories imply that the impact was incredibly hard. These people describe being shocked, stopping their car, and looking around for the wounded (or more probably dead) owl, but finding nothing. No feathers or blood on the windshield, nothing on the road or nearby.

If an owl does fly into a window, it can leave distinct markings on the glass. In 2011, a woman returned to her home in Kendal, UK to find a nearly perfect imprint of an owl on a window. An owl had crashed into the glass, leaving a ghostly white image, complete with eyes, beak, tail, and fully outstretched wings. Owls produce a talc-like substance called powder down; it's layered close to their skin and protects their growing down feathers. This powder created the haunting silhouette on the glass.[19]

It's rather common to see an owl zip across a car windshield at night. It has happened to me a few times, and usually there's nothing paranormal about it. What might be of significance is what was happening in the moments leading up to this sighting. I've said this repeatedly throughout this book, but when I hear people tell me about seeing an owl, I'll ask what they were thinking or saying right before it appeared.

Ben tells his stories

I am friends with a man who has only recently come to a place where he can openly admit the unusual events in his life. I understand this tension all too well, the need to share your own defining experiences and knowing full well that the rest of the world doesn't want to hear it. His name is Ben, and there are a lot of odd similarities in our lives and our experiences, enough that it seems beyond coincidence. There are a few folks that I feel a special bond with, and he is one of them. He told me a very interesting owl and windshield story.

He was driving an SUV full of children home from his daughter's birthday party at a skating rink. During the drive, the kids pleaded with Ben to tell them some stories. So, for the first time ever, he spoke about some of the strange things that had happened in his life, events that imply some sort of ongoing contact experiences. He was worried about scaring them so, he told his stories in a sort of "campfire" way. He shared with me:

> It was very emotional for me to tell these stories because, prior to that moment, I had never even hinted to my kids that I've had these experiences since childhood. I told them a ton of stories, with my missing time event as the finale. The stories were well received by all of the kids and I was feeling relief that I had crossed a milestone. I felt like I finally sort of came out to my kids, like I had left the door open for them to take away what they wanted from the stories. I was glad I had framed it in a way that I didn't overwhelm them.

Right as he finished speaking, an owl swooped in front of his windshield. It came down over the top of the car and flew in the headlight beams. All the kids let out a collective *whoa!* Ben said it was obnoxiously close, and after a moment of gliding out in front of the vehicle, it flew off and disappeared into the woods.

Ben was no stranger to synchronicities, so his immediate playful thought was, "Oh come on, an owl? How cliché! Couldn't you have sent something more original, like a bear?" Right then, a huge black dog ran across the road, and one of the kids shouted, "Look a bear!"

There wasn't any lag time, it all happened within seconds—finishing his stories, the owl, the dog, and the bear comment.

Reflecting on this account, Ben felt that telling his stories was something hugely important. Admitting to others what he's experienced has been terribly difficult for him, to the point where he feels it's a weakness. It has been, and he suspects always will be, a part of who he is. He took a small step forward while driving that night, and it felt like he received a knowing nod from the other world. The way Ben tells it, that owl was a synchronistic trail marker, acknowledging his effort to admit his own truth to others, especially his own children.

Ben has another significant story, it began when he took his kids out hiking on some nearby trails. While wandering through the forest, an owl appeared and followed them as they walked. It accompanied them for miles, swooping in and out of the trees, flying farther down the trail and perching above them, then watching as they hiked by. His children were excited by its presence, but there was something very mysterious about it.

Later that evening, as he tucked his children in for the night, Ben read them a book. They had picked it out at random prior to him coming upstairs. The book, titled *Say Boo!*, was about a ghost named Ben who could not remember how to say "Boo!" In the story, Halloween was nearing, and Ben the ghost was desperate to find his voice.[20]

Ben was reading from the book and said, "Ben looked up and saw a large owl sitting on a branch." Just as he read those words aloud, his dog started to bark frantically at the back door. He put the book down and went downstairs to let the dog out. When he opened the door, he had the uneasy sense he was being watched.

He looked up and immediately found the source of the feeling. There was an owl looking down at him from a large pine tree, and Ben feels certain it was the same owl that had been following him and his children all day. The words "Ben looked up and saw a large owl sitting on a branch," had been the last thing he said right before opening the door and seeing this owl.

In the writing process for this book, I've worked hard to be faithful to the witnesses and their stories. Ben and I did a lot of back and forth emailing to make sure the details of these two accounts were accurate. It was during this process that Ben had a realization and exclaimed, "Now that these two stories are written out and next to each other, *they have the same lesson!*"

Speaking one's truth gets acknowledged by the universe. When Ben the father found his voice and finally told his stories in a car full of children, an owl appeared. When Ben the ghost from the children's book found his voice, an owl also appeared.

Owl on an LA freeway

I was contacted by a friend named Cynthia the morning after an odd owl event. She and I both felt like this owl sighting was somehow related to my writing about owls. She is the same woman who picked up a tiny owl from the middle of a road, described earlier in this book. Unlike that story from years earlier, she is now well aware of the UFO connections in her life.

Cynthia was on her way home from a meetup of other experiencers organized by abduction researcher Barbara Lamb. She was together with a friend, both of whom have had ongoing experiences that imply UFO abduction, and both have had odd encounters with owls. They were driving at night on a freeway in Los Angeles. There came a point in the conversation when they started talking about God, and right then they both watched an owl swoop low across their field of view, frighteningly close to their windshield. She looked at the clock and it read 11:11. Don't ask me why, but this number has a curious way of showing up connected to these kind of odd events.

This account mirrors my experience with Kristen in the opening story, where a conversation about God seems to manifest an owl sighting. Her story also parallels an account later in this book of a woman who saw a big white owl while in a car full of experiencers after leaving Dr. John Mack's first support group meeting.

Incidentally, within these studies the number 11:11 is noted with a frequency that defies mere coincidence. The number might show up on digital clocks, license plates, or receipts from the grocery store. Obviously there is nothing unusual about the number, but many people observe it with a prevalence that seems highly unusual. It might be that the observer has a heightened awareness, and is unconsciously drawn to notice this number with an increased frequency.

Other number sequences are also reported, like 3:33 and 12:34. This phenomenon is common among UFO experiencers (and the maybe people), though plenty of others notice similar ongoing patterns. There are no answers as to why people are seeing these repeating numbers so frequently. This qualifies as a synchronicity, and although subtle, this a paranormal event in its own right.

Edgar Cayce mentioned 1111 only one time in his psychic readings. He spoke these words in 1929:

> The first lesson for six months should be One-One-One-One; Oneness of God, oneness of man's relation, oneness of force, oneness of time, oneness of purpose, Oneness in every effort—Oneness—Oneness!

Edgar Cayce (1877–1945) was an American mystic who allegedly possessed the ability to answer questions while in a trance on subjects as varied as reincarnation and Atlantis. He was known as the sleeping prophet, and what he did would be now be referred to as channeling. Much of the modern new age movement traces back to the impact of Cayce. His spoken words were transcribed by his secretary, who possibly wrote down the literal "one, one, one, one" instead of 11:11, as we would see it on a digital clock in present times.[21]

UFO experiencers will also report a pattern of waking up to see the number 3:33 on their bedside clock. Why that time shows up so often is an unknown. One thought is that this might be happening in conjunction with an unremembered abduction event, and the conspicuous time might be meant as a marker or clue.

"I see you"

Brigitte Barclay is an experiencer from England, and she had an owl event that was both mystifying and frightening. This happened October 9th, 2011, and in the UK that's written out as a tidy 9-10-11, and anyone with an eye to curious number sequences should take note. At that point she was well beyond the "maybe" status, and very aware of her lifetime of experiences. Like any powerful synchronicity, or dream for that matter, her owl story is tangled up in a series of other odd events.

That evening Brigitte went to a local electronics store to get a combination printer-scanner. She wanted to talk with the salesperson, but he was busy with another customer. After a long wait without any help, she decided to come back later.

It was nighttime when she left the store, and as she approached her car in the parking lot, she saw something sitting on the pavement near the rear tire. When she got closer, she saw it was a printer-scanner—it was out of the box and seemed to be brand new.

Her immediate thought was that someone had been watching her in the store and was playing a trick of some sort. She was flooded with paranoia and quickly got into her car to drive away, but was so shaken that she couldn't start the engine. Had she really seen the exact item she'd been looking for sitting next to her car? Awash in self-doubt, she got back out and touched the printer-scanner to prove to herself it was real. Why was it sitting there? She scanned the parking lot wondering if anyone was watching her. Then she picked it up, put it on the front seat, and drove away in an anxious state of shock.

The route home ran along narrow roads through rolling farmland. As she drove, she tried to make sense of what had just happened in the parking lot. Her mind was reeling as she approached a corner in the road, then she heard a sudden loud voice in her head saying: "*I see you.*"

At that moment, a big owl appeared in front of her and hit the windshield with a mighty boom!

The bird bounced off and disappeared. Brigitte's heart was pounding as she stopped the car, and she felt a desperate need to find the owl. There was no traffic, so she backed up slowly and looked for any sign of the it in the tall grass alongside the road, but there was nothing.

When she got home, she immediately told her teenage son what had happened. The boy had witnessed a lot of unusual things with his mother, and was adamant that this was a bad omen. He wouldn't let that printer-scanner in the house.

There's more to this story. The corner where she'd hit the owl was less than a mile from where she'd had a UFO sighting a few years earlier. Brigitte stopped her car to watch a large glowing white orb floating above the tree line. She got out, walked towards it, and stood within about 10 meters of the object, which she estimated was over a meter in diameter. As she approached, it moved silently down from the trees and floated away across a farmer's field.

The owl in this story is at the center of a swirling muddle of synchro-weirdness, and the outlying threads lead across the ocean to two of Brigitte's friends. These are a man and woman, both in America, both are experiencers, and both have pivotal roles in this strange story. They had an online Skype conversation on October 9th, and it began when the woman typed the letters "I C U" into the chatbox.

They later realized the time count of the comment lined up, as best as anyone can tell, precisely when Brigitte heard the words "I see you" in her head, and the next second an owl hit her windshield.

During their Skype call, the woman was at home in California, sitting outside with her computer. It was a clear blue day, and she watched an odd little cloud floating across the sky. The moment it was directly above her, a massive thunderclap boomed overhead, startling both of them.

I asked her if she thought the thunder happened at the same moment the owl hit the windshield, and she blurted out, "*Yes!*" Then she cautiously backpedaled, "Well, obviously I don't know, but that little cloud was just so weird. It doesn't make sense that it could've produced such a crazy loud burst of thunder."

I reached out and talked with each of the players in this tightly woven drama. The man told me he'd spoken with Brigitte the day after the owl hit her windshield, and he recognized it had upset her terribly. I sent him a late-night email with some questions. He was up early the next morning for his job, and replied to me, suggesting we talk on the phone. Minutes later, while driving in the pre-dawn darkness, a large owl appeared in the headlight beams and nearly hit his windshield.

The three people in this story all told me about a bizarre set of synchronicities and dreams that brought them together, and what followed was a frenetic welling up of irrational emotions. I could hear the confusion in their voices as they tried to express that they hadn't acted like themselves. They all confessed that, on some level, they'd behaved oddly during this time of intensified weirdness. It was as if some outside source was busily creating stresses in their interactions with each other.

There is a lot more to this story, including UFO sightings, prescient number sequences, psychic events, and an oppressive mood of unease. And they were all seeing owls.

Owl wings are wider than a car

As noted in the chapter on screen memories, there a plenty of stories of impossibly large owls, the four-foot-tall kind, standing in the middle of a lonely road at night, forcing the driver to stop. Sometimes these owls will fly away, and the witness will describe a huge wingspan that might be as wide as an entire lane on the highway. In these reports, the bird rarely flies off to the side, but instead leads the driver further down the road, or flies up and directly over the car itself.

One person, who had very recently seen a UFO, stopped his car for one of these four-foot-tall owls. This was at night quite close to his home. As he approached it, the owl took off and flew right over his car. He described an enormous wingspan that could be seen out both side windows from his position in the driver's seat. I can't help but be puzzled over this account, and how difficult it would be to actually see out both side windows at once when a bird's wings in flight might only be seen in that position for a microsecond. His UFO account from a few weeks earlier is quite frightening, where he and his wife both experienced missing time and a feeling of panic.

There is something nerve-racking woven into these accounts, and I'm cautious not to judge them. Brigette's experiences were both scary and emotionally charged, and she certainly framed them as disturbing, but are they malevolent? Confronting the unknown means confronting fears, and it's easy to imagine evil lurking in the darkness.

When I first stepped into this arena of researchers, experiencers, and zealots, I desperately wanted to remain unbiased as I pressed forward, and I reached out to Dr. Leo Sprinkle for advice. He's one of the elder statesmen in this field, and one of the most radiant, big-hearted men I've ever met.

I asked him, "How can I stay objective in this new role of researcher?" He calmly stated, "You can't. No matter how you want to act, you'll be absolutely subjective. Just know that." This might seem obvious, but it was exactly what I needed at that moment, and his advice has allowed me to be a lot less rigid in the way I frame this mystery.

Chapter 6:

Owls and Synchronicity

Synchronicity is essentially a shiny new word

for what we would have earlier called magic.

—Jeffrey Kripal [22]

Carl Jung coined the term *synchronicity* to describe the meaningful coincidences in his life and work. This is his definition: "Synchronicity is the coming together of inner and outer events in a way that cannot be explained by cause and effect and that is meaningful to the observer."

Anyone who has had direct contact with the UFO phenomenon will often report a long list of unusual repercussions, things that imply an overall depth well beyond what you would expect from a metal spaceship filled with little scientists. One side effect that gets repeated by abductees with a near absolute consistency is an increase in synchronicities, and I've been aware of this pattern for years because of how it's invaded my life. I spoke about this to a close friend, rather pompously declaring that UFO abductees attract far more synchronicities than the rest of the population.

She rolled her eyes and wisely replied, "But that's true of *anyone* on a spiritual path."

I realized instantly she was right, and I saw my own narrow-minded focus. Her astute reply forced me to look at the bigger picture. Following that line of thought would mean *UFO abduction is a spiritual path.* I realize how high and mighty that sounds, but after talking with so many experiencers, I can't help but see this as true.

So many elements of the UFO abduction phenomenon correspond in a tidy way to the journey of the student seeking enlightenment. There is a similar checklist of points that get reported over and over, starting with the upheaval and confusion of being chosen. What then follows is an initiation, deep introspection, the dark night of the soul, being tested, a transformation, and a profound sense of mission. Eventually, there's a *crack in the cosmic egg*, as if the cement that held an old reality together crumbles, and gets replaced by an expanded consciousness with deeper insights. These same elements are at the core of a long list of spiritual and shamanic traditions, and the magic of synchronicity is part of this list.

For me, synchronicity is like a compass on a foggy morning in the open ocean. It's a tool to orient yourself and recalibrate your direction of travel. If you are in the flow, following one synchronicity should lead to another. I had a beautiful conversation with an abductee, and she described her own long line of synchronicities as if they were all strung together. She pantomimed pulling on that golden thread, tugging and reeling it in. She told me, "At the end of this thread is your destiny."

If UFO abduction is a spiritual path, then you should expect messengers, symbols, archetypes, and totems showing up along that path. In my direct experience, that means owls.

Powerful synchronicities have happened throughout my life, but they took on a heightened fury after seeing all those owls with Kristen in 2006. That event was the starting point of me looking into my own experiences.

Leading up to the owls with Kristin, I was in a place of questioning and yearning. This was a terribly anxious time because I knew I needed to look into the UFO stuff that had been going on in my life. I was pushing it away, actively denying it, and seeing those owls was the first crack in the dam.

The synchronicities increased in frequency and tenor. I was confronted with something that the world I'd grown up in told me was impossible, but it was happening nonetheless. I was getting hit with so much weirdness I couldn't deny it anymore. It was only then that I started to examine my confusing UFO memories.

Looking into these experiences opened the floodgates, and in those years I was hit with so many synchronicities and so many owl sightings, that it felt like madness. A trap door had opened under me, and I'd fallen into the unknown. 2009 was a brutal year, where the synchronicities were all piling up one after another, to the point where I was drowning. I feared for my sanity in that frenetic chapter of my life. I am much more at peace as I write this, and in the aftermath of so much turmoil, I no longer see reality as I once did.

Those experiences were terribly difficult, and I'm seeing similar challenges as a pattern in the lives of people who've reached out to me with their owl and UFO stories. It starts with the individual being in a place of questioning and yearning, struggling with some sort of anxiety in their lives. And then an event happens, and after, the individual changes. For me, the event was the synchronistic power of seeing all those owls with Kristen, and after, I changed, I was different.

This pattern isn't anything I uncovered on my own. It comes from an author named Gibbs Williams, who wrote a great big book on synchronicity titled *Demystifying Meaningful Coincidences*. Gibbs has been a psychoanalyst for over forty years, and he had his patients keep detailed diaries, then he studied the role of the synchronicities in their lives. He found a clear pattern. There was a yearning, a questioning, a longing. Then there was an event—a synchronicity—and because of it, those people changed.

Symphonic music has a similar tipping point. There is a change in the music and something totally new emerges. The tempo builds to a point of instability and then a *crescendo* happens (imagine crashing cymbals). Afterwards, the music flows with a new equilibrium and harmony. It would be nice if the human experience could match the well-ordered flow of an orchestra, but it rarely works that way. This change can be sloppy and frantic, but nonetheless real.

This pattern matches my experience in 2006 of seeing the owls in the mountains with Kristen. Leading up to that first night under the stars, there was a building realization that I needed to look into the UFO events throughout my life, but I just couldn't allow myself to go there. This was a time of restlessness and anxiety, there was a pressure building, and I knew there was going to come a point where I could no longer deny the implications of those stories. Then the owl event happened with Kristen, and after that, my life had changed. There was now a palpable sense of *knowing* that reality was far more mysterious than I'd ever dared imagine.

In the aftermath of those owls, Kristen and I were both on an emotional roller coaster, and I feel like I was more deeply affected than her.

She moved out of our little valley in the autumn of 2006 to spend the winter back in her home town. We emailed after she left, but it was sporadic and awkward. During the time we spent together, Kristen had never once heard me mention any of my UFO experiences, especially the ones that might imply abduction. I called her late one night in the winter of 2006, and she was on a train when she answered. I was incredibly tense at that moment, and I blurted out what I'd been trying to deal with, this fear of looking into my own experiences, knowing full well that I would be opening Pandora's Box. I told her about seeing UFOs, my missing time event, and waking to see five gray aliens in my yard.

She listened to me as I nervously babbled about the blatant implications of UFO abduction, and it must have been obvious that I desperately wanted to cling to the thick layers of denial. After I'd talked myself out, I took a breath and waited for her reply. She was, as is her way, quite direct with me. She said, "Quit your goddamn whining and *do something*."

This was exactly what I needed to hear in that moment, and perhaps this one piece of advice is the reason why I met Kristen. I did do something, and this book is the outcome of that *doing*.

Like the journals of Gibbs Williams' patients, the owls seen with Kristen played the role of a powerful synchronicity. The pattern is clear to me. I'd been in a place of deep yearning leading up to those owls, and afterward something changed.

I had a friend call me out on this pattern. I'd written and spoken about it a lot on my blog, and it frustrated him. His point was that everyone is in a place of yearning all the time. He said I wasn't being scientific, and my response was *what do I care, I'm not a scientist*. I'm not trying to approach this muddle of divergent experiences with science as a tool. Instead, I see my role as more of a folklorist. Stories are being told to me by real people, and I sense even deeper stories taking place below the water line.

I took his feedback seriously and realized there were more than a few examples where I'd been too eager to connect the dots. From that point forward, any time I point out the yearning followed by a change, the events must very plainly fit that pattern. I am trying to be clear in how these ideas are explored, but also clear that this is a personal journey. This is not science, and I don't pretend that it is.

The scientific community has either ignored or denounced the UFO phenomenon for close to 70 years. With very few exceptions, the people who try to wrestle with this stuff using any kind of scientific rigor end up framing it merely as metal spaceships from another planet. They want to measure burn marks in a farmer's field. They don't want to cloud their tidy documentation with the strange invasion of consciousness that gets reported when you listen carefully to what experiencers are saying.

This stuff is a swirling mess that will challenge any thinking person's rigid perceptions. It's a boiling soup of contradictory ingredients like UFO abduction, synchronicity, archetypes, shamanic initiation, totem animals, altered reality, psychic visions, powerful mind control—*and owls*.

I ask the same questions to anyone who has seen a UFO, an owl, or has experienced a profound synchronicity. What was happening in your life leading up to the event? And, what were you thinking in the moments before the event? The follow-up would be, how did your life change after the event? The answers to these questions can be eerily consistent.

I spoke to one woman who told of driving late at night to see her mother. She was crying as she drove, feeling overwhelmed by the world and all its challenges. She sobbed out, *"There must be more than just this, there must be!"* When she got out of her car at her mother's home, she saw a beautifully radiant craft gliding silently just above the tree tops. Again, the witness was in a place of questioning and yearning right before the event. It might be incorrect to call this example a synchronicity, it plays out more as a form of manifestation.

Marriage proposal and ghostly owls

Another woman shared a story of driving at night with her boyfriend. They were on a lonely dirt road when they saw something in the headlights.

She asked, "What are those children doing out so late, and why are they dressed like ghosts?"

Her boyfriend said, "Those are owls."

She described them as about four feet tall, and their movements were *kind of flowing*. They continued on their way, and didn't discuss what happened for several years. When they finally did talk about it, he remembered the owls as lit from above from a bright streetlight, but she thought that was ridiculous, given they were on a remote dirt road.

There is something suspicious about two witnesses that are mixed up over whether they saw children dressed as ghosts or owls. What they remember is playing out like two different but simultaneous screen memories. Add to that the woman saw a football field-sized UFO glide right over her during the Hudson Valley flap of the 1980s. She also shared a handful of other suspiciously odd owl stories.

The date of the "ghost children" event is clearly remembered by her boyfriend—now her husband—because that was the night he proposed to her. Curiously, she isn't quite sure if it was that night. Though I haven't heard exactly this same detail before, the marriage proposal part, this certainly seems to match the tenor of other accounts. There is plenty of testimony where these kind of events will manifest at emotionally charged moments.

Here's another odd pattern. When I ask UFO witnesses what they were thinking in the moments before their sighting, it's quite normal to get the reply, "Well, I was thinking that I wanted to see a UFO."

Another consistency is that after seeing a UFO, people's lives will change. Some people will start acting more altruistic, they'll become vegetarians, stop swatting bugs, or volunteer at the local animal adoption center. Witnesses will commonly report a deeper sense of spirituality, a feeling of profound knowing, and a sense of mission—though they may have no idea what that mission might be. More often than not, they'll also describe the onset of outright psychic powers.

Owls, synchronicities, and UFOs all seem to be playing a similar role: they can change people. This is obviously a bold statement, and it certainly doesn't play itself out with 100 percent percent consistency, but there is enough of a pattern that I've come to see these curious elements as the same thing.

My iPad

As I proceed forward, I'm getting all kinds of synchronicities that seem to be intertwined with the investigation itself. Part of doing the research means digging through books. I'm indebted to this new chapter of technology because I can simply order an eBook, and within minutes it's on my iPad. This is helpful because it has a nice search option, so I can easily find specific words. The word I'm searching is *owl*, and when I type it in, a lot of other words show up too. The word *knowledge* comes up, because it has "owl" within its letters.

But I'm not interested in knowledge, so I use my fingertip to swipe past knowledge. This is a word that gets used a lot in the kind of books I'm collecting, so I need to do a lot of swiping to move beyond knowledge. It was while I was persistently trying to get past knowledge that I recognized this was a metaphor for how I'm proceeding with this research. To get to anything of any real depth, I have to bypass my logical mind. I have to move beyond *knowledge*.

I'm trying to follow my intuition, because if I depended on my logical mind, I would look at this stuff and say, "Owls and UFOs? What? This is stupid. UFO abductions? This might involve me? No way, this can't be true—I *can't* go there!"

But I have been going there. I've been proceeding forward and trying to trust my heart.

Chapter 7:

Dr. Kirby Surprise

As I type this, there is a book on my desk with the very straightforward title of *Synchronicity*. The author is Dr. Kirby Surprise (yes, that's his real name). He puts forth a bold premise on what might be at the source of this enigmatic phenomenon. He proposes that a synchronicity is produced by the individual, that it's one's own intention that actually makes these events emerge into being.

I sought out Dr. Surprise after hearing him promote his book on a series of online radio programs. I initially wanted to interview him for my own podcast series. In my first email to him I said that, from my research, the people who claim the UFO contact experience seem to be having more synchronicities than the rest of the population. His reply got my attention, here is part of his first email to me:

> Getting across the idea of synchronistic experience as self created is why I do this… Overall, my personal myths and experiences with UFOs and would sound considerably stranger and more complex than the usual UFO abduction and conspiracy fare.

What? I was flabbergasted. The guy who writes a book on synchronicity *says he's had his own personal experiences with UFOs!* He seemed to be proving my point that UFOs and synchronicities are somehow connected. I got his book and a quick look at the index showed that the term UFO is never mentioned. But on page 255 he wrote, "I like to make owls."

He was describing how to create your own synchronistic experience of a self-generated owl sighting. He treats synchronicity as something that can be playfully engaged through intention by anyone reading his book. Manifesting owls, his example, is presented as a game where synchronistic experiences are created by the observer.

This game has a simple but wide frame of reference. You look for them, and focus on their ability to present themselves in any, and every, place where you turn your attention. There are no "others" in this game. It's only you and the effect you have on the synchronistic experiences around you.[23]

Even without his personal example of owls, this resonated strongly with my own direct experiences. Have I been unknowingly playing this game? Are there no "others" in this? Is it all just me? Yet, it seemed odd that a book titled *Synchronicity* gives instructions on how to manifest owls, and the author has his own UFO experiences. I began to wonder, had I somehow manifested Dr. Kirby Surprise as my own spirit-totem to match my research?

There have been ongoing and carefully controlled scientific studies showing that the consciousness of the experimenter can directly and measurably influence the results of an experiment. This is well known but little understood.

An example would be a simple study involving a subject performing a set number of coin tosses, with the intention of getting heads more often than tails, and then tabulating the results. Logic would dictate that the results should be perfectly random, but that's not what happens. Instead, there is a consistent and measurable outcome of the coin landing as heads more than tails. Something is going on; it seems evident that the mind of the coin tosser is influencing physical reality in a way we don't understand. The effects of focus and intention are clear, but how it works is still unknown.

This means that the person on the receiving end of the synchronicity is making it happen. So, a gambler can have a lucky streak, a paranoid will truly find evidence of conspiracies, and someone struggling with the unknown will literally see owls. Dr. Surprise writes:

Seeing your reflection in the synchronistic experience of a series of coin tosses or dice throws in a laboratory is hard because of the simplicity of the experiment. Only the real world offers the depth and variation of events needed for true work with SE. The meaning of these events is particular to the observer. Synchronistic experiences can be very seductive. They tell you exactly what you most want to hear. [24]

This is my direct experience. I've been researching the connection between owls and UFOs, and most of the stories to back up my inquiry have been arriving in my lap with a weird synchronistic flurry. I spoke at length with Dr. Surprise for this book. He has a doctorate in counseling psychology and has worked in advanced outpatient programs where he assesses, diagnoses, and treats psychotic and delusional disorders. Seeing as I'm someone who feels strongly that I've been repeatedly abducted by aliens, his credentials were a nice fit for me and my seemingly delusional experiences. He patiently heard me out as I explained my mixed up involvement with owls, synchronicities, and UFOs. His response was less of a clinician and much more of a mystic.

He was very aware of the owl's mythic role in our collective psyche; as spirit animals they represent magic, the unconscious and spirit messengers. He was also aware that the UFO phenomenon plays a very similar role. To him, it wasn't a surprise that my immersion into these two iconic subjects meant a lot of powerful experiences would reflect back at me.

He speculated on my intense interest in UFOs and owls. If I had been creating an intention and a focus (and I certainly had been), I would produce an opening for something to fill. My emotional and obsessive energy had been driving these experiences, and it overwhelmed me. He said that we're in a Holodeck created by our own brains. We need to be aware that the same part of the brain that controls dreaming also controls our everyday processing.

I tried to explain that this hasn't been an aimless static of odd events. Instead, it all seems directed to achieve some set result. It feels like orchestrated magic. Both owls and synchronicities led me toward clues, and these lead to me back to myself—and finally trusting in the reality of my own UFO experiences.

I spoke with Dr. Surprise on the most owl-rific night of the year, Halloween. This conversation didn't feel like therapist and patient. It felt like shaman and initiate. He agreed that these synchronistic experiences can have a deeply personal power. The owls are a metaphor of an underlying pattern. There is no fine line between the inner and external world. The owls and the UFOs resonate with us, *because they are us!* During our conversation, he casually pointed out that owls and UFOs are naturally paired together on a cultural or ancient level. The symbol of the owl is exactly what the UFOs are to us. Here is an excerpt from our phone interview:

> Owls are also the classic symbol for the unconscious. Owls are the things that live in the dark shadowy areas. They pass through the night. They're wise. They're slightly dangerous and creepy. They're messengers. They convey things. They've always been seen as omens and portents, they've always been held as these messengers between the known and the unknown. They are in exactly the same psychological and emotional position in the past for our ancestors, as the UFOs are to us today. They are these mysterious magical things that we don't quite understand that live in the darkness. They are both generally seen more at night, but when they manifest in the day, it's a big frickin' deal. And they mean something, they are always taken as: *Wow, that's really something amazing!* And, symbolically in every culture, owls are the messengers from the unconscious.

Dr. Surprise went on to describe his own ideas on how he can manifest synchronicities in the form of owls, how thoughts and intentions have an effect on reality itself. In his book, he treats this as a playful game. Here, he describes owls from the point of view of his shamanic work.

> I make them. They're thought-forms. You build them out of matter and energy, out of emotional energy and mental pattern. You can play with them. They are familiars. They are exactly what every tradition does with spirit animals. You are taking matter and energy from these other planes that is, in some reflective way, your emotion and thoughts, and creating a technology with it. And then using this technology to change the randomness of events in the environment. And this is a process that is not some big magical Hogwarts thing that you need to learn. This is something that the organism itself does normally. All thought, all emotion produces these forms. All of it produces effects on these planes, and all of it

changes the underlying structure of physical reality from the brain. And I think that the extreme manifestations of it, you may occasionally get something physical. You know, lights in the skies.

Dr. Surprise had his own run-ins with UFOs when he was around 20 years old. He described some things that seem consistent with what a lot of other contactees and abductees have said, but his point of view implies a personal responsibility as to the source of the mystery. He feels strongly that he was manifesting these experiences. The UFOs he saw were lights in the nighttime sky, just little dots that would zig-zag and wiggle in motions that defied any logical explanation. He would take his friends out into a field at night and say, "Okay, look over there, there's going to be some lights showing up." And they did show up as if on his command, terrifying his friends.

Dr. Surprise has been meditating from the age of nine, and he seems to have unknowingly tapped into some playful side of his own unconscious. I asked what he thought was happening.

Well, it was actually quite a bit more psychotic sounding than just seeing UFOs. In fact, in psychiatry, there's a term called thoughts of reference, or ideas of reference, and basically that's the psychiatric version of synchronistic events.

Now, that happens with me, to this day in fact, to the point where whatever I'm thinking is sort of reflected in the environment. It seemed insane to me at the time that I could talk to whatever these beings were, through coincidences in the environment. I was presented with this originally as mythology; it came at the point where I had this meditative breakthrough. I could give you the technical sort of explanation of what happened to me, but it might be over the reader's head, unless they were hardcore shamans and theosophists. Basically I hit a space where I started broadcasting and getting reflective events out of the environment, and not knowing I was doing this. When I hit into this, this trail of events got to the point where it could become conversational with the environment.

Obviously something was reading my mind and playing with me, and it's friendly, it's funny, it's a lot smarter and much more well-informed than I am. How is this possible? How could you manipulate time, space, events, coincidence, and then put them together with matching patterns of thought?

He eventually formed a mythology in his mind that some sort of extraterrestrial intelligence was using a technology that was not limited to mere matter and energy. This would be what people have mistaken for angels or spirits for thousands of years. These were the spirit realms that shamans and mystics have tried to describe. At that chapter in his life, he felt that these higher beings were talking to him.

> The coincidences follow whatever mythology you create, so I literally created this UFO mythology. In the beginning, my idea was that there was actually something or someone out there. They must be out there with whatever kind of spaceships or craft they have, and I could walk out in a field at night and look up in the sky and lights would fly by, and I could do this very consistently. I got into this sort of wishful thinking mythology of, "Gee, if you could just figure enough of this out, maybe they'll come and meet you and do the whole ET routine with them." Which of course never happened.
>
> As I tried to piece this together over time, over months and months and months, and nothing physical appeared; the messages and coincidences and talking to the environment continued, but the messages changed, because my internal concept of what was going on was changing. I was still the parakeet in its cage pecking at the mirror, thinking it's another bird.

Eventually, this internal mythology changed from ETs communicating from their UFOs to his present, much more nuanced ideas about synchronicity.

> It still seems, if I want to personify it, that I'm being instructed, guided, talked to, joked with, teased, and cajoled by things that are vastly more intelligent than I am. But now I understand that what I'm actually seeing is the larger and vaster workings of my own unconscious in my own mind, in a sort of cooperative playful way.

The ideas that Dr. Surprise presented in his book and personal conversations might seem pretty far out, but it all fits so cleanly with my own personal experiences. I need to grit my teeth to grok his model of reality, where consciousness is directly influencing physical existence. Yet I can't help but see my own collision of owls and UFOs conforming to the intention I give them.

Dr. Surprise and I talked about the odd motion of these unknown lights in the sky. I've had my own experience of seeing something that closely matches what he was manifesting as a 20-year-old. We were finishing each other's sentences as we described what we had seen. Little dots sliding across the sky in an oddly smooth way that obviously wasn't an airplane, helicopter, or satellite.

Here's my own example of seeing odd little lights in the nighttime sky. I was at the home of Christopher Bledsoe, Sr. in North Carolina, having spent the day with him and two other UFO researchers, both women. He's had experiences of such bizarre intensity than I can barely wrap my mind around the enormity of what he has endured.

After the sun went down, we were all sitting around in the backyard of Bledsoe's home. His wife and kids were there too, and we were all talking about UFOs. At around 11 p.m., Chris calmly pointed at an orange light in the western sky and hinted that this might be something odd. The light looked like a normal aircraft, it was nothing more than a small blinking dot moving slowly to the north.

One of the researchers and I walked across the dark yard to get a better view through an opening in the trees. At first glance, the dot seemed to be just an aircraft with a slight blinking quality. But after looking for a few seconds, we were both aware that the light was moving in a weirdly halting way, sliding forward and quickly backing up.

The researcher stammered, "Oooh, look at that. This is giving me the chills!" It smoothly skimmed across the sky in a liquid gliding motion, stopping and backing up a half step, and then easing across the sky again. It had the quality of a little water bug skimming across a pond, rather than any normal aircraft in flight. We probably watched it for less than a minute, and it eventually moved off to the north and out of our view.

This sighting happened among a crew of UFO researchers and abductees, all of us having spent the day completely focused on the phenomenon, and later that night we saw this odd little light in the sky. Could we have manifested that herky-jerky orange dot above us? Or, was the source of the phenomenon (whatever that might be) simply allowing us to get a glimpse of something as a way to reassure us that this stuff is really happening?

I had the chance to ask abduction researcher Budd Hopkins how he dealt with the really strange outlying weirdness. He rolled his eyes and said the threads run off everywhere, and then he made a wide hand gesture like water splashing outwards. He said it was his job, as an author and researcher, to rein it all in, to try and make sense of the bigger picture. With that he gestured again, as if pulling everything back into his cupped hands.

I see it as my job to do the opposite, to examine all those threads running off everywhere, and follow where they lead. When confronting these clustered events, it seems as if some synchro-gong has been struck, and the reverberations rattle every connection along every thread in the web. This all must tie back into an unknown focal point, the same way an entire orchestra is connected to the conductor, following his lead for every nuance in the grand performance.

Chapter 8:

Owls equal UFOs equal Synchronicity

After wallowing in all this overlapping weirdness, a question arises: *Are owls, UFOs, and synchronicity all the same thing?* The pragmatic answer is obviously they are not, but on an intuitive level, I can't be so sure. There is a blurring of these disparate elements, and each has a similar power. For this research, I have been treating all of these as if they are the same thing. This is a thought experiment, simply to see if this avenue of inquiry will bear fruit. What I'm finding is this stuff is all tangled up and intertwined in ways that leave me confounded. Owls, UFOs, and synchronicity all have the power to change a person, all functioning in the same way, to redirect the lives of the people experiencing their power.

Where does an account of seeing a UFO end and an owl sighting begin? Author Nick Redfern has lamented over the complexities of doing UFO research. He says, "It's not that it's weird, it's *too* weird." The things that get reported go way beyond the motives of a little scientist in a flying saucer. Nick has also said he feels like he's really onto something in his research when synchronicities begin to invade his life.

Time is Art

I connected with a husband and wife team who are producing a documentary with the working title of *Time is Art: Synchronicity & the Collective Dream.* The film project is evolving as a highly artistic endeavor, and I'm convinced that the creative process is somehow tied into both synchronicities as well as UFO contact. The wife, Katy Walker, told me about shooting footage in the Mission District of San Francisco, a neighborhood well known for its murals. Their story begins while they were getting video footage of these artistic murals. This street art was passionate and weird, and they were both impressed.

One mural was a montage of Native Americans ceremonies, a tiny white owl, a UFO, and even a skinny gray alien. Another was a colorful set of huge stylized owls. In the minutes after shooting these artistic renderings of both UFOs and owls, they set the camera down without realizing it was still running. Later, to their surprise, they found something unusual. The camera had caught a structured craft that was descending smoothly behind a tree. This high definition footage was brightly lit in full daylight, and even though it's only seen for a few seconds, it's clearly not a helicopter, airplane, or balloon. At the time, they had no idea they'd captured this image, only noticing it days later.

video frame captured during the filming of a documentary on synchronicity

I can't speak to the authenticity of this footage, but they seem quite convinced it's genuine. Also, they haven't used this short clip for any kind of self-promotion.

Both Katy and her husband have had some odd life events, enough that I am putting them in the *maybe* category. Katy tells of hiding in an attic of a cottage for three hours in a mental standoff with skinny beings. She struggled to push them out of her consciousness, refusing to go with them. This terrifying incident happened in eastern Germany in 1998, and it was proceeded by a blinding light through a window right after her friend, Oliver, left the cottage to investigate some odd noises outside.

They never spoke about the incident, and Katy wonders it their memories were somehow erased, because their behavior seems so strange. "I don't know what happened when he came back. I just know it was a very long time and I was angry he didn't have an explanation for why he was gone so long."

111

Katy's extremely frightening experiences were featured in *The Synchronicity Highway: Exploring Coincidence, the Paranormal and Alien Contact* by the husband and wife team Rob and Trish McGregor. This is a book about synchronicity with "alien contact" right in the title.[25]

So we have two *maybe* people, creating a documentary on synchronicity, shooting images of UFOs, aliens, and owls; and then unknowingly video-taping a UFO in flight. This is a perfect example of what I've been finding (or more correctly, *what's been finding me*), a collision of all these conflicting elements.

The name Chris

Chris Knowles and Chris Knowles are both researchers from Boston, and both are looking into the UFO mystery. These overlapping names make me pay attention.

Christina Knowles is an abduction researcher who has also had her own direct contact experience. This combination is very common, and these life events consistently bring about a powerful *sense of mission* in the experiencer. She is one of the very few abduction researchers that, when I ask, "Do you have any reports of *real owls* interacting with abductees?" She answers, "Yes." Now this doesn't happen very often, researchers will almost always say no. She has recognized a pattern, where some of the abductees she's been working with are seeing real owls, and they'll lock eyes and then describe receiving a psychic download from the owls. The nature of most of these messages is that we humans need to be better stewards of our planet. This is the same message abductees consistently report receiving from aliens while aboard ships, but it's very interesting to me that the source is an owl.

Christopher Knowles, also from Boston, is an author, artist, blogger, and researcher who is hard to categorize. He's been exploring how ancient mythology is emerging in our present-day movies and comic books. This guy has some of the most far-reaching and perceptive insights into the overall UFO phenomenon of anyone out there. His mother would collect owl figurines, hardly proof of anything paranormal, but this little detail shows up often. He's also had a lot of very strange life experiences, some involving UFOs. Unlike Christina, who is very much an abductee, I am cautiously putting Christopher in the *maybe* category.

Also, the name Knowles has 'owl' embedded right in it.

My research doesn't have a big pool of data. I've collected a lot, but I don't have 10,000 owl stories told to me by abductees. But of this limited pool, there is a very weird disproportion, way more than what could be random, of people either named Christopher, Christian, Christina, Kristin, or Chris. There may be no other word in Western culture that is more heavily loaded with mythic resonance than the first five letters of these names.

The English name Christopher has its roots in the Greek name *Christóforos*, meaning *Christ-bearer*. Throughout this book, anytime any one with some variation of the name Chris shows up, it will get noted as part of this pattern.

Christopher Bledsoe, Sr. (one of the many named Chris), mentioned at the end of the last chapter, is a UFO abductee with an incredible set of experiences. Both he and his son, Christopher Jr., had concurrent missing time experiences, as well as seeing small glowing humanoid beings on the night of January 8th, 2007. This happened while fishing along the Cape Fear River in North Carolina with three other witnesses. The entire crew saw multiple UFOs at close range.

This is an extremely well-documented case, and there is such an abundance of weirdness stemming from that night that it would be impossible to summarize in just a few paragraphs. The events were traumatic, and Chris isolated himself. He withdrew from his previous life, hiding away in the back corner room of his house for almost a year.

I visited Chris at his home in 2013 and sat with him in that back room. He shared his feelings of terrible isolation and hopelessness. Then he said, "See that bush right there." He pointed to the window where there was a bush outside pressed right up to the glass. He told me, "You know, right after all that happened, there were two owls living in that hickory bush. I would see them all the time, and I would hear them all the time. They were always right there in that bush."

At this point, he had no idea I was the owl guy, and all I could do was listen to his story. He said that he would often hear a third owl off in the forest nearby. He described these as big brown owls that would make strong hooting calls. Chris was born and raised in the house right next door and he stated that he had never, in all his life, seen owls in this area.

I find it absolutely fascinating that this soft-spoken man had a pair of owls take up residence right outside the room where he sought solace after such a profound UFO contact event. I've been finding this detail, owls showing up around the time of UFO contact, over and over again. I struggle to understand the role the owls might be playing in these elusive storylines.

During those reclusive months, Chris had a terrible time relating to his family and ended up seeking support with a citizens band radio. He used this radio as a way to communicate with people in the outside world. He even built a 131-foot tall metal-framed tower with an antenna to boost his radio system's receiving power. There was a thick cable connecting the tower to the CB equipment in that lonely back room.

After he finished the tower, one lone owl was repeatedly seen in full daylight sitting high in the framework. He said the owl had an eerie presence and seemed to be continually staring at him. He's not sure if this was one of the pair of owls outside the window in the hickory bush.

On June 25th, 2011, the day of his 28th wedding anniversary, just as Chris stepped out of that back room, lightning struck the antenna. The current followed the cable, and that back corner of the house was blown away, exploding in flames. All the CB equipment was destroyed in the fire, as well as a lot of paper documentation from his abduction case. Chris told me that if he had been in that room, as he usually was, he would have been killed instantly. After the lightning strike, he never saw owls around the house again. He feels that they were some sort of warning.

Chris had another curious owl experience when he was ten years old. He had been to a Christmas service at a local church and was in the parking lot at night, waiting for his mother to pick him up. He was alone leaning against a tree, and as his mother pulled in, he looked up and saw a huge owl on a branch within reach of where he stood. It hadn't been there when he got to the tree, and he didn't hear it land. They locked eyes and stared at each other. Chris told me this story in a face-to-face conversation, and said this memory was seared into his soul. It was obvious this event still resonated strongly with him, even after over 40 years.

Then he told me that a little over a week later, he was shot and killed. It happened on New Year's Day while hunting with some local boys. He was accidentally shot in the back from six feet away with a twenty-gauge shotgun. He was rushed to the hospital and died on the operating table while the doctors were trying to remove the lead pellets. He told me, "I was inside of an orb. I used to describe it as a clear bubble, but I know it was an orb now."

He remembers standing on a solid surface, looking out into space and watching the earth get smaller and smaller.

The owl at the church, the hunting accident, and his 2007 abduction experience all happened along the same rural road, all within a mile and half of each other.

There's more. Chris, along with his entire family, saw a white owl at his father's funeral, and this matches the lore of death that's also part of the owl's mythology. More on this story later in the book.

After I posted the initial essay about owls on my site in the summer of 2013, someone pointed me to a blog posting from researcher and abductee, Chris Holly (another Chris). It turns out that my essay was a trigger for her to write about her own owl experiences. She wrote:

> Something else that I never connected with my experiences with the unknown until I read about it on the internet by others who shared the same experience… Owls, I always saw and heard owls, mainly white owls, wherever I lived.[26]

She has been blogging about her research at her site, *Chris Holly's Paranormal World*. She's had a lifetime of odd events, including an initial experience that has involved a close-up UFO sighting with multiple witnesses, missing time, and physical aftereffects. This distressing event happened while she was a teenager growing up on Long Island.

In her posting, she wrote that during her childhood it was common to see an owl outside at night, "I would look out my window where I would see a beautiful white owl perched on a big old oak tree that stood outside my bedroom window." As a little girl, Chris repeatedly told her parents about this owl. As an adult, she questioned her mother, now in her 80s, about her seeing the owl all those years ago.

> When my mother realized I was actually seeing a white owl all those times as a child she looked at me sort of shocked and admitted she never really believed that it was true.

As a researcher, I've heard this many times, children will try to report something extremely odd to their parents, and they'll casually dismiss the whole thing. Sadly, what gets reinforced is that it's better to shut up and not say anything. My advice to anyone who hears a child sharing an unusual story is to listen and to take that young person very seriously. There may be a mundane explanation, but anyone, either a child or an adult, knows full well that they're stepping out of the boundaries of what is acceptable by bringing up something that seems impossible. I encourage you to listen, and listen closely to what they are sharing with you.

Chris had another odd owl experience, this one witnessed by a group of friends. She was in her 30s and living in East Islip, New York, and this was close to where she had lived as a child. She was hosting a Christmas party (there's that "Chris" again) in her home. There was a large window on the side of her living room facing the driveway, which was lined with trees.

> One of my friends walked over to the window as it had started to lightly snow when she yelped: "Oh my God look at this giant white owl!" The people attending my party all ran over to look out the window and there on a branch close to the window sat an absolutely beautiful large white owl. It sat there on the gray tree limb with snow falling gently around it looking more like an oil painting than a real creature. My guests were fascinated by the owl as it was the first white owl they had ever seen up close and could not get over how it simply sat there staring back through the window at us. My group of friends stood looking at this owl in silence until one of them broke the silence by asking if the owl was "creeping anyone else out?" A few of my friends admitted they had an uncomfortable feeling as the owl peered through the window at them.

I thought it was strange they had never seen a white owl before and equally strange they thought it was creepy. I had seen them literally all my life including a few times at the house I was in when this event at the party happened. I thought everyone on Long Island saw white owls all the time. It was at that party that I realized it was not a frequent event for other people.

Chris had another owl experience while living in Schweinfurt, Germany. This would have been in the 1970s, and it happened in the early evening just before nightfall, when everything was still and gray. She was walking home from the grocery store when she heard the familiar hoot of an owl.

I looked up and there in a tree next to where I was walking sat a large owl. He was not as white as the owls I usually saw but he was big and did have many white feathers. He looked at me and I looked at him and I kept on walking... I did think at the time that seeing this owl was a bit strange but I did not know what to do about it. About three weeks or so after seeing that owl I had a very strange event occur with another lost time event along with a run-in in my apartment building with extremely strange beings. Now years later I finally understand that all of these things may be connected.

Chris went on to explain her concerns over how seeing an owl might be an ominous harbinger for an impending contact experience.

I have read many things concerning seeing owls, from it being a warnings or type of message as well as being connected to alien abduction. The fact I have suffered from many lost time events in my life and have seen unidentified crafts in my past does give me pause when I think about how I have seen white owls my entire life too... and trust me I will do all I can to prevent another strange encounter.

Chris is very much a UFO abductee. Her experiences have been deeply challenging and she certainly doesn't frame this phenomenon in love and light. She writes about her experiences and her research on her website, and she also hosts a podcast series where she interviews other abductees. All this and a lifetime of owl sightings. In a lot of ways, she reminds me of myself.

Stacey, owls, and a psychic medium

These experiences can manifest in a frenetic swarm of weirdness, and there is one story that defines the collision with me and this owl stuff. October of 2009 stands alone as the absolute height of my own synchro-mania. At that point in my life, I was totally freaked out—it felt like the world was coming unraveled around me.

This strange set of events began in the summer of 2009. I had been trying to set up an appointment with a psychic medium named Marla Frees. I felt drawn to contact Marla after listening to her doing interviews for Whitley Strieber on his website. We had played phone tag for over a month, and due to our conflicting schedules the first available time slot was on Sunday, October 4th. We were all set up for a one-hour psychic session, and I was hopeful that she might offer some clues to the oppressive weirdness that had invaded my life.

The opening salvo happened on the morning of Saturday, October 3rd, when I read a post about owls on a website called, simply enough, *Synchronicity*. I scrolled down and saw a comment from a woman named Stacey, who said: "...a couple years ago I had the privilege to spend time in a giant owls 'nest' for lack of a better word, with over thirty barn and horned owls watching me. It was one of the most profound moments of my life!"

Well, this got my attention, and I contacted her through email asking to hear her story. Minutes later, she sent me an essay she'd written about her experience. In it, she described walking through a meadow surrounded by trees and there were owls seemingly on every branch looking down on her. She wrote: "There were too many to count. I had stumbled upon a holy shrine and I was the initiate."

Needless to say, I was impressed. She was with a man named Christian and he saw the owls, too. Our back and forth emailing got sort of frenzied, and at one point she said on the same night she'd seen the owls, both she and Christian had also *seen a UFO*.

I was flabbergasted because I hadn't once mentioned UFOs in our conversation, it was Stacey who brought it up. I told her this was especially strange because I had a blog focused on UFOs, owls, and synchronicity.

With that, Stacey replied: "My friend Marla (who interviews for Whitley Strieber's website) has great stories to tell... she's tapped in." Hearing this felt like I'd fallen into a bottomless pit. Stacey had no way of knowing that I had a psychic appointment in less than 24 hours with her friend Marla.

The following day my head was still ringing like a gong. I have very few memories of that hour on the phone with Marla, I do know that at one point she started crying. She explained that something was terribly wrong, and I needed to take these experiences very seriously. I wish I had recorded this psychic reading, all I can clearly remember was that the intensity of it was overwhelming. I have a single piece of paper with notes from that hour long session, and the one thing that stands out on that page was something Marla said to me: "*You are here for profound reasons.*"

This cluster of events begins with an owl story on a website called Synchronicity, and within minutes it felt like I was a shiny metal ball bouncing around in a pinball machine of owls, UFOs, a guy named Christian, and a crying psychic.[27]

Struggling with the mystery

The UFO riddle holds a sort of power within it, something that forces any thinking person to contemplate life's grand mysteries—the same questions that have followed us throughout the ages. If you start out talking about little lights in the sky, you should very quickly start talking about God. You should end up wrestling with the really big questions. Who are we? Why are we here? What does it all mean?

I have a friend who meditates, goes to spiritual retreats, has a guru, and all that stuff. When we talk, we both really get into it. We push each other, both of us struggling to articulate elusive metaphysical concepts, and the conversation ends up getting deeper and deeper. We fall into a kind of spiritual one-upmanship, and at some point he'll get frustrated with me, and say, "I can't believe you don't meditate!" And I'll snap back, "I can't believe you don't read UFO books!"

People will ask me, "Do you think this UFO stuff is real?" The easy answer is, "Yes, it's real." I can say that with conviction because of my own sightings and the overwhelming glut of evidence. Again, yes, this stuff is real, but I'm at a point where I struggle with what the word *real* actually means. To me, what might be real has become just as slippery as the overall mystery itself. So much of what I'm looking at plays out as theatrical, absurd, or beyond the edge of comprehension. What might be real becomes so abstract that it leaves me questioning the source of all existence. The word *real* is the first for letters of *reality*, and my definition of that crumbled ages ago.

The problem is, how does anyone keep their brain focused on the enormity of this mystery? All I can do is examine the little details, and sometimes I can barely grasp those. There comes a point when the trapdoor opens up, and I'm falling. I can only truly wrap my mind around this mystery for a few fleeting seconds. In those moments of clarity, I can't understand why I'm not running down the street screaming, "They're here!"

We're staring at a Rorschach inkblot. You'll see whatever baggage you bring to it, and it'll mirror back your own ideas and beliefs. The one thing I know for sure is that everyone's got a different take on this phenomenon and nobody agrees on everything. So when you enter this community—and I'm picturing all the contradictory characters milling around at a UFO conference—nobody is going to have the same conclusions. Everyone is telling a different story, but I feel strongly that at the core there is a real experience taking place. That's the only thing I can say for sure, that *something real is happening*. Beyond that, it's all speculation.

A rational scientist would look at all this UFO and owl weirdness and fight to squeeze it into the tidy box of logic. In doing so, they would need to leave out all the really weird stuff. A poet might be better suited to play with all the elusive strangeness. This might make some pragmatic readers cringe, but sometimes great truths can only be fully revealed through poetry, mythology, or metaphor.

There is some unknowable facet of reality that creates synchronicity, and I'm impelled to follow this magic compass. I'm being given clues, and they are telling me to step off the well-worn path and into the darkest part of the forest. This research, and all its associated weirdness, has been my own deeply personal inward exploration.

Chapter 9:

Back to Back Reports

Digging into the weird connections between owls and UFOs has unleashed all kinds of synchronicities, and these seem to be intertwined with the research itself. These synchronicities have forced me to recognize that something is happening—and it feels important.

I've received a set of stories that echo each other with a remarkable similarity that's impossible to ignore. I didn't really do much to search these stories, they just fell into my lap, sometimes less than 24 hours apart. This chapter features three different back-to-back stories, and each plainly mirrors the other in details and mood. There is a weird power to this pattern of parallel reports, so much so that they seem to define a grander truth than the stories themselves.

Two white owls

I know a man who's had a curious set of life events that oddly parallel my own, including lots of owl sightings. He reached me by phone and told me I needed to talk to someone who had "The mother of all owl stories." That got my attention. He gave me the contact info for a woman named Leslie (a pseudonym) and told me he thought she'd be open to sharing some of her odd experiences. Leslie and I exchanged hellos on the Facebook chat-box, and during our initial back and forth, I sent her a link to my timeline. This is a page on my blog where I list some of my own life events. I sent this at 6:04 p.m. on May 13th, 2013. She replied back 29 minutes later with this:

> ... I read the timeline on your blog, went outside onto my porch to get a little air and got swooped by a white owl! Well then, what do you think of that?!

I got back to her and said, at this point, I thought it was freakin' normal! She has a large white owl fly over her within minutes of our first hello, she's spent years on that porch and nothing like that had ever happened before. The synchro-weirdness connecting me to owls had been manifesting with such a deluge that this felt completely ordinary.

Leslie is a certified clinical hypnotherapist and works helping patients with issues like quitting smoking, weight loss, and stress management. But most of her clients are coming to her seeking help in dealing with memories that imply UFO contact.

Leslie has strong psychic skills and she uses them in her therapeutic practice. She was mentored by her adoptive father who taught her to develop these skills through simple little games, like find the pebble under the shell and guess the card. She began doing this with her own son, hoping to encourage his psychic intuition. Her son had started meditating the year before, at the young age of five. This parallels the experiences of Dr. Kirby Surprise who started meditating at age nine, and then went on to have his own odd UFO experiences.

The first time Leslie sat with her son and played these psychic games, he was six years old. They were sitting together in their backyard and he was picking it up quite fast. As they were working with the cards, a big white owl flew into a nearby tree, perched on a branch, and watched them. This owl stayed with Leslie and her son for the next three years. When she would drive to the grocery store, she could watch the owl following in her rearview mirror. While at the store, the owl would wait on a lamp post in the parking lot, and then follow her home again. It lived in a tree in their yard and was always around, seemingly paying close attention to whatever they were doing.

This was a magical time for her family. That white owl would follow her everywhere, sometimes getting just a few feet away from her and her son. During this time, Leslie was also doing fieldwork where she would go out at night with the intention of seeing UFOs. This was done in rural locations with a small team of comrades. They would set up equipment in the day so they could get a fix on the horizon and nearby vantage points, then return at night hoping to see something unusual. The white owl would show up at these sky-watching gatherings, too.

Eventually Leslie and her family left that home. She moved out of state to study advanced hypnotherapy. A few days after leaving, her old next-door neighbor called and told her that the owl was dead. He'd found it in her backyard lying on its back with its wings spread wide. Both Leslie and her son were heartbroken. Reflecting back after many years, she feels the owl was performing some task, its job had been completed, and at that point it died.

Leslie had another recent owl experience. She lives in a fairly big city, and she was walking her dog one morning down a sidewalk in a busy residential part of town. She sensed something behind her and turned around to see an owl standing on the sidewalk. She thought it must have fallen out of a tree, and she was worried about it, but didn't know what to do. After a moment she turned and continued along on her walk. Then the owl flew right over her, and landed directly in front of her in the center of the sidewalk, blocking her way.

She walked up close, near enough to touch it. She sensed that there was something wrong, that the owl was sick. It was a little over a foot tall, but its height was hard to gauge because it was sort of drooped over in a despondent pose. Curiously, her dog showed no reaction at all, and this was unusual because she was quite high-strung and eager to chase anything in her path.

Leslie stopped a stranger on the street and asked if she could use his cell phone. She wasn't carrying hers, and she was surprised at her assertiveness. He handed her his phone, and she searched out an animal rescue service to come deal with this owl. As she was using this man's phone, he lit up a cigarette. She found a number to call, explained about the owl, and they said, "Wait right there." With a weird swiftness, a van pulled up and two guys from animal control hopped out and approached the owl. This all happened before the man had finished his cigarette!

These two guys efficiently slipped a bag over the owl and carried him to the van. They explain that they were connected to both veterinary services and a nearby wildlife sanctuary, and just as suddenly they were gone. Leslie feels strongly that this owl had purposely plopped itself in her path, choosing her because it needed help.

Like so many other people who've had these weird owl experiences, Leslie has had a lifetime of direct UFO contact and powerful synchronicities. She also has a profound *sense of mission,* something she feels is tied into her contact events, and this is consistent with nearly every experiencer I've ever spoken with.

Her experiences can be traced back to before she was born. When her mother was nine months pregnant with Leslie, she saw something in the sky, and even though she was frightened, she felt compelled to go outside in the middle of the night. She was suddenly in the presence of two small gray aliens, and they escorted her out into the apple orchard behind her house. These beings walked her through the trees to a clearing where there was a landed flying saucer. She has a jumble of memories of being aboard the craft, and the distinct feeling of the cold floor under her bare feet.

The next thing her mother remembers was collapsing in her front yard and screaming for help. Her neighbors, who had seen the UFO, found her on the grass as she was going into labor. She was rushed to the hospital and Leslie was born that night.

Leslie's mother was deeply traumatized over the events of that night, as well as ongoing contact throughout the entirety of her pregnancy. She couldn't come to terms with what had happened, and she was unable to bond with her newborn daughter. Several years later, Leslie's mother dropped her and her sisters off at the doorstep of an adoption services office and disappeared.

I cautiously asked Leslie what this was like, and I marveled at her answer. She said she was never angry at her mother and that she understood that it would have been impossible for her to cope. This happened in the early 1960s, and at that time there was absolutely no outlet for anyone with these experiences. She explained that she sought out and eventually met her mother when she was a young adult. It was during these meetings when she heard about the trauma surrounding her birth.

My initial meeting with Leslie was in the early evening on Monday, May 13th, 2013. The following day at 2:29 in the afternoon, I got an email from a woman named Shonagh Home, who wrote:

> I went on your website and was thunderstruck to see all the articles about owls. If you read my book, the entire thing is a series of synchronicities with the owl.

It was only minutes after getting this email that Shonagh and I were talking on the phone. Shonagh is a shaman and author, and her autobiographical book is titled *Love and Spirit Medicine*. It's a memoir of her visionary journeys using sacred mushrooms to access the spirit world. Her mentor in these psychedelic realms has been a giant white owl. Her story is extremely strange, but what really amazed me was how closely her experience paralleled Leslie's, who I had met less than 24 hours earlier.[28]

Shonagh spent half of her life in New York City, seduced by all the powerful external forces that have come to define our culture of consumerism. She was married with two daughters and enjoyed the quintessential Manhattan lifestyle. In 2001 her husband moved the family to Seattle, and things began to crumble. She was cut off from the life she loved and her marriage soon dissolved. She sank into her own dark night of the soul, and the years that followed were a powerful catalyst for self-reflection.

These life events set Shonagh on a spiritual journey inward. She started to meditate, and sought out books and teachers to help her better understand her deeper self. This eventually led her to shamanism as a life path. Shonagh studied with a shaman teacher in the Yucatan. He took her to meet with a Mayan shaman for a blessing ceremony. After it was over, Shonagh thanked him, and he gave her a necklace that held an owl pendant. She politely accepted the gift, but couldn't help but wonder, why an owl?

Shamanic practice involves accessing altered states of consciousness to connect with the spirits. Shonagh briefly explored ayahuasca, then turned her attention to the sacred use of psilocybin mushrooms. She was so moved by her first experience that she began a monthly ritual with this medicine. She called it, "Going through the portal to sit on God's lap and talk to the spirits." Over the course of Shonagh's explorations, she experienced the presence of the owl around her and began to think of it as a guardian of sorts. During some of these medicine journeys, she could hear owls hooting in the near vicinity.

Shonagh was beginning to see owls, hear owls, and have owl synchronicities everywhere she looked. It felt as though she had reached a place where the veils between the worlds were lifting. The owl can be a powerful ally for any shaman who performs their work at a soul level. It's the owl's ability to see in the dark that can guide the shaman as they traverse the realms of spirit. Shonagh was familiar with spirit allies, but it wasn't until she began working with the mushroom medicine that she developed a relationship with the owl. The mushroom journeys were about engaging the realms of spirit, and the owl was taking on the role of a wise protector and guide.

As Shonagh got deeper into her practices, she realized that everything society had taught her was being stripped away. She was seeking, and getting closer to her true self. Using the mushrooms in sacred ceremonies had been transformative, yet she needed to go even further. Up until that point, all her mushroom journeys had been taken in the company of a partner, or under the watchful eye of a shaman mentor. She came to a critical juncture in her explorations when her medicine partner, who had become her lover, pulled away. In a state of grief, she made a life-changing decision to take the medicine alone. This meant walking a pathway to her deepest depths, without the assuring presence of another.

She took that leap on a snowy evening in January. That day she had received a package from a Native American friend and artisan, who had gifted her with the tail of a snowy white owl a couple of months earlier. Her friend had used the feathers to create a ceremonial fan with a beaded handle, and she received the finished piece that afternoon. She lit a small bundle of sage, smudged herself and her bedroom with the smoke, then cleared the room with her white owl fan. She was nervous about going it completely alone, but she knew this time she had to go all the way. She asked the white owl spirit to protect her, and then sat down and ate five grams of mushrooms. This is considered a *heroic* dose. Shonagh wrote:

> A half-hour or so later I felt the medicine begin to kick in. I said to the mushrooms, "Please hear me. I come to you with no skin left, just my wounded heart... I come to you for your council and your teaching."
>
> ... Almost immediately, I saw a white sphere in the distance making its way to me. As it neared I saw it had wings and then I realized it was the white owl. She stood before me and became a beautiful woman clothed in white owl feathers with long, flowing

white hair. She radiated warmth and kindness, and said, "I am White Owl. I am your medicine and I will work with you, Daughter Who Longs."

My heart opened to her and I radiated my gratitude. I opened my eyes in that moment and my entire bedroom was encased in luminous white owl feathers. It was such a beautiful sight to behold. I was completely contained and protected. She was to be my guardian throughout the entire journey and her love for me was beyond anything I could possibly describe in words.

Shonagh let herself cry and felt a huge soft wing folding her into her guide's breast, like a mother owl would protect a fledgling. The White Owl took Shonagh to the top of a tree that held the yellow leaves of autumn, then they went down the trunk and deep into the luminous green earth. Mother Earth gently spoke to Shonagh, telling her, "You are dying, Daughter Who Longs."

This startled me, and I looked at her and she said, "Yes, daughter. You must know. The girl in you must die." I began to cry. I understood then why the tree had yellow leaves. It was a time of shedding, of passing from one phase into another...

"You will be birthed tonight," White Owl said. "You will be birthed from Daughter Who Longs to Daughter Who Knows. I will help you." At that she took me to a place where we were standing in a landscape of crystalline white snow.

She stood before me and said, "I am removing the veil, goddess." She removed two veils from me. I was incredulous that she called me "goddess" and she laughed and said, "Yes! You are a goddess! You are my sister. I will work with you not as something greater than yourself. I will work with you as your sister."

I felt myself radiating luminous blue light when the veils came off. Then I was catapulted into what I can only describe as the Cosmos, the Universe, the All."

This psychedelic journey took Shonagh to the third phase of womanhood. She was leaving the maiden and the mother behind, removing those two veils, and she was entering the phase of the crone. From fledgling to autumn to the snows of winter, from life to death to rebirth, she was guided down this eternal path by an owl, who now called her "goddess."

Like many UFO abductees, there is a deep transformative after-effect from Shonagh's White Owl event. The experiencer is in a place of questioning or longing, an event happens, and then a change. This plays out exactly with Shonagh—she is transfigured by the giant owl, and reborn as something new. The message couldn't be more plain. She goes from *Daughter Who Longs* to *Daughter Who Knows,* with the help of an owl.

Shonagh's whole transformative event plays out with an eerie similarity to a UFO abduction. It began with a white sphere seen in the distance making its way toward Shonagh, and then she found herself in an unusual white room. Like almost all accounts of alien contact, the communication with the white owl was entirely telepathic.

I asked Shonagh if she has ever seen a UFO, and I wasn't at all surprised when she described seeing one the previous summer. She had just finished working with a client and was now lying down on her back, gazing up to the night sky. She noticed a triangle of stars, and the center was an empty black void—then there was a bright flash of light right in the middle, like an explosion. In that moment, she knew she was receiving a communication. She couldn't say what it was, but she was in a state of pure calm and trust. Then it exploded again twice more. She thought, "Holy shit. I just saw a real space ship!"

I've also asked Shonagh if she's ever had any UFO abduction experiences, and she's quick to say no. What is curious is that the story arc of her life plays out like what so many abductees have lived. The journey from the dark night of the soul to a spiritual transformation is something I have heard over and over within my abduction research. The white being in another realm that radiates unconditional love, being catapulted into *The All,* and especially seeing a UFO; these are right out of the pages of most any abductee's autobiography. I fully recognize that these glowing examples don't represent the darker experiences of many (or even most) UFO abductees. The shaman and the abductee are being led along a terribly challenging path, and if both are being confronted with initiation rights, the question arises: What is the role of the initiate?

I have a hard time separating Leslie's story with her white owl from Shonagh's story and her white owl. Leslie is very much an abductee, but I don't think Shonagh is. She's much more in the *maybe* category.

I spoke with Leslie on Monday, and Shonagh on Tuesday. I connected with both women in less than twenty-four hours. Now, here's where things get really interesting: both of them were born the same year and in the same place, 1963 in Ontario. Both are working psychics and using these skills to help people. Both have had a lot of powerful synchronicities. Both have seen UFOs, and both have seen owls. They were both adopted, and they've both had profound transformative experiences with a large white owl. I'll also add that both women have striking blue eyes.

It's these kinds of clustered synchronicities that keep me on this path. To me, they are proof of something at play and that reality itself is much more dynamic than I once believed.

The two hammocks

I spoke to a woman named Susan Kornacki after hinting to me on Facebook that she'd had a profound owl experience. We had communicated off and on over the last few years, and I followed up with a set of phone calls. Susan has had a lifetime of UFO contact experiences, and like so many with these ongoing events, she is profoundly dedicated to serving and helping mankind. Her sense of mission is palpable in almost every every word. When we spoke, she said she had three owl experiences that were important to her.

The first wasn't her own, but one that had been ingrained into her family lore. Her grandfather wasn't much of a talker, but he did have one story he would tell over and over. He had over twenty grandchildren, and all of them were captivated by this story. He was always out in nature, all of his life, and it defined his very being. He had spent the afternoon doing what he loved, he was alone in the woods fishing, yet the whole time he had an odd feeling. He sensed a distinct presence, as if there was something right there with him. He looked around and there was nothing, but he swore he wasn't alone.

While driving home that same day, he heard a voice saying, "You need to take a left." That didn't make sense because that wasn't the way home. He looked to his side and there was an owl sitting in the passenger seat. The shock of a talking owl in his car, right next to him, caused him to turn right and he got into an accident. Then the owl was gone, and he never knew if it somehow flew out of the car, or just disappeared. He was convinced that the owl was trying to help him avoid an accident, but he was too startled to follow its directions.

Because of her grandfather's often repeated story, owls have always had a magical place in Susan's heart, and this magic played out on Easter Sunday in 2010. Susan was at big a family gathering not too far from her home. Her daughter and ex-husband David were also there. Over the previous couple of days, Susan had been feeling a weird sensation intensifying in her back, and while at this party she suddenly felt a tremendous rush of powerful energy running up her spine. She described it as a " Tesla coil going off!" Immediately, she told everyone she had to leave. She left alone without her daughter, David agreeing to drop her off at Susan's later in the afternoon.

Susan arrived back home in a state of confusion at about 4 p.m. She was overwhelmed by the frenetic energy in her spine, and had no idea what was happening. She went out to her backyard and got into a hammock, which was set-up between two trees. The moment she lied down, she watched an owl fly above her into one of the trees connected to the hammock. Then another owl landed in the other tree that held the other side of the hammock, and those owls began a back and forth chorus of calls with her lying between them. Susan explained:

> I just kind of surrendered. I laid back into the hammock, and I
> knew what was going on. I knew that they were taking this energy
> and calibrating it, they were helping me to ground it, to have it be
> more complete. The sound of the owls, and the energy was moving
> back and forth, and I was right in the middle.

I can't help but see Susan as some sort of energy storing component, like a battery on a circuit board between two electrically charged owls. This went on for over half an hour, and David arrived home with their daughter. When they walked into the backyard, Susan thought for sure the owls would fly away, but they didn't. David walked up to Susan in the hammock, concerned that she'd left the party so abruptly. He asked if she was alright. She replied, "I am now."

Then she asked what was above them. He said he heard two owls. She explained that they arrived at the exact moment she got in the hammock. When she asked David what he thought they were doing, he said, "It sounds like they're helping."

> I've never had anything like that happen before, animals coming to—I don't want to say heal me—it was more than that, these weren't just balancing the energy but they were also part of the information that was moving in my body. They were a part of it. It was amazing. This energy was overwhelming. I had no frame of reference for what to do with it.

Susan didn't understand what she was feeling, but thought that these intense sensations might match some sort of Kundalini rush, but she couldn't say for sure.

Leading up to this owl event, Susan had started to dabble in energy healing. This traced back to one of her UFO contact experiences. She clearly remembers the aliens showing her that she could move this psychic energy through her hands. She was in a place of yearning and felt a need to follow this path, to see if she could actually make this therapeutic work happen as a career.

Susan, with the help of the owls, seems to be an energy healer who is coming into her own. The explosion of energy in her spine certainly plays out like a Kundalini awakening, and this might have been an energetic blockage being cleared away, allowing a freer more dynamic flow of energy. She opened up, and those two owls were playing some role. Either they were part of some activation process, transmuting something within Susan, or they were attracted to something radiating out of her the moment she put herself in that hammock.

It was after the event with the owls that people started coming to see her for energy healings. She wasn't advertising or anything, they seemed to find her out of the blue. She just went with it, because now she could feel these energies a lot more clearly and cleanly, even though she'd never had any formal training. It was simply an internal knowing about what to do to help people.

Susan described the first odd sensations in her spine beginning on the Friday before the owl event. The feelings were painful, and she even made a joke, "What is this, *a crucifixion?*" That would have been Good Friday, and the owl event happened two days later, on Easter Sunday. When I pointed out this glaring metaphor to Susan, she seemed genuinely surprised. She's never been in any way religious, so the irony hadn't occurred to her. There is no day in the Western world with more overt *death and rebirth* symbolism than Easter Sunday.

She was home alone on January 1st, 2012, lost in a mood of unease. She didn't understand what she was feeling or what was happening, it felt like something was draining out of her. She casually glanced out a window, and made direct eye contact with an owl—it was looking right at her. Susan was on the second floor, and the owl was on a branch just outside the window. Their eyes were locked for the next 15 minutes. She actually said they *engaged* one another, and there was an *information transfer.*

In the moments after seeing that owl, she started feeling better. She somehow knew the owl was picking up on her mood, and there had been some kind of communication. Susan felt strongly that the owl was connecting to the trees and also connecting with all the various beings out there. She was in her house, and the message from the owl was to come out, leave the confines of her safe home—a call to *pull out to nature.*

Leading up to seeing the owl, Susan had been feeling a deep pull to change her life and follow a new path. Right after seeing the owl, things began to shift. Very soon after she acted on that pull and moved to Hawaii. This had been a long suppressed dream, stretching back to her childhood.

I spoke to Susan on a Wednesday. On Thursday, my friend Suzanne connected me to someone else who had a story she thought I would find interesting, hinting this woman had a lot of unusual life events. I didn't hesitate, and within minutes I was chatting on Facebook with a woman from Massachusetts named Kelly. I need to add that each of the people linked here—myself, Susan, Suzanne, and Kelly—have all had UFO contact experiences.

My interest peaked when I realized that Kelly had her own profound experience involving a hammock. Her story took place on a gorgeous Saturday afternoon in September 2008. She was lying in the hammock in her backyard, gazing at the crystal blue sky, hoping to catch a glimpse of something above her, something she could honestly declare as special, a sighting that would confirm her past experiences.

Kelly looked up from the hammock in contemplation for a good half hour to no avail. She was pleading to the sky, but nothing happened. Then she had a simple thought, she should just ask. She spoke a simple request: "Please show me something out of this world. Something I'll *know* is special, without question. I will close my eyes, count down from ten to one, and when I open my eyes, there it'll be, right there for me to see."

She had made similar pleas at other uncertain times in her life, each time asking from a place of pure intent. She'd had good results from these heartfelt appeals. The answers came in the form of unexplained, paranormal-type events, and she hoped to get a similar reply on that sunny afternoon. Alas, nothing happened. She made the same appeal for a sign in the heavens three times, but nothing presented itself. She calmly thought, "I guess this isn't going to work for me this time."

Right at that moment, her eight-year-old son walked up and plopped himself down right next to her in the hammock. He asked, "What're you doing, Mom?"

"Well, I'm trying to ask to see something really special. Something extraordinary. Maybe you can help me?"

As they lay there, side by side, Kelly gently explained what she had been doing. They both closed their eyes and she described how it worked. They made the same wish and then started the countdown together. When they got to three, her son interrupted, "Wait mom, I didn't do it right. I don't think it'll work."

Then without hesitation, he took the lead and they both closed their eyes as he spoke with a sincere intention, *"Dear God, please show us a UFO."*

Kelly hadn't addressed her request to anyone or anything, not to God, and she never said the word UFO. Then he exclaimed, "5-4-3-2-1!"

When they opened their eyes, there was something shiny directly in front of them, sitting low in the sky, like it was there for them to see. They were both ecstatic, pointing at it together. What they saw was a motionless, noiseless, brilliant white light. It was like an intensely bright star, but this was the middle of the day.

She asked her son to run and get the binoculars from the house. She repeated, "Thank you" over and over as he raced away. Seemingly within seconds he was back, and looking through the binoculars she saw something beautiful and surreal. She described it as a highly reflective, cone-shaped object, shining like a diamond with a million facets. Like a prism reflecting every color imaginable, and even colors beyond imagination. It was totally stationary in the clear blue sky.

When her son looked through the binoculars, he let out a breathless "Whoa!"

She called her husband to come outside. When he stepped out of the house and onto the deck, the light started moving. They both beckoned him to the hammock. They handed him the binoculars and he watched for a long time, eventually moving up to the deck for a better vantage point. He remained focused on the slowly moving bright object until it was no longer visible through the trees. Her husband, ever the skeptic, had no explanation for what it could have been.

Kelly didn't just see something, she felt something too. The whole thing left her with feelings of wonder, awe, curiosity, and gratitude. She asked for confirmation, and that's precisely what she received. The event changed her.

I spoke with two women, one day apart, both with hammock stories and both with UFO contact experiences. Both events happened in Massachusetts, less than 43 miles apart. Each event began with them alone, and then their child and husband arrived (In Susan's case, her ex-husband). And both experiences were profoundly emotional.

These two women had even met on Facebook, become friends and chatted, all without either one knowing the other's hammock experiences. Curiously, if you look at side by side pictures of Susan and Kelly, they look like sisters, almost like twins.

But for me the most resonant thing is that despite all the similarities in their experiences, one woman saw owls and the other saw a UFO, both while lying in a hammock. It feels like the owls and UFO are mirroring each other—playing the same metaphysical role.

I woke with a start the night after writing this back-to-back hammock story. My heart was pounding, and I had this total knowing that *this was the most important owl story I had collected*. Now, this feeling tapered off with the cold light of dawn, so I can't say if it's true, but that was my thought in the moment.

The two balconies

I spoke with a woman named Tori (a pseudonym) about an experience while she was staying by herself in a vacation home near a ski resort. This set of events took place over the last weekend in September 2014, and the whole thing was preceded by a sense of foreboding. She felt nervous because she was going to be there all alone, and this was unlike her.

Tori was jolted awake at around three o'clock on Monday morning. Her dog was barking hysterically, and this was unusual behavior. She spent a long time calming the it down before she could go back to sleep. An hour later she woke again, this time to the dog growling. It was then that she saw a glow coming from the hall. She thought she must have left a light on downstairs, but she hadn't noticed anything before.

Then something caught her eye out the big wall of windows next to her bed. There was a dot of light in the sky, and it was moving around in an odd way. This was still before sunrise, and she watched this bright shiny object darting around in the dark sky while lying in bed. It would move in close, and she saw it as a silvery metallic craft, then zip further away until it was only a tiny dot of light. The entire wall on one side of the bedroom was made up of tall windows, this included a big glass door that opened onto a deck, so she had a wide view of the sky. She watched for about 45 minutes, and then it disappeared. At that point, she promptly fell asleep.

Tori woke again at 7:30, now fully daylight, and she watched an enormous gray owl flying in giant circles above the golf course next to the house. The huge windows framed the whole scene in a way that she could clearly watch the flight of this slow circling owl. She watched from her bed for a long time, and she had an odd feeling that it was looking at her.

Eventually she spoke aloud, "Go away, you're scaring me." At that point, the owl flew towards her and landed right on the deck outside her window. It was standing with its back to her. Tori wanted to open the door and shoo it away. She was just about to get up, when the owl began hopping backwards, still facing away from her. She had the distinct feeling it was trying to hide its face. It waddled right up close to the glass, turned its head, and her instantaneous thought was, "*It's a woman!*"

The owl stood still and stared at her for a long while. She was clear that it wasn't simply a female bird looking in at her, *it was a woman*, a person—and it scared her. She was moving away in the bed, trying to distance herself from the window. At one point her eyes were averted, and when she looked back the owl was gone.

Tori described the owl as mostly gray and about two feet tall. This matches a great gray owl, a common enough bird given her location. Parts of this story suggests she had seen a real bird, but some of it seems like a screen memory. The days leading up to this odd set of events included a flurry of psychic weirdness. She told of guessing someone's birthday, she didn't know why, she was suddenly prompted to say it out loud. This same psychic birthday knowing has happened to me, and both of us were correct about the date.

Tori called me two days after seeing the owl walk backwards on her balcony. We spoke on the phone for over an hour, and during that time my computer would ping with each incoming email. I checked while we were talking, and I had four separate messages, and each were accounts of owls and UFOs. I get a lot of personal reports like this, but four in one hour is sort of over the top—especially while immersed in conversation about *exactly the same* subject.

Tori got back to me the day after we spoke. She described seeing unusual twinkling lights from the balcony of her high-rise apartment the night before, the same day we spoke. They appeared right as she was telling her mother and grandmother about her UFO sighting and the strange owl landing on her balcony.

I noticed something in my conversations with Tori. She was telling a scary story, but there was a sense of wonder in how she shared it. This shows up in other witnesses too, this tone of amazement. It was obvious that she had experienced something both frightening and awe-inspiring.

A little over a week after talking with Tori, I received an email from a woman in Brazil named Suzana, and she described a series of events from early in 2014. She lives on the top floor of a large apartment complex, and the view across from her balcony is of two towers, one at each end of the same building. She stepped out onto her balcony at night and saw a V-shaped object appear between the two towers, and she was instantly flooded with a powerful feeling of joy and peace.

The object didn't fly in from anywhere, it simply appeared in the center of the space between the towers. It had yellow lights, one on the front and two or three on the wings. She watched as it began moving, it drifted slowly until it was hidden behind one of the towers. She ran to the edge of her terrace in the hopes of seeing it again, but it had never reappeared. It was a clear night with no clouds, and she had no idea where it could've gone. Then, silently to herself, she asked, "Gosh, where are you guys?" At that moment two enormous white owls flew past the terrace.

Suzana had been living in that apartment for more than a year and had never seen any owls. They were close to her as they flew past, and they made a distinct whistling sound. She remembered hearing this same noise a few times earlier, but never while seeing owls. That whistling noise would be their calling for her in the upcoming weeks.

In her letter to me, Suzana wrote:

> After seeing the UFO and the owls, a feeling of connection of both UFO and owls filled my heart and mind. Could these birds be a materialization of the beings inside the object I saw? There must be a strong connection to both!
>
> I went to sleep with a wonderful feeling of peace and joy, which was with me for many days. Every time I'd remember the sight, the same feeling would fill my heart and mind. But I wanted answers! Why did my "friends" appear? What do they want me to know? Was it just a confirmation that they are around in these chaotic moments we are living? Why the white owls?

After this night, the owls would come back, sit on an extension
of the building wall and just stare at me while I watched with
amazement. and I tried to show my feelings of peace and joy.

These two owls were close enough that Suzana could scare them with
her movements, so she was careful not to startle them. She didn't want
them to leave, and her descriptions were brimming with emotion. She told
me something interesting:

I would do my best to keep my vibration in joy and peace, because
I had the feeling they were there because of my vibration.

Earlier in this book, I speculated that perhaps owls sensed some
heightened resonance in the experiencer, and they were attracted to it.
This may account for why abductees are seeing so many owls. Suzana
described exactly what I had wondered about, *the owls were there because of her vibration.*

On one of the nights, one of the owls flew onto her porch with a rat in
its beak. She mentally said, "I'm not going to watch you eat that rat, so
you better fly to another place." And it did, it flew to the building next to
hers.

Suzana always knew when they were around because of their distinctive whistling. Once at night, one of the owls almost flew in her window.
She felt blessed to have such sweet friendly visits, they arrived nearly
every night, and this went on for a long time. One night she was frightened by a cockroach on her terrace, so for the next few weeks she
wouldn't go out there, and the owls never returned.

Suzana shared her thoughts about why she'd contacted me:

They want us to speak up and tell our stories, and the relation to
our experiences with them… That's what they WANT! … Maybe
the owl and UFO experience I went through was just a way of
reaching your blog… I feel you are a catalyst.

She went on to compliment the work I have been doing, thanking me
for speaking out. I was honored, and at the same time I recognize that my

blog, my written work, and my audio interviews all seem to be influenced by some outside force. I am cautious about saying this, but I feel strangely compelled to do this work, and this book you hold in your hand is a direct result of this odd urge. Suzana went on:

> You are making me think about how I've been so reluctant to write about what I know and receive from them. I need to have more courage and not hide under the carpet, to loose my fear of being pointing at me as crazy!... I have to work on my fear of speaking my truth... Don't you think they have good reasons in asking me to contact you?

Both of these balcony sightings, with Tori and Suzana, involve seeing owls right after seeing a UFO. This is a bit out of the ordinary, because most of the reports of this type involve the witness seeing the owl *first*, and *then* the UFO.

These back-to-back stories have an amplified power. The way they arrived was so thick with synchro-intensity that it feels like it was orchestrated for my benefit. I realize how presumptuous that sounds, but they each delivered a mighty wallop, and I was left astonished.

All three of these back-to-back stories happened to women; the white owls with Leslie and Shonagh, the hammock experiences with Susan and Kelly, and the balcony events with Tori and Suzana. This pattern plays out within the entirety of my research, more women than men are telling me their owl experiences, and I'm not sure why. One thought is that women are better communicators than men, and they're more likely to reach out to share their experiences. Men might be having just as many weird owl events, but perhaps they keep it to themselves. Or, it could be that the mythic power of the owl is truly connected to the feminine.

Maybe our ancestors saw this same pattern of owls favoring women, and this lore manifested in our ancient goddesses, like Lilith, Athena, Minerva, and Lakshmi—each with an owl companion. Whatever the reason, women certainly outnumber men in this owl research. Of those women, there is a curious number with bird names, like Dove, Sparrow, Cardinal, and even Bird itself!

Chapter 10:

Owls in the Sacred Sites of England

Maria Wheatley comes from a long family linage of dowsers, all living in among the ancient sacred sites of southern England's Wiltshire county. Her research has been centered around the ley lines and energy patterns in hallowed places like Avebury and Stonehenge. She has also researched crop circles. I heard her describing her fieldwork on a podcast, and as I listened, I thought to myself, "Oh this woman simply must have an owl story!"

I found her contact info and I sent an email. I explained I was researching UFOs and owls, and I asked if she had any personal experiences that might fit this inquiry. Within a few minutes she replied:

> I have seen a large expanding UFO that involved an owl! So I was amazed as I read your email.
>
> It was 1991 or 1992, it was midsummer's eve around sunset and a friend and I decided to visit Oliver's Castle near Devizes in Wiltshire. Nearby is a wooded area with trails, we were about to enter the woods when suddenly a majestic barn owl swooped in front of us, crossing the path and then went up into a nearby tree. We both sensed it was blocking our path, as if denying us entry.
>
> We took the unspoken advice and instead went to the nearby hilltop [known as Oliver's Castle], which offers outstanding views due to its high elevation. We were admiring the view when we noted an amber light heading north. After a short while, the light became stationary and then expanded and expanded until it was very large. There seemed to be swirling light at the bottom and looked like a cigar shape.
>
> Then in a split second it returned to its former size and sped off! My friend was spooked, so we hurried down the hill and raced off

in the car. Had it not been for the owl blocking the path, we would have missed an extraordinary event!

This is a wonderful example of a combined owl and UFO event. Like many sightings of this kind, it had a sense of psychic knowing, they both felt the owl was sending a *message*, it was denying their entry into the forest.

In the aftermath of this event, Maria was able to do tarot readings with an increased ease and effectiveness. The fellow she was with that evening claimed to have developed greater psychic knowing. It was as if some dial in his brain had been turned way up, and for a few weeks, he was reading people's minds. This scared him and he didn't like it. Eventually, both Maria and her friend's psychic abilities eased off from their intense high, but Maria feels she's gained heightened clairvoyant capabilities and insights from that owl and UFO event. Maria's story plays out as a mirrored counterpoint to another white owl event in the sacred areas of southern England.

In 1997, Bert Janssen had been actively researching the crop circles of Wiltshire for three summers in a row. He was at a point where he felt he'd come to a dead-end in his ability to follow the mystery any further. Then all that changed. Here are Bert's own words explaining what happened:

> This was my third year, and I thought this is my last year, I've done it all now, I've seen it, three years of [researching] crop circles, it's enough. Then something happens that will draw you back the next year.
>
> What happened to me, I saw for the first time in my life, in Wiltshire, an orb, a ball of light. And not just flashing by, this was amber and it was floating over a field in the near dark of the evening.

Bert watched in amazement as this floating orb cruised around above the fields. It would slow down and then accelerate. Very similar to what Maria saw, the orb was amber and growing larger as he watched. It would grow to the size of a huge balloon, then shrink back down to the size of a grapefruit.

> I watched it for a few minutes, floating over the field, then it moved along and disappeared behind a shed. I was sure it would reappear

again, because the shed should have blocked the view for a just a few seconds, but it never reappeared. And I thought, 'That's really strange, why did it disappear at that shed?'

He went to the shed and tried to get in, but the only door was locked. He put his ear to the door and heard an eerie hissing noise. He was alone and it was getting dark, and he left with plans to come back in the daylight.

He returned the next day and walked around to the back side of the shed. He saw a small window without any glass, it was up high, about the same height the orb had traveled as it passed behind the shed. He thought, "Can it be that the ball of light could have gone through that window and into the shed?"

The open window was up on the second floor, and Bert desperately needed to know what was inside. He had to break into the shed through the front door, and once inside, he heard the same eerie hissing noise. He climbed a ladder to a loft, the level of that open window, and discovered the source of the hissing.

To my great surprise and shock, I found a nest of white owls! I thought, this cannot be true. So the ball of light is totally connected to these white owls. So for me the white owl and the balls of light that are seen in Wiltshire, they are somehow interchangeable. That's why I am paying so much attention when I do see a white owl, because I'm not always sure it is a white owl. Could it be that I am actually looking at something else, and it only presents itself as a white owl.[29]

This is a perfect example of what is at the core of my research. I can't help but see the *window* as a metaphor. UFO researchers are forever struggling with the source of these craft, and one idea (that I like) that gets batted around is that these craft enter our dimensional reality through some kind of cosmic *window*. In almost all the world's mythologies, owls can be seen, like the shaman, as having the ability to traverse in and out of *the beyond*, crossing some veil, or passing through a window. The owl, the UFO, and the shaman all have this metaphoric (or literal) ability. I very much see both Maria and Bert in the role of the modern-day shaman.

Bert, together with his wife Heather, herself a shaman, had another powerful white owl experience in crop circle country in 2011. They followed an owl while driving at night. It lead them on a journey through the rolling hills and narrow roads of Wiltshire. At one point, Heather experienced a vision of the ground zipping below her, getting closer and then further away. It took a moment to realize what she was experiencing—she was *seeing through the eyes of the owl* as it flew over the undulating fields. That same night she saw what she can only describe as a *hell hound*, a mythic beast of ancient Briton. This unleashed a cluster of intense synchronicities that culminated in a beautiful crop circle in a field near where they had chased the white owl.

This is yet another example of the paradox syndrome. So many strange things were happening around Bert and Heather that it took on a form of confirmation—something profound had arisen out of all the frenetic events.

Another powerful detail from Bert's 1997 white owl experience: it happened at a point of questioning and personal disillusionment over the crop circle mystery. He was ready to walk away from the whole messy subject, but both an owl and a UFO (in the form of an orange orb) changed him. He describes the night in 2011 with his wife, where they saw the white owl and hell hound, as a sort of epiphany. Something was interacting directly with him and his wife, leading them into the darkness in a way that reframed their role in the overall mystery.[30]

Now, 18 years after his owl and orange orb event, Burt is still active in this subject. He's now less of a pragmatic researcher, and more a mentor to people seeking spiritual answers. His story is a delightful counterpoint to Maria's experience. Bert had an orange orb lead him to white owls, and Maria had a white owl lead her to an orange orb!

I've asked a few crop circle researchers the same question I ask everyone else—if they've had any odd owl experiences. Very few have any stories to tell. I asked this question of pioneering crop circle researcher Colin Andrews, and I was disappointed when he told me no, he'd never had any unusual owl experiences, nor did he recall any from his research.

This surprised me, because I see the landscape of Wiltshire, the focal point of so many powerful crop circles, as being outright magical. I wrongly assumed that this place should be flooded with curious owl events. He did say that he's had a lot of hummingbird experiences (another mythic bird), and that's interesting to me. But what's much more interesting is that Colin has had abduction experiences, something that he first shared publicly in 2011. The fact that the man who coined the term *crop circle* has also had lifelong interactions with elusive non-human entities didn't surprise me in the least.

I've come across a few owl stories in crop circle country, just fewer than I expected. The story of Maria on the hilltop near Oliver's castle is a perfect example, as are the stories shared by Bert and his wife Heather.

There is a presumption by the uninformed that these circles are created by UFOs, to the point of assuming that they are pressed into the crop by landed flying saucers. This simply doesn't show up in the research, although floating balls of translucent light are commonly reported. UFO accounts connected to the crop circles of Wiltshire are decidedly rare. There are some, but like the owl reports, fewer than I would have expected.

Robbert van den Broeke is a young Dutch experiencer who has lived a life of bizarre involvement with the unknown. His case has been documented by multiple researchers, but the utter strangeness of what has taken place around him leaves him open to criticism by skeptics. He seems to have the ability to predict the arrival of crop circles, and these formations usually appear close to his home in Holland. Foreseeing these circles is often accompanied by depression, and he will suffer for several days prior to the arrival of a new formation. This was the case on the night of September 10th when Robbert suddenly *knew* he should drive to a nearby field, at the time he was with researcher Roy Boschman.

Dutch parapsychologist Richard Krebber was called and accompanied them that night and was there when they found the newly formed circle. Krebber had brought along his fully-charged iPhone and witnessed its battery draining within the circle, experiencing firsthand the commonly reported failure of electronic devices within new crop formations.

The moon was nearly full as these men stood together inside the flattened series of circles in a mustard-seed field. Robbert felt something mystical watching them, and seconds later they all saw a large owl swooping down very low over the formation, circling it three times—counterclockwise, which was the same direction as the flattened plants.

Robbert had the distinct feeling that this owl's consciousness was somehow connected to a larger consciousness, which was both observing the men and energizing the new formation. At that point all three men felt a distinct warmth in their legs. Krebber also reported feeling a tingling in his arms and especially his hand, accompanied by an unusual, but pleasant sensation, of something stretching his body upwards.

Twenty-two days later, Robbert sensed there was going to be another crop circle, feeling it would show up on the night of October 2nd. Again, he went searching with Boschman. Robbert saw a field of flowers and three circles in his mind's eye, then he both heard and saw the name Zwarteberg (Black Hill). He knew of a Black Hill Road, but could only guess the direction they should drive. As the men drove toward the spot, Robbert said that he hoped they would see another owl.

Even though it was dark, they eventually found a place that seemed to match Robbert's vision. They stopped alongside a field of mustard-seed and got out of the car. Boschman saw an owl flying across the field, as if it was trying to draw their attention to something. They walked to where the owl was last seen, and found a flattened circle closely matching what Robbert had described in his vision.[31]

Four owls on four posts

I had my own brush with owls in Wiltshire, albeit indirectly, in the summer of 2014. I was staying in traditional little inns while traveling through the English countryside. Dinner was served at these adorable establishments, but there was one evening I was busy until late. I arrived back at the inn minutes after the kitchen had closed, but still in time for dessert and a pint of stout. I was the only one in the small dining area, and i could see that the waitress was staring at me. She eventually asked, "Are you one of those crop circle people?"

I replied, "Well, sort of."

She explained that each summer the inn gets a lot of *croppies* (the self-adopted name for the crop circle enthusiasts), and she was more than a little mystified by them. I've met plenty of croppies, and many would certainly qualify as eccentric. I explained that I'd spent the day at a crop circle conference on the campus of Marlborough College, three miles from the inn.

Then I told her I was working on a book about owls. She thought that was odd because the other evening, when she was pulling into her driveway, she saw a set of owls. She lives on a nearby farm, and there are four posts alongside her driveway, and there was a big owl on each of the posts, so there were four of them all lined up. They didn't fly away as she pulled in. Instead, they just sat there as she lit them up, one by one, with her headlights.

I asked when that was, and she said two nights ago. I realized right away that was the same day I had arrived at the inn.

At that point I mumbled, "*Oh, that was me.*"

She looked at me quizzically and said, "What? Do you think you somehow manifested those owls?"

"Well, maybe."

It was obvious she was skeptical of what I'd just said, and I asked if she sees a lot of owls. She said not very often, but they are around. I asked if she had ever seen four in a row like that, and she said, "No, never."

I then went on to explain some of the weirdness of my research, and how owls seem to show up in all kinds of strange ways, sometimes seeming to be in direct connection to me. We talked together as I ate my dessert and drank my stout, and we kept talking for a good while after I finished both. I guess I made my point because by the time I was leaving the dining room, she seemed to take me seriously and said, "Maybe you did manifest those owls."

She spoke about growing up in Wiltshire and how the area is rich in ancient folklore. She was dubious of most of these tales, but it was part of living here. She told me a story about a friend who was hunting rabbits, and was about to shoot towards a hedge row when a small orange orb appeared, floating near where he was pointing his gun. Seeing something so strange caused him to pause. At that point, a fellow walked out from behind the bushes along a footpath. If he had fired his rifle, he probably would have shot that man, so the little glowing orb might have saved a life.

August 10th and three crop circle events

I've had some odd crop circle experiences, and there is one date that shows up repeatedly. It started in the summer of 2002 while I was working alone at my desk. A curious thought burst into my mind, something I've come to call a psychic flash. The words, "We need a crop circle here!" suddenly appeared in my head. I didn't know where it came from, but the notion felt playful. The next morning, August 10th, 2002, a crop circle was found in a field of wheat near the small town of Teton, Idaho. This was 31 miles from my home, and by western standards, this was quite close to me.

I visited the site that afternoon, and there were 16 circles in a simple cross pattern set down in a field of wheat. I met a researcher there who told of seeing a grapefruit-sized metallic sphere hovering above the site. She also spoke to the neighbors and heard from multiple witnesses that a bright orange light had appeared in the area of the formation at around three in the morning. The formation was discovered when the sun came up that same day. Alas, no owls that I know of in this event.

Woodborough Hill owl formation
August 10th 2009

On August 10th, 2009, a crop circle appeared in Wiltshire, UK with the stylized face of an owl centered in the design. This was called the Woodborough Hill formation, and it happened in the heart of crop circle country. This was a rare circle because it reappeared the next year. The same design could be seen from above in the field the following summer.

Chute Causeway formation
August 10th 2013

Whatever had affected the crop had produced a visual echo of sorts. Beyond the owl in the design, there was no connection to me with this event.

On August 10th 2013, a crop circle, known as the *Chute Causeway Formation*, appeared in a farmer's field in Wiltshire. This rather complex set of events involves a crop circle, a friend, myself, and an owl. My friend Cynthia is a self-proclaimed *croppie* who has gone to the UK for several summers in a row to chase the phenomenon. She was staying at a traditional English inn with a crew of like-minded croppies, and on the night of August 9th, they all meditated for the appearance of a crop circle. They were asking for a circle with the theme of peace. She woke up at four in the morning (on August 10th) and, while lying in bed, she formally asked out loud to be taken to see the creation of a crop circle.

She then felt a weird rotating sensation and what she feels was the onset of an out of body experience. Then she blacked out. Later that morning, Cynthia awoke with a start. She had the sensation of being dropped back into her bed. She consciously recalled being on board a craft accompanied by a palpable feeling of tilting in a circular motion.

Later that day, Cynthia and her comrades heard a new circle had formed the night before. The whole crew went together to the site, and she describes standing in that circle as one of the most profoundly mystical experiences of her life.

I had a parallel experience on the other side of the ocean. At about nine in the evening of Aug 9th, I was standing in my next-door neighbor's yard in Idaho, when I saw a great horned owl land on tree. Two friends and I watched the owl for a few minutes, and then it flew off. It was a perfectly lovely sighting. The bird was silhouetted against the twilight sky at the very top of a spruce tree, very close to where we stood.

I am pretty quick to find some deeper meaning to any owl I might see, but at that moment I couldn't find any significance to that sighting, so I dismissed it as nothing more than a pleasant chance to see an owl. It was only later, after talking with Cynthia at length about her experience in England, that I realized this might have a connection to the owl sighting in my neighbor's yard.

Allowing for the time difference, 9 p.m. Mountain Time (August 9th) lines up with 4 a.m. GMT (August 10th). That means I had a close-up owl sighting that happened at precisely the same time my friend described having an out of body experience eight time zones away.

Also of note, a Dutch researcher, known as *R71,* made a technical drawing of the Chute Causeway circle. He worked from aerial photos and posted his image online on the same day the circle appeared. What turned up in the diagram were six little peace signs. These weren't in the field. They only emerged after he used a computer to connect points within the design. So, a group of people meditated with the intention of manifesting a crop circle with the theme of peace, and that night a circle appeared nearby with peace signs hidden within the design.

This little cluster of crop circle events began with a psychic flash, followed by a formation appearing in Teton Idaho on August 10th, 2002. Seven years later to the day, a giant owl crop circle appeared in the UK,

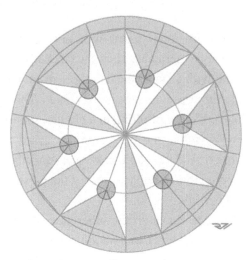

Chute Causeway diagram with peace signs

on August 10th, 2009. Four years later to the day, a circle with hidden peace signs appears on August 10th, 2013, and it coincided with a beautiful owl sighting in my neighbor's yard.

If we follow the model presented by Dr. Kirby Surprise, synchronicities are somehow generated by the observer. They are influencing reality in some unknown way that produces these eerie effects. Could it be that some deep part of ourselves is calling out to an owl, asking it to make itself known at the very top of a spruce tree? We are in need of a message—and we give it to ourselves.

Synchronicities are every bit as mysterious as UFOs or crop circles, but are these other events also being self-generated by the individual? The collective unconscious might be the source, or maybe it's some connection between the individual and our ancient past. There might be a well of mythological archetypes, and the seeker is tapping into this without knowing it, and they are plucking up the appropriate symbol for their own needs. It's as if there's a cosmic turbine chugging away in some realm we can't perceive, but our intention might occasionally influence this machine and it'll spit out sparks, and we see those flashes in the guise of the paranormal.

PART II

RECOGNIZING OWLS

Chapter 11:

Owl Mythology

Myth is the secret opening through which the
inexhaustible energies of the cosmos pour into
human manifestation.

—Joseph Campbell

When asked to define mythology in one sentence, comparative mythologist Joseph Campbell said that would be like trying to define life in a single sentence. He then went on to say that his simplest on-the-street definition of myth would be a story told almost exclusively in symbolic terms.

Mythology as a word has two parts, the prefix myth, by most definitions means something that isn't true. All too often, the word myth implies a purely fictitious narrative, a fable that's been told and re-told throughout ancient cultures. When using the term myth, most people will hear it as something without any meaningful value. The suffix ology means "the study of," so mythology is the study of myths.

Joseph Campbell spoke of two schools of thought on the idea of myth. The objectivist would view myth as nothing more than primitive fairy tales, something obsolete—a dusty book on a shelf, full of old legends to be scrutinized by the rational academic. The other school, the subjectivists, would see myths as something much more vital, a timeless reflection of universal truths, values, and archetypes. Myths carry a significance in our lives, playing an important role. As I proceed forward, I will be weighting the subjectivist side of the scale with a disproportionate zeal.

If the ideas in this book seem biased towards the mystical, that's because they are. Campbell also said, "Myths are clues to the spiritual potentialities of the human life."[32]

The owl has two major symbolic meanings, one is wisdom, the other is death. These divergent ideas probably stem from the owl itself. With their huge eyes and intense gaze, they have an aura of intelligence and serenity. A biologist would see those eyes as well-evolved tools for hunting in the dark. The poet would see those same eyes as being able to penetrate your soul. Owls don't simply appear as wise, they seem *too* wise. So much so that they come across as mystical.

The owl can see into the darkness, and this is the overriding metaphor for its spiritual powers. It can see into the other world, the underworld, the realm of the dead, or the dark world. Like the shaman, the owl can travel to these other realms and then come back with a message. The owl as messenger is interwoven into much of this lore, whether delivering wisdom or a portent of death.

The ancient owl motif is connected to the feminine. The day is masculine and the night is feminine, with the sun and moon as counterparts. The 28-day lunar cycle equates to a woman's cycle. Owls tend to gravitate towards goddesses and fertility icons. In ancient Babylon, the hooting of an owl at night was thought to mean the cries of a woman who had died in childbirth, now searching for her lost baby. This is a grim insight into an age where giving birth was dangerous, too often the cause of a young woman's death.

Owls and the night

The owl, as a symbol, can be a total downer. This role is paralleled across the ages and across almost every mythic tradition: the owl is an evil omen. Nighttime had an entirely different meaning before the electric lightbulb, and all sorts of folklore evolved that painted the darkness as something ominous and sinister. The owl represents the night, and thus it became the totem for all the menacing things hidden in the dark. That includes the internal darkness of the mind and the subconscious.

153

The Sleep of Reason Produces Monsters
Fransisco Goya

Spanish artist Fransisco de Goya was no stranger to metaphoric symbolism. He used owls (along with bats and cats) in a depiction of a nightmare. In his 1799 etching, *The Sleep of Reason Produces Monsters*, a group of sinister owls hover over the tortured sleeper.

Darkness, the domain of the owl, is equated with death, and this connection is easy to understand. The owl is a creature of the night, rarely seen in the daylight. Death, darkness, and owls can all be seen as sinister. Even today, seeing an owl can be unsettling, there is something about them that projects a menacing intensity.

For many of the world's cultures, the owl is an ominous sign. Some traditions believed that merely hearing its screech in the night was a harbinger of death. In China, the owl is called *the bird who snatches away souls*, and in Hungary, it's called *the bird of death*. This storyline continues in present-day accounts from real people. I've collected a wealth of reports of owls showing up in conjunction with the death of a loved one, so much so that they've got their own chapter in this book.

The ancient Egyptians believed that owls were guardians and protectors of the dead. This same tradition reappears across the Atlantic with the Aztecs (curiously, both cultures were pyramid builders). Many Egyptians felt that when someone sees an owl, they will receive a message, another example of the ever-present theme of the owl as messenger.

Egyptian hieroglyph for night

The hieroglyph of an owl represented night, cold, and a state of passivity. The owl was used as the written mark for the sun after it had set, a time when the world was crossing through darkness. The owl hieroglyph is unique because it shows the front of the owl's face. You can see both eyes, while all other bird hieroglyphs are seen in profile, with only one eye showing. For reasons unknown, owl mummies have been found throughout Egypt, often with their heads cut off.

Owls and the goddess

The Hindu religion has its own owl symbolism, and unlike most of the world's dark mythologies, it's positive and good-natured. A white owl is the vahana, or mount, ridden by Lakshmi, the Hindu Goddess of wealth, fortune, and prosperity (both material and spiritual). She is the wife of Vishnu and the embodiment of beauty. She brings good luck and protects her devotees from all kinds of misery and money-related sorrows. When depicted in art, her expression is always calm and loving. By keeping the white owl as her sacred vehicle, she teaches us to open our eyes to the light of the wisdom residing within us.

In the West, we can trace the wise owl meme to Athena, the Greek goddess of wisdom. Her companion was the little owl, and that's the actual genus and species—the little owl, *athene noctua*. In Latin, noctua means owl, so the literal translation for the little owl is the owl of Athena. This virgin goddess symbolized and embodied wisdom, so her little owl sidekick has taken on that quality too, even today. Athena is the companion of heroes and the goddess of heroic endeavor. Beyond wisdom, she also represents courage, inspiration, civilization, mathematics, and the arts.

The Roman goddess Minerva takes on Athena's role as the symbol of wisdom. Like Athena, Minerva is a virgin goddess and is depicted with an owl as her sacred companion, usually perched on her hand. She is also said to have the power to transform into an owl.

In many ways, Lakshmi can be seen as a parallel goddess to Athena and Minerva. They all have owls, and they also have a kind of buoyant optimism about them and their lore. These are three rare examples of the mythic owl seen in a positive light.

The Parthenon, the ancient Temple of Athena, still stands in Athens, her namesake city (though it's not known which was named first, the city or the goddess). It sits proudly on a hilltop known as the Acropolis. The structure, now almost 2,500 years old, was thought to have had families of little owls nesting within its roof lines. The owl's connection to Athena might be because these birds made her temple their home. Saying someone is "Bringing owls to Athens" is an old expression in Greece, a sarcastic way of saying they are doing something totally unnecessary.

The Parthenon itself was built atop the ruins of an older temple, which historians call the Pre-Parthenon or Older Parthenon. This earlier temple was destroyed in the Persian invasion of 480 BCE. The rebuilt temple is aligned to the star cluster Hyades. In Greek mythology, the Hyades were the five daughters of Atlas and half-sisters to the Pleiades. In the 5th century AD, the Parthenon was converted into a Christian church and dedicated to Christ's mother Mary, another virgin goddess.

The owl was a symbolic protector in ancient Greece. If an owl flew over Greek soldiers before a battle, they took it as a sign of imminent victory. The owl as a good omen was put to use by the Greek army. The commanders would keep a collection of caged owls hidden away, and these would be released over the soldiers in the hours before combat as a way to exploit their superstitions.

The Death of Socrates

The Death of Socrates (1787) is an oil painting by Jacques Louis David. I have stood before this enormous canvas many times; it takes up an entire wall in the French Neoclassicism gallery at the Metropolitan Museum in New York City. This grand image depicts Socrates surrounded by his pupils in a gloomy dungeon in the moments before his death. He is reaching for a chalice of hemlock while giving his final lesson on the immortal soul.

Plato, who first used the term *archetype*, is also in the painting, hunched over in a mournful pose at the foot of his teacher Socrates. There is a student, Citro, seated on a simple bench next to Socrates with his hand on his thigh. Chiseled into this stone bench is an owl, with text in Greek that reads *Athenaion*, meaning "of Athens." Below this is David's signature. The artist was well versed in symbology, and this grand painting is all about wisdom and its convergence with death. So the owl, the symbol of Athens, is threefold appropriate.

Owl coin

The first widely minted coin in human history was known as *the owl*. It featured the profile of Athena on one side and a little owl on the other. This is where we get the term heads or tails—Athena's head on one side and an owl, with its tail prominently displayed, on the other. The coin toss was used, then as now, as a way to randomly solve simple issues. This thick heavy silver coin, the four drachma, was the primary form of international trade for over 300 years, from 430 to 99 BCE. The present-day

Athenian coin from the fifth century BCE

Greek one-euro coin features the very same ancient Athenian owl on the tail's side.

To the right of the owl are the Greek letters AOE (alpha, theta, epsilon), which means *Of the Athenians,* or more simply, *Athens.* There is a sprig of olive leaves above and to the left of the owl's head, probably placed there to commemorate success in battle. There is also a crescent moon, depicting the owl's connection to the night. The crescent moon might also symbolize clairvoyance, knowing without thinking, and the feminine.

Are these ancient memes still at play? Presently, the US dollar holds the honor of the most widely traded form of currency on our planet, so it plays the same role the owl coin did in ancient times. Looking closely at the front side of a paper one dollar bill, tucked in near the numeral one in the upper right corner is a tiny owl—at least that's what it appears to be. All that can be seen is a little speck of an owl-like head, it's peeking above a crescent-shaped flourish that frames the numeral one. This tiny owl head might be nothing more than part of the decorative motif in the background. A similar shape is seen repeating at other places on the bill. It's worth noting that, like the Athenian coin, the dollar bill has olive leaves above and left of the owl's head, and also a crescent.

President Theodore Roosevelt, ever the naturalist, stuffed and mounted a snowy owl while still in his teens. It's rumored that he carried an Athenian owl coin in his pocket all throughout his Presidency. During the early years of the 20th century that the US coins were redesigned, with a nod to the classical Greek design elements. From 1917 to 1930, the US quarter featured Lady Liberty, an obvious representation of Athena. She is standing in the same pose as a marble sculpture of Athena from the Parthenon. Both coins, the ancient Greek owl and this modern US quarter, feature the goddess Athena on the heads side. The tail side of the American quarter also has a bird, albeit an eagle. The eagle is the masculine counterpart to the owl, and also the symbol of Athena's father, Zeus.

Ancient Rome

Even though Minerva and her companion owl represented wisdom, Roman superstitions also portrayed owls as harbingers of doom. For example, the hoot of an owl was thought to foretell imminent death, and this is consistent across much of the ancient folklore. Romans also saw owls as having magical powers, and by placing one of their feathers near someone as they slept, they would be prompted to reveal their secrets. And, nailing a dead owl to the door of a house would ward off evil.

The deaths of Julius Caesar, Augustus, Commodus Aurelius, and Agrippa were all said to have been predicted by an owl.

"Yesterday, the bird of night did sit. Even at noonday, upon the market place, Hooting and shrieking." This quote from Shakespeare's *Julius Caesar* came as the conspirators plotted the death of their leader. This omen may be a bit of old English folklore transposed onto a story of ancient Rome.

Strix was the ancient Roman word for owl or witch. The legend was that these evil women could turn into an owl, fly at night, and suck the blood of babies. Strixes are not vampires in the popular sense; they haven't risen from the grave, instead they are demons that can transform into an owl-like creature, and they are most often women. This is a good example of the sinister aspects of the ancient owl lore. Strix is also a genus of owls, and this includes the largest owl on earth, the great gray. The Latin definition for Strix is a screech owl, an evil spirit, or witch. The ancient Greek word Strix means screecher or shrieking night-bird.

In some ancient Hebrew literature, Lilith was the first wife of Adam. She took on this role after he and Eve were evicted from The Garden. In old Jewish folklore, Lilith was symbolized by an owl, and her name in

Hebrew means Night Monster. She was portrayed as an evil spirit who would steal children in the night. Lilith bore the children of Adam, and all were demons. The name Lilith is found in the Dead Sea Scrolls, it's noted among a long list of monsters and evil spirits.

Stealing babies is part of traditional Celtic fairy folklore as well as the modern UFO report. I've heard repeated accounts of parents panicking when their child is somehow missing from their crib. The police are called, a search takes place, and a few hours later the child is mysteriously found back in its crib. These nightmare events happen in the homes of abductees, sometimes in conjunction with UFO sightings.

Owls in the Bible

Owls get mentioned in the Bible around a dozen times, sometimes fewer, depending on the translation. It's hard to find any significance to the owl in the Bible, it seems to be used as nothing more than a spooky adjective. There are some poetic passages where the author is trying to describe something as gloomy, and the owl gets plugged in as a kind of dismal set piece.

Owls show up as something awful in the book of Job 30:29 (KJV): "I am a brother to dragons, and a companion to owls." (Although some translations will say: "I am a brother of jackals and a companion of ostriches.") This line is in among a long litany of passages that are about as depressing and miserable as anything ever written. It's prefaced with lines like: "When I looked for good, then evil came unto me: and when I waited for light, there came darkness." (Job 30:26) Owls are part of Job's dark night of the soul. These morbid passages, according to many scholars, are signs of clinical depression on the part of the author.

Owls get used again in the Book of Isaiah for similarly dreary descriptions. Isaiah 34:8 (NIV) begins: "For the Lord has a day of vengeance, a year of retribution..." and a bunch of really grim stuff follows, including: "The desert owl and screech owl will possess it; the great owl and the raven will nest there. God will stretch out over Edom the measuring line of chaos and the plumb line of desolation." (34:11) "And thorns shall come up in her palaces, nettles and brambles in the fortresses thereof: and it shall be an habitation of dragons, and a court for owls." (34:13 KJV)

Owls in the Bible are repeatedly equated to gloom and doom, and this mythos continues to this day.

The Bible also says not to eat owls. The Lord told Moses and Aaron what animals are okay to eat and what are unclean, or *detestable*. The reason Kosher Jews don't eat pork is because of these passages in the Old Testament. But, if you read further, God also says not to eat owls, and he's pretty specific about this. The book of Leviticus 11:13-18 (ESV) says: "And these you shall detest among the birds; they shall not be eaten; they are detestable: ... the little owl, ...the short-eared owl, the barn owl, the tawny owl..."

According to these passages, God says you shouldn't eat a big long list of *detestables*. Beyond just pigs and owls, these include other birds, bats, animals, and insects.

Owls in fairy tales

Grimm's Fairy Tales was first published in 1812 by the German brothers Jacob and Wilhelm Grimm. The brothers traveled Europe, transcribing folklore and fairy tales from common villagers. These included Little Red Riding Hood, Hansel and Gretel, Cinderella, and Snow White.

In the first edition of their book, there is a strange little story simply titled *The Owl*. This exceedingly sparse tale is barely two pages long. A great horned owl flies into a barn, and all the townsfolk believe it's a monster. Anyone who dares to enters the barn and sees it runs away in terror. The bravest men in the village are called to the task, but none have the courage to approach the bird. After they all fail, the locals contemplate their doom.

> And now there was no one left who dared to put himself in such danger. "The monster," said they, "has poisoned and mortally wounded the very strongest man among us, by snapping at him and just breathing on him! Are we, too, to risk our lives?" They took counsel as to what they ought to do to prevent the whole town being destroyed... So they set fire to the barn at all four corners, and with it the owl was miserably burnt.[33]

This is a typical example from folklore of the owl as something horrible. Curiously, I found this account on page 123 in the version used as reference, and this has been a highly synchronistic number, both in my research and my life.

Owl folklore of the British Isles

In England up until the nineteenth century, it was believed that the screech of an owl heard out the window of a sick person meant imminent death. Like ancient Rome, the English also had a custom of nailing an owl to a door to ward off evil.

Just before the murder of Duncan in Shakespeare's *Macbeth*, Lady Macbeth says, "It was the owl that shrieked, the fatal bellman, Which gives the stern'st good-night."

In modern times, the owl still makes a symbolic appearance at weddings in Scotland. A live owl is sometimes part of the ceremony, its role is to deliver the wedding rings to the best man. At the start of the service, the owl sits on its perch at the back of the church, alongside its trainer. When the best man is asked for the rings, he turns and the owl is released, it flies silently the length of the church to settle on his arm. There is a leather strap on one of the bird's legs, and this holds the two rings for the bride and groom. These are untied and handed to the officiating priest. In this way, when the young couple put on the rings, they are being blessed with the wisdom of the owl.[34]

The Americas

Throughout the Americas, the native cultures saw the owl as equated with sorcery, evil, and death. To an Apache, dreaming of an owl meant that death was approaching. In the Cherokee traditions, it's said that if you are outside in the daylight and an owl flies over your head, a family member or loved one would die within days. Cherokee shamans saw screech owls as able to bring sickness as punishment. The Hopis see the burrowing owl as their god of the dead, the guardian of fires and tender of all underground things, including seed germination. Their name for the burrowing owl is Ko'ko, which means watcher of the dark.

The northwest coast Kwagulth people believe that owls represent both a deceased person and their newly-released soul. The Kwakiutl Indians were convinced that owls were the souls of people and should therefore not be harmed, for when an owl was killed, the person to whom the soul belonged would also die. California Newuks believe that after death, the brave and virtuous became great horned owls. The wicked, however, were doomed to become barn owls. In the Sierras, native peoples believed the great horned owl captured the souls of the dead and carried them to the underworld. The Hocak people will tell misbehaving children, *the owls will get you*. And there's an old saying in Mexico that is still in use today, *when the owl cries, the Indian dies.*

Not all of these Native American owl traditions are linked to death. Many mythologies are rich with themes of bravery, confidence, and warrior rituals. Owls can be seen as both guardians and messengers. In Arizona, Zuni mothers will place an owl feather next to their baby to help it sleep, again a symbol of the night. In Hawaiian mythology, Puapueo was a benevolent deity who organized the owls on the island of Kauai to chase the mischievous Menehune, tiny leprechaun-like creatures, back into the caves and forest.

In South America, the Mayans saw owls as the symbol of death. The Mayan underworld had nine levels, the lowest ruled by Ah Puch, the god of death. Ah Puch was symbolized by three animals, the moan bird, the dog, and the owl. The Aztecs also saw the owl as a ruler of the underworld, and holding godly powers as messengers of the *Place of Fright*. The Aztec god of death, Mictlantecuhtli, was often depicted with owls. The Gran Chaco is a native culture in South America which held that the voice of an owl brings the message, *Beware! I am bringing harm to you!*
35

I had the chance to speak with retired police officer Jonathan Redbird Dover. He worked for over a decade on the Navajo reservation, and his beat was the four-corners area of the desert southwest. He spoke at a UFO conference, along with his partner, about how the tribal police have traditionally been quite open to paranormal reports on the reservation. They investigated claims of UFOs, mysterious entities, and Bigfoot—just like they would any other crime scene.

We stood together in an open courtyard and I asked him about the belief system surrounding the owl in his culture. Much of what he shared matched what I had already found in my research. He said owls are seen as something dark and foreboding, as omens of death, and are considered wicked. I told him I was finding something different, it has been much more playful and mystical. As I said that, an attractive young woman walked by with a huge owl graphic filling the entire front of her t-shirt.

I looked at the officer and said, "See what my life is like." We both recognized the humor in the moment, this tidy synchronicity making its point for me.

It was at this same week-long UFO conference in Arizona in 2013 that I asked pretty much every person I met if they'd ever had any odd experiences with owls. Early on at the event, I'd asked that question of author and researcher Rosemary Ellen Guiley. She shared some interesting owl experiences while researching sacred sites in New York State. The next day, she ran up to me and said she had overheard someone talking about owls, and I simply had to find him. She described him as a big, young Native American who was covered in tattoos. This didn't match the typical attendee at this conference, who were mostly blue-haired senior citizens, so I figured he should be easy to spot.

A few days later, well after the daily conference events had ended, probably nearing midnight, I saw him. He was sitting quietly in a chair, all alone at the end of a long empty hallway. I walked up and introduced myself, and asked what brought him to a UFO event like this. He told me he wasn't attending the conference, he was only using the internet on his phone. He was a member of the Yavapai Nation, and the conference center was on the reservation and open at all times to the tribal members.

I sat in the chair next to him and told him that I was researching unusual owl experiences, and that a friend had overheard him talking about owls, and I was curious. Little by little, he told me his story. A few years earlier, he had the unsettling experience of an owl that would follow him wherever he went. He calmly explained that it hung around his house and it would always be there, always looking down at him. If he were at a friend's house, a store, or a gas station, the owl would follow him, as if it were keeping watch. It would be perched there, staring at him—and this wasn't out in the countryside, this was urban Phoenix.

He got so frustrated with the owl that he would throw rocks at it, trying to scare it off. When he told this to his mother, she was filled with dread. She warned him not to mess with any owls, they were powerful medicine, and it could mean something terrible was about to happen. The owl holds an ominous place among the totem animals of his native lore.

I asked him what he was doing during this time of his life. He calmly told me he'd been involved with a dark element in the urban gangs of Phoenix. He was swallowed up in the drug culture, dealing and selling among a dangerous set of players. I asked him about his mindset at that time, and he explained that he was young and wild, and would never back down from any kind of fight. He didn't care if he lived or died, and he was amazed he survived those years.

It was during this time of his heaviest gang activity that ominous owl was following him the closest. Eventually he was arrested, and while in prison he met a mentor of sorts who helped him see the value of his own life. He was clean when he got, out and the owl hasn't shown up since.

Aleister Crowley

The community of UFO enthusiasts is quite small, and their interests tend to wander all over the map, intersecting with a wide range of other esoteric subjects. Within this tiny group, few people have attained the legendary status of British occultist Aleister Crowley (1875-1947). Separating the myth from this bigger than life character is nearly impossible, especially when using the internet as a research tool. Crowley was responsible for founding the religion and philosophy of *Thelema*. This lead to his establishing the *Ordo Templi Orientis*, an initiatory fraternity that used magical rituals and ceremonies to impart spiritual teachings.

He was infamous for the use of ritual sex magic and hallucinogens to achieve states of altered consciousness. Beyond just an occultist, he was (among a lot of other things) a poet, painter, playwright, novelist, mountaineer, world traveler, Freemason, yoga master, ritual magician, openly bisexual, spy for the British Empire, and heroin addict. His mother used the term *beast* to describe her unruly son. Crowley later referred to him-self (with much glee) as the *Great Beast*.

At some point around 1919, Crowley drew a little pencil sketch of a big headed entity that has come to be known as *Lam*. This drawing has been a point of contention for researchers because very little is known of its source. It emerged while Crowley was living in America, specifically when he engaged in a six-month-long magical episode known as *The Amalantrah Working*. This involved a combination of occult rituals, sex, and drugs to induce a visionary experience, and this drawing is said to depict a being summoned during these arcane rites.

The image of Lam, drawn by Aleister Crowley

 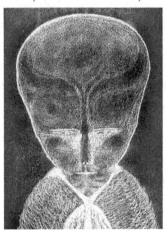

pencil sketch   *reversed*

This image was featured as the frontispiece for an edition of Helena Blavatsky's *The Voice of the Silence,* with commentary from Crowley on the same page. This eerie sketch seems to be titled *The Way*, with text below explaining: "LAM is the Tibetan word for Way or Path..." It was later stated that the figure was Crowley's guru and painted from life.[36]

The similarity of Lam to the prototypical gray alien is pretty obvious, and the subject of endless speculation among the more conspiratorial UFO enthusiasts. Although dismissed by scholars, it's become a sort of internet "truism" that Crowley literally manifested a gray alien during an occult sex ritual. Blogger and researcher Regan Lee (one of those *maybe* people) pointed out something unusual about this sketch. If you look just above Lam's brow, you can see the shape of a gray alien eyes in the shaded texture on the forehead. Once you notice that, it's hard to see the smaller eyes any more. Things get weirder. When the picture is reversed, a stylized image of a horned owl emerges. This insight came from author and researcher Christopher Knowles (another one of those *maybe* people). Granted, at this point, I'm seeing owls everywhere, but let me add that the name Crowley has OWL embedded right in it, as does Knowles.

The Shroud of Turin

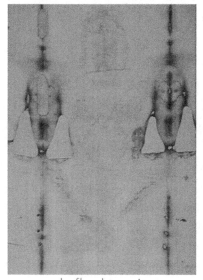 

owls flanking Jesus   reversed image

The Shroud of Turin

An owl emerges, well two owls really, in another mythic image, the Shroud of Turin. Like seeing the owl in Lam's head, the power of this image requires a photographic reversal to bring out the details. This image is said to be none other than Jesus himself, supposedly imprinted onto the cloth that covered his lifeless body after the Crucifixion.

These two owls (one much clearer than the other) are seen on the shroud, flanking Jesus on his right and left, seemingly perched on his elbows. Unlike the representation of Jesus, which emerges in the negative, the owls are seen more clearly without the photographic reversal.

167

The owls are found within the symmetrical triangular stains on the shroud. These were created by fire damage when the church, Sainte Chapelle in Chambéry France, burned in 1532. The whispered lore being that the fire was started by Satan himself. The shroud was held in a box on the altar and some silver fittings melted and damaged fabric. The shroud was folded when it happened, creating symmetrical stained patterns. Rounded triangular patches of white cloth were sewn in place by nuns to repair the shroud. These created the sides of the owls.

I can't help but see the resemblance between the Shroud of Turin and the Burney Relief, the latter being an ancient clay tablet showing a curvy female Babylonian demon, also flanked by two sentinel owls.

Queen of the night

If you google the words *owl* and *goddess*, the Burney Relief will come up at the top of the list. I know because I've been obsessed with these words and any clues to how they might connect. I was in London in 2014, and my hotel was just a few blocks away from the British Museum, home to the Burney Relief. Curiously, I was staying at the Hotel Athens—Athens named after Athena, the Greek goddess with a little owl. Anyway, I walked to the museum and found the clay tablet within minutes. Given all that has been written about it, I was surprised that it's rather small.

What I saw behind the glass was a Mesopotamian terra-cotta plaque depicting a nude woman with wings and talons for feet. She is perched upon two reclining lions, and flanked by two owls. The relief, also known as *The Queen of the Night*, has been dated at between 1800 and 1750 BCE. It originates from somewhere in southern Iraq, but the exact site where it was found is unknown. There is debate if she is a goddess or a demon. Scholars wonder if the winged-woman represents Lilith, Lilitu, or Inanna. Or, it might be Ishtar, goddess of sexual love and war, or perhaps her sister and rival, the goddess Ereshkigal, who ruled the underworld.

Beyond her creepy owl feet, there isn't much that makes this image all that ominous, let alone demonic. There are ancient tales of shapeshifting owl ladies flying around at night, drinking the blood of babies, and that's certainly sinister. If this woman with owl talons for feet does represent

The Burney Relief

Lilith, then this is a good example of the same dark mythos being very much alive for nearly 4,000 years. Owls as a symbol for something ominous are still showing up today in spooky Hollywood movies and children's Halloween decorations.

The hybrid bird goddess is one of the earliest symbols of any kind. Figurines with characteristics similar to Ishtar and Athena have been cataloged and dated to well before recorded history, tracing back as far as 7,000 BCE. The exact origins of these myths are unknown, but open to endless speculation, making this kind of research terribly difficult.[37]

I recognize the temptation to cherry-pick from the deep pool of diverse owl mythology, and eagerly latch onto any conclusion that matches my own avenue of thought—there's an absurd glut of data, and with so many

169

clues comes the challenge of finding a deeper meaning. It would be very easy to make the map fit the territory.

Owls are like puffy clouds on a summer afternoon. You can look up and see whatever you want. There is so much mythology, folklore, and mysticism connected to the owl that anyone could come up with any conclusion that fits their mood. I know myself well enough to declare that I am *not* objective or neutral, and pretending that I am won't make it so. This has been my own deeply personal exploration into the unknown.

I asked author Brad Steiger about the mythic lore of the owls. He replied:

> The symbolism of the owl is so multifaceted and layered with the residue of so many cultures that any one interpretation is impossible. Even as a totem, the owl has different meanings depending upon the vision obtained during the Vision Quest. Using any animal as a universal symbol is nearly impossible. The lamb represents Jesus Christ to one individual and lamb chops to a hungry meat eater.

Chapter 12:

Owls as Archetype

We've used archetypal forms, from the dawn of man right through to today. There are ancient books ornamented with symbols and prehistoric cave walls are painted with sym-bols. Egyptian hieroglyphs are more than just a phonetic way to describe a spoken word, these are all symbols and they all mean something. Certain things have meant the same thing in the human psyche for all of eternity, it creates a thought form, which can be imbued with energy, and which can interact with your subconscious in the same way that a key can interact with a lock. Seeing an owl is seeing a symbol, and perhaps it can unlock something inside you. This archetypal symbol carries information and meaning much beyond simply a bird with big eyes.[38]

—Jef Harvey

Pretty much all the research for this book involves asking this one question, "Have you ever had any odd owl experiences?" If you ask that of an abduction researcher, they'll say yes, and they'll go on to describe typical screen memory events with owls showing up throughout their reports.

If you ask someone who's had the direct contact experience that same question, you might end up hearing some bizarre stories, weird stuff that goes way beyond the four-foot-tall owl in the road at night. It's certainly not every abductee that'll have these kinds of owl experiences, but it's enough that there is a pattern of what seems to be, as far as I can tell, *real* owls interacting with the abductees.

Dr. John Mack's 1994 book on UFO contact, *Abduction,* featured the extremely intense accounts of a man named Peter Faust (how's that for an archetypal name). I've talked on the phone with him only once, and we've shared a handful of emails over the years. I initially reached out to him during some of my darkest times as I tried to come to terms with my own memories. He's been wonderfully supportive and insightful, and I appreciate his help.

As part of this book project, I sent Peter an email, asking him the same question I've been asking everyone—*have you ever had any odd owl experiences?* He replied:

> That is what got me in the door, so to say, to begin looking at this in my life. When I lived in Hawaii, there was a big old owl (that's what I thought at the time) that would come to the sliding glass door off my bedroom at night. Of course under regression when I looked at the owl it was a whole other creature. So yeah, me and owls and ETs have a connection.

The owl described by Peter fits cleanly into the screen memory category, an image projected into his mind, presumably so he wouldn't be terrified of seeing a creepy gray alien. How this is done is a mystery, and *why* is an equally difficult question. Also of note is that it was an owl (or the image of an owl) that played the role of catalyst for Peter to begin looking at his bizarre life experiences. This matches the role of the owl in my own odyssey of awakening.

The question is, why owls? As noted earlier, the presentation of an owl could be nothing more than a convenient disguise. It's a common enough animal, especially at night. What a UFO researcher will say is that owls have great big eyes, and these are similar to the big penetrating eyes of the aliens. They're choosing the owl as a sort of costume, because an owl resembles a gray alien. This has been repeated so many times, that it has become a sort of dogma, a sort of truth. I question that, we don't truly know why they are choosing the owl. The similarity to the big-eyed alien might be the reason for the screen image of the owl, but this just feels too simple.

I suspect this kind of contact experience has been ongoing throughout the entirety of human history, and the reverence for the owl in folklore and mythology can be traced back to experiences like what Peter described. The shamans and sages throughout time might have confronted similar owls, staring in at them from their own doorways.

Perhaps the owl isn't chosen for its likeness to the gray alien, but because of its *archetypal* power. The owl might serve some theatrical purpose, a presentation so the experiencer can drink in its evocative essence. The symbolic power of the owl might have been implanted into our psyche at the dawn of human existence.

The idea of *the owl as archetype* jumped out at me while listening to UFO experiencer Jacquelin Smith channeling the spirit of an owl. The concept of the archetype seemed like a message specifically meant for me. Dipping into the symbolic lore of the owl has provided some of the juiciest clues along my path. Jacquelin, speaking as an owl, said of the aliens:

> They are using the owl symbolically, but the owl is still the owl frequency, to mirror to us in an archetypal sense, because humans think of owls in a certain way, right? There is an archetypal image that is mirrored to the humans, this goes on at a subconscious level and connects with the human's genetic memory bank. Because humans think with symbols, they are touching us on that level, and that goes back to the beginning of humankind, and how we see owls.

Archetype is an elusive concept. There are ideas and themes that have resonated within the core of humanity throughout time, and they continually bubble up to the surface. In ancient Greece, Plato introduced the term archetype to define a philosophical idea, referring to pure forms that embody the fundamental characteristics of a thing. These pure forms are invisible to the eye, but they exist in the realm of their idealized states. If our souls have existed eternally, we would then retain a memory to recognize them. Plato contends that all the feelings that accompany our existence are but recollections of what our souls already know.

Carl Jung later built upon Plato's ideas about the archetype. He saw the archetype as psychological, framing it as a collectively inherited unconscious idea or image. The archetype is universally present in both our individual and collective psyches.

The collective unconscious is a unique component to Jung's ideas about the mind, and it serves as a form of psychological inheritance. It contains all of the knowledge and experiences we share as a species. He proposed that archetypes exist within the *collective unconscious*. According to Jung, archetypes are unlearned, innate, universal, and hereditary. These function as a way to organize and translate the world within us, and the world around us. The owl is an archetype that holds the mythic power of the ages. It's been scratched onto ancient cave walls, and presently it's a companion to young Harry Potter.

Across all the world's traditions, owls are seen as messengers from another realm. Their ability to see into the darkness is a metaphor for their roles as gatekeeper or interloper. The message they deliver might be to confirm the reality of these other realms. Owls are wise and foreboding, and this could also be said of the alien. Are these elusive visitors using the image of the owl because we can tap into this grand lineage of their symbolic meaning?

I can't help but imagine an owl standing before the ancient shaman at the entrance to his cave, just as it stood before Peter's big sliding glass door. Trying to unravel the source of an archetype is like trying to know the source of a dream; all one can say is there's a source out there. To say any more would be folly.

If the abduction experience has been with humanity from its inception, could it be that the mythic power of the owl grew out of the screen memories of the ancients? If people have always been having these contact experiences, then they've surely been sharing them around the fire with their fellow villagers. Perhaps the owl hype has been generated by the aliens. Whitley Strieber's owl vision on the snowy window sill implies some vital purpose, and it could be one more in a long line of campfire stories meant to embed itself into the psyches of anyone listening.

A few questions arise—is the image of the owl something the aliens use as a sort of "default" setting for deceiving the abductee? Is there a reason the owl is used sometimes, and deer is used at other times? Is there an archetypal reason one image might be chosen over another? Is it the abductee that's generating the owl as a screen memory, as if their own psyche needs one image more than another?

Could it be that the human psyche reacts instantly to the presence of the alien, and a sort of defense mechanism takes over, plucking the owl image out of hidden corners of our minds? Is the owl image generated to protect the observer? This makes some sense because one's sanity might be in jeopardy just by looking at an alien in their proximity. I have spoken to more than a few people who have seen an alien in what would be ordinary waking consciousness, and what they describe is so distressing that it produces a sort of existential agony.

If it's the abductee who creates the costume, is it grabbed from the ether in its archetypal *pure form* in the way Plato would describe it? There are no easy answers to any of these questions, but I suspect it's more a blurring of multiple points rather than one simplistic explanation. For instance, when an owl spirit stands at the door of the shaman's hut, is this shaman about to be abducted and taken aboard a flying saucer? And when the abductee sees a giant owl standing outside his window, is he about to be initiated into some deeper form of psychic knowing?

The owl as a symbol

Jim Sparks (a pen name) is an author and abductee with a seemingly endless inventory of experiences, all remembered consciously. He's a somewhat controversial figure in this field because he seems to have *too many* memories. When asked about how the aliens communicate with symbols, Jim replied:

> They create holograms or images that literally hang in the air. For lack of a better explanation, I call it a hologram. Sometimes before an abduction, not always, I would get the courtesy of a symbol just before being pulled—I like calling it being pulled [as opposed to] abducted—to let me know what kind of abduction it would be. An example, a hologram of an owl would appear. When I would see something like that, that would tell me it's time for school.[39]

In its simplest form, the owl is a symbol for education. The image of a cartoon owl with a little graduation cap is commonplace in elementary school classrooms at the end of each year, the wise owl as an allegory for education. Again, this traces back to the wisdom goddess Athena and her owl.

If an abduction researcher is hearing repeated stories of four-foot-tall owls showing up in the presence of contact events, the assumption is that these are screen memories. If the same researcher hears repeated stories of seemingly normal owls (in size and behavior) in the presence of an abductee, they might conclude that it's merely a coincidence.

On the other hand, if the village shaman was asked to comfort a young tribe member who was seeing giant owls at the door of his teepee, he would look at these issues very differently than the modern abduction researcher. The owl might be something much more enigmatic than just a convenient disguise. The owl could be seen in its role as a mythic totem, a manifestation of something symbolic or emblematic.

Like the archetype, looking at the owl as a *totem* forces the observer to look within for clues. The owl as a spirit guide is powerful medicine throughout all the world's sacred traditions. Beyond its physical presence, the owl represents ideas: wisdom, shape-shifting, and second sight. Owls are symbolic of seeing into the darkness, the unknown, or the unconscious. They are guides that stand at the gateway to hidden realms. They represent a life in transition, messengers of change, and a call to explore the unknown. All this might ring true for both the UFO abductee and the shamanic initiate.

Seeing an owl on a dark lonely road or peering in a window at night might be unusual, but not impossible. The whole event could be easily dismissed by the abductee. Deer, raccoons, and cats are also commonly reported, and these all have big nocturnal eyes, and each could be shrugged off as something normal. It gets more bizarre—clowns and Jesus show up as screen memories too, and each has a spirit lore and an archetypal presence that might serve as a clue to the abductee on their journey into these unknown realms. This journey might be on board a flying saucer, to an alternate reality, or to a deeper part within the initiate's own psyche.

Seeing a deer has a feminine mythic power. As a totem they imply gentleness, moving through life's obstacles with grace and gratitude. Deer is a symbol of balance and a return to the forest. The Roman goddess Diana, and her Greek counterpart Artemis, are both virgins and both are depicted with a fawn. Diana was the woodland goddess, having the power to talk to and control animals. She also represents the moon and birthing, and is often portrayed with a moon crown, a symbol of the night and a woman's monthly cycle. Diana didn't much like men, and lived in the forest with her water nymphs, all of whom, like Diana, had taken a vow of chastity. Anytime I come across someone named Diana in this research, I look for any hint that she's playing the role of a woodland goddess. Later in this book, there is a story of a wounded owl rescued by a woman named Diana.

Raccoons wear a mask, and as a spirit guide they represent *the disguise*. The bandit is bold and confident. They are telling the observer to seek guidance, to be curious, and to question without fear.

Cats, like owls, are symbolic of what hides in the darkness—or the unknown. I've heard more than one person say that their cat can see into other dimensions. Cats explore in the night, they are watchful, independent, and psychic. They are associated with mystery and occult magic.

Clowns are the personification of the Trickster. Jesus is about as heavily laden with symbolic power as anything in the western world. I have read accounts of a naked man wearing a giant oversized cowboy hat showing up as a screen memory. I'm not quite sure how to interpret such an overtly masculine image except maybe as the flip-side to the divine feminine of the deer. Each of these screen memories holds a symbolic power that might be meant specifically for the observer. Or, I might be reading way too much into these ideas—trying to untangle a hodgepodge of clues that lead nowhere.

In her memoir, *Owl of Minerva*, British author and philosopher Mary Midgley wrote:

> I have borrowed the owl for my title from Hegel, who is well known to have remarked that, 'the owl of Minerva spreads its wings only with the falling of the dusk.' This is a potent and mysterious symbol that might have various meanings. But the thought

for which I want to use it as that of wisdom, and therefore philosophy, comes into its own when things become dark and difficult
rather than clear and straightforward. That—it seems to me—is
why it is so important.

Midgley goes on to lament that too many thinkers only want to attend
to what is clear, and they turn their backs on things that are dark and
doubtful. She is eager to look beyond the brightly lit successes of science,
and instead explore the dark landscapes of meaning and thought. Midgley
wrote:

> It seems to me that we have here the old story of the man who
> keeps looking for his car keys under the same lamp-post. Someone
> asks him, 'Is that where you dropped them?'
> 'No,' he replies, 'but it's a much easier place to look.' [40]

This analogy plays out in the realm of UFO research too, with the
pragmatic investigator staying only under the brightly lit lamp-post, while
the core of the mystery is somewhere off in the darkness.

Midgley looks to the owl as a guide into this shadow realm. Owls,
being associated with the night, are used in many cultures as symbols for
two things—first for death, and second, rather differently, for wisdom.
Going into the darkness brings danger. But, if you must go there, then
surely it's wise to have a companion that can penetrate the darkness.

The owl, by this interpretation, is an ally for any traveler stepping off
the path and entering the darkest part of the forest. One should expect the
owl to show up, either symbolically or literally, whenever a seeker digs
into the deepest mysteries. If this plays out to its fullest, the screen
memory of a four-foot-tall owl might mean the observer is being told that
their journey is difficult rather than clear and straightforward.

> Animal symbols will show up at certain times, almost like reality
> is a dream and animals can be placed into the dream when needed.

This short statement above rings true. It came in an email from a man
named David, who was describing the role of the owl shortly after the
death of his father-in-law. I sense that the scriptwriters of reality can easily pencil in symbolic imagery right into the storyline of our lives. If they

need to punctuate something within the narrative, they'll add whatever is required for the desired effect. I see something else in that statement—if you change the word *animal* to either *UFO* or *synchronicity*, it still rings true.

From some shamanic perspectives, if a person is experiencing hellishly terrifying abductions, then owls popping up should be no surprise. The ominous totem matches the menacing events. This owl medicine could be seen as part of a transformative experience, using the trauma to prod (or initiate) the abductee to become a wise elder, shaman, or a teacher of sacred traditions. If someone is fully engaged and grappling with something as elusive as UFO abductions, the owl should be all over it in every way.

The somewhat nebulous ideas of *archetypes* and *totems* might be intellectually stimulating, but a real owl is very concrete. The experience of seeing an owl along with a UFO (or something equally mystical) gives a spiritual authority to a mere critter. Sometimes the arrival of a sacred animal has implications that can seem elusive, and other times it can be quite obvious.

Something very unusual happened on Tuesday, October 29th, 2013, approximately three dozen orcas surrounded a commuter ferry as it crossed Puget Sound, from Seattle to Bainbridge Island. This ferry was carrying sacred tribal artifacts, returning them to the ancestral home of Chief Sealth, also known as Chief Seattle. These items had been dug up nearly 60 years earlier from the winter village of the Suquamish tribe and home of Chief Seattle. Since that time they had been on display in a Seattle museum.

Suquamish Tribal Chairman Leonard Forsman just happened to be on board the ferry that day; he was returning home to the island after an unrelated event in the city. He spoke about watching the pod of killer whales, "They were pretty happily splashing around, flipping their tails in the water," he said. "We believe they were welcoming the artifacts home."

Here we have an event that made the national news involving a sacred animal, and none of the headlines shied away from the obvious mystical implications. Even the usually dry prose of the Associated Press hinted that this was something magical.[41]

The orcas, like the owls, are animals considered devoid of any higher consciousness by the watchdogs of our consensus reality. Nonetheless they are showing up as totems at a critical moment. They are presenting themselves as a beautiful example of this attuned symbolic power. This wasn't a dream vision of orcas, they were physically there, playing the role of escort for something sacred on its journey home.

The overall UFO mystery has such a sweeping strangeness, and it overlaps with so many other arcane subjects, so much so that it feels impossible to leave anything out of this big bucket of weirdness. This enigma is complicated and bottomless, forcing me to examine anything with even a hint of relevance. Looking into the owl's symbolic and archetypal lore has offered up some of the most engaging insights of this journey.

During this investigation, I have repeatedly asked myself, *why owls?* I may have gotten an answer. The owl as archetype seems to be the cleanest overall solution to this puzzle. When looking at it this way, everything seems to click into place. What is so striking is that the idea of the archetype was given to me through a soft-spoken woman who was channeling the higher spirit of the owl itself.

Chapter 13:

Owls in Pop Culture

The artist's task is to save the soul of mankind; and
anything less is a dithering while Rome burns. It is
the artists, who are self-selected for being able to
journey into *The Other*, and if the artists cannot find
the way, then the way cannot be found.

—Terence McKenna

When you look up *myth* in the dictionary, one of the meanings is "a widely held but false belief or idea." The rest of the definitions are similarly dismissive. The conventional idea of myth is that it's a fallacy, an old fairy tale in a book on a shelf. Joseph Campbell argued that myth is instead something alive and vital. He said, "Mythology is not a lie, mythology is poetry, it is metaphorical."[42]

There is an assumption that we are adrift in an age without myth, but I see exactly the opposite. We are instead awash in myth, it's emerging out of movies, television, and comic books. Our pop culture entertainment, crass as it might be, is dripping with mythic power.

Academics might sit together in a symposium and ponder the source and evolution of classical folklore, asking such questions as how certain stories traveled from Egypt to Greece and then to Rome. But why aren't they looking at what's happening now? Hollywood is churning out a new mythology by mining our ancient past as well as our tabloid headlines. There is a feverish power in our pop culture, and this is a reflection of

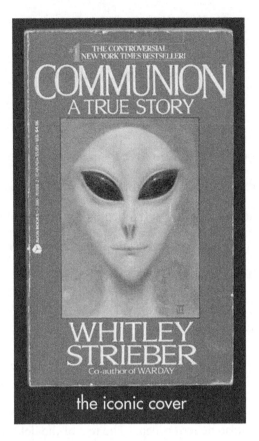

the iconic cover

ourselves. Our new mythology includes UFOs in the same way our by-gone lore includes owls.

The first instance in our popular culture where the owl was directly connected with the UFO abduction phenomenon was in the 1987 best-selling book, *Communion*, written by Whitley Strieber. It's impossible to overstate the cultural impact of this book. Over the next quarter of a century, the idea of the owl as some sort of stand-in for the prototypical big-eyed gray alien has subtly seeped its way into our current folklore. This is in sharp contrast to the actual cover of that book, which was anything but subtle—the image of that iconic gray alien is forever seared into the consciousness of our pop culture, as instantly recognized as Ronald McDonald or Santa Claus.

Strieber had the elusive memory of an owl looking in at him from his bedroom window. When he and his wife checked the spot where the owl should have been standing, there was undisturbed snow, making the *physical reality* of that owl impossible. Nonetheless, the *mythic reality* was there. Strieber seems to have had the same owl experience that the sages and mystics have had throughout time. He was tapping into something universal, and it seems that Hollywood has been tapping into his first-person story too.

The Fourth Kind

In 2011, I received an extremely well-written personal report from a young man named Kevin. He described several odd experiences, including a disturbing missing time event shared by him and a close friend while driving across the desert. There are no UFOs in his experiences, but what he described clearly matches what gets reported by abductees.

We started an email correspondence and something happened in this exchange. Kevin began to confide with me in a way that I have come to recognize. People will share things with me that they may never have told anyone else. I end up playing a sympathetic role in the lives of some people, and I take this role seriously. I'm not a psychiatrist or any kind of trained professional, so it feels like all I can do is listen carefully.

During this email exchange I asked Kevin the same question I've asked everybody else: had he ever had any odd experiences with owls. Here was his reply: "When that movie, *The Fourth Kind*, came out, and I saw the trailer for it, I nearly lost my mind."

The Fourth Kind is a 2009 horror film about UFO abductions. It used a lot of creepy owl imagery as part of its plot, clearly portraying the owl as a screen memory implanted by sinister aliens. Here's more of what Kevin wrote:

> All my life I've had weird experiences with owls. Especially great snowy owls. All over. Places they shouldn't have been. And a lot of them when I was driving by myself. Many of those times when I could have lost time and never noticed it. White owls have sat outside my window. They've been in my room. They've flown right in front of my car several times, a few times looking impossibly huge. I used to tell people about the owls.

One thing was that people didn't believe that I saw so many white owls and that I saw them in such weird places. Another thing was that I was always alone when I saw them. They both excited me and made me very, VERY afraid.

When I saw the trailer for that movie, I became very frightened. But I was intrigued. I downloaded the movie and watched it by myself one night. That was a huge mistake. I didn't sleep that night. I didn't sleep the next night, either. And by the third night, I was dreaming about owls and aliens. I was a wreck for a couple of weeks after that. I was afraid. I've seen all sorts of abduction stuff, read lots of books, studied up on that sort of thing for many, many years. But I've never reacted like that.

Kevin is reporting what I have heard over and over again, that he's been seeing owls with a regularity that goes way beyond mere chance. He describes a confusing mix of what are probably real owls (flying in front of his car) and what might well be screen memories (seeing them in his room). That movie obviously had a triggering effect, but it's probably impossible to untangle all the elusive elements and truly know what might be hidden.

The plot of *The Fourth Kind* is centered around a therapist and her clients, many who have apparently suffered UFO abductions. When the movie was released, there was a promotional barrage claiming that this was a true story. The film begins with the title card "supported by actual case material" and that it contained "actual footage" from case histories. Sadly, this was a publicity stunt—the film was a work of fiction. It was dismissed with contempt by the UFO research community, where most everyone saw it as exploitative and inaccurate.

Still, I have to assume that the scriptwriters flipped through a few UFO books for inspiration and found some owl references in abduction reports. Whitley Strieber's *Communion*, with his account of an owl out his window on the night of his initial abduction memories, was most probably one of these books, and these spooky owls became a central motif in the plot. I see this as a clear example of UFO literature influencing Hollywood. What seems more interesting is Kevin's emotional reaction to the owl imagery in this movie.

Not of This Earth

An owl plays its standard movie role as the harbinger of doom in Roger Corman's 1957 low-budget thriller, *Not of This Earth*. The film begins with a young woman walking on a darkened street. She hears a hooting owl, we see stock footage of an owl, and a few seconds later she is confronted by a human-seeming alien. He takes off his dark glasses and zaps her with his eyes. She passes out and the alien drains her of blood.

So, we have an owl showing up in the moments leading up to alien contact, perfectly personifying the owl/UFO mythos from my research. I see no conspiracy. This B-movie simply uses the owl as a bit of spooky foreshadowing, and that's that. Owls are no stranger to creepy movies; they are as iconic as cobwebs and creaky doors. Much like this film, the 1935 classic *The Bride of Frankenstein* has an owl cameo early in the story, again foreshadowing death. This is a wonderful vignette of classic horror.

But on a deeper level, these dramas play out in what gets reported by real people. Some experiencers will see an owl in the moments leading up to a UFO sighting, or they'll hear an owl out their window, and the next moment they have little gray aliens in their bedroom. These reports are eerily consistent, and they point to something cryptic within the overall mystery.

The alien in the film is played as the quintessential Man in Black. He wears a black suit and strange dark sunglasses. He speaks in a halting cadence and drives a big black car. In the first few minutes of the film there is mind-control, penetrating eyes, and even telepathic communication. This alien is here on Earth, doing creepy medical procedures to unwitting humans in an effort to save his dying race back on his devastated home planet. All these elements are part of the modern UFO lore, but were virtually unknown to the general public in 1957.

Twin Peaks

The owls are not what they seem.

This line was spoken by a mysterious giant to FBI special agent Dale Cooper, played by Kyle MacLachlan, as he lays bleeding on the floor in the cult TV series *Twin Peaks*. This episode was directed by the series creator, David Lynch, and aired on September 30th, 1990.

This show was purposely meant to be eerie and open-ended, littered with clues that seemingly lead nowhere. This line about the owls is an elusive tidbit within the overall narrative, but where did it come from? Lynch is notoriously tight-lipped about his inspirations and the hidden meanings within his works. The show got progressively weirder as it went on, with hints of UFOs and government conspiracies.

Like *The Fourth Kind*, the references to owls and UFOs in Twin Peaks can most probably be traced back to Strieber's *Communion*. The scriptwriters for Twin Peaks must have been aware of the eerie mood created by Strieber in his first-person re-telling of UFO contact experiences. Communion came out three years before the pilot episode of Twin Peaks, allowing one to inspire the other. Both the TV series and Strieber's book are curiously similar in their elusive mood, both generate lots of questions but very few answers.

The character of Major Briggs (played by Don S. Davis) shows up in Twin Peaks on a classified investigation for the Air Force. He even says he was involved in Project Blue Book, a real-life Air Force report on UFOs that publicly concluded: "There was no evidence indicating that sightings categorized as 'unidentified' were extraterrestrial vehicles." Most researchers dismiss Blue Book as an orchestrated effort by the government to deny the UFO reality. According to Major Briggs, a signal was picked up by deep space monitoring equipment, but it wasn't coming from outer space. Instead, it was emanating from the forest surrounding the little town of Twin Peaks. So we have an overt UFO thread woven into the series. Major Briggs gets abducted in the second season, though not by aliens, and is interrogated about the meaning of the owl cave.

Owls are seen as a harbinger of death in most Native American traditions, and this lore was interwoven throughout Twin Peaks. There is an evil character in the series known as Killer BOB (played by Frank Silva); he's a demon that possesses people and commits murder. The name is capitalized because it's an acronym, it means Beware Of Bob. Like so many tales from the Native Americans, BOB can shape-shift into an owl.

It's worth noting that David Lynch is an ardent meditator, and he's more than hinted that he gets inspiration from this non-ordinary state of consciousness. If these symbolic owls emerged from his travels inward, he's not saying. The series is meant to be obscure, so it's near impossible to find any literal meaning to the line, "The owls are not what they seem."

186

Fire in the Sky

Niara Terela Isley has had lifelong abduction experiences. She's also had the added trauma of MILABs (Military Abductions), along with a horrifying set of experiences while serving in the Air Force. She authored the book, *Facing the Shadow, Embracing the Light* (2013), where she shares both the harrowing events and her spiritual path as she worked to move beyond the suffering.

When I asked Niara about any odd owl experiences, she told me a story of when she was about nine years old. She woke up one morning with pain behind her right ear. She touched it and felt a defined little bump. She was scared, wondering if she had cancer and was going to die. Then she forgot all about it and later thought the bump was nothing more than a natural part of her skull.

This memory came screaming back when she saw the film *Fire in the Sky* (1993), a depiction of the Travis Walton abduction event from 1975. She was sitting in the dark theater and had an emotional reaction to a moment early in the movie when the camera briefly passes a stuffed owl. It's only seen for a few seconds in the interior of a bar in a quiet western town.

She told me, "I remember sitting in my seat in the dark theater, seeing an owl flash on the screen, and then feeling pushed back in my seat with all the breath squeezed out of my body. That *real* memory of how the bump [in my ear] appeared suddenly popped into my mind out of no-where. It was a shock!"[43]

The fleeting close-up of a stuffed barn owl appears at the 4:09 time count. The only dialog until that point was spoken by a dusty cigar smok-ing local on the porch of the bar as he watches a truck screech to a halt on the quiet main street. The man says, "What the hell was that all about?" Then he watches as a set of UFO witnesses get out of their truck and walk awkwardly into the bar.

The man recognizes something is wrong and says, "Hey Mike, in a hurry?" Seconds later, the owl appears.

When I watched this scene as research, I had been terribly stressed that this book (the one you are reading) had morphed into something over-whelming. It had swallowed me up and there was no end in sight. That line, directed at "Mike" really hit home. Was that a message for me about my own impatience?

Tracey Torme (son of crooner Mel Torme) adapted Walton's 1978 book, *The Walton Experience,* for the big screen. Torme also wrote the script for the 1992 television mini-series, *Intruders*, another adaptation of a book about alien abduction. The protagonist in the teleplay is a psychiatrist, played by Richard Crenna, who is confronted with patients dealing with the trauma of UFO abduction. His character is a composite of Budd Hopkins and Dr. John Mack. Curiously, *Intruders* has the eerie hooting of a great horned owl in the lead up to two separate abduction events.

Torme was asked about the owls in both these movies, and he said there was nothing to it, at least not consciously. This seems perfectly reasonable given that owls are standard fare in scary movies.

There are two ways to look at the emergence of owls in movies about alien abduction. They could be a completely practical decision on the part of the scriptwriter and production team to add some depth to the storyline. They could be taking a cue from sources like Strieber's *Communion* and simply sneaking it into the plot. *Twin Peaks* and *The Fourth Kind* both seem to fit this model. Or, it could be that owls arrived in the storyline unconsciously. A set decorator simply hung an owl picture on a wall, or the sound editor spliced in a hooting owl to help create a spooky mood. I have a strong preference for the unconscious option. It's just more fun.

Owls and Hollywood

In the book, *Silver Screen Saucers*, author Robbie Graham addresses the main issue used by debunkers, that gullible UFO witnesses are merely parroting things they have seen on TV or in a darkened theater. The subtitle of the book is, *Sorting Fact from Fantasy in Hollywood's UFO Movies*. Robbie argues that cinema, more so than any other medium, has shaped our expectations of how we think about alien life and visitation. UFO movies are influenced by real factors, some cultural and some conspiratorial. After all his research, he's concluded that the UFO witnesses and experiencers are *not* influenced by pop culture. Instead, it's the other way around. Robbie writes:

It is my observation that UFOlogy informs Hollywood more than Hollywood informs ufology, which is to say that Hollywood engages with UFO lore in a parasitic fashion, feeding on the rich veins of a seventy year old subculture... This perspective contrasts with the popular assumption that the UFO subculture feeds on— and thrives as a result of—images projected by the entertainment industry. This is not quite the case.[44]

In Hollywood's UFO movies, broadly speaking, art imitates life.

Contact

In the 1997 movie *Contact*, there is a scene early on where the young Ellie Arroway (played by Jena Malone) talks to her father (played by David Morse). She is lying in bed and asks her father this question, "Hey dad, do you think there are people on other planets?" Right at this moment the father leans forward, and behind his head is a small picture of an owl thumb tacked to the wall.

Later as an adult, Ellie (played by Jodie Foster) is a scientist obsessively searching for extraterrestrial life, very much something an abductee might do. The film culminates with her entering a giant alien-designed machine and being transported (abducted?) to another dimension. In this psychedelic realm of distorted time, she meets an alien, appearing before her in the form of her deceased father. So, the person who resonated an archetypal owl image in her childhood later shows up, from beyond death, as a *screen image* conjured by the aliens.

If that owl picture was placed on the bedroom wall on purpose, it's a perfect use of foreshadowing on the part of the filmmakers, exactly matching the owl/alien connection I am trying to explore in this book. If it emerged by accident, all the better—the owl as a symbol welling up from the ether is much more intriguing!

Disney's Pinocchio

An owl shows up right before the arrival of a star-being in Disney's *Pinocchio* (1940). Jiminy Cricket sings the yearning lyrics of 'When You Wish Upon a Star' and then gets hypnotized by a big-eyed owl clock on

189

the wall of Geppetto's workshop. Within seconds, he sees a curiously bright star in the sky out the window. This twinkling light descends from the heavens, enters the room as a shimmering orb, and then transforms into the Blue Fairy.

This scene plays out as an alien bedroom visitation, where in some sense, the DNA of the inanimate Pinocchio is upgraded into some in-between state, no longer a puppet, but not yet a real human. This mirrors a lot of the ancient alien lore, with implications that beings from the stars have tampered with genetics to create modern humans. Jesus was also ushered in at birth by a star from the heavens, and like Jesus, the finale of *Pinocchio* involves death and resurrection.

The owl, a symbol for alien contact, punctuates the arrival of the Blue Fairy. Tall, blond, and beautiful, she personifies the Pleiadian Nordic, a race of aliens that show up in the abduction literature. These angel-like beings are known for their loving benevolence. Also, the work of Jacques Vallee is required reading for a comparison of the modern UFO abduction stories and ancient faerie mythologies.[45]

Steven Spielberg's 2001 film, *A.I. Artificial Intelligence*, is a sci-fi reworking of the Pinocchio story. The initial script used by Spielberg came from Mr. *2001* himself, Stanley Kubrick. The alien/blue fairy connection is hammered home in the culmination of this film, where spindly aliens with big heads look on as a virtual reality blue fairy resurrects a real boy. These fairy-tale movies aren't meant to imply some grand conspiracy. It's more that the same curious elements that make up the modern UFO abduction lore have been part of our mythology and consciousness throughout the ages.

The artists and the unconscious

I've talked with lots of people who claim the direct UFO contact experience. Beyond the owl question, I'll also ask them if they are a creative type. With very few exceptions, they'll almost always reply yes. They'll be painters, writers, poets, illustrators, or musicians. A lot of abductees seem to be artists, and this plays out in the larger mystery.

We should expect artists to be more sensitive and more open to abstract thoughts and ideas. If they are more open, they should be capable of tapping into the mystical static bouncing around the collective ether.

True inspiration is a mystery, and any artist can describe how getting lost in this zone can create a sort of timeless trance where things flow magically. An artist's best work comes from that mindless place, unhindered by logic and intellect. This could be the concert violinist standing on stage, or the illustrator hunched over in the corner with a sketchbook.

Although it almost always falls short, the Hollywood machine is continually trying to come up with the next UFO-themed movie or TV show. But where do these ideas come from?

There are three avenues of thought. One says the scriptwriter simply dig through some UFO books and uses them for inspiration for a story. There's plenty of evidence for this. The creative team for *The-Files* had a room at the production offices filled with UFO books. The writers would mine these shelves for inspiration, and anyone familiar with this literature can pick out the many references that were inserted into the show.

The second is that UFO movies are a deliberate part of a deep conspiracy to seed the public with carefully crafted ideas and themes. Script writers submit to the whispered directions of government secret keepers from on high. There seems to be some evidence this happens, but my sense is that it's rare.

The third, and most interesting option, is that the real magic of storytelling flows from an unknowable place. The artistic scriptwriter is tapping into some grand reservoir of archetypal themes, and this might include UFOs and owls.

I sought out blogger and author Christopher Knowles when I was trying to formulate some ideas about a graphic novel project. A few years ago, I was planning to write and illustrate a comic book involving both UFOs and owls. I also wanted to include some mythic elements, but quickly realized I was forcing these themes into the story. I called Chris and explained my frustrations. He replied that I shouldn't try to insert any kind of mythology. Instead, I should write from my heart. His advice was forceful, *just let the ideas flow out of you, if you truly let go, those mythic elements will emerge on their own.*

Occult researcher Paul Weston addressed this same mystery: "Where do artists get their inspiration? Certain ideas appear to be hanging in the air waiting to interface with human consciousness." [46]

The Owl Service

Sometimes the owl imagery in popular culture is connected to the modern UFO lore, and other times its roots can be traced back to the legends of our ancestors. One beautiful example of this entwining of folklore and contemporary storytelling is *The Owl Service*. This was a popular fantasy novel for young adults from 1967, written by British author and mythologist Alan Garner. It's an adaptation of an ancient Welsh myth, but updated to modern day Wales. Garner has been very clear that the book was meant as an "expression of myth."

Author and researcher Nick Redfern remembered this book from his youth in England. He told me, "Alan Garner was really popular in that time, he was like a weirder version of J.K. Rowling." A dominating theme of Garner's work is that time does not flow like a river, from past to future, but that an emotionally-loaded experience can repeat itself throughout history in different guises, with each character interpreting the original event from their contemporary perspective.

The story revolves around the emotional tensions of three kids, two boys and a girl, in a rural manor house in Wales. They find a set of dinner plates hidden in the attic, and these are decorated with a cryptic owl pattern; thus the title of the story, *The Owl Service*. Once they find these plates, they unwittingly begin to re-enact an ancient Welsh myth in which a woman made of flowers is caught in a love triangle—and then she's transformed into an owl by a magician. The children seem to awaken the legend by finding these mysterious plates. They each live out the roles of an almost forgotten owl mythology, and they are eventually overtaken by obsession and madness.

The story was based on a real-life experience of Garner's. He found an old set of Welsh plates with an owl design, and from this spun the entire book. The design on the plates found by Garner look like flowers, but if viewed another way, they appear to be a set of evil owls. This seems intentional on the part of whoever designed the plates. One must assume the artisan was depicting elements of the very same legend which Garner had modernized in his novel.

The beautiful maiden Blodeuwedd is the centerpiece of this medieval Welsh myth. She was created from flowers to be the wife of warrior and magician Liew. What follows is a story of adultery, mad passions, magic, murder, and resurrection. Liew is killed by his wife, but doesn't die, he is instead turned into an eagle (the masculine symbol of the day). Blodeuwedd is punished for plotting the death of Liew, and she is turned into an owl (the feminine symbol of the night).

The Owl Service was made into an eight-part television series for the BBC, shown over the winter of 1969-1970. Garner wrote the teleplay, and the production is drenched in an eerie mystique. The themes are quite arresting, and it seems remarkable that this production was targeted at young adults, because the whole thing is just so bizarre. The series was all shot on location using film, something unusual for British television at a time when most of its production involved videotape and indoor sets. The mood is decidedly gloomy and claustrophobic.

Watching this series, I was astonished at its power—the characters seem trapped in a shadow box of a lost, haunted realm. On one level, it's a beautiful piece of film-making, on another, it's like peering into a dream.

Jenny Randles wrote about how synchronicities invaded this BBC production:

> The making of the serial for TV was littered with owl situations. Every time fate took the crew to a particular location, something involving an owl would turn up there, a hidden door-knocker, an ornament banging shutters at midnight, or a live owl rescued from a bird attack which had taken up refuge in the room they were then using as the focal point of the programme! Such amazing things merely scratch the surface of the mysteries surrounding the series. The book, film serial, legend and real-life all seemed to fuse in some incredible sense, just as Alan Garner's theories and writings suggest that they might.[47]

The key cast members would later comment on the lasting impact the series had on their lives. The Welsh actor Raymond Llewellyn, said in 2008 that his role of the troubled gardener Huw has haunted him ever since. Michael Holden (who played the Welsh boy, Gwyn) said that it felt like "we were personally living the whole thing." Gillian Hills (who played Alison) said, "It was all so real, it was frightening." Garner was on the set during the entire production, and Wells said of his presence, "He was enthusiastic, he sort of shone from inside and had intense blue eyes. He willed us to become his characters. We were meant to live our parts."

Also of note, the actress Gillian Hills holds a special place in cinema history for her small but pivotal roles in both Michelangelo Antonioni's *Blow Up* (1966) and Stanley Kubrick's *A Clockwork Orange* (1971). She was in *those* scenes.

There is no UFO imagery in *The Owl Service* (unless you factor in the saucer shape of those plates themselves), but everything about it is a cautionary tale of the power of myth and how it can force itself into the narratives of our lives. Any actual owl imagery in the story is minimal, but the archetypal mood is palpable throughout.

The Hobbit and Sword and the Stone

Author J.R.R. Tolkien made a drawing of an owl to allay the fears of his eight-year-old son Michael, who had been having nightmares of an evil owl in his room. This owl would perch atop high furniture and picture frames, glaring down at the boy. Tolkien named the bird *Owlamoo and* said, "I tried to draw Owlamoo from his descriptions, which seemed to rob it of terror." He created this highly stylized owl in 1928, nine years before the publication of *The Hobbit* in 1937. Any abduction researcher would take a keen interest in a child with recurring nightmares involving glaring owls, the implication being that this might be some sort of screen memory for an alien bedroom visitation.[48]

Owls get mentioned only a few times in *The Hobbit*. When Bilbo Baggins was spying on the Trolls, he was to "hoot twice like a barn-owl and once like a screech-owl." as a way to signal the Dwarves. For an author so profoundly steeped in magic and myth, the owl is, for the most part, absent from any of Tolkien's books.

Drawing by author J.R.R. Tolkien from 1928

The owl plays a much bigger role in a counterpart work of English fantasy. T. H. White published *The Sword and the Stone* in 1938, initially as a stand-alone work but it eventually became the first part of a trilogy, *The Once and Future King*. This initial book is a fantasy re-telling of the boyhood of King Arthur under the tutelage of the wizard Merlin.

White's novel features a talking owl, Archimedes, as Merlin's side-kick. The name Archimedes is an overt nod to the ancient Greek mathematician physicist, engineer, inventor, and astronomer. The wizard and his owl represent two separate lines of ancient wisdom traditions—Merlin as the master of esoteric magic and Archimedes as Greek rationalism. The imagery of the wizard and his little owl is wonderful in its symbolism. It perfectly personifies the western cultural idea of the *wise owl*.

Walt Disney later adapted White's story to an animated film, releasing it on Christmas Day 1963. An apt date, given that it's the story of a boy who performs a miracle and is later crowned a king.

Both Tolkien and White present a wizard with a long white beard and a tall pointed hat, and both authors use legend and fantasy to define something idealized in the English character. These two enduring works emerged right on the heels of each other—*The Hobbit* in 1937, *The Sword and the Stone* in 1938. One year later, in 1939, England would be at war with Germany. Neither work is a harbinger of doom (like the folklore of the owl), and neither is propaganda, but each seems more a glorified call to define what is best within its home culture.

Also, White's *The Once and Future King* was the inspiration for the Broadway musical *Camelot*, as well as *Monty Python and the Holy Grail*.

Harry Potter

Harry Potter, the young orphaned wizard, is the main character in a series of seven best-selling fantasy novels. Like Merlin in *The Sword and the Stone*, young Harry has an owl as a companion. Hedwig, a snowy owl, was gifted to him on his eleventh birthday, and she delivers his mail. So, the most popular series of books in the history of publication features *an owl as messenger*, the centerpiece of owl mythology. This is a perfect example of ancient mythology emerging right now in our mass consciousness.

Now don't read too much into this, but J.K. Rowling, the author of the Harry Potter series, has the letters *o-w-l* embedded right into her name. This little coincidence is more of an insight into the way my quirky mind works than evidence of the supernatural.

The owl, even in its fictionalized form, whether storybook or Hollywood, seems to play the same role, that of delivering a message from the great beyond. The owl as a messenger is both a metaphoric fable and a literal truth. Yes, truth is a strong word, but this feels accurate given of the wealth of firsthand accounts I've received from sincere people. I've heard enough owl experiences that I now see this as a certainty, but what it all might mean is still a mystery.

The UFO is both a fable and a truth. It's a fable in our Hollywood depictions, and a truth in the abundant evidence accumulated over the centuries. Both aspects, fable and truth, are vying for a place in our collective psyches. Pop culture has become our modern mythmaker and, for good or for bad, we absorb its output.

Chapter 14:

Owls and Conspiracy

There's a little hotdog stand in the middle of the Pentagon's central courtyard. It was lovingly dubbed *Cafe Ground Zero* by its patronage because the Soviets were rumored to be using this building as the targeting location for their missiles. The Russians supposedly scrutinized satellite imagery of the courtyard and deduced that top military brass were entering this small building each day at exactly the same time. Thus they aimed their nuclear missiles at what must be the site of super-secret strategy meetings. Little did they know that this was merely the place where admirals and generals would congregate for lunch. Although this makes for a nice story, it has never been substantiated, and it's most probably a bit of modern folklore.

The five-sided shape of the pentagon also holds, within its design, a five pointed star—the pentagram. Both these symbols are rich in ancient myth and meaning. The upright pentagram, in some traditions, represents the five wounds of Christ. The inverted pentagram has a much more sinister lore, being associated with witchcraft and Satan worship. The hotdog stand, like the massive building that surrounds it, is also pentagon shaped. So it's a pentagon within a pentagon.

Sitting atop the five-sided cafe is a wooden owl, and according to government sources, it's there to ward off birds. This owl is perched on a pole in the *exact center* of the headquarters of the United States Department of Defense. Conspiracy theorists, read into this what you will.

As an aside—as if it were even necessary to add—the US government has a strict policy of denial when it comes to the reality of UFOs. The problem is there are a whole lot of people who've had dramatic sightings of strange things in the sky. These folks have had the firsthand experience of seeing something jaw-dropping, but which our government states does not exist.[49]

If their eyes aren't lying to them, then officialdom is. Following this line of thought, the very next thing to ask is, *what else are they lying about?* Once that door is open, all sorts of paranoid conjecture comes tumbling out. Some of it is nutty, and some of it is well-grounded in compelling research. The UFO witness is well-primed to drink from the deep well of conspiratorial craziness. Add internet access to the mix and the rabbit hole is bottomless.

I am absolutely certain that conspiracies of all sorts have been carried out against the public. This includes layers of disinformation surrounding the UFO reality. The conspiracy subculture blurs with UFO research, and these two avenues of thought can feed off each other in ways that produce a kind of madness. The problem is, some of the stories—even the most outlandish—might be true.

The Capitol

The Capitol building in Washington, D.C. is situated at the center of a series of roads and open parks. When viewed from above, the symmetrical design looks very much like an owl, and an angry one at that. The Capitol building itself is positioned at about this owl's heart.

The original street design and locations of the major monuments of Washington D.C. were created by French-born civil engineer, Pierre Charles L'Enfant. His plans included the site of the Capitol, the White House, and The Grand Avenue, now known as The National Mall. These plans were later added to and revised by both George Washington and Thomas Jefferson. This meddling infuriated L'Enfant's pride, and he was prone to passionate outbursts (he was French, after all). It's difficult to know who actually takes credit for the owl outline around the Capital, but it seems that these three men were all involved. Both Washington and L'Enfant were Freemasons, but whether Jefferson was a member of this fraternal order has never been conclusively answered.

As an emblem of wisdom, the owl would be a perfectly logical symbol for the epicenter of the American government, so there might be nothing at all conspiratorial in this imagery. These were learned men steeped in classical history, so they would be aware of the owl and its connection to ancient Greece, the goddess Athena, and the Roman counterpart Minerva.

We get the word *capitol* from the *Capitolium*, the main temple of ancient Rome, seated on the Capitoline Hill. This monumental site was dedicated to the Supreme Capitoline Triad, and there is a marble sculpture in

Palestrina Italy of these three deities seated side by side. In the center is Jupiter, the king of the gods. He is seated with an eagle, a masculine symbol of power and the sky. To his left is Queen Juno, his wife and sister, the goddess of sky and stars with a peacock at her side. The tail feathers of the peacock symbolize the vault of heaven and the eyes of the stars.

And to Jupiter's right is his virgin daughter, Minerva. Like Athena in Athens, she has a companion little owl, a feminine symbol of wisdom and the night.

Bohemian Grove

When I tell people I am working on a book about owls, one of the first things they'll say is, "You mean like the big owl at Bohemian Grove?"

No other item in this book has presented me with as much wildly conflicting information as this huge stone figure. Yes, it seems there is a big owl there, and it looms above a stone altar, but I have found no connection to UFOs. However, there's plenty of conspiratorial speculation surrounding it.

Bohemian Grove is a secluded retreat on the coastline of Northern California, taking up a little over four square miles of glorious Redwood forest. This exclusive site belongs to a private men's club in San Francisco, known as the *Bohemian Club*. Each year, for two weeks in mid-July, the Bohemian Grove hosts an exclusive gathering of some of the most powerful men in the world.

Dr. Glenn Seaborg, both a Bohemian Grove member as well as a Manhattan Project scientist, described the Grove as the place, "where all the important people in the United States decide an agenda for our country for the following year." [50]

Within this closed-off haven for the super-elite is a 45-foot tall stone shaped like an owl. This much is well known and on the public record. Trying to figure out what actually goes on at this annual outing in the woods is tricky; rumor and speculation run wild. On one end of the continuum, the meetings are attended by a bunch of wealthy power brokers who make merry in a very private setting. On the other end are dark tales of pagan worship, occult rituals, and human sacrifice—all while plotting global domination.

Giant stone owl at Bohemain Grove

Whatever the truth might be, a consistent thread in all accounts (benign or incendiary) is that there's a lot of heavy drinking during those two weeks.

The San Francisco club house is adorned with an owl emblem on the outside, and its letterhead also features an owl. There's even a bar across the street called *The White Owl*. All this imagery can easily be traced back to Athena and wisdom.

The club emblem is an owl with the motto *Weaving Spiders Come Not Here*. This comes from the Greek myth of Arachne, a mortal woman who boasted that her weaving skill was greater than that of Athena. A contest took place, and Arachne's weaving was filled with imagery depicting ways that the gods had misled and abused mortals. Athena, also the goddess of arts and crafts, saw that Arachne's creation was not only mocking the gods, but it was far more beautiful than her own. Enraged, Athena turned Arachne into a spider. The scientific term for spiders, *arachnids,* traces back to the myth of Arachne.

This giant stone owl (although some reports describe it made of cement) known as *Moloch*, is named after a god of the Canaanites, an evil deity that required the sacrifice of human children. But the ancient literature presents Moloch as a bull, not an owl. No easy answers, but since the Bohemian Club is shrouded under so many layers of secrecy, it's easy to assume the worst. Given the state of the world today, many of these assumptions might be true.

The Hadron Collider

The $6.5 billion Large Hadron Collider, located on the border of France and Switzerland, had an emergency in November 2009. The entire 17-mile long underground particle collider, designed to peer into the secrets of the universe, went into emergency shutdown because the electrical systems were overheating.

There is an outdoor and, and it seems that a bird swooped down, grabbed a piece of French bread from physicists enjoying their lunch. It then flew over the external electrical system and dropped the bread on a compensating capacitor, right where the main electricity supply enters the collider. This caused a short circuit, triggering failsafe devices to shut down the elaborate cooling system for the gigantic atom smasher. Whatever happened, I'm impressed by the accuracy of that bit of baguette.

A spokesman for CERN, the European Organization for Nuclear Research, said the facility was up and running again after a few hours. They also stated that "the bird escaped unharmed, but lost its bread."

The bird is believed to be an owl.

The question arises, did an owl terminate an experiment that would have ripped a hole in the fabric of reality? It might be that the entirety of humanity was saved from a sucking vortex of doom, all thanks to a benevolent owl. Some reports say the bird was a pigeon (the proper name would be *rock dove*), and the dove is an equally mythic bird, the totem of peace. And a piece of bread is symbolic of the body of Christ.

Mythology can be dismissed as nothing more than old books filled with even older stories. Yet it can also be seen as something alive and evolving. Myth is so ever-present that for the most part it's invisible. Our ancient myths blur with our modern pop culture, the roots tracing back to the first spark of humanity.

The present-day UFO myth is just as vital and tangible as the lightning thrown down from the heavens by Zeus. Our movies and comic books, alongside well-footnoted volumes about UFO abduction, are nurturing something. A powerful story is being kept alive. We are being told, over and over, that there is more to all of this than we dare imagine.

PART IV

OWLS AS SIGNPOSTS

Chapter 15:

Owls Get Mixed up with Aliens and UFOs

The intuitive mind is a sacred gift and the rational mind is a faithful servant. We have created a society that honors the servant and has forgotten the gift.

—Albert Einstein

It's easy to equate an owl with a flying saucer in purely speculative ways. Both owls and UFOs are described as flying with an eerie silence, as well as an unnatural smoothness of motion. It's also easy to connect the owl and the gray alien, as both project a menacing aura, and both have big eyes. Owls, aliens, and UFOs all seem to want to get mistaken for each other. When digging into the accounts, these overlapping connections become a mystifying jumble.

I've talked with a woman named Jujuolui at several UFO conferences over the years, and she is very open about her contact experiences. She also tells of having a lot of owl encounters and feels certain these are linked to her interactions with the gray aliens and their craft. Some of these owls seem like screen memories, where they take on some of the visual characteristics of the grays.

Jujuolui told me how she awoke one night to the sounds of a hooting owl. Waking up in the middle of the night is unusual for her, unless there is a contact event unfolding. Her initial thought was that this wasn't an owl on her roof, but instead an alien being making a hooting noise.

She was compelled to get out of bed, go outside and take a picture of what she assumed was a gray alien. She told me, "If it were a normal owl, I would not have done this, I would've ignored it and kept sleeping!"

UFO experiencer felt she
was told to take a photo
in the darkness

Jujuolui felt she was being *told* to point and click her camera in the direction of the house. It was pitch black outside and she took a picture with the bright flash. When she looked at the image on the back of her digital camera, there was a big owl perched on the edge of the roof. She was then *told* to take another picture, and she thought, "Surely, if this were an owl it wouldn't stay so close to me for another picture, especially after the first flash of the camera! I took another picture, and sure enough, there it was!" That owl on the roof was positioned directly above her bed.

The photo is clearly a real owl, but I can't dismiss her feelings of being compelled to go out into the night with her camera. Was this feeling somehow projected into her from an outside source? If so, what would be the purpose? She left her house thinking she was going to take a picture of an alien being, but instead got a picture of an owl. She told me this house was the site of a tremendous amount of experiences, mostly with the gray beings. She says they are like a second family to her.

An owl person

An experiencer was interviewed by author Linda Zimmermann for her 2013 book, *In the Night Sky*. This witness used the phrase "owl person" to describe the four-foot-tall being that would stand at the foot of his bed as he lay there, paralyzed and unable to scream.

> This "owl person" terrified him. It just stared at him with those frighteningly big eyes, and the next thing he knew it was morning.
> These encounters went on month after month, sometimes only once a week, sometimes two nights in a row, but always in the

same manner… the terrifying owl eyes that stared at him from the foot of the bed. Then five or six hours would pass as if it was only a second, and he would wake up and it would be morning. He knew these were not dreams, but how could this be reality?

…The awful stress of these encounters wore him down to the point where he thought he was going to lose his mind.

The witness was asked to sketch this owl person, and what he drew looks very much like the quintessential gray alien from countless other reports. What seems telling is that he equated this unknown visitor to an owl. There was no screen memory, he was clearly seeing an alien being, but needing some context, he called it an owl. He also described being stared at from his bedroom window by something with huge squirrel-like eyes. This disturbing "squirrel person" would have had to have been about four feet tall to peer into his window. Zimmermann noted that:

Just for the record, the squirrel person did not have fur or a bushy tail… I also have to state that the 'owl person' did not have feathers, wings, or a beak, and he only used that term because of the round head and relatively large eyes. Trust me, if someone told me they were literally seeing four-foot-tall squirrels and owls, their story would not make it into this book![51]

Well, beyond squirrels, plenty of four-foot-tall owl stories have made it into *this* book! So many that I could only share a small percentage of these very compelling reports.

The motion of owls and grays

Contactee Peter Maxwell Slattery described an emotional reaction while watching a YouTube video showing a group of baby owls. He got so freaked out that he couldn't watch it. These little owlets moved their heads in an odd bobbing manner, and it brought up unnerving memories. Peter tells of seeing gray aliens in full consciousness, and he says they have a distinct motion to their heads. He described watching a gray being peering around the edge of a doorway (something I've heard other experiencers describe), and it was bobbing its head in the same unsettling way as the owlets. Unlike any other bird, owls have uniquely fluid neck movements, and this adds to their mystique.

Peter tried to mimic these motions to me on a video Skype call, tilting his head toward one shoulder and then the other, but he couldn't match the odd movements of both the owls and the grays. I watched his gestures and his expressions of frustration as he tried to act out something that obviously bothered him. Also of note, I looked at the time counter for our video call right as Peter was describing this unsettling head bobbing, it read 1:23:45. This has been a highly synchronistic number for me, making me pay close attention. Not too long after having this talk with Peter, I actually saw a set of three baby owls looking down at me from a nest near my home. I was very aware that these fuzzy owlets seemed to be making the same bobbing motion that Peter had described. I couldn't help but be struck by the eerie way they moved their heads, giving me a visual insight to the many accounts I've heard over the years.

Owls and an eerie smooth flight

Earlier in this book, abductee Lucretia Heart told of watching a gray alien morph into an owl in full daylight. She has another owl story that happened in her backyard at twilight. Lucretia saw something next to a tree that seemed whitish-gray and curiously large. It looked like it was perched on the back of a lawn chair, or maybe in a very low tree limb. It seemed about four feet tall, but she thought it might have been smaller. In the dim blue light of dusk, it looked like a person standing there, about two acres away, but she couldn't be sure. She turned her head for just a moment, and when she looked back, it was silently skimming above the tall grass, heading towards her. She was instantly seized with panic.

What she was seeing was a smoothly gliding gray form, its big head about four feet off the ground, streaking across the field at about the speed of someone running fast. She was freaked out, and it took her a moment to realize what she was seeing was a big owl flying across her yard, its belly skimming the top of the tall grass, creating the illusion of legs below the grass line.

What set her off was the imagery of something she had seen before. Gray aliens will sometimes move around without walking, instead they'll smoothly float just a little bit above the ground, as if on an invisible hovercraft. This floating is rarely mentioned in the literature, and witnesses describe this weird gliding motion as terribly distressing.

It took a long time for her panic reaction to subside—the emotional trigger had tapped into something deep. She has seen aliens moving in this way during multiple experiences. At one point, she saw a gray being gliding over lumpy uneven terrain, but its movement was smooth and level. She later went back to where she had seen this entity skimming above the ground, she followed the path it had traveled, and there was a wide abrupt ditch that it had zipped across. If it were running, it would've needed to step down and then back up again, but her memory is of a velvety smooth motion without any dip at the point of the ditch.

She is pretty sure she's seen this same owl on many occasions in and around her yard. She's gotten a good look at it, and it's a great gray, the tallest species of owl in the world. She estimates the size at about two feet from head to toe, with an amazingly large wingspan. She notes that even though the owl is speckled gray in daylight, at night it appears as a ghostly white.

Lucretia tried hard to explain her feelings whenever she saw this owl, it was like the atmosphere changed, and it was extremely odd. This is something that gets repeated a lot, pretty much anyone who sees an owl in the wild says the same thing—they are struck by an *otherworldly vibe*. Owls fly so smoothly and so silently that the observer is left with a weird sense of awe. I have experienced this same reverent emotion many times.

It's striking that Lucretia saw a great gray owl and, for a moment, thought it was a gray alien. The deeper I immerse myself into these murky waters, the more I see a curious blurring between the owl and the alien, something I can't ignore. It feels like they are innately paired together, something that goes beyond their obvious resemblance but plays out in their unsettling presence. Seeing either has an almost mystical power.

Looking for an owl and finding a UFO

I spoke to a woman at length about a conjoined owl and UFO experience. She is a respected academic who has asked to remain anonymous. Her sighting happened on a Friday evening in 2014. There had been some drama leading up to this event, earlier that day she had been appointed to a rather prestigious position at a respected university. She teaches religious studies, so I took note that her sighting happened on August 15th, a date celebrated by the Catholic Church as the *Feast of the Assumption of the Blessed Virgin Mary*. This day commemorates the death of Mary and her bodily assumption into Heaven. It's the most important of all Marian feasts and a Holy Day of Obligation, and earlier the same day, this woman attended Mass and prayed for strength.

As an aside, I know two other women who've both had what they call their *awakening experience* on August 15th, and both accounts involve UFOs.

That evening, she sat with her husband looking out over the ocean. She was as much celebrating her new position as unwinding after a long, emotional day. They were sitting together on a dock enjoying a beautiful evening when she heard the hooting of an owl. She was surprised that there would be an owl so close to the ocean, so she scanned the trees behind her, but saw nothing. She looked up and saw something sparkling in the sky directly above her. It wasn't yet dark, and she clearly saw a silvery object shining high in the heavens.

At first, she didn't mention anything to her very rational husband, she just watched as it made odd maneuvers across the sky. After about two minutes, she asked, "What's that?" Then they watched the object together for the next ten minutes. He's a no-nonsense engineer type, and was genuinely perplexed. He said, "Well, it's not traveling in any kind of linear trajectory."

Later, both the local paper and television news reported that people had seen a silvery disc-shaped UFO that same evening. Curiously, in the days right after the sighting, she'd completely forgotten about the hooting owl. She received an essay early the next week from a colleague at another university. The text recounted Whitley Strieber's memory of a barn owl on a snowy windowsill the morning after his initial contact event.

While reading his account, she suddenly remembered she saw that silvery object while she was looking for an owl. At that moment she heard a ping from her computer—*it was me* sending her a Facebook message asking if I could call her. She agreed and we were talking within minutes.

We'd never communicated; I sent her the text because an experiencer friend had told me I should talk with her. The first thing I asked was if she'd ever had any owl or UFO experiences, and I could hear the astonishment in her voice. She told me what had just happened, and I was astonished too.

She'd just been hit hard with a bunch of overlapping owl and UFO events, and my contacting her was the most intense of all. She told me later, "The call was such a weird synchronicity. That was part of the strangeness of the whole experience, I had never had somebody so directly talk to me like that, just contact me out of the blue."

I can come across pretty strong, and I asked if I scared her on that call. She said, "I wasn't afraid, but I knew right away that you were a person who is in the synchronicity flow all the time, that's how it felt.'

Budd Hopkins' Kitchen

Pioneering abduction researcher Budd Hopkins had a framed photo of a group of owls on his kitchen wall. These were common barn owls, perhaps the spookiest looking of any owl. These white-faced birds look eerily like the image of the big-eyed gray alien that has permeated our popular culture. I was with Budd at his home in 2008 when he pointed to that picture, commenting on how weird those owls looked. Then he said to me, *"I don't know what's going on in those minds, I don't understand what they're thinking."* [52]

Years later, I saw a video documentary that featured Budd, and it showed him going through a collection of drawings made by UFO abductees. He was standing alongside a cabinet of flat files, and one by one, he was holding these illustrations up for the camera. He got to a particularly creepy painting of a group of spindly gray aliens all standing together. He pointed to the big black eyes and said, "The terror comes from the fact that when people look at them, *they don't know what's going on in those minds, they don't understand what they're thinking."* [53]

Point Pleasant and the Mothman

During 1966 and 1967, Point Pleasant, West Virginia, was the epicenter of strange reports of a giant winged creature. These sightings came to be known as *Mothman*, and this frightening episode seemed to culminate in the December 1967 collapse of the Silver Bridge into the Ohio River, a tragedy that claimed 46 lives. Some have speculated that these phantom sightings were a harbinger of the bridge collapse event, as if the power of the impending disaster had somehow manifested a sinister apparition.

There was a barrage of paranormal strangeness that surrounded these events, including UFOs, and this was documented in John Keel's 1975 book, *The Mothman Prophecies*. One thing that was consistently reported by the locals was that Mothman seemed to delight in pursuing automobiles, a habit that is definitely not bird-like, but more consistent with UFOs. The Mothman itself was dismissed by many skeptics as nothing more than a big owl. Here's an excerpt from one of Keel's earlier books:

> In late December 1966 a rare arctic snow owl was shot by a farmer in Gallipolis Ferry, West Virginia. This was two feet tall and had a five foot wingspan. "Mothman" witnesses converged on the farmer for a look at the owl and all of them declared that it in no way resembled what they had seen.
>
> In July 1967 another rare bird turned up. This one was a turkey vulture and stood a foot tall. It was found by a group of boys near New Haven, West Virginia. Again, the "Mothman" witnesses looked and shook their heads.
>
> We do suspect that a few alleged "Mothman" witnesses did mistake owls for "Mothman." While driving through the TNT Area late one night in November 1967, we were startled ourselves when a huge owl suddenly flapped into the air next to the road. It was so big that it was carrying a full-grown rabbit in its talons. Perhaps if a similar owl suddenly fluttered in front of a car filled with teenagers they might mistake it for something larger and more dramatic.[54]

I received an account from a man who had a sighting of an orange orb, along with approximately two hours of missing time. Within a month of this event, while driving at night, he saw the prototypical four-foot-tall owl standing in the middle of the road. He was quite close to the Mothman sightings along the Ohio River, but this was 43 years later.

The owl flew off without incident, but its enormous size made him curious. This sighting plays out as a probable screen memory, something he was unaware of at the time. He did a little research and found a few reports of giant owls sighted up and down the Ohio River Valley. These sightings might imply a possible *cryptid,* an animal whose existence is disputed or unsubstantiated, like Sasquatch or the Loch Ness Monster. He considered that the Mothman events surrounding Point Pleasant could all trace back to people seeing an as-yet undiscovered species of giant owl living in the forests of Ohio. He reasoned that what he saw was so big that it could've easily been mistaken for a winged humanoid. So, we have a UFO witness with missing time, pondering that the ubiquitous four-foot-tall owl might be the source of the Mothman lore.

There are more examples of skeptics using the owl as a convenient scapegoat for an outright dismissal of anything unusual. The Flatwoods Monster (also known as the Braxton County Monster) from 1952 was shrugged off as a bunch of confused witnesses seeing a great gray owl. The 1955 Kelly-Hopkinsville encounter, where two families saw odd lights in the sky and weird entities in rural Kentucky, were blamed on nothing more than people seeing owls. These are two classic cases from the beginning of the modern era of the UFO. Both accounts have flying craft seen by multiple witnesses in conjunction with entities on the ground, something quite unusual during those early years of UFO accounts. It seems that in the case of Point Pleasant and elsewhere, the skeptics are eager to use owls as a stand-in for aliens.

The Owlman

Much like Point Pleasant, Cornwall in England has had its own reports of a man-sized flying creature with glowing red eyes. All of these unsettling encounters are clustered near the tiny seaside village of Mawnan Smith, specifically around the 13th Century St Mawnan Church, about a mile outside the village.

This ominous creature has become known as the *Owlman,* with the initial sighting on Easter weekend in April 1976. The eyewitnesses were a pair of sisters, nine-year-old Vicky and twelve-year-old June, who were in the area on holiday with their family. The girls were walking through the area when they saw a large winged creature hovering above the Mawnan church tower. The terrified girls ran back to their father and described what they had seen. It was obvious that his daughters had experienced something terribly distressing, so he ended their vacation and immediately returned home. The father would not allow either of his daughters to be interviewed. He did, however, provided a local researcher with a drawing of the creature made by June.

Owlman witness sketches

April 3rd 1976

June 17th 1976

Two months later, on July 3rd, two 14-year-old girls were camping together in the trees near the Mawnan church. They heard a hissing sound and saw a figure that looked like an owl as big as a man, with pointed ears and red eyes. Years later, one of the girls, Sally Chapman, wrote about her sighting as an adult:

> I wanted to run but couldn't. It was EVIL, intensely so. When it moved … its arms or wings or whatever went out and it just rose through the trees. Straight up through the evergreens, it didn't flap, it didn't make a sound.[55]

Sightings of this owl-like humanoid continued on the following day when it was described as silvery gray. There were more sightings two years later, in June and August of 1978, all within the vicinity of the church. In later years, odd UFOs have been reported, each time seen from the grounds of the Mawnan church. Twice, these were described as a "block of light," either pulsating blue-white (in 2003) or as rectangular orange-red (in 1996).

A woman contacted researcher Nick Redfern with a profound account that deepens the mystery around this seemingly haunted location. It happened a few minutes after 11:00 p.m. in 1998 while driving home after visiting a friend in Mawnan Smith. She had barely left the little village when she saw something appear just off the road. It was about the size of a large beach-ball and glowing bright orange. The next thing she knew, she was somehow parked on the shoulder, only to realize that she had two hours of time that couldn't be accounted for.[56]

While emerging from her disorientation, she saw a huge owl-like creature with somewhat human qualities. It was hovering in the air, about fifteen feet off the ground. Like Sally Chapman's account from 1976, the creature was not moving its wings to keep aloft.

This account initially reads like a textbook contact account, where the missing time would suggest an abduction event. The addition of the Owlman makes the mystery even more complex, implying that this giant winged creature is somehow connected with the UFO phenomenon. It might be that the Owlman is nothing more than a screen memory, a slightly nuanced owl display projected into the minds of the observers. The question would be: Why are all these strange sightings clustered in such a defined area? One answer would be: *Maybe the entirety of the UFO mystery is not what it seems.*

These Owlman reports are bizarre in ways that go way beyond just a big owl. That the creature consistently took flight simply by spreading its wings and floating upward is positively eerie. This is similar to what I have heard in other odd sightings. One abductee told me about approaching something he initially thought was a crouched man in a darkened parking lot. However, when he got closer it appeared as more of a shadow figure. His mind said *owl*, but he knew that wasn't what he was seeing. It spread its wings and lifted upwards, and although there was no flapping, he felt a sort of pressure. This sensation was unlike anything he'd ever experienced, and it reminded him of standing on the side of a highway and being pushed back by the force of a passing semi-truck. Then he "watched as it seemed to float away."

The Owlman sightings of Cornwall are markedly similar to the Mothman flap of Point Pleasant. Reports from both events describe the creature as exuding an atmosphere of absolute menace. I have corresponded with a man who had what he feels is more of a Mothman sighting near Norwich, England. He told me that "the event was dripping in dread." In the aftermath of seeing this being, his life came unraveled. I will also say that this man has shared enough with me, including a UFO sighting, that I would consider him one of the *maybe people.*

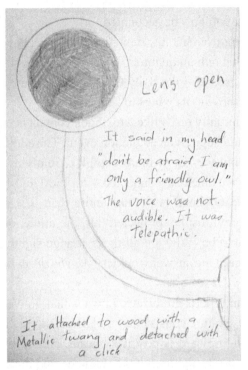

Witness sketch from an event in 1957

"I am only a friendly owl"

I heard from a woman who described a very odd nighttime event that happened when she was about five years old. She was awake and lying in bed alone in her room when she saw a metal object zip down from the sky and clamp itself onto the outside of her window. She tried to scream for her mother when a voice spoke in her head, "Do not be afraid, I am only a friendly owl."

She knew it was no owl, but all the fear left when she heard those words. She stayed still in the bed and stared at it. She was looking at a round lens on a curved metal stalk. The lens seemed to be peering at her through the window, when suddenly three mechanical shutters closed and re-opened, as if it blinked. She was curious, got out of bed and moved towards the window, but the object detached itself and zoomed back into the sky with incredible speed.

This woman has shared enough of her life experiences that I see her as one more of the *maybe people*. She leads a very devout spiritual life, and is dedicated to the protection of nesting sea bird habitats. She's a very compassionate woman, and I'm seeing this kind of sensitivity as a pattern among experiencers.

In this case, we have a weird metal eye speaking telepathically, telling a frightened little girl it's an owl. I've spoken with a lot of people who have seen an owl staring in at them through their windows, often at highly charged moments. They assume these are real owls, but could they instead be looking at a flying metal eye that uses some form of mind control to project the image of an owl? This report seems so odd, but perhaps this is commonplace. Maybe this is an instance when the alien's psychic projection technology wasn't working so well.

Beeping UFOs

Lindy Tucker is both a UFO researcher and witness. Over the years she's heard a set of odd metallic beeping sounds, and most of these unsettling noises have happened simultaneously with sightings of unknown flying objects. Lindy first heard these beeping sounds in her own backyard in Orton, Ontario.

She first saw unusual lights in the sky on March 3rd, 1975, but there was no sound in association with this sighting. These sightings reoccurred over the following months, and it was on April 26th that she first heard a loud, penetrating beeping. These noises became an ongoing event, and on the evening of June 14th, 1975, she made an audio recording of this beeping sound right outside her home. Since that event, she has collected other recordings made by UFO witnesses, and these all have what seems to be the same beeping noise. It's these sounds that have been the focus of her research.

Almost a decade before Lindy taped these noises in her backyard, the US Air Force analyzed a set of very similar beeping recordings, and their findings were published in the now famous Condon Report of 1968. They concluded that these sounds were being produced by a Northern saw-whet owl, a bird that is barely seven inches tall. These adorable little owls make a repeated tooting whistle, and given their small size, this can be surprisingly loud. I have listened to recordings of the saw-whet owl and the beeping UFO sounds back-to-back, and they are quite similar. Yet when listening closely, the owl has a flute-like quality, while the UFO sounds seem more mechanized. This is my non-scientific take when comparing the two using headphones.

A detailed investigation of five UFO related beeping recordings was conducted by tenured Aerospace Professor Ronald Stearman at the University of Texas at Austin. At that time, Stearman had access to some of the most sophisticated audio analytic equipment on any American campus. The outcome of these studies showed that the sounds from each of the UFO recordings are remarkably similar. These were compared to the more easily obtained sounds of a saw-whet owl, which were also very similar to each other. When carefully examined, the owl and UFO beeping had incompatible audio signatures. After an extensive analysis of the acoustics, Stearman ruled out the Air Force's saw-whet owl explanation.

The fact that the Air Force would attempt to dismiss UFO sounds by blaming them on an owl was enough to get my attention, but there's more. Lindy's 1975 recording of this beeping sound in her yard also includes the unmistakable *call of a great horned owl!* Along with some crickets, there is a low steady hooting that overlaps the metallic beeping. I have long been hoping to find a photograph or video that shows both an owl and UFO in the same frame. So far, any visual corroboration has eluded me, but this recording is a close second! A friend of mine (also an abductee with a few odd owl experiences) thought it sounded like the owl and UFO were talking to each other.

This 1975 audio was recorded right in Lindy's backyard. She was there along with fellow researcher Chris Purton, then a Professor of Astronomy at York University in Toronto. This is one more *Chris* that shows up with a direct connection to owls and UFOs. This recording and others can be heard online at Lindy's website, *Beeping UFOs*.[57]

Witnesses report that the UFO beeping sounds can be unusually loud, much louder than what a tiny owl could produce. These sounds have also been heard broadcasting over AM, FM, CB, longwave, and shortwave radios, all in the proximity of a UFO sighting. Unusual electrical failures have been reported too, things like car radios and engines, flashlights, hearing aids, indoor lighting, and tape recorders have either faltered or shut off entirely, seemingly as a result of these beeping sounds.

Lindy has a recording from a New Hampshire family who tried using their video camcorder to record a huge, triangular-shaped craft that flew over their house in the spring of 1992. Unfortunately, for some unknown reason, the video was entirely black. The audio on the tape, however, has the same steady beeping noises.

These sounds aren't always connected with UFO sightings, but are most often heard in "flap" areas at times of high activity. Witnesses will leave their homes in search of the sound, which might have no visible source. Sometimes these folks will report an inexplicable fear and run back inside, as if the sensations are too intense. Some witnesses have reported this beeping can be extremely loud, and they can feel the sounds penetrating their chest. All these unusual effects are something a little saw-whet owl probably couldn't quite muster.

Lindy described an unnerving event that points to something much deeper at play than just some noises made by a UFO. She had written up a report in 1994 for the MUFON UFO Journal titled "Tracing Sound to UFO Encounters." This article detailed both her research and personal experiences, but the paper copy had been misplaced and she was frantically searching to send it off to meet the deadline. It was the middle of the day as she dug through her cluttered desk for her copy of the report. It took some searching, but she eventually found it—and at the exact moment her fingertips touched the paper, *the beeping noises started outside her home.* All the windows were open, and the sound was loud and steady. This precise timing and significance of the beeping was not lost on Lindy.[58]

Whatever's happening, it's in some way intertwined with us and with our consciousness. Accounts like this, including the cameo role of a hooting great horned owl, defy any simple explanation.

Saving a wounded owl

Kenneth Arnold was unwittingly responsible for the term *flying saucer* when he described what he saw to reporters in the summer of 1947. His sighting kicked off a media frenzy and ushered in the modern era of the UFO that forever changed popular consciousness. What folks might not know is that *Kenneth Arnold had a pet owl!*

Arnold built a cage for his daughter Kim so she could raise an injured great horned owl that had fallen from its nest. It's remarkable that this key player in UFO history would have an owl living at his home. Reflecting back, Kim says she thought it was incredible that her father would actually let her keep such a wild creature. She described the cage he built as an expression of his character, something truly wonderful.[59]

Helping an injured owl shows up in a more recent case. On the evening of February 17th, 2013, in the foothills of North Carolina, a young couple and their three-month-old child were driving home from a birthday party. The sun was down and they were in their neighborhood when they saw a slow-moving triangle-shaped object just above the height of the nearby houses.

The husband, Jacob (a pseudonym), pulled off the road and watched the craft from a distance. They were parked and watched in amazement. Then it moved right above their car and stayed positioned there for at least two minutes. At that point, his wife freaked out, screaming and praying while holding their crying baby.

Jacob raced home to drop off his wife and child and get his video camera, but by the time he got back out of his house, it was gone. He described the triangle-shaped craft as having three white lights, one in each corner, and a larger red light in the center. He guessed each side of the triangle was about 25 feet long, and it was hovering around 15 feet above his car—so low he could have hit it with a football.

The next night he heard an owl in his yard, something he'd never noticed before, and it was there hooting again for the following three nights. Some months after this, Jacob and his wife were driving on a busy highway when they saw an owl in the ditch right along the side of the road. He was worried it was injured and might stumble into traffic, so they pulled over. Jacob took off his hoodie and used it to wrap up the bird. He said the owl didn't struggle—it was totally calm and let him carry it to the car. His wife drove the few minutes to their home while the owl was sitting on the floorboard at Jacob's feet.

They unwrapped the owl in their driveway, and it just stood there looking at them. It was a big handsome barred owl. After a few minutes, it opened its wings and calmly flew to a tree branch in their next-door neighbor's yard. It stayed in that branch for three days, staring at them.

On February 19th, 2014, Jacob again heard an owl hooting in his yard. He checked the date and realized this was exactly one year to the day that he'd heard the same hooting after the triangle sighting. As before, the owl stayed in his yard for three days.

Jacob spoke to me about how unsettling all this has been, not just the initial sighting, but everything that followed with all the owls. Since seeing the triangle, he's had recurring dreams that he has been chosen. When I asked what changed since his experience, he said that his Christian faith has become stronger. He also shared something I've heard a lot, the fears of a parent that their child might have some deeper involvement with the phenomenon. This is the most difficult thing about this research: how can I offer solace to a parent with these kinds of worries? The emotions are powerful, and my heart is heavy that I'm unable to give any meaningful advice.

Jacob works with animals. He trains dogs, and this is another thing I see as a pattern with folks with these types of experiences. It's a sort of sympathetic calling. Many seem to work or volunteer at animal shelters, train horses, or rescue abandoned pets.

Like Kim Arnold, Jacob came to the aid of a wounded owl. I have collected a handful of similar stories where people with some connection to the UFO lore will rescue an owl. It might be an up-close sighting or out-and-out contact. All these accounts have the feel of a children's fable, where helping an animal in need is a test, and their simple act of kindness will later turn out to be more important than they could've ever imagined.

The owl, directly or indirectly, gets woven into these reports in ways that seem scripted, as if they are meant to be clues to something deeper.

Owls are signposts along the path, but a signpost isn't very interesting on its own, it's just a stick of wood pounded in the ground with a sign attached at the top. It's the message on the sign that needs to be acknowledged. "Bridge Out" or "Danger Ahead" might be very important. The challenge is to separate the owl (or the UFO for that matter) from the message, and then to interpret any vital meaning.

Chapter 16:

Owls and Shamanism

David Weatherly is an author and paranormal researcher. When I asked him *have you ever had any odd owl experiences*, he shared a story that exemplifies the weirdness of this stuff. He told me about going to interview a witness named Joan. She was a young mother who had been having ongoing UFO sightings around her home, and this was his first visit to meet her. David pulled his truck into the driveway just as the sun was setting. He described shutting off the engine and, while still in the driver's seat, putting a set of fresh batteries in a small voice recorder in his lap.

Here's what he told me:

> As I was looking down to do this, I heard a heavy thud and felt a slight shake as though something had fallen on the vehicle. Looking up quickly, I was shocked to see an owl perched on the hood. It turned its head and looked directly at me. I recognized the species, a great horned owl. This one was at least a foot tall. It looked at me, paused, turned its head and looked forward down the street, then repeated these movements. It never made a sound and after a moment, it launched into the air.
>
> It was an unusual incident and I wasn't sure what had caused the owl to land on my vehicle moments after I had turned the engine off. I didn't mention this incident to Joan when I went in to conduct the interview.
>
> Sitting in Joan's kitchen, I listened quietly as she began to give me details of her UFO sightings. Like many people who report repeated encounters, Joan had experienced some odd things in her life. On two occasions, she had experienced missing time, lapses in her routine that she simply couldn't explain and didn't have any clear memory of.
>
> Once she had told me about her sightings, I brought up her children. Joan had two kids (a daughter age 12 and a son age 7). Her

daughter had not mentioned anything unusual since the UFO activity had begun. Her son however, had started to talk about lights in the sky and the little men. He had also developed an imaginary friend, a common thing for young children to do, but the timing was rather curious.

As I sat talking to Joan, her son came in to the kitchen. He calmly reported to his mother, "It's at my window again Mommy."

Joan assured him that "it" was already gone. She excused herself for a moment and walked with her son to his room. When she returned to the kitchen, she explained that a large owl had started coming to her son's window and perching on the sill outside.

David asked Joan if she'd ever seen the owl herself, she said she hadn't, but her daughter had witnessed it a few times. Her neighbor had also told her that he'd seen a large owl in her yard. When David pressed her for more details, she said the owl had started to appear right around the time of her first UFO sighting.

I spoke with David for a recorded interview in July of 2012, and we both agreed that there's an overlap between UFO events and a wide range of other paranormal experiences. During our back-and-forth dialog David told me he'd had a near-death experience in his youth. When I heard that, an alarm bell went off in my head, and I blurted out, *"Wait, are you a shaman?"* Without any hesitation, he answered: "Yes, I am."

David went on to explain that during his childhood, he had a strong interest in magical traditions. As a young man he studied shamanism with elders from numerous cultures including Tibet, Native America, Europe, and Africa. Even though we had met a few times, I knew none of this history before conducting our formal interview.

This shamanism thing keeps showing up in ways that seem to imply a deeper message is trying to emerge, and David's story with the owl embodies so much of this mystery.

Nobody volunteers to be the village shaman. Instead, they are chosen by the elders. In most cultures, the role is thrust on a youth who shows signs of higher psychic or spiritual capacity. Many anthropologists paint shamanic initiation rites as something brutal, a ceremony to shatter the recruit's fragile sense of reality. This might be through a metaphoric death and rebirth ritual, and only afterwards will the young shaman take on the role of intermediary between worlds. I've heard researchers declare that you cannot become a shaman unless you've had an actual near-death experience. This means the young initiate would've already crossed over into another world, and would have a path in place to follow later in life. When David told me he'd had a near-death experience in his youth, I immediately saw this as part of his initiation, the literal transformation from young boy to young shaman.

Here's an edited excerpt from our three-hour long interview:

Mike: So here's my final question, if I had to ask a shaman any question, it would be this: *What is the meaning of all the owls?* I see a lot of owls, I mean, more than other people, and at prescient moments. And I don't think they are UFO screen memories, I think these are *real* owls.

David: So what you are saying is that you don't feel like they are screen memories.

Mike: No, they are *real* owls.

David: When you look at totem animals, you'll find slightly different interpretations depending on the cultural background, but you also find some commonalities. Now, the owl in a lot of North American mythologies is symbolic of death and all the things associated with that, like the other-world and the spirit world. It's also a very feminine energy, and it's often associated with people who have psychic or mediumship abilities. It's a night totem, so it's associated with the moon and lunar energy. I'm just talking in generalities, there are differences when you look at more western cultures. What's your cultural heritage?

Mike: My father was Scottish, both my grandparents on his side were born in Scotland. The lineage is Scottish as far as we can trace it back. My mother was born in Denmark, and her ancestry is all Danish.

223

David: Oh, now that's cool. The owl in shamanic definition is pretty interesting. If you take the crow, you'll find very similar definitions and interpretations in America and in Europe. The same is true for other animals like the deer. But the owl is curious, the interpretations are very different on the two continents. Things that are associated with it in North America are a bit more ominous. A lot of Native American tribes think it's a bad omen if you see an owl, meaning someone is going to die. Some of the native mythology, for instance in the South Western tribes like the Apache, have a whole owl-man monster that exists in their creation myth. But if you go to Europe and look at the owl it's a bit more noble and it's often associated with the goddess of wisdom [Athena], and it's more associated with the ability to be clairvoyant. And it's often symbolic of being aware of your surroundings. So I would say that with your background the owls would fall into that category for you. Now you can take all these things that I've said and sit with it and derive your own interpretation. But I would certainly say that anytime you see one, you really need to *pay attention* on multiple levels.

Mike: (*laughing*) Sorry, I didn't mean to laugh.

David: And *pay attention* to what's going on at the moment when you spot it, what's happening that day. But also what's going on in your life at the time.

I need to point out that David's advice was exactly what I had been doing at the time. When researching not only owl sightings, but UFOs and synchronicities, I had been asking witnesses the same questions I was asking myself, *what was happening in the moments leading up to the experience?* So I find it very reassuring that David was telling me the same thing, confirming the way I've been framing my own research.

Mike: That's funny, because you said, "pay attention" and I was literally getting ready to reply, and I had just written down "pay attention" on this piece of paper in front of me.

(*Now David laughed*)

Mike: So that's what I've come away with. I don't have a good answer, the only answer I do have is pay attention.

At this point I shared a story from 2009 where I saw five owls all at one time in Montana. This happened along with my friend Peter, and it's told later in this book. Our conversation continued:

David: Those kind of things make it very clear that this is a very defined and connected totem for you... and that is what you need to look at and be conscious of in those moments. Chronicle those things because they are valuable, you'll see patterns emerge and you'll see greater levels of understanding develop from those experiences.

Mike: When you say chronicle them, that's interesting because I have been, and it's been in the form of this blog. I really take the blog seriously, it's not hidden away in a diary. I am publicly declaring it and it gives it a different resonance. It feels like I am doing an experiment, I have to take this seriously and I am trying to be as honest as I can be on this blog.

David: (laughing) You are following the shamanic process. It's sort of akin to the shaman sitting down and telling the village stories.

When he said that—*you are following the shamanic process*—it felt like a bell ringing in my head, like I'd just solved the puzzle on a game show and won the grand prize. I'm not exaggerating. His reply was the answer I'd been desperately seeking. David and I concluded the taped interview, but we continued the back-and-forth exchange on a Facebook chatbox:

Mike: During the recorded interview I thought you said: "the owls are a shamanic initiation" But what you really said was: "you are following the shamanic process."

David: During taping, I didn't outright say you were going through a shamanic initiation because that's a very personal thing. I didn't know if you would want it shared. But essentially it's the same thing. Following the shamanic process does by nature lead to initiatory experiences.

Mike: The thing is, the answer that all my owl sightings would be a *shamanic initiation* just feels exactly right!

David: The important thing is the message you heard and how much it resonated with you.

Mike: Well, the message—a shamanic initiation—resonated absolutely perfectly at a soul level! I trust that means something.

In pretty much every one of my audio interviews, I've asked each guest the same two questions. The first would be about my own experiences; I'll ask: *What's up with all the owls?* The other is: *How do you define the role of the shaman?*

During that recorded interview, David answered both of these questions in one fell swoop, in a deeply personal way. He told me that the owl is both *a path* and *a shamanic initiation.* He was very clear that I am on that path, and it is my own initiation.[60]

I'd been asking everyone what the owls meant, and none of their answers rang true, but when David told me that it could be a shamanic initiation, that answer came with a clear psychic knowing. Am I being initiated? I was never dragged away by the village elders to take part in any ritual. Or was I? Could there be buried memories of an abduction that might fit into this shamanic framework? The UFO mystery has certainly played a role in my life, and it has ushered in a whole new set of ideas. I now have a completely altered view of reality, and of my own consciousness.

Spiritual awakening is as good a term as any for what I've experienced, but what does that mean and where do I go with it?

As stated previously, I'll ask witnesses two questions: *What was going on in your life leading up to the sighting?* Then I'll follow up with: *What has changed in your life since the sighting?* I've heard a few witnesses say that before seeing a UFO their life had been going poorly, they'd been feeling stuck and confused. Now, it would be perfect if the next thing they said was that after their sighting that they had become unstuck and saw things clearly, but I haven't heard that reply yet. What I have heard with consistency is that the sighting forced them to look much deeper into the meaning of reality itself. They'll start meditating, begin reading spiritual books, or take college courses in advanced physics. It's very common that they'll quit their job and begin an entirely new life, working to help people with a new dedication to these more mystical ideals. It's also pretty common that they'll write a book.

I need to add one more amazing event tied to David Weatherly and me. During the editing process for the original 2013 essay *Owls and the UFO Abductee*, I asked David to review the text. I had written a lot about shamanism, and I wanted his input to make sure I wasn't talking out of my hat. I sent him a document of my work-in-progress, and a few days later he sent me this:

> I think you'll find it interesting to know that I actually read your essay last night just as the sun was going down. I have a window right by my desk. I'd say I was about halfway through the piece when I noticed a bird flying by out of the corner of my eye. I watched it fly in an arc away from the window and then back around. It landed on a tree nearby and that's when I got a clear look at what it was, an owl! First one I've ever seen here at my house, where I've lived for over 20 years.

So, a shaman sees an owl while fact-checking the ideas of a UFO abductee on shamanism and owls. This is the same shaman who had an owl land on the hood of his truck and stare into his eyes the moment he arrived at the home of a family having UFO experiences.

As I proceed forward in this research, I keep on bumping into this shamanism stuff, and I recognize it's somehow intertwined with the deeper mystery of both owls and UFOs. The presence of the owl seems intimately connected to the role of the shaman. The owl has large eyes that allow it to peer into the night, and this is a metaphor for the mission of the shaman. We are all confronted with darkness, and the many fears behind its curtain. Like the owl, it's the shaman's responsibility to access that hidden realm and return with a message.

The shaman's role

The late mythologist Joseph Campbell saw the role of the shaman as something vitally important within ancient societies, and he argued that our modern culture is adrift without it. He pointed out that one of the markings of the young shaman was a psychological break from reality. He wrote:

> The shaman is the person, male or female, who in his late child-hood or early youth has an overwhelming psychological experience that turns him totally inward. It's a kind of schizophrenic crack-up. The whole unconscious opens up, and the shaman falls into it. This shaman experience has been described many, many times. It occurs all the way from Siberia right through the Americas down to Tierra del Fuego.[61]

In our modern world, we simply can't tolerate the idea of a child falling into their own deeper selves. It isn't considered that this turn inward could prove vitally important to the greater community. The idea of *shaman sickness* is well understood in indigenous cultures, but westerners have no reference point and treat it as mental illness. Beyond the emotional collapse, a potential shaman might be recognized by the village elders because of powerful visionary experiences. These might be the appearance of an animal guide that is identified within the tribe's shamanic mythology. This is very often an owl.

It's easy to imagine a frightened tribesman in a jungle village telling of an owl taking him on a vision quest, but what about a traumatized insurance salesman in Ohio telling of aliens taking him aboard a flying saucer? The question is, *are these the same stories?* And the follow up would be, *will these initiates someday play a similar role?*

Joe Lewels, Ph.D., is the author of two books that had a big impact on how I think about UFOs—*The God Hypothesis* and *Rulers of the Earth*. He has been doing abduction research for decades, but I contacted him specifically to ask about shamanism. He had spent time with Harvard psychiatrist Dr. John Mack, and they traveled together throughout Mexico and South America, talking to shamans about their connections with other realms. Dr. Mack was doing research for his 1999 book, *Passport to the Cosmos*, where he argued that direct UFO contact could be compared to a shamanic initiation (more on his work later in this chapter).

After his years of research, Joe now frames alien abduction as something deeply spiritual. I asked him if he's had any UFO contact experiences, and he said he'd asked himself that same question many times, and feels strongly that he hasn't.

Here is an excerpt from my conversation with Joe. He was articulating what I have been feeling.

> I see what's called the alien abduction phenomenon, and I don't like that term, let's say experiences with non-human intelligence. The people who are having these experiences are, many times rather unwillingly, being dragged into a shamanic apprenticeship. The people having these experiences are being taught how to heal, their consciousness is being elevated, and they are being given opportunities to help people. Many of them will leave their jobs and then become Reiki masters and massage therapists and hypnotherapists. All of these can be seen as forms of shamanic activity...
>
> We need shamans, and if society doesn't provide it, the universe will.

My first Reiki session

I have been speaking with all kinds of people who tell of UFO contact and, beyond what Joe listed, a lot of them are channelers, dowsers, psychic mediums, animal communicators, energy healers, medical intuitives, and past life regressionist—or they've written a book with a focus on expanded consciousness. It seems that the UFO occupants are trying to influence humanity by seeding our population with shamans, or at least people with certain shamanic skills.

One thing I see with a remarkable consistency within this pool of UFO experiencers is that a lot of them are practicing Reiki masters. Reiki is an ancient Japanese technique for stress reduction, relaxation, and healing. The practitioner will use their hands to connect to an unseen energy within the patient's body.

The word Reiki is made of two Japanese words: Rei which means *God's Wisdom* or *the Higher Power,* and Ki, which is *life force energy*. The outcome from this kind of treatment can be as simple as feelings of peace and well being, while other times people experience miraculous healings.

I had my first Reiki session in 2013 with a woman in my little town. She simply stood near me for about 15 minutes with her hands above my body. A the end, she told me, "Well, what I'm getting is that you are having a Kundalini awakening." In its simplest definition, this would be a more eastern way of saying spiritual awakening.

As we talked, I asked if she'd ever had any odd owl experiences. She said, "Not really, except for what happened last night while I was out for a walk, that was pretty intense." This got my attention, and I said I needed to hear what happened. She explained that, the night before, a huge owl had led her down a path. It flew ahead of her, stopping several times on tree branches waiting for her to catch up.

I calmly told her, "That was me. That owl was all about *this*, us here right now."

She thought for a moment and agreed. Later that night she contacted me to tell me about seeing another big owl perched on a nearby fence post. It watched her intently as she walked by. This happened on the evening of the same day we'd had our session together.

So, my local Reiki practitioner had seen two big owls, two nights in a row, with my Reiki session sandwiched in the middle. I asked her if she thought she might be a UFO abductee, and she said no.

Stanislav Grof

Stanislav Grof is a psychiatrist and one of the initial investigators in the field of transpersonal psychology. He was at the forefront of LSD research in the 1960s as well as playing a pivotal role in the pioneering investigations of non-ordinary states of consciousness. He developed holotropic breathwork after LSD was criminalized in the late 60s. This is a disciplined breathing technique used to induce a mystical state. Grof noted that the dreamlike imagery in these altered states, what he called *holotropic states*, often contained solutions to the pressing questions of the mind. These solutions very often come in the form of a non-ordinary experience, and sometimes they even include owls. Grof wrote:

> Synchronistic events are particularly frequent in the lives of people who experience holotropic states of consciousness in their meditation, psychedelic sessions, experiential psychotherapy, or spontaneous psycho-spiritual crises. Transpersonal and perinatal experiences are often associated with extraordinary coincidences....
>
> Similarly, when we have a powerful experience of a shamanic type that involves an animal spirit guide, this animal can suddenly keep appearing in our life in various forms with a frequency that is beyond any reasonable probability. In one of our six-day training modules, a participating psychologist experienced in her holotropic breathwork session a powerful shamanic sequence in which an owl played an important role as her power animal and spirit guide. That same day, she returned from a walk in the forest with remnants of an owl. When she was driving home after the module had ended, she noticed by the side of the road a large wounded bird. She stopped the car and came closer; it was a large owl with a broken wing. The owl allowed her to pick him up and take him to the car without showing any signs of resistance. She took care of the bird until he was able to fly and return to his natural environment.[62]

Finding a wounded owl, actually picking it up and healing it, has the feel of a fable spoken by an elder around the campfire. The owl in Grof's example emerged at a time of deep self-examination while using techniques to induce a non-ordinary state of consciousness. It feels like dream symbolism had manifested in the real world for some experiential purpose. This could be a clue, an archetype, a metaphor—or perhaps a gateway lesson to the role of the shaman.

An abductee's experience aboard an alien craft is consistently described as something beyond normal waking consciousness. These people will struggle to articulate the utter strangeness of their experience, as if some aspect of their mind has been altered. Or, it might be *reality itself* that's been altered, much like descriptions of the Oz-Factor.

The near-death experience

The near-death experience (NDE) can be seen as yet another non-ordinary state of consciousness. The hospital patient on the operating table who momentarily slips beyond the confines of life will come back and tell a story with a long list of similarities described in other accounts. These include: entering a white realm, meeting dead relatives, experiencing oneness, communication through telepathy, and a feeling of timelessness.

A set of divergent narratives are at play, and they seem to parallel certain mystical traditions. Like being abducted from your bedroom by aliens, "going into the light" has become part of our modern folklore.

There is also a pattern of what happens in the aftermath of these defining events—things like a sense of renewed life purpose, changes in spiritual ideas, a sense of mission, a total shift in life direction, a new environmental awareness, emotional difficulties, psychic experiences, and weird synchronicities. UFO abduction, near-death experiences, and shamanic initiation all include these points, as if the source is the same thing.

The UFO abductee, near-death experiencer, and shamanic initiate will struggle to describe what has happened in their journeys. They'll say that mere words can't explain the magnitude of what they've experienced. It seems they're trying to explain a different dimension, something well beyond the normal physical plane we call reality. These events aren't being described as something hallucinatory, but as something entirely real, as if it's more real than real. It's as if this physical realm we occupy is the illusion, and that other realm is the real world.

Dr. Suzanne Gordon is a near-death experience researcher, who, curiously enough, has had her own NDE, psychic experiences and a very intense close-up UFO sighting. She has spoken to hundreds of people who've had the NDE, only to return to this physical realm and succumb to a sort of metaphysical anguish. She refers to this suffering as the trauma of enlightenment.

I know more than a few folks who've had the one-two punch of both UFO abduction and the NDE. (Jacquelin Smith is an example, and her story is told later in this book). These people are either deeply empathic, outright psychic, or most often both. There is an unmistakable pattern where these double-whammy people are now working as therapists, energy healers, or psychic mediums. They've dedicated their lives to helping others, and like the shaman, they have lived the role of the owl.

A flying saucer is simply a craft that can take someone to another realm. But so is the magic mushroom, shamanic initiation, and even death. There are people who have traveled on these elusive craft, traversing across ethereal barriers into other realms and returning with a message. This is the mythology of the owl, the messenger.

These messengers are here, right now, among us. They are playing the vital role of the shaman, a role that has been with us throughout the ages, but their stage is no longer the campfire at the center of the village, where they would have once been respected. It's now happening in therapist offices and on massage tables. This good work goes on despite being ignored (or scorned) by the majority in our modern society. Yet, I sense a change in recent history; little by little, the ridicule is fading away. What was once considered the lunatic fringe of energy healers and psychic mediums is steadily becoming commonplace.

I sense a similar growing acceptance among the general public concerning accounts of UFO abduction. In decades past, these claims were met with vicious contempt, but this is less true today. While strong skepticism certainly remains, it doesn't seem to have the venom of just a few years ago.

Dr. John Mack

Dr. John Mack was a Pulitzer Prize-winning professor of psychiatry at Harvard Medical School, his research with Dr. Joe Lewells was noted earlier in this chapter. Dr. Mack wrote two books on the alien contact experience, the first was *Abduction* (1994), an account of his years working as a clinician with UFO experiencers. In his final book, *Passport to the Cosmos* (1999), Dr. Mack compares and contrasts the initiation rites of the shaman to what is being reported by UFO abductees. I read *Passport to the Cosmos* when it came out and it had a powerful impact on the way I frame the more challenging aspects of this mystery. His book mentions owls a lot, either in the context of the screen memory or as the totem animal of the shaman.

As part of his research, Dr. Mack sought out traditional shamans to better understand the phenomenon. He asked specifically about the skinny gray beings, and all these shamans gave a similar answer: "We know about this, this is commonplace in our lives, and we know about these beings, we've had the experiences."

Dr. Mack spoke with Native American medicine man, Sequoyah Trueblood, who lives on the Kahnawake reservation in Canada. He asked him, "Well, Sequoyah, you've known 150 medicine men, or so, in your life. How many of them have had these kinds of encounter experiences?"

Sequoyah replied, "All of them." [63]

That's a bold statement, and the implications are staggering. I contacted Sequoyah Trueblood to verify what he said, and he confirmed it as correct. He spoke calmly, detached from the rigid constraints of the modern UFO abduction researcher. He told me that medicine men and shamans all over the world are in communication with beings from other realms and other dimensions. It seems too simplistic to say that they are all UFO abductees, but more that they have all interacted with these beings on a deep level. These relationships certainly involve what we know as the classic gray aliens from the present-day abduction lore, but also nature elementals and the spirits of ancestors.

He said, "When you carry that pipe you can no longer hold judgement. You have opened a door to let these beings in from their other realms. When you are open, these things happen."

Sequoyah explained that the word shaman comes from *saman*, a term used by the indigenous Buryat people in Siberia. In their language, it means a person who lives in two worlds at the same time. This could also be said of the UFO contactee.

Author Sarangerel Odigan studied shamanism with the Buryat and wrote that the, "Owl is believed to be a patron of shamans." [64]

I need to add that my phone conversation with Sequoyah came within minutes of me seeing a beautiful barred owl in a tree near my home. When I told him this, he said that it didn't surprise him in the slightest.

The first experiencer support group

I spoke at length with a woman named Elizabeth about her lifelong UFO contact experiences. Like so many others, she has had some powerful owl events as well.

She told me about driving down a rural road with her father when she was about 15 or 16 years old. They drove past a barn at twilight and saw a set of large birds swirling around near the roofline. They stopped and got out of the car in hopes of identifying the birds, and quickly recognized them as owls. Soon the owls were flying over them, and Elizabeth and her father both got down on the grass, lying together on their backs in a low trench and looking up at the sky. They counted twelve owls, and they flew above them for about 20 minutes. They would swoop down one at a time, gliding low and close, just above them. Her father took photos and later identified them by their wing markings as barred owls. This happened over 30 years ago, and I could hear the elation in Elizabeth's voice as she described the sensation of these owls all lining up and silently passing over her and her father, one after another, like planes in a flight pattern over an airport.

Elizabeth tells of having a strong ability to communicate with animals, and this seems to play out in her many owl sightings. Her dad is a biologist and skilled naturalist, and she followed in his footsteps. She made it very clear to me that her father was also an abductee.

Elizabeth was living in the Boston area in 1989 when five gray aliens appeared in her bedroom at night. She called this her awakening experience, and it lead her to contact Budd Hopkins in New York, who put her in touch with Dr. John Mack. She started working together with Dr. Mack in 1990.

She went to the very first experiencers support meeting at Dr. Mack's home. This would have been very similar to any other support group, like alcoholics anonymous, where people sit together in a circle and share their experiences with the hope of finding solace and companionship. Elizabeth was intimidated by a member of this group, one man was big and awkward, and her initial impression was that he was scary.

When the meeting ended, she left with a small crew of attendees that had carpooled together. As they were pulling out of the driveway, they all asked each other what they thought of the meeting. Elizabeth commented about the big scary guy, "Well, I don't want to be a member of any club he's a part of."

At that moment an impossibly large snowy owl flew above their car. It was low and close, coming from behind and flying right out in front of them. Elizabeth was amazed at the size—the wingspan seemed to be as wide as the car itself. It flew in front of them on a quiet tree-lined street, all lit up by the car headlights. They watched this giant white bird lead their way for what seemed like a very long time before it turned off into the tall trees alongside the street.

Everyone in the car felt the same thing, that owl was *meant* to fly down the road in front of them. One person even said that she thought, "The owl was trying to tell us we're on the right path."

So, after the very first experiencer group meeting at the home of Dr. John Mack, a car full of abductees is guided down a road by a giant white owl. I can't help but think this owl was sitting on the roof of Dr. Mack's house, patiently waiting for this moment to make its dramatic appearance. Elizabeth has never seen an owl that large before or since.

She continued with the support group, and eventually found a deep connection with that big scary guy. He became one of Elizabeth's closest and dearest friends.

Many of the reports in this book describe folks seeing white owls. There are really only two species that would match this description, the barn owl and the snowy owl. Both have wide ranges spanning over vast sections of the globe. The snowy owl spends the summer in the far northern latitudes, and migrates south each winter. The barn owl is a fairly common bird on every continent, but neither of these birds are truly white. The snowy owl is speckled with small black dots, and the barn owl has a pale tan coloring on its wings and back. In both species, the underside of their wings and bellies are almost pure white. If these owls are illuminated in flight by car headlights, they can appear ghostly white.

Within many of the world's shamanic traditions, especially the Native American lore, the white owl has a deeper spiritual role than other owls. If one sees a white owl, then it's thought to be delivering an inward message. The communication isn't meant for anything worldly—it's a message for the soul.

Like so many others who have had these experiences, Elizabeth is a practicing Reiki master. She is also a spirit medium, psychic healer, and an animal communicator. She feels that her skill as an animal communicator has somehow played a part in her many owl sightings.

When asked about her psychic abilities, she feels it traces back to her contact experiences. Pretty much all her communication with the UFO occupants has been telepathic, and this has somehow influenced the workings of her inner-mind. She says that when you interact with these alien beings using psychic means, the doors of consciousness get blown wide open. This allows all kinds of other things to rush in through that open gateway.

Another experiencer, Kim Carlsberg, addressed these same issues by saying: "Once you're opened up, you're opened up to everything."

Would it be accurate to declare Elizabeth a shaman? That's tricky to answer, but like so many others, she certainly seems to be filling the shamanic role with her many clairvoyant skills. She feels her contact experiences are the source of these skills, and she has been using them to help people, a pattern seen in a lot of experiencers.

I can imagine the UFO occupants looking down at Earth from their view-screens, and seeing that we humans are in a heap of trouble. Instead of downloading scientists and politicians with the pragmatic solutions to all our global problems, they are instead planting the seeds for a new crop of shamans. Or, the UFO occupants might be part of a team of entities that are hidden from our normal perception, and they've been working since the dawn of man to create shamans. Both these scenarios are overly simplistic, but something is interacting with these people and—against all kinds of societal pressures—they are following a shamanic path.

Chapter 17:

Mushrooms and Meditation

I am friends with a woman named Artemesia (a pseudonym), and like so many in this research, she's had a lot of very similar experiences to my own. Even though we've never met, we've spent a lot of time on the phone, and the timelines of our lives overlap to the point of absurdity. In the fall of 1999, she and her boyfriend Chris went on a vision quest in Yellowstone National Park. This involved taking psychedelic mushrooms with the formal intention that it served a spiritual purpose, so this wasn't just two nature-lovers getting stoned for kicks.

They had spent the day in an altered state, and when the sun went down, they were deep in the backcountry, far from any trails. They were wandering around one of the thermal areas of the park when they decided to head back to the safety of their car, but quickly realized they were lost. They struggled to find a way through the dark, sulfurous fog, mud, and a tangle of fallen trees. They struggled to find a way back and eventually entered a meadow of easier travel only to see an unusual grouping of big boulders in this open area. Artemesia sensed something was wrong, and she got out her headlamp, turned it on, and saw a lot of eyes shining back at her. She heard grunts and realized she and Chris had wandered into a field of buffalo. She writes:

> I turned off the light right away so as not to piss them off, and just as I did so a huge, and I mean huge owl swept down out of a nearby snaggy dead looking lodgepole and buzzed right over our heads, actually knocking off my friend Chris's hat with either its wing beat wind or by its actual talons, we weren't sure which. But it was close. I was really freaked out. We had to backtrack and do more log walking over thermal bog in total darkness with no head-lamps to get to 'safe' ground, away from the bison.

We discussed it all later, and the owl, though it was only one small feature in the whole afternoon of visions and adventure, stood out as highly significant for both of us. At the time I wondered if it really was an owl, if it was sent to warn us, or if it might have been something else. It was easy to think like that due to the 'vision quest' context that already encompassed the whole event.

The use of psychedelic drugs might make a pragmatic researcher throw this report in the trash, but I'm not so quick to dismiss. The story seems to hold some clues. The fact that she and Chris were consciously setting out to have a "vision quest" seems relevant. This kind of seeking can be seen as a ritual act, and with it comes a genuine power. Especially when, in a moment of real danger, an owl knocks someone's hat right off their head! Could this owl have saved their lives?

I was told another story where a life might have been saved by an owl. A man named Kevin was driving at night on a lonely highway in the desert, fighting to stay awake. He had the window open to keep from falling asleep, but it wasn't working. Right as he was nodding off, he saw what he thought was an upright log in the middle of the road, and then wings flapping. Kevin was suddenly jolted awake when the wing of an owl slapped him in the face through the open window.

Back to Artemesia. At the time of this experience, she was unaware of any UFO events in her life. Since then, she has seen what can only be described as alien beings while at the same time receiving telepathic communication. This happened in a full waking state and wasn't retrieved through hypnosis. This event (among others) has forced her to recognize her own direct contact experiences.

This same woman had another very interesting owl experience, again with a guy named Chris. *Two different owl events, two different guys named Chris.* This is one more example (or two more, really) of owl stories that involve someone named Chris.

The shamanic journey

Mushrooms play an important role in the life of Shonagh Home. She is a practicing shaman, and she has also had an intense set of owl experiences that are both visionary and literal. Her story of awakening and transformation is covered in depth in Chapter 9, Back to Back Reports.

Like any shaman, she ritually travels into a non-ordinary state of consciousness, a place where the rules of our perceived reality no longer apply. Shonagh uses high doses of psilocybin mushrooms in sacred ceremonies to step beyond the veil, and a giant white owl has been her guide in the most powerful journeys. She sees the owl, along with the mushroom medicine, as a powerful ally in her shamanic work.

Although she's seen a UFO, Shonagh says she has never had any abduction experiences, but these medicine journeys, along with some of the events in her waking life, closely parallel what I've heard from UFO abductees. Would this make her one of the *maybe people?* Well, maybe.

I've heard from another shaman who tells of interacting with beings from UFOs in non-ordinary reality. But he also says: "I'm sure I've never been abducted, I think I would know. A shamanic person is able to remember and process extreme spiritual experiences without going insane, swimming in waters of consciousness where a 'normal' person would drown. If you want to take someone away, do strange things to them and bring them home with amnesia, a shaman is the wrong person to choose!"

He's implying that if a shaman gets abducted by aliens, they would have the transcendental skills to break through the missing time and access those hidden experiences, and that might be true. I've also spoken to shamans who are very open about their UFO contact experiences. They describe a familiar conflicting narrative of both trauma and ecstasy, including missing time and a long list of symbolic elements. This story has been lived by many, all throughout the ages.

There is an obvious transformative power to UFO contact, but an intense synchronicity can also produce a jolt to the system. The heightened state from a profound synchronicity could be just as valid, perhaps more so, because your experience is spontaneous. UFO contact, mushroom trip, or synchronicity all have the power to change someone. There are a host of other non-ordinary states that can transform, including the NDE, OBE, trauma, and deep meditation.

Angela is one more of these *maybe people*. Even though her experiences hint at UFO contact, she told me she is not an abductee. She's had a lot of very strange life events, and this unusual owl experience from when she was 22 is a typical example. She took mushrooms with a group of friends. The mood was both recreational and sacred. It happened at night in a forest, and they were sitting together in a circle, all fully in the psychedelic throes of the hallucinogen. She told me a great horned owl landed in the middle of the circle of tripping friends and just stood there. Her description was that it was well over three feet tall, which is impossibly large for any owl. Here again, we have the overlapping of people on mushrooms and a very bizarre owl experience.

Are the non-ordinary states of consciousness created by mushrooms similar to the distorted reality described by UFO abductees? Could owls be attracted to some weird vibe produced by these trippy states? Does someone in the throes of a hallucinatory ritual give off some subtle glow that can be seen by an owl? Is the seeker manifesting the owl? There is a shorthand to both the UFO and the entheogenic medicines—they are said to *open a window or doorway* to another realm. Psychedelic visions, owls, UFOs, and shamanic initiation are all overlapping and blending together, making any one interpretation nearly impossible. Yet these experiencers, either reluctant or willing, are being transformed.

Owls and spiritual transformation

I received an email from a woman named Lauren who had found the owl essay on my site. She wrote:

> I stopped reading the essay because I just have to tell my owl story too, and I feel overwhelmed with emotion. I experienced the owl after ingesting a lot of psychedelic mushrooms, psilocybin. What it felt like was that an owl had flown into my brain. I don't know how else to describe it. It lasted for several hours and the owl was largely the only vision I experienced during that particular trip. I was inside my house, lying on the floor.

241

At this time in my life, I was addicted to alcohol, pills and anything that would get me high. After this experience with the owl and several more trips on psilocybin, I stopped taking all drugs and drinking. I'm still sober four years later.

The owl has appeared at other times in my life since then—a real owl, in my yard. And also in my dreams.

In a follow-up email, Lauren shared more:

I was in a very dark place in my life when mushrooms and consequently owls entered into the picture... The owl I saw during that first trip was flying and it seemed to fly into my head, and I emerged later, a changed person... Some would say that the owl and the other visions that followed were some part of my unconscious mind, but no, the owl was something outside of me, some power that came to me and helped me. I am sure of that.

She was very clear that the mushrooms, along with the owl imagery, had saved her life. She also described other mushroom trips where what seemed to be a flying saucer made of a clear substance landed in her room. Another time she had the impression that a huge saucer had landed just out her window. The whole experience left her with a feeling of love, and she wondered if she might have been aboard the saucer with them. This trippy imagery could be dismissed as nothing more than the psychedelic effects of the drugs, but it's the mythic symbolism that fascinates me.

She repeated that before these experiences, she had absolutely no interest in owls or UFOs, let alone God or spirituality. Whatever happened not only ended her drinking, but left her convinced that there is a spiritual reality to life.

I continue to occasionally see owls (real ones!), and they always make an appearance on an auspicious occasion... And just a few days ago, on Halloween, as I was thinking of writing to you, I saw one sitting on a telephone wire, and he looked right at me. It seems to me that owls look directly at you in a way that no other bird does.

...The UFO experiences I've had gave me that impression that maybe flying saucers are a vehicle, literally and metaphorically, that God uses to communicate with us.

By that definition, *the flying saucer would be God's messenger*, and that's the same role played by the owl.

I contacted Lauren to review the text I'd written, the account you've just read. She emailed her reply, saying I'd captured her experience accurately and gave me permission to share her story. At that point, it had been almost five months since either of us had exchanged any emails. Then she added this:

Two days before I received your latest email, a barred owl appeared in my yard. It flew by just a few feet in front of me and landed in a tree. I watched it for a while... I see owls so infrequently that it always seems like such an event, and such a blessing.

I am at the point where I no longer see this as simply coincidence. To me, this is a form of confirmation, and it keeps me moving forward. Every spiritual seeker is following their own path, and the tools they use along the way have their own ecstasies—as well as dangers. Those owls, both real and psychedelic, appeared in Lauren's journey in a way that replicates the traditions of our ancient past. Her experiences are feeding me and my own need for a deeper knowing.

The UFO encounter that changed Bill Hicks

"I have had seven balls of light come off a UFO, lead me on their ship, explain to me telepathically we are all one and there's no such thing as death..."

That line was delivered by the late Bill Hicks in 1991 as part of his stand-up comedy routine. The first question would be, was that a joke? And the next question would be, was that line true? The UFO experience happened to Hicks, along with his childhood friend Kevin Booth, on the day of the Harmonic Convergence in 1987. At the time they were tripping heavily on psychedelic mushrooms.

Having corresponded at length with Kevin, I feel certain neither he nor Bill were physically abducted at the hands of alien beings. Nonetheless, the power of this mystical event had a huge impact on both their lives.

Bill Hicks died of cancer in February 1994 at the age of 32. His role as a comedian was something far more forceful than just a guy on stage telling jokes. It was as if he were pleading with the audience to live a life without fear. He had an intense stage presence, he was sweaty and seemed uncomfortable in his own skin. He smoked and made jokes about it—*I'm a heavy smoker. I go through two lighters a day.* He was brilliant in his direct attack on consumerism and pop culture. It's easy to say a comedian is "dangerous," but this is the perfect word for how he confronted his audience with the darkest underbelly of America, while at the same time, imploring for a deeper spirituality.

Kevin wrote a book about his lifelong friendship with Bill Hicks, called *Agent of Evolution*. This book has the word "Evolution" right in its title, and some of that traces back to this mushroom and UFO experience. Kevin wrote:

> I think Bill always thought he could get somewhere else. This was the moment it was proved to him. It's easy to point out the obvious: You took five grams of mushrooms, of course you are going to see spaceships and all kinds of other shit that doesn't exist. That's why they call them hallucinogens. They cause hallucinations.
>
> That's a valid argument. But we were taking hallucinogens to help boost consciousness. It was more like a key opening a door. The door was there without the drugs. What the mushrooms would do is they would allow two or more people to get in sync and open the door together and walk through it together and experience what's in the next room together.

They purposely chose the day of the Harmonic Convergence because "everyone else around the world was all supposed to be logging on to the same metaphysical chat room at the same time. It was part of the mental telepathy." They sat together outside on Kevin's family ranch in Texas, treating the event as a sacred ritual.

Kevin explained: "We took five grams. Five grams of dried mushrooms is a lot. If you wanted to punch a hole through the fabric of space-time, five grams is good. But don't try it yourself... unless you are ready and willing to cross the threshold."

What unfolded was a shared UFO experience, and Kevin's description is ridiculous, like something out of a bad science fiction movie. The inside of the ship was like a conch shell, and they walked together down a spiraling ramp through a hallway of light and then toward a circle of light. It was here that they met lustrous glowing beings.

> Bill and I were both in the ship. He was asking questions like: "Why are you here? Why is this happening?" I remember coming out with explanations of time travel and a firm belief that the barriers to time travel and communication were all inside your mind. Basically anything was possible. These beings were bridging the gap between belief and non-belief. Between love and hate.
>
> At the time I was thinking that my head conjured up this image just for me to see, then Bill indicated to me he had seen and experienced the exact same thing.
>
> After that we realized that we were able to communicate completely telepathically.

Bill had taken mushrooms two times before a performance. The first time he was aware of something more than just an ability to make people laugh, he felt he could read the collective mind of the audience. This was powerful, but the "telepathy" experience with the UFO was way more intense. He took mushrooms before another performance, but this time it was horrible and he never did it again.

Back to the psychedelic experience aboard the ship:

> This was very specific. For the first time ever, Bill and I were able to say things and hear each other back, able to ask questions and get answers. We had a perfectly normal conversation without either one opening our mouths. We were perfectly in sync. It was like a miracle. We communicated like this for a while. Neither of us saying anything...

It went from being the two of us being able to communicate with each other, to us being dialed into a network where now we were in open communication with hundreds, thousands, maybe millions of minds at the same time. There was something identifiable in it, like we could trace where the voices were coming from and who they were. Everybody was sharing this moment because they wanted to. It seemed as real as the words on this page. It was freeing. And it was unbelievable. We just laid on the floor and stayed tapped into whatever we had tapped into.

Bill changed after taking those mushrooms. Kevin stated, "The UFO experience during the harmonic convergence had an extremely powerful impression on Bill that lasted throughout his short life. It's as if a heavy burden had been lifted from him and everything he had always believed but couldn't prove had been affirmed, and he could move on with confidence to the next phase of his life."

Kevin wrote: "The spaceship, that was the most important thing that ever happened to Bill. He saw the 'source of light that exists in all of us.' Later he said, 'God, I hope that was just the first of many things just like that.'"

Bill would talk about the UFO experience during his stand-up routine. Kevin wrote: "I think the crowds were confused by it. Was it a metaphor? Was it a joke? Where was the punchline? But the first time he talked about it during a show, I was proud and amazed but also a little bit embarrassed."

The works of ethnobotanist and psychonaut Terence McKenna fascinated Bill, and he would often quote him from stage when he described this UFO experience. Said McKenna: "If you take mushrooms you're climbing on board a starship manned by every shaman who ever did it in front of you, and this is quite a crew, and they've really pulled some stunts over the millennia, and it's all there, the tapes, to be played." So when Bill talked about mushrooms and evolving and UFOs, he wasn't joking.

In June 1993, Bill was diagnosed with pancreatic cancer that had spread to his liver. After being told by Bill of the seriousness of his illness, Kevin became obsessed with the hope a miracle was going to happen. It was during this time that Kevin spoke with Bill by phone. They talked about an upcoming planetary alignment that month, another Harmonic Convergence. Bill wanted to do something together for it, but he was too sick. Instead, Kevin took mushrooms and walked along a creek near his home.

It was on that hiking trail that Kevin did something he would normally never do: he prayed out loud, "Please God, give me some sort of sign to let me know if Bill is going to survive this." At that exact moment, a large owl landed on a branch and started hooting. It was right up close, directly in front of Kevin. This was full daylight, and the owl just sat there, staring right at him. Later that day, Kevin spoke to Bill over the phone. He told him about this owl experience, and Bill went silent like it was bad news.

Later that night, Kevin spoke to a mutual friend and described seeing the owl. He was told of the owl folklore, that it could be seen as a bad omen, a harbinger of death. He realized that Bill had been very aware of the owl's symbolic meaning during their call.

Kevin told me: "I like to think of myself as a logical person, and I didn't make a big deal out of it. Literally the next day, again in broad daylight, right by my house, another owl sat down directly in front of me and this time the hair on the back of my neck stood up."

After that, he had another owl incident at his family ranch. He never told Bill about these follow-up owl experiences.

In one of his final phone conversations with Bill, Kevin described another UFO experience while on mushrooms. It happened above Red River New Mexico in the Sangre de Cristo Mountains. He was with his girlfriend and they were hiking at night with his two big wolf dogs.

> I don't know why I did this, but I had an entire ritual planned out that included eating the local trout at a specific time—followed by eating the mushrooms—and then all of us hiked up a long dark snow-covered trail to the top of a mountain where there was a plateau we would frequent while skiing, but never at night.
>
> The UFO encounter with Bill on... the harmonic convergence was a very comforting, happy spiritual experience. The encounter on the mountain that night was something totally different. It was scary, physical, and left us wanting to run for our lives. All I can

recollect was a loud harsh sound—almost like a military aircraft. Bright lights and it was if the ground fell out from under our feet.

The next thing Kevin remembers was waking up and thinking that the only reason they weren't abducted was that his extremely badass wolf dogs acted as their protectors. He felt that whatever happened that night was metal and physical and was meant for a different reason than the earlier encounter with Bill.

> My girlfriend and I did not speak one word for almost an hour and ran down the snow-covered mountain trail in total darkness. Once we saw the lights of the city, we stopped and just like the time with Bill—we both had the same recollection. At this time I stopped and prayed and asked if Bill would survive. I know its sounds like cheap New Age bullshit, but I visualized a giant crystal talking to me—almost like a cheap Star Trek prop—but it said: "Bill is going to die, but that nothing was going to change—everything would be the same and that all of the negativity surrounding his death was all my fears and ego and the fears and egos of others."
>
> When I returned to Austin I told Bill about the UFO experience, but this was only days before he passed, and it was as if he was beyond the point of UFOs having any meaning. It was as if he was halfway through the looking glass.

I asked Kevin a question that might be more suited for UFO abductees. I wanted to know if Bill felt a sense of mission, and he replied:

> There is no question that Bill was a man on a mission. He believed that since all people are connected by one consciousness it was important to raise that one consciousness… Bill's ultimate expectation was that once mankind could raise its vibration to a higher level we could as one leave the planet and pursue the stars.

One more thing, I had sent Kevin a short set of questions, and the sun was setting when he opened the email. He saw an owl out his window as he was answering those questions—he even got a picture.

An Owl in Brendan's living room

I've been in contact with a man named Brendan, and he's had a lot of very odd owl experiences. He shared a couple of stories in his first email to me, and this one caught my attention.

> One morning I got up, made my coffee and wandered sleepily into the living room. Imagine my surprise when something huge flew over my head. I made a hasty retreat and closed the door. I then slowly peeked in and saw a barn owl sitting on the window ledge. All the windows were closed so it must have come down the chimney. I opened a window, left the room and it made its own way out. I felt honored to see a barn owl up close in daylight but this was not to be the only time.

Here's one more odd experience, it starts while walking his dog through the woods near his home on a beautiful foggy day. He writes:

> After a while, a deer walked out in front of us on the path. I decided to turn around and go back, so that the deer could go on her way in peace. When I got home, I put my dog in the kitchen and then a voice inside me said, walk to the top of the field, so I did. I just started walking blindly through the mist until I found myself standing in front of a tree at the end of the field. In the tree was the barn owl. It looked at me and then jumped onto the ground in front of me. Imagine the scene, a man alone in a misty field standing under a tree with an owl! For about a minute I had the incredible privilege of locking eyes with a wild barn owl and then it flew silently away. This was definitely a spiritual event but its implications are not yet clear to me.

These events happened, along with some other owl sightings, right after what he calls his *Kundalini Awakening*. Beyond his owl experiences, he has described dreams that sound suspiciously like UFO abduction memories. I asked Brendan if he thought he was a UFO abductee, and he said no. Then I asked if he was a shaman, and he was very cautious with his answer. He implied it wasn't for him to say, that this title must be awarded by his community. That said, he's had a long list of textbook experiences that point to a shamanic awakening; this includes a time of spiritual sickness, bonding with a spirit entity, a kundalini awakening, and unmistakable visits from power animals.

He recently wrote me about his pull to take the entheogenic mushroom, Amanita muscaria. He treated the occasion as a sacred shamanic ceremony, and felt that the spirit of the mushroom was incredibly communicative both before, during and after. He wrote to me:

> The night before I took it I had powerful dreams. I was shown a UFO sitting in a forest. A woman came to me, pointed at it and said emphatically, *this* is the advanced meditation!

Owls and meditation

I've received a few accounts of an owl showing up right after meditation. One was shared by a man named Christopher (yet another one), who was 22 years old at the time, and living on the Big Island in Hawaii. This was the very first time he'd ever tried a sitting meditation. After about 20 minutes, he felt very peaceful. Then he stood up, walked out onto the front porch and saw a white owl flying in swooping circles. It landed in a palm tree right next to the house and sat there. He sensed the owl was looking at him.

Christopher said, "I had never meditated before, and I had never seen an owl before." It was right at that time that he went on, what he calls, an underworld journey. He said he was blasted out beyond the ordinary singular sense of himself.

Something was showing him a hidden parallel experience. He saw two things going on at once, and it scared him. He was seeing a "simultaneous reality alongside the hum-drum Judeo-Christian program that was running the show." This all happened in quick succession, his first meditation, the white owl, and his awakening experience.

This story, like others, seems to imply a kind of shamanic initiation. Christopher was offered a glimpse beyond the normal pale framework of reality, with an owl showing up as a marker—or perhaps a trigger. The owl was integral to the event, charging the moment with power and meaning.

I heard from another man who told me about a similar experience after meditating alone outdoors in the middle of a field, something he loves to do. After his time in meditation, he opened his eyes, stood up and felt moved to say these words aloud, "My work, it's for my own upliftment and that of this planet, if you are in alignment with this upliftment, you are more than welcome to manifest yourselves, your mentoring will be truly appreciated. If you are not in alignment with this upliftment, please do not come around, you are not welcome!"

Right after saying that, he saw a small group of crows flying in circles, they were swooping and diving. It looked like they were attacking something hidden in the tall grass. He walked towards the commotion and saw a big snowy owl on the ground. It was staring at him while completely ignoring the crows. When he got closer, the owl took off and flew around him, its eyes locked on him the whole time it was in flight. It landed nearby, and he got a lovely set of photos.

We're always with you

Below is an email I received in 2013 from a man named George Poirier, and it's posted in its entirety. Although there are no UFOs, this is a perfect example of the mystical that seems connected with the owl. It hits a check-list of points that have been reoccurring in my own life, as well as in this research. The shaman's path, initiation, life changes, messages from the beyond, and the thinning of the veils.

> I'm 64 years old, and have had unusual shamanic experiences since I was a small child. Many of my childhood experiences included different types of animals. I don't recall any of them being owls.
>
> At age 40 I began to go through multiple initiation events that changed my life profoundly. After 20 years as an entrepreneur, I became a Mind/Body healer.

In 2002 my partner and I moved to the Blue Ridge mountains in Western North Carolina. From almost the day we arrived we were besieged with owls. They appeared at all hours of the day and night. My partner and I are both very sensitive and felt that the veil where we lived was very thin.

After much discussion I thought that the owls were conveying a message about the power of silence. My partner thought that the message was about being aware of "who" was watching from the other side. We both agreed that the owl medicine had to do with the ability to see behind the veil. From 2002 to 2006 those owls never let up.

In 2007 we left to move to Georgia. The very day we were leaving, I was driving home from running an errand, when an owl flew right at my windshield forcing me to a complete stop. It perched on a tree to my right and the telepathic message was we're always with you.

On April 13th 2006 I facilitated a breathwork session with an old client and friend. The next morning he suffered a heart attack and died. The next day a huge great horned owl perched ten yards from our back fence during the day and stayed there for several days. Maybe my friend came to say goodbye.

I don't know what all this means beyond what I detailed here to you. I don't recall any abduction experiences.

This single email chronicles a lot. A flood of owls mark a life change, and a call to do healing work. And, an owl arrives, seemingly as a messenger from beyond the veil of death. Although George never describes himself as a shaman, his work certainly fits that role. And even though he shrugs off having had any abduction experiences, he does describe the same kind of spiritual awakening that seems to go hand in hand with UFO contact. When an abductee has a profound owl event, is there some heightened *vibe* that attracts this mysterious bird? It would seem that both the enlightened initiate and the UFO abductee might share this same spark.

So, is it the abduction event that attracts the owls, or the follow-up enlightenment? All this owl stuff might not be related to UFOs at all, but instead to a heightened spiritual openness.

Chapter 18:

Manifesting Owls

This book had its genesis in a long format essay which was posted on my blog on the morning of July 3rd, 2013. After it went up online, I sent out a bunch of notices through Facebook, letting some of my friends and contacts know there was a new post on my blog. This essay was a big deal for me! It was hard work, and I was proud of how it turned out. What I didn't expect was the immediate response, not so much from the folks reading it, but from the owls themselves. It felt like I was putting myself out there with some bold ideas, and a confirming echo was bouncing back.

At 8:37 p.m., the same day the owl essay was posted, I got an email from my sister. She lives on the east coast and knows only a little bit about my research into owls, synchronicities, and UFOs. Her email was short and a little panicky. She'd just heard a friend of the family share a story from his college days. She wrote:

> ...he had an experience where there were owls involved and he is missing a couple of hours... OMG call me!

At 9:09 that same night, I got this message through Facebook:

> I totally just SAW the owl. I went outside and called my BF on the phone (Shawn, the ufologist) and no joke I saw the owl... It was off in the distance in a big tree but I saw it fly up into the tree and could see it sitting on a branch ... I was telling Shawn, "OMG I just read Mike's essay!"

This came from Adrienne Dumas. Her owl and UFO experiences were featured in the very essay that was posted earlier that morning.[65] Curiously, she was talking with her boyfriend Shawn when she saw an owl.

253

He's had his own powerful sighting of a giant triangular craft, and is now immersed in the study of UFOs.

Owls two nights in a row

A day later, on the morning of Friday, July 5th, I saw a grainy picture of an owl perched on a power line, it showed up on my Facebook page. It was a camera-phone image taken at night from a friend of mine, Melissa, and she's had a lot of UFO contact experiences. It was posted earlier that same morning, at 2:59 a.m. East Coast time. She wrote:

> I can't explain it, about 15 minutes ago while in my car this huge owl came right over my windshield. It talked to me... hooted ... then did a shrill two part cry and flew away. WTF?

Early in the morning on the next day, Saturday, July 6th, I saw another very similar grainy picture of an owl from Melissa. This one was also taken at night and it showed an owl on a wooden dock. The image was titled: *Second one. Second night in a row.*

I contacted Melissa to hear the story behind these two back-to-back owl sightings. She had read my owl essay on Tuesday, July 4th, and then went to visit a friend named Laura around midnight that same day. They hadn't seen each other in a while, and they talked until close to three in the morning. Melissa needed to unload about the challenges of her ongoing visitor encounters. Laura was a good listening ear, having seen UFOs with her father when she was younger.

Their heart-to-heart went late into the night, and it was one of those conversations that got really deep. They talked about aliens and animal spirit guides—especially birds. Laura explained how she had lived a life full of synchronous hawk experiences. Laura's father had Native American lineage, and he would always tell her that animals will choose you, and these will be your spirit totems. Melissa replied that she loved birds, and if she had to choose her own totem, it would be an owl. She said this shortly before her owl sighting.

The streets were empty as Melissa drove home. She was startled when an owl suddenly swooped down out of the darkness and passed close to the windshield. She jammed on the brakes and watched it float up and land on a power line. She rolled down her window and got a photo as the owl was hooting. She felt amazing as she drove off—nothing like this had ever happened to her before, and she saw the experience as a gift. Minutes later, she posted the grainy image on Facebook.

The next night, she drove with her fiancé to one of her favorite spots, a quiet road that ended at a lake. They parked in front of a wooden dock talking about their lives and how fitting into society could be so hard. They hadn't been there long when Melissa looked up and saw a big owl right in front of the car. It was perched on the wooden railing of the dock. They were both surprised because it wasn't there when they pulled up, and they hadn't seen it land. How could they have not noticed it until right then?

Melissa told her fiancé that she had seen an owl the previous night. Then it swooped down off the railing toward their headlights, as if it were picking something up right in front of the car.

There are elements in this story that feel choreographed for maximum impact. It was just before the first owl sighting that Melissa's friend Laura had told her that her spirit totem would choose her, and less than an hour later, it showed up on a *power* line. The follow-up sighting feels like the scriptwriter of reality needed two exclamation marks to punctuate the storyline.

Owls had already played a role in Melissa's life leading up to this two-night event. It was seven years earlier, in 2006, that she suddenly became obsessed with owls, buying little figurines, nicknacks, and pictures. This was right at the time when her UFO contact experiences kicked into high gear. Curiously, 2006 was the start of my own obsession with owls, as well as a profound increase in synchronicities.

Seeing owls in connection to me

Like Melissa and Adrienne, I've had a lot of people contact me and tell of seeing owls (*real* owls) in connection to their reading my online essay about owls and UFOs. Beyond the essay, plenty of folks have told me they've seen or heard an owl right as they are listening to one of my podcasts, or while watching one of my presentations online.

This has been showing up as an undeniable pattern, and you'll read a bunch more examples peppered throughout this book. When I hear one of these echoing accounts, my very first thought is to wonder if the reader is an abductee, and I make a point of asking. What I'm finding is that a lot of these folks, but not all, will answer yes and then describe a lifetime of UFO contact experiences. Others will say they aren't abductees but still share some extremely odd stories, putting them into the *maybe* category. The remainder might have no UFO events in their lives, but they very much come across as spiritual seekers.

I've spoken on the phone to a lot of experiencers, both as part of my research and also where we simply share stories. More than once they'll call the next morning to tell me they either heard or saw an owl shortly after hanging up the phone. I'm amazed at how normal all this now feels. Maybe I shouldn't, but at this point I've come to expect it.

The blog has been a chronicle of my challenges and inner turmoil, and I've been trying to describe all these experiences and emotions honestly. There are folks out there who identify with what I've been saying, and then they'll reach out to me. I've received a lot of emails that begin with a line like this, *I was trying to decide whether or not I should contact you when I saw an owl land on a branch just outside my window.* How do I process this kind of repeating strangeness?

At this point, I really don't need to see any more owls. I'm already convinced there's something going on. What is amazing is that so many other people are having these owl experiences in connection to me. It's this deeper layer of synchro-weirdness that forces me to pay very close attention to my own path. I have a responsibility to this research, to my own experience, and especially to all the others who are dealing with something similar. I've found no conclusive answers, only more questions—and a deep knowing that something is pulling on the puppet strings of our reality.

Halloween owl

A woman named Lauren contacted me by email in December of 2013 with a long list of curious owl sightings. One of these happened in 2009 while sitting in her yard; she had a baby barred owl fly down from a tree and land right at her feet. She got down on the ground, crawled right up to the little owl, and said hello.

Another happened in 2010 on, of all nights, Halloween. Lauren's kids were putting their costumes on when a barred owl landed on a branch close to a window, and the whole family watched it for about ten minutes. She intuitively felt it was the same owl she had seen as a baby, now all grown up, and it was telling her goodbye. She hadn't seen any owls since that night, but that changed with this next account.

The day before sending me the email, she'd heard me being interviewed on an audio podcast. That lead her to print out my online essay about owls, and she read it that night. The next morning she wrote to tell me what happened:

> I was home alone, and when I looked out the bathroom window, I saw a big barred owl perched in a tree directly in front of me. It stared in my direction for about ten to fifteen minutes... I was floored because I'd just listened to your interview and read your essay, and then there was an owl right outside my bathroom window the following morning!

Like Halloween three years earlier, she couldn't help but wonder if this was the same owl she had seen as a baby.

> ... I have no way to tell if it was, but it did feel familiar somehow... It was a very profound synchronicity for me—it was a moment when I felt as though what was happening was "real" and was happening for a reason. I still have no idea why these synchronicities occur, what causes them to occur, or what their intended meaning might be, or if there's any intended meaning at all.

Along with owls and synchronicity, Lauren went on to share a long list of other odd life events, enough that I sense she would be one of the maybe people. Also, I have a handful of accounts of owls showing up on Halloween, and this seems a little bit too perfect, where the folklore matches the reality. Earlier in the book, another woman, also named Lauren, told of seeing an owl on Halloween.[66]

The origins of Halloween date back over 2,000 years to the ancient Celtic festival of Samhain (pronounced sow-in). This time marks the autumn harvest and the beginning of winter, and this transition between the seasons was seen as a bridge to the realm of the dead. The Celts started their calendar on November 1st, and the final night of the year was a time when the boundary between the living and the dead became blurred. It was believed that on this night the presence of otherworldly spirits made it easier for Druid priests to make psychic divinations. This ancient lore is mirrored by the mythic role of the owl. In other words, it's not just that owls are seen on Halloween, it's that the owl has a direct connection to the night itself.

Here's another similar story, this one from a woman in Australia. Like the previous account, she heard me interviewed on an audio podcast, and it lead her to read my essay. Here's what happened:

> Last night I read your article on owls and was very interested in the whole synchronistic phenomenon concerning the owls. In the past 20 years I've had astonishing and truly amazing experiences with synchronicity. I've been through very hard times and sometimes nearly lost my usual intense belief in the Divine. It was the always perfectly timed synchronistic acts that kept me going through dark times and that restored my faith and gave me hope for a better future...
>
> By the time I got to page 31 in your essay, I wondered if I would also have an owl experience like the people you mentioned. I was reading this sentence: "It was a beautiful night and she heard the very clear sound of two owls hooting."
>
> At that VERY moment I heard an owl's hoot outside as I was reading. Needless to say I was overwhelmed! The owl (which I haven't heard before) kept on hooting until I finished reading your article. It stopped and I lay awake for a long time waiting to hear his call again, but he probably left to synchronistically surprise somebody else.

These two accounts from two women seeing and hearing owls in connection to my owl essay are examples of what I am getting almost daily. Both women are framing these owl experiences as outright mystical events. Their letters culminate in bold statements like, *these things are happening for a reason,* and, *they've restored my faith.*

I've listened to a lot of people share their owl experiences, and even though these are just stories of seeing a bird, they almost always get described as a blessing, an honor, a gift, or an outright spiritual event. Almost all the accounts I receive have a similar mystical undercurrent. For me, the consistency of these stories represents a kind of confirmation. These experiences go way beyond owls, they are tapping into something much deeper.

It's understandable that my website would attract people with a similar mindset and similar experiences. This is an emotional subject, and some readers will describe how they feel a connection to my life journey. I get a lot of feedback saying as much, and it makes me all the more committed to my role in this, whatever it might mean.

I've spoken to lifelong abductees at conferences, and asked them that same question—have you ever had any odd experiences with owls? Sometimes they'll say never, except for the beautiful owl they saw the night before. It feels like there's a synchronistic power that can anticipate my question, and this power can present people with owls, as if preparing them for connecting with me.

A dream owl with a pen

I received an email from a man whose life has an eerie parallel to my own. We are the same age, and some of the key dates of each of our experiences line up with a curious symmetry. Like me, he works as a professional illustrator and our drawing style is oddly similar. While he doesn't say it directly, what he shares certainly points to some sort of suppressed UFO contact. Like so many others, he fits into that elusive maybe category. Here's what he said in his email (italics my own):

> I've been wanting to write to you for a few months, but kept chickening out. Then two nights ago I had a very vivid dream that an owl dropped a five-foot fountain pen in front of me (I've attached a drawing). I figured that was probably my subconscious or something telling me to just do it.

dream image from a fellow illustrator

I have only seen three owls in my life. The first was huge, like a five-foot wingspan, and flew silently over my head at about the same time I was making a weird little 16mm movie. The film, from 1987, featured a man's face, wearing a white mask with large black eyes painted on it, and it slowly appeared at night in the bedroom window of a terrorized woman.

I don't want to read too much into his weird little movie, but that imagery is kind of obvious. I mean, isn't it? His letter continued:

The second was when I was driving with my son about three months ago. The owl flew in front of our car and alighted onto a neighbor's chimney. I had been listening to your podcast just before.

And the third was four days ago when I was looking out the back window and pondering writing to you and an owl suddenly landed on the telephone wires behind our house. I feel stupid writing this, it seems like just goofy coincidence, but, what the heck, there it is.

I no longer believe that there's any such thing as a "goofy coincidence," especially since they continue to pile up around me.

Diana in the driveway

Here's another odd set of events that came from a reader of my blog. Like everything in this chapter, it also includes me. On August 4th, 2012, I had my photograph taken sitting near a great horned owl (it's my the "about the author" image at the end of this book). I was at an event where a local raptor rescue center was taking part in a community fundraiser. The ornithologists from the center had a series of birds on display in a big open barn. There was a golden eagle, a falcon, and a great horned owl. This owl had been rescued after someone found it with an injured left wing. It was nursed back to health but was unable to fly, so it couldn't be released back into the wild. Now it lives at the raptor center and occasionally gets taken to elementary schools and other public events, like the one on that day

In the photograph, you can clearly see the owl's wing hangs awkwardly at its side. I posted this image on my blog and Facebook the same day it was taken.

Four days later, I got a letter from a woman named Diana. That morning she was in her house trying to transfer one of my audio interviews onto her iPod, but the download was going slow. She went outside to take the trash to the curb and saw what she thought was a bundle of something in the driveway, when she got closer she realized it was an injured owl. The poor creature could barely move because of an open wound under its right wing. The owl would flop onto its back and as it struggled to get upright, she saw the wing twisting awkwardly. There was almost nothing holding it in place.

She got a dog carrier, and after some struggles got the bird into the container using a rake. She went back into the house to search out a local veterinarian that was affiliated with wildlife rescue. After that, she transferred the podcast to her MP3 player. She put the dog carrier with the injured owl in the car, and drove to the vet. Here's the weird part—during the drive both she and the owl were listening to my voice.

The similarities between her story and my photo are positively bizarre. Both stories feature a wildlife rescue, a great horned owl with an injured wing, and both owls got to listen to my voice. She was also clear that she had not seen the photograph of me and the injured owl before contacting me with her experience. She told me what episode she was listening to, and it involved me and the guest, Lorin Cutts, talking about owls and how they interact with UFO abductees. Very much like me, Lorin has had a long list of extremely strange owl experiences.

I can't ignore the fact that the woman who shared this story was named Diana. In Roman mythology, the goddess Diana was associated with wild animals and woodlands, and she had the power to talk to animals.

People finding wounded owls show up a few times in these accounts. There is a story in Chapter 9, from an abductee named Leslie about an owl plopping itself in front of her on the sidewalk, as if it were demanding to be rescued.

I gave my first-ever-presentation about owls and UFOs on the stage at the annual International UFO Congress in February of 2014. The next day, I heard from more than one person that after my talk there had been an owl perched on a tall light pole in the parking lot of the conference center.

I've had people see owls right before calling me on the phone or right after. Same goes for emails, same goes for watching a talk of mine on YouTube or DVD. I've had more than one person tell me they saw an owl fly across their windshield while driving and listening to one of my podcasts.

People are seeing owls in ways that seem to be directly connected to me. I fully realize that there are plenty of owls out there, and it isn't really all that unusual to see them every now and again. Yes, sometimes an owl is just an owl, and there is no deeper meaning. But there seems to be a difference in how some of these sightings play out, as if an owl is punctuating the moment for dramatic effect.

Giant red UFO eyes

It gets even stranger. I received an email from a man who saw something a little harder to dismiss than an owl. Daniel (a pseudonym) was at his desk early in the morning just before sunrise. He was watching the YouTube video of my 2014 presentation on owls and UFOs while at the same time checking his email. He scrolled way down "as if drawn to do so" to find an unopened message that he didn't remember receiving. At the bottom of that email was a logo with an owl, and he thought this was a funny synchronicity.

It was at this point that Daniel felt compelled to contact me. He began writing an email at the same time my video presentation was playing. Just as he typed the word owl, he looked out the window to see something shocking. Two large red lights were hovering beyond the trees in his yard, maybe 100 yards away. Daniel said these lights "looked like giant eyes."

He slowly walked up close to the window to see two more red lights about eight feet below the ones he first noticed. There were now four lights high off the street beyond the trees with a misty white glow that seemed to be radiating toward him. These lights were positioned as if in the corners of a large square, and he sensed some sort of dimensional void in the center.

Daniel tried to take a picture, but as he turned his camera on, the lights slowly and silently moved off and disappeared. He ran downstairs and was shaking as he told his wife what had just happened. He went back upstairs and looked out the window, but there was nothing. At this point, his yard was starting to light up with the approaching dawn. He took a picture from the same position he had seen the red lights, and when he looked at the photo, he saw the ghostly image of a face within the faint glow of sunlight and the pattern of tree branches. I've examined this image and even at a glance it doesn't take much to see the face of a gray alien or a human skull in the photo. This could be easily dismissed as nothing more than seeing a face in the clouds, but it gets even stranger.

Daniel had paused the YouTube video before running downstairs to his wife, and the frozen image on the screen was something I had drawn, and it looked eerily similar to the face that emerged from the photo in his yard. The paused image was an illustration depicting one of my own experiences. In 2009, I was diagnosed with a slight cataract in the lens of my right eye. This tiny growth created a very clear image that only I could see, and it looked like the face of a gray alien or a human skull—and strangely, it also looked a little bit like me. I write a lot more about this face near the end of the book, in a sub-chapter titled: *My confirmation event.*

In short, Daniel sees what can only be described as a UFO at the moment he typed the word owl. This happened while watching me give a presentation on UFOs and owls. Then he sees the impression of a gray alien's face in a photo taken out the window, a face that matches something I had drawn.

After all that, Daniel wrote: "I'm freaked out now. I've never seen anything like this before, and that's not why I was contacting you." He wanted to tell me of metaphysical experiences and some challenging dream-related things that had invaded his life. He painted a dark picture to the lead-up to seeing the red lights out his window. Daniel ended his initial email telling me his middle name is Christopher.

Owls and spiritual awakening

What follows is one more example of the mystical power of these events. A man who works in the social sciences contacted me with a remarkable story. His name is John and he described a lifelong curiosity about the subject of UFOs. In recent months, however, this interest had become an obsession. His inquiry had always stayed close to the "nuts and bolts" stuff, avoiding anything related to consciousness or spirituality. In his online searching for UFO information, he kept coming across a YouTube video, the same one noted by Daniel in the previous account. It's a 110-minute long presentation I had given in the UK in 2014. The talk was titled Owls, Synchronicity and the UFO Abductee. John wrote to me:

> Before I watched the video, I thought that I wouldn't like it because of the subject matter. However, once I was done watching it, I honestly felt very moved. The idea that synchronicities were special and meaningful was something that I hadn't heard before, but it struck me and resonated. I had experienced them so much more in the last several years. So much so, that I couldn't ignore them and actually felt like I could almost predict them.

Right after the video ended, the phone rang. It was a dear friend named Jamie. Although they hadn't spoken with each other in months, she felt compelled to call him that night, at that moment. During their conversation, he told her about watching my UFO presentation, but didn't mention owls. Jamie then recounted an experience she had while driving in a rural area with her parents when she was still a teenager. They came upon something big, hovering less than 15 feet over the center of the road. Nobody in the car said anything, they all just sat there and stared. She described the craft as an elongated triangle, almost almond-shaped. She likened the color to something iridescent, like the surface of a soap bubble reflecting light. They watched in silence for a little while, and the next thing she remembered was being at their destination. This was about 20 minutes of traveling time, but it was an hour later. She said that it took a while before anyone could say anything, and all they could do was ask each other *what the heck was that?* Nobody talked about it after that.

Jamie had never told John about any of this. John said:

> Soon after she told me, I felt compelled to ask her about owls. I simply asked her, "Do you ever see owls?" She said, "Oh yeah, I used to have an owl sit on my window sill all the time, it stared at me and sometimes really scared the crap out of me." She explained that it had been quite a long time since she's seen any owls.
>
> We went on to have a deep conversation that night about these topics, and I was feeling quite jazzed about the whole thing when we got off the phone. About a half hour later, she texted me and simply said, "OMG!!!"
>
> I knew exactly what had happened before she said any more. She told me that right after our previous phone conversation, an owl had landed on her window sill and was looking at her. She confirmed what I already knew. Strangely, I wasn't at all surprised. It was just supposed to have happened, almost as if we made it happen. So amazing!
>
> I've now been completely transformed in my understanding of this whole phenomenon and actually have begun to question if I've been an abductee myself. I've had some very unexplainable things happen that lead me to believe that something strange has been happening my whole life. I recently told a friend that the most amazing thing of all this is that the "scientist" in me was simply searching for answers about the phenomenon, but instead what I've found is a spiritual awakening.

John went on to thank me in a way that left me feeling quite humbled. I recognize my responsibility to share what happens along this path, because there are others out there confronting this same mystery.

John watched a video of me talking about my personal experiences with owls, and it triggered a set of events that transformed his ideas about reality itself. He said: "I feel compelled to explore my consciousness and to pay very close attention to synchronicity." This one email sums up so much of what has been unfolding as I proceed forward—a blurring of owls, synchronicity, and UFOs, and it all culminates in a spiritual awakening.

There have been times during this research where I've wallowed in doubt about the reality of this owl stuff. Some connections seemed too tenuous and were easy to dismiss. But all these accounts of owls showing up for other people in conjunction with me was different, it was like a very real form of proof. It told me that I was on to something, and that I needed to keep pulling on that golden thread and dig even deeper.

Chapter 19:

Owls and Death

In the follow-up to the 1987 publication of *Communion*, Whitley Strieber received what he estimates to be a quarter of a million letters from readers. That book, specifically its jarring cover image of the bald alien with the huge black eyes, acted as a trigger to people all over the world. There was an emotional need to share what had happened to them, and in that era before email they wrote out their experiences on paper. At a certain point, the post office began coming to his home with big canvas bags packed with letters, each with someone's deeply personal accounts.

Anne Strieber, Whitley's wife, took on the role of reading and categorizing these letters. She would sit at her desk, day after day, year after year, patiently trying to make sense of this outpouring of stories that define what we now call alien abduction. Within these letters was a repeating pattern of people interacting with their dead friends and relatives while in the presence of the aliens.

Anne had a large chalkboard next to her desk where she would make notes, and there came a day when she wrote, "This has something to do with what we call death." This simple statement became one of the most important realizations for this husband and wife team as they grappled with the mystery of contact.

Whitley wrote this in his 2012 book *Solving the Communion Enigma*:

> It does have something to do with death. In fact, it has to do with the next state in the evolution of this species, which involves a leap ahead into a completely new relationship with ourselves, in which mysteries like death take on an entirely new meaning.[67]

This same statement could be made about owls. All across the globe and all across the ages, they have been connected to mysteries of death, either as an omen preceding someone dying, or as a sign of the departed after their passing. A young Native American told me that three owls had shown up around his family's home the night his brother died. He saw these sentinels as three generations of owls: a youth, an adult, and an elder. This symbolic appearance of owls at the moment of a tribe member's death was well understood by everyone on the reservation.

My mother and an owl story

I held my mother's hand as she slipped peacefully away from this life. My sister was on the opposite side of the bed, holding her other hand as she took her last breath. She had been unconscious for several days after having an aneurysm in her brain, and during that time she was in a hospice room at an assisted living facility in North Carolina. It was early in the morning when it happened, and all of us, my brother, my sister, and I, felt a sense of relief that her suffering was over. She had been slowly succumbing to the terrible effects of Alzheimer's, and she spent her final years confused and frightened.

I was staying at my sister's home, with her and my older brother, my only siblings. The rest of that day was a blur of trying to sleep and trying to make sense of all the busy requirements that followed. That evening we all sat together side-by-side on a big couch on my sister's backyard deck. We were joined by one of her closest friends, Ruthie, who lived across the street. She was sitting directly opposite us. It was a calm summer evening, and the mood was somber but pleasant.

Ruthie is very Southern and very proper. There came a point where she took a deep breath and then formally addressed all of us, me and my two siblings, all facing her on the couch. She spoke with calm seriousness, "I need to tell you that I know there is an afterlife, I absolutely know this. I know because of an experience *I had with an owl*."

Right then my sister flinched, she was visibly reacting to Ruthie's statement. She exclaimed, "Oh my god, What? *An owl?*"

My brother, sitting on the other side, gave me this look as if I'd somehow put Ruthie up to this. Both of them were well aware of my owl research, and neither of them quite understood what I was doing. I was 50 years old, and right then I still felt like the quirky little brother.

My immediate thought was, *oh this again*. Ruthie obviously saw our odd reactions, and I spoke up to explain, "Okay, this is very strange. You don't know this, but I've been doing research on owls and how they play a role in mythology and folklore, including things like death and UFOs. But, please, I want to hear what happened."

Ruthie explained that a few years earlier, after her father had died, she was in a terrible state of grieving. She was trying to find some solace, and she would walk alone on a nature trail that winds around the neighborhood. She did this every day for about two weeks, and each day she would see an owl, which was always perched in plain view.

> I didn't know owls were out during the day and especially that one that would let me get so close without flying away. I came to feel like he was my owl.
>
> There came a day when I was out on that trail, just like all those days before, and a hooting made me look up, and he was sitting on a very low branch just staring at me. He wasn't flying off, and I knew this was a special event. I knew that The Lord had let Daddy send me a message that all was well. I feel so fortunate that such a beautiful bird was chosen as the messenger.
>
> The message came as a feeling—a confirmation that Daddy was at peace. I didn't see the owl again after that day, and I felt certain that I had received my message.

Hearing Ruthie's story, I felt a deep connection with her and what I feel is a powerful truth. She didn't need to convince me of anything, I was already fully immersed in a sense of knowing, and this was extremely helpful in my own time of grieving.

I had been spending the previous days either at my sister's home or at the hospice care room. One of us, either my brother, sister, or myself, were always by our mother's side. During these days, I would get up early each morning and drink coffee with my sister at her kitchen table. I would check my email and then read aloud the daily owl stories I was receiving from people. My sister seemed fascinated, but at the same time baffled. These accounts were filled with dreams, premonitions, UFOs, and death. So when Ruthie spoke of *her owl*, my sister was fully aware of the stories

I had been collecting for this book project. My brother was also aware, but I knew enough not to share too much with him. I sensed this bothered him, so I had kept any talk of owls to a minimum whenever we were together.

I can't help but feel that hearing Ruthie's beautiful owl experience was somehow staged for the benefit of my siblings. It felt as if it had been orchestrated by some sympathetic force, partly to comfort us, and partly so my brother and sister would both get an insight of what I had been going through for the last few years. Owls, whether real, symbolic, or in a story told by someone else, have been continually showing up at highly charged moments in my life. When I tried to explain this to my siblings, I could tell they didn't understand. But now they've been presented with a deeply moving example, with me sitting in between them when it happened.

White owl at the cemetery gate

Christopher Bledsoe, Sr. has had both UFO contact and owl experiences. Some of his unusual owl sightings are covered previously in this book. He also had an owl event that played out very similar to Ruthie's.

I met Chris in May 2013, while I was in his home state of North Carolina. I was there for two weeks, visiting my mother in the assisted living center near Charlotte. This was two months before her death.

I hadn't yet met Chris, I only knew him from some online audio interviews where he described his many experiences. His heartfelt accounts fascinated me, and I simply called him up, explained who I was, and he invited me to his home. I felt completely welcome during my two-day visit. His home was bustling with family, kids, neighbors, and dogs.

During my time there, Chris, myself, and two other researchers walked across his back yard so he could introduce all of us to his parents. His mother and father lived right next door in the house where he grew up, so he had lived his entire life in this one spot.

His father had been dealing with health issues, and now spending a lot of time in the shade on the back deck. He had a beautiful slow, sweet southern accent, and we all sat and chatted together on a calm spring afternoon. His father, like pretty much everyone in the family, had seen

UFOs around these homes. He spoke about watching a shiny craft from that very spot. He pointed up at the sky and described what he had seen.

His father died peacefully in early December of that same year. Chris and his family had a powerful experience in the limousine on their way home from the funeral service. It was a cold rainy afternoon, and as they pulled away from the gravesite, Chris's wife spotted a huge barn owl sitting on a low branch in a tree alongside the road. Everyone in the limo saw the owl—it was looking down at them, perched on the one branch on that tree that allowed for an unobstructed view, as if it wanted to be seen by everybody.

Chris said it was amazing to see such a big owl, in full daylight, in the pouring rain, at that significant moment. He said that everyone in the limousine felt this was a sign that his father was okay. He described the distinct sensation of being watched, but it wasn't a negative feeling.

Pretty much everyone in his family has either seen a UFO sighting, or has had direct contact. This means a car full of experiencers all saw an owl moments after a ritual ceremony for a UFO witness.

Researching death

Dr. Peter Fenwick is a neuropsychiatrist and Fellow of the Royal College of Psychiatrists, and Britain's leading clinical authority on near-death experiences. Together with his wife Elizabeth, a counselor, they wrote about a remarkable owl event that very much ties into his research on death.

This story happened to a British woman a few months after her mother had died. The first appearance of this owl was on an April morning when she noticed a commotion in her garden. There was a flock of birds dive-bombing an owl that sat quietly on a low branch of an oak tree. She describes what took place.

> When I stepped out into the garden, there was a great flapping of wings and the owl flew down and landed in front of me on the grass. It was a large tawny owl about 12 inches high. It looked up at me with big brown eyes and mewed. It seemed very tame.

271

During the day, every time I went outside, the owl would come down and stand in front of me. It was almost as if it was trying to say something. The big brown eyes looked so human and reminded me of my mother, also brown-haired, who had died the previous summer.

This reaction is remarkably common: someone experiencing a loss *will see an owl as their departed loved one.* That night, as she and her husband slept, the owl returned. Their bedroom window was open and the owl came inside and sat on the sill, behavior her husband didn't like at all.

The next morning, I opened the kitchen windows. No sooner had I opened the large window over the sink, than there was a great flurry of wings and the owl flew right into the kitchen… I opened the outside door, hoping to coax it outside, but it seemed to be quite at home in the kitchen. It flew down to the other end, and sat on the curtain rail watching me. It had a tremendous wing-span and it was remarkable that nothing was knocked over. Eventually it flew out of the window and sat on the back porch.

When we went out to the car later that morning, it came straight down and perched on the flowerpot I was carrying. As we drove out, it sat on the gatepost watching us.[68]

The owl returned that night to sit at their bedroom window and then the porch the next morning, but after a few days it left and never came back.

Dr. Fenwick has a wealth of examples of birds showing up within his research. Dying patients will sometimes see a bird out of the corner of their eye, and then tell their loved ones, "I can see a bird, and they will take my soul when I die." He has also seen a pattern of other birds, not just owls, arriving after a death. They show up as if to comfort the surviving loved ones. Dr. Fenwick explains:

They are usually a bird that the person liked, and they somehow or another appear in the home, sometimes they come down the chimney, sometimes they come in through an open window, and the other animals in the home behave in a very strange way to them. These birds are not chased by the cat, and the dog doesn't bark at them. It is as if they are familiar in some way. And when the person who is bereaved comes into the room, they know that the bird is carrying the soul of the person who has just died.[69]

Dr. Fenwick tells of a friend in Massachusetts whose husband had died. Shortly thereafter, a big snowy owl came and sat in a nearby tree outside the family's home. During the days leading up to the funeral, this owl simply sat there and watched. The owl made the local news, and there were people from all over Massachusetts coming there and taking pictures. As soon as the funeral was over, the owl left.

These owl accounts from Dr. Fenwick closely parallel what I have been finding. I heard one story of a husband and wife who saw an owl perched on the top of the door to their house. It was sitting awkwardly there, clinging to the door frame all afternoon. Later they learned a close friend had died right at that same time. There is death symbolism of both the owl and the doorway.

My father and a mourning dove

My father died peacefully in May of 2012. He was 85 years old. This happened 14 months before my mother's passing. My dad lived a rich and full life, but like my mom, his last few years were difficult because of challenging health issues. This wasn't sad for my siblings and I, instead we were relieved his suffering was over.

After getting the phone call from my brother about dad's passing, I got on a plane and traveled to my sister's home. My parents were living in an assisted living community a few miles down the road from my sister. As a family, we worked hard to make our father's service something uplifting and inspiring. We had a bagpiper play *Scotland the Brave* and *Amazing Grace.*

I drove to the funeral with my sister. When we arrived at the chapel, a mourning dove flew across our path, directly in front of the windshield. I mumbled, "A dove." It was the only bird to pass that close to me in the full eight days I spent with my family, and believe me when I say I pay attention to this kind of stuff.

We parked, went into the chapel, and a few minutes later I went back to my sister's car to get a small table that would hold my father's ashes for the service. There, on top of the car parked right next to my sister's van, was a mourning dove. It sat there staring at me, very close. There's no way to know, but my sense was that this was the same bird that crossed our path minutes earlier. I spoke aloud to this dove, telling it that I was very aware of its message. I talked softly, as if it was my father, and said thank you. The dove is a mythic symbol of peace. Even its name, *mourning dove,* was resonant in that moment.

In the New Testament, the dove shows up as a messenger at the baptism of Jesus, "And the Holy Spirit, in bodily form, descended on him like a dove. And a voice from heaven said, 'You are my dearly loved Son, and you bring me great joy.'" Luke 3:22 (NLT). Part of me wanted to delete this Bible passage, it felt a little bit too churchy. I'm leaving it in because I cried while typing it out.

ReNae and the Ashtar Command

For the most part, this research has been nothing more than me collecting a lot of owl stories, and at the onset pretty much all of these accounts were somehow tied into UFOs. I knew from the mythology that owls were associated with death, but at that point I didn't have any accounts that actually demonstrated this. There came a day when I received a heartfelt account from a fellow named David. He told of seeing an owl on a telephone pole looking down on his father-in-law's farm—this happened within hours of the man's death. The owl was perched right in the center of the property, and neither he nor his wife ReNae (who had grown up on the farm) had ever seen an owl there before. He felt that this owl was his wife's father, *as a spirit symbol,* looking at the farm he loved one last time before he left.

This was exactly the email I had been waiting for, an account associating the owl with death—without any of the UFO baggage. I wrote David back, thanking him for sharing. Within minutes, I received a reply:

> I am reading your website for the first time and am not sure if you are connecting UFOs to owls, but an interesting feature of my wife's life is she was very psychic. She just passed away two months ago. We met years ago when she was having encounters with Ashtar, this was some alien in a spaceship. She never claimed to be an abductee, this Ashtar stuff was more of a mental thing. I do not know if there is any relevance here but just wanted to throw that in.

So my very first account of owls and death had a direct connection to UFOs. David summed up Ashtar as "some alien in a spaceship," and that's a pretty good one-sentence definition. *The Ashtar Command* is a common element reported by UFO contactees and psychics. A benevolent light-being named Ashtar is said to be the source of a huge volume of spiritual messages. This information comes from different channelers, and it's presented with thick brush-strokes of love and light. This aspect of the phenomenon gets dismissed with contempt by most UFO researchers. Yes, it sounds pretty flaky, but I'm not so quick to judge. There's an eerie consistency within the material that comes through a divergent set of channelers. I'm less focused on the content of the communications, and more intrigued that so many psychics are coming forward with such similar messages, all claiming Ashtar as the source.

I expressed my sympathy to David, explaining that my mother had died a month earlier. He directed me to his wife's close friend Diana, feeling she was better able to share ReNae's Ashtar experiences than he could. When I spoke with Diana, she not only described how ReNae had channeled the Ashtar Command, but she also told me her own owl and UFO story.

When Diana was a small girl, this would have been in the late 1940s, her father cut down a big beautiful oak tree in their yard because an owl would sit in its branches. We talked about how odd this seemed, because

275

an owl could just move to another tree. She once asked her brother if he remembered why her father cut down that tree, and he said it was because it was close to an office used by their father, and the owl was making too much noise. This also seems odd, because an owl should only make noise at night.

Diana then went onto explain that on a corner in her old neighborhood, about 20 yards from that oak tree with the owl, was a site where she had always known that a space ship had landed. I was a little confused and I pressed for more details. She said that every time she walked past this spot, she could clearly visualize a classic disc shaped craft—it was shiny metal and not very large. I asked if there had been talk among the neighbors about any kind of UFO landing there, and she said no, that it was just a strong *knowing* that she'd always had about that one spot.

A white owl and a message

The second story I found (or that found me) of owls and death was told by a woman with the pen name Gypsy Woman. She saw a big white owl out her window right as she was jolted out of a sound sleep. It was perched on a bare branch, aligned perfectly for her to see it from her bed. The next morning, she again woke with a start, and right as she sat up the phone rang. Answering, she received the news of a family member's death. When I followed up and talked to her, she too had a UFO connection.

Gypsy Woman told me of seeing multiple UFOs, including a close up daylight sighting. Add to this a visit from Men In Black, a near-death experience, and psychic abilities. It's as if her lifetime of unusual experiences created an opening that morning for an owl to land on that bare branch. It could be that this owl was delivering a message, sad though it may have been, to someone with the life experiences that would allow her to receive it.[70]

Lonn Friend and his mother's passing

Lonn Friend is an author and rock and roll journalist who writes about the heavy metal scene. He also runs a rather introspective podcast series, *Energize*. I heard an episode where he spoke about synchronicities, death, and owls. His questioning and insights were deeply heartfelt. He explored the symbolic connection between owls and that *other world*, the place of the departed, and how these signs had emerged in a flurry around him.[71]

What follows is another example of the *paradox syndrome*. Within Lonn's story is a cluster of overlapping events, and I recognize the power in what he shared. I was meant to connect with Lonn—that is not a sense, but a knowing, and in pulling on the threads of his experience, I've unraveled emotional clues tied to my own life.

Lonn's mother died on August 10th 2013 after an unsuccessful cancer surgery. His last words to her were, "Don't be afraid, you're going to the Shire." She loved Tolkien and understood the sentiment. The Shire is the home of the Hobbits, an oasis of peace within the mythical world of Middle Earth.

On the 21st of August, Lonn's aunt Esther died during heart surgery— he called her his Angel aunt. Esther was his mother's older sister, born 11 years earlier, and she died 11 days after. These dates hit home for me— my mother had died 11 days earlier than Lonn's mother, on July 31st.

My mother's death, July 31st 2013.
Lonn's mother's death, Aug 10th 2013.
Lonn's aunt Esther's death, Aug 21st 2013.

These emotionally charged dates are separated by an eerily tidy 11-11, the number of days between them. This didn't feel random, and it created a palpable connection to Lonn's experiences and emotions and my own. I'll also add that August 10th is a big-deal day for me in this confusing pool of synchro-weirdness. Earlier in this book there is sub-chapter titled: *August 10th and three crop circle events.*

On August 27th, Lonn's cousin Jill, the daughter of Aunt Esther, brought her mother's ashes home to Los Angeles to be buried at Forest Lawn Cemetery alongside her parents, Lonn's grandparents. Lonn, along with his brother, was at the graveside holding his mother's ashes during the service. Later that same day there was a beautiful ceremony where Lonn scattered his mother's ashes on a plateau off in the desert. To get to the remote site, they drove up Los Robles Road, which translates to *The Oaks*. The hospital where Lonn's mother died was Los Robles hospital in Thousand Oaks California. The word *oak* was repeating.

After the service, a close friend of Lonn's, Robert Cruz, drove him back from the desert and dropped him off at his mother's apartment in Oak Park California. Lonn spent the night in his mother's home. He was awakened at around two in the morning by the gentle hooting of an owl just outside the bedroom window, it was perched in an oak tree. This was one more reference to *oak*.

Even though it was the middle of the night, he got up and logged into Facebook, and asked about this owl. Within minutes, Robert Cruz replied and said that the cooing of a sitting owl, in Native American lore, means that the departed have crossed over safely. Robert, who is native American with strong intuitive skills, told Lonn that his mother's sister was also with her.

Shortly thereafter, Lonn went to Las Vegas with his daughter and the rest of the family for Thanksgiving dinner. On Thanksgiving Day he received a text from his cousin Jill who was now back in Florida. He replied right away and asked, "What's up?"

Jill told Lonn that she was shaking. She had been having a hard time because she missed her mother so terribly. The night before, Jill was lamenting to a close friend that she hadn't received any kind of a sign from her mother, and she was desperate for some reassuring message. All her friend could do was tell her to be patient. But now, as Jill was talking to Lonn on the phone, *she was staring at a little owl in her garage.*

She told her cousin that she went into the garage, moved a bucket (another death metaphor) from a shelf, and right behind it stood a little owl.

Jill told Lonn, "Listen to me, this owl, it's staring at me, it's still sitting on this shelf. I've been in Florida for 27 years and I've never seen an owl!"

Eastern screech owl in a Florida garage

The garage hadn't been open since the day before, so she didn't know how it could've gotten in. She took a cell phone picture and sent it to Lonn. The whole time she was talking to the owl as if it was her mother—and she said to it, "Mom, I'm talking to Lonny on the phone!" The owl would blink as a reply. The photo shows a little eastern screech owl sitting on a cardboard box, it was only about eight inches tall, and like any owl, it looked vaguely menacing.

The owl appeared at 6:30 a.m. on Thanksgiving Day 2013. It was on the only shelf in the garage used by Jill, the rest of the space being her husband's. This little owl was still there when Jill and her husband returned from a holiday dinner with family. It was later that night when she went into the garage and told the owl, "Mom, it's okay, you can go now. I know you're okay. Thank you for visiting me. I love you." Only then did the owl leave.

The next day, Lonn checked into a hotel. Like most places in Las Vegas, it had a theme, stylized like an opulent French library with bookshelves lining the walls. He randomly pulled a book off a shelf, a children's book about owls. He was in a place of awe with these reoccurring synchronicities; he showed the book to his daughter, who simply shrugged as if she accepted the way the universe wants to communicate.

If you merely peek into the mythologies about owls, you'll immediately see that the owl is closely connected to death. According to the Kikuyu tribe of Kenya, owls are harbingers of death—if one sees an owl or even hears its hoot, someone is going to die. This is similar to folklore from all around the world; owls as a harbinger or omen of death.

Yet within my research, this is rare. It happens, but such reports are far outnumbered by instances of owls appearing *after* someone dies. Owls will make their presence known, they'll be conspicuous in a way that makes it impossible for the observer to miss. What is consistent is that these witnesses, in the moment of grieving, won't describe what they see as an owl, *but as their departed loved one.* Our world can seem restrained and mechanized, but even nonspiritual people can see an owl and then immediately talk to it as if it were their dead parent. There is a pattern of grieving, then an owl experience, and then a sense of peace.

Talking to owls

I have a funny story that happened at a doctor's office. I was there for a minor outpatient surgery, and they give me a valium beforehand, so I was sort of talkative during the actual procedure. I spoke (or more correctly, slurred) about my owl research. The doctor and assistant humored me and asked a few questions. I shied away from any mention of UFOs, instead saying I was writing about owl mythology, which seems honest, but avoided the loony factor of flying saucers. I told them that I'd been collecting reports of people seeing an owl shortly after the death of a loved one, and how they'll talk to the owl as if it was the departed, usually their father or mother. Jill talking to the owl in her garage is a perfect example.

Later that same day, the doctor got back to me with a curious story. She explained that right after I'd left the office, her receptionist told her that an owl had landed on her back porch the night before. This was a few days after her dog had died, and she went out side and talked to the owl *as if it were her dog,* telling the owl how much she missed him. The receptionist chose that moment to tell her story, without any prompting from the doctor, and she described the solace of being able to talk to her dog one last time. The doctor cautiously implied that, for her, this was a very weird coincidence. All I could do was nod knowingly, because this kind of thing wasn't weird for me—it was perfectly normal.

I've received a lot of owls stories, and most are connected to UFOs. A lesser number tell of owls showing up in connection to the passing of a loved one. These are deeply heartfelt accounts, and I recognize the emotion in each and every one. I am so grateful to everyone who've shared their experiences with me, and I've done my best to honor the spirit of these stories. It's as if the owl is a form of shorthand, a symbol for something that can only be known intuitively. That owls show up in the context of death must mean something. The owl seems to be reflecting the ultimate questions—*why are we here,* and *what happens when we die?*

When people return from a near-death experience, they'll describe it as timeless realm. It's nearly impossible to convey the power of their round-trip visit using something as limiting as language. From these firsthand accounts, death itself parallels other experiences of crossing the veil. The psychedelic mushroom, the shamanic initiation, meditation, and UFO contact are all realms beyond our ordinary consciousness. Visiting these regions has the power to completely transform the traveler, and the owl seems to be the totem for these perilous journeys.

PART V

OWLS AND THE DEEPER MIND

Chapter 20:

Owls in Dreams

It is still true, as I predicted in 1947, that no flying
saucer has ever been 'captured' or even 'proved.'…
They are unknown, the hidden world, that all of us
at one time or another are aware exists, and which
intrudes on our lives to make us think.

—Ray Palmer[72]

Anne Strieber read upwards of a quarter of a million letters after the publication of her husband's book *Communion* in 1987. These were heartfelt accounts sent by people describing their own contact experiences at the hands of alien visitors. She said the most common phrase in all those letters was: "I had a dream that wasn't a dream."

I've had long talks with people who feel they've had direct UFO contact, and at some point in the conversation I'll hear about their dreams. These are often described using terms like "hyper-vivid" and "more real than real." There are a few ways to look at this. Abductees might wake in the morning with memories of being aboard a craft and interacting with aliens, and they could be remembering a real experience that took place during the night. What is dismissed as a dream might have truly happened. These memories might play out as dream-like, but with a heightened urgency. Or their contact memories might be so bizarre, and so beyond belief, that the abductee can only frame it as a dream.

Another thought is that some outside source has co-opted their dream-time, and a metaphoric drama will play out with a conspicuous meaning. It's as if the aliens are beaming a specific story down from their flying saucer and projecting it into the mind of the sleeping experiencer. The dreamer will live out something vivid and visionary, and this might be described as decidedly different than an ordinary dream, as if the storyline is terribly important. These stage-managed dreams could be created by the aliens for the purpose of delivering a very specific message to the abductee, often through symbolic imagery. It might be that the UFO occupants are avoiding full waking contact, and are instead imparting information directly into the subconscious. There might be a reason for this kind of indirect transmission, as if dreamtime is a better way to receive certain messages.

Nobody truly knows why we dream, but it's something we all do every night. It's recognized that the stressful issues in our lives get reflected back at us, albeit distorted, during dreamtime, demanding our attention. Anyone dealing with either trauma or enlightenment should expect this drama to well up in their dreams. If someone has truly experienced contact with an alien life form, only to have the memories of those events erased, you would have to assume that parts of that experience would be seared into the hidden corners of the mind. The dreamscape might be a sort of pressure valve, so when something can no longer remain buried, it escapes the unconscious and bursts out into our dreams. If there is a message the dreamer needs to hear, who better than the owl to play the messenger.

The dream diary

My girlfriend Andrea has had a lifetime of unusual experiences, and she also deals with profoundly vivid dreams. She told me she kept a diary where she wrote down what she felt were her most significant dreams, and there have been a lot of them. I asked if I could see what she had written. She printed it out and handed it to me. The very first dream account reads:

February 11th, 2007
A Black Owl pulling me through the sky over a forest area by
my right arm. We stopped to rest on a tree limb and the owl
cuddled with me.

The remainder of that dream document is a flurry of owls, UFOs, and
aliens all playing out in a kind of mythic theater. In the following years,
Andrea's dream journaling has taken on a kind of urgency. She documents her nightly journeys nearly every morning, all with a similar cast
of spirit animals, and Jungian archetypes.

Awakened by an owl

I've had more than one abductee tell me how they cringe at the sight
of an owl, or the sound of their hooting. Are they responding at a gut level
to owls (either real or screen memories) showing up in relation to direct
visitation?

I was contacted by a man named Will who's had a lifetime of encounters, and owls have played a role in some these experiences. He said that
his contact experiences "were often preceded or followed by the sound of
owls on top of my house hooting." Like many others, he describes the
mid-90s as a busy time with a lot of nighttime visitations.[73]

On several occasions this noise was loud enough that he'd go outside,
stand in the yard, shine a strong light up at the roof, and see owls sitting
up there, sometimes as many as three. He described them as the size of
10 year-old children. This is unusually large for any owl. He is now, understandably, apprehensive about the sound of owls at night.

> I was once awoken from a very lucid and awful abduction dream
> by the hooting of an owl. At first I found it hard to differentiate the
> dream from reality. But once I got up I could clearly hear the owl
> hooting. When I looked out the window with a flashlight, I saw a
> giant owl staring at me at eye level from the neighbor's chimney...
> I cannot tell if the experience was a dream or real. Perhaps this
> distinction doesn't apply to me because all my dreams seem real

until I begin to "surface" out of them, like coming out of deep water to the surface world.

It seems that most of my owl experiences happen after an abduction. The owls are real, in my estimation, not a screen memory. However, who knows? They simply seem drawn to my roof right after an abduction. Then they make a lot of noise, although none of the neighbors seem to notice. Such events occurred in suburban San Francisco, which is quite tightly packed with homes.

He tells of being brought out of an abduction dream by an owl. This owl *woke him up*, both literally and metaphorically. What I find most intriguing is that Will describes these experiences as a blurring of dreamtime and reality. It's as if there is some force out there that can turn a dial and control the way we perceive physical existence.

One of the challenges of doing this kind of research is that so many fascinating details emerge from this in-between world. Abductees will consistently describe their experiences as dream-like, yet they'll also say they are extremely vivid. People are having real experiences, I'm convinced of that, but it seems like the contact itself takes place beyond our surface world, as if their consciousness gets transported to some deeper realm, and then returned.

Grizzly bear dreams

Owls have been showing up in my own dreams. My days have been consumed with writing and obsessing about owls, so it shouldn't be any surprise that they'll appear in my unconscious too. I had a funny dream where I looked down and saw my big toenail had gotten really long, and instead of using a clipper, I simply peeled at it with my fingers. The piece I picked off looked exactly like an owl in flight! No mystical insights, it's just what happens when you write a book about owls.

On the other hand, I had a recent dream with a power that hit me hard. I woke up on May 15th 2014, and wrote this in my blog, "I had a dream last night that was interrupted, or maybe punctuated, by the call of a great horned owl. I'm writing this within minutes of getting out of bed."

The dream started in a bland suburban setting, and I was standing out in the driveway of a house that I assume was mine. The other homes were spaced sort of far apart, it was summer and the lawns were green. The sun was low in the sky and everything was calm. Then I saw a grizzly bear poking around on the lawn across the street. At first I didn't feel nervous or threatened, it was something amazing to see. Then this big thing was lumbering towards me, and I retreated into the garage.

I hurried into the house using the inside garage door, only to realize there were six other doors all lined up, and all connected to the garage. The bear came in and tried to break through each door. The doors, from one to the other, got progressively more flimsy and each lock was harder to latch closed.

The bear was right outside each of these doors and, like me, it was going from door to door, and I could see it as I pulled them closed. As I moved on, the doors would barely close, as if they were sized wrong for the frame, or the knobs were broken, and parts would fall off as I tried to get them shut. The final door was nothing more than a thin sheet of plywood, far too small for the frame, and barely hanging in place on faulty hinges. The wood was warped and rotten, and I could see the bear over the top and sides, slowly coming towards me, his big paws reaching through the open spaces as I frantically tried to get it locked.

Then I heard the hooting cry of an owl, steady and clear. I could hear it as this bear was tearing away at the final door with its claws.

It was at that point I woke up, but the hooting continued. I lay there in bed, with the pale light of dawn easing through the only window in my bedroom. I was hearing the unmistakable call of a great horned owl, and it must have been on the telephone pole right outside my window.

Let me state this clearly: A real owl woke me up right as a grizzly bear in a dream was about to rip down a door and kill me!

I was going to get up to look out the window, but the owl stopped hooting before I could muster the energy to climb out of bed. I lay awake for a long time, deeply impressed at the symbolism of the dream, and that a real owl would invade my dreamscape just as a huge bear was about to pull down the final flimsy barrier between me and it. (Bear? Barrier?)

I had lived in that cabin for over 20 years, and I've occasionally heard an owl, and very rarely seen one nearby. But starting that morning with that owl, I began hearing them right outside my bedroom window. This had never happened in the two decades I've called this my home.

I've wrestled with all kinds of ideas on what the owl might mean, and my favorite interpretation is that the owl plays the role of a metaphysical alarm clock. That morning a real owl went beyond metaphor and truly played that role.

This dream was awash in symbolism. Maybe the bear is *the truth,* and the flimsy doors are the crumbling barriers between me and that truth? And the owl was saying—quite literally—*wake up!*

Bear can be spelled bare, as in the naked truth, and bear also means to suffer a burden. Anyway, this was sure how it felt.

Later in the day, I heard from a friend who also had a grizzly bear dream that same night. His name is Jack, and he's had a lifetime of what sure seems to be UFO abduction events. His dream began in an idyllic forest where he sees a grizzly bear on the opposite side of a river, it's just sniffing around and he feels no threat. The whole scene is beautiful and majestic.

The next thing he remembers is a small house, and he walking up to the side door and knocking. He peers through a window and sees a tiny woman walking up to the door, and there's a massive grizzly bear behind her. She opens the door, and the bear came outside. With that Jack moved behind the corner of the house. He knew if he runs or panics, the bear will chase him down and kill him.

He kept moving away and the bear followed him, and they both end up in front of the garage. The bear has done nothing threatening, it's just lumbering along and sniffing around, but Jack is very aware of the danger. Then the bear looks up at him, he thinks, *"Oh Fuck!"* and wakes up.

There are so many similar elements in our two dreams, the grizzly bear and the garage being the most obvious. Both Jack and I were in agreement that the bears in our dreams represented *fear*, or more specifically *fear of the unknown*. I sense this lumbering fear is something deep inside, an *unknown truth*, and it's pursuing both of us.

Jack's dream emerged as he was planning to undergo hypnotic regression in an attempt to retrieve what might be buried UFO abduction memories. This has been, understandably, a looming stress.

In June of 2014, Jack traveled to California with his partner Suzanne. Part of the reason for this trip was to meet with abduction researcher Yvonne Smith to explore his experiences. He sought out hypnosis in the hopes of uncovering more information concerning some odd memories from his youth. During the hour-long session, he had only fleeting images of what might have been some sort of alien contact experience. He saw skinny beings, but mostly just their arms and bodies. Yvonne asked what their faces looked like, but their image was somehow blocked from Jack's perception. These impressions brought up emotions so intense that he cried.

Later that same day, Jack and Suzanne had dinner with the author Whitley Strieber and his wife, Anne. That very night, after Yvonne Smith's hypnosis session and dinner with the Striebers, Jack had another symbolic dream worth noting, this time with owls. He was in some sort of a barn looking up at the rafters, and there was a big owl sitting on the cross beam centered under an A-frame roofline. He got the feeling he should step back to see a wider view of the barn. It was then he saw a tiny owl lying down asleep on its side. It was on a small shelf of wood tucked under the edge of the roof.

Jack sensed the larger owl was telling him to let the baby owl lie there—*just let it sleep*. The roof was sheltering something, hiding it just below the surface, and he felt it meant that those memories should stay hidden. The owl's message wasn't a warning, but more like advice, that it might be better to leave it alone. He said he'd never had an owl show up in any of his dreams before that night.

Curiously, Jack's partner Suzanne—who is also an abductee—had her own experience of an owl in a barn. She has an eerie memory from when she was still in pre-school. She remembers being compelled to walk away from her schoolyard, and she entered a spooky old barn where she encountered an owl. It was sitting up in the rafters, and she has a clear memory of it tilting its head towards her. She isn't sure if she truly saw an owl or not, yet she simply *knew* there was an owl in there. When she emerged from the barn it was after dark and her parents had called the police and started an organized search for her. She is unclear what might have happened, but it seems there was missing time along with an owl, whether real or just an impression, she doesn't know.

Here's one more story involving Jack, Suzanne, and owls. She told me they'd both been hearing an odd high-pitched whinny sound outside their bedroom window. They heard it frequently for over a year. After some online research, Jack thought it was most likely a baby raccoon. It was months later that Suzanne read an online article that included various owl sounds, and when she heard the call of the eastern screech owl, she realized that was what they'd been hearing all along.

A few nights later, Suzanne heard the noise again and went outside in hopes of recording the audio on her phone. She told me, "I was going to record it to share with you, so you could hear what I've been hearing."

Suzanne clearly heard two owls communicating from two adjoining trees in the neighbor's yard. As she approached one of the trees, she said, "Suddenly, I saw a glowing orange orb appear right where I was looking. It blinked on and blinked out, then both owls stopped hooting!"

She described it as if someone had shined an orange flashlight through the leaves of the tree. She said, "It was pretty high up, maybe 30 feet. It was a bright orange light, about the size of an orange." She waited a while but never found the source of the light, and didn't hear the owls again.

An owl and dream analysis

I heard an owl story from William Konkolesky, a young man who has long been aware of his role as a UFO abductee. It happened while he was a college student, a peak time of contact activity in his life. He was walking on a path in a forested area alongside the campus. As he walked, a big round thing dropped straight down in front of him, no more than three feet from his face. His immediate thought was that this falling ball was a beehive, but right at eye level huge wings emerged and he watched an owl glide away, following the path without flapping its wings. What baffled him was how that owl could drop straight down.

On the surface, there's not all that much to this story, except he was very clear that it happened at a time of intense abduction activity. To examine it superficially seems tenuous, but there are some symbolic gems. I've come to see some of these experiences as playing out with a sort of dream logic. Instead of asking a pragmatic UFO investigator to make sense of this, it might be better to ask the gypsy fortune teller. Perhaps the skills of a dream interpreter would be a better way to analyze William's owl experience. At this point, scrutinizing reality as if it were a dream has become normal for me.

The cartoon owl will often get drawn wearing a square graduation cap. So, the college setting coincides with the simplest caricature of the wise owl.

The beehive as a symbol has a lot of meanings. Both the Masons and Mormons see it as representing industry, and the roots of that interpretation trace back to ancient Rome. This is a tidy analogy because the hive itself is buzzing with industrious little honeybees all working together. The more interesting mythic beehive symbolism is that of death and rebirth. The residents of the hive seem to die off each winter and are reborn each spring, thus the metaphor. Actually, honey bees don't die, but there is an annual dormancy of the hive, each winter the bees will all huddle together for warmth, but it appears they've been resurrected.

UFOs are most often described as eerily silent, but if a flying saucer does make a noise, it's sometimes described as a buzzing, like the sound from a beehive.

The forest is a symbol of the dangers young people must confront if they are to become adults. The forest represents the darkness that must be traveled symbolically to reach spiritual goals—it's a place of testing. The path itself is the life journey, and the owl is the messenger from unknown realms.

So, this young man on a quest for wisdom (college), enters a place of testing and darkness (the forest), is confronted with death and rebirth (the beehive), only to see it as a messenger (the owl), leading him along his life's journey (the path). All this at a time of profound contact with aliens (again, the owl). Now, I might be way off base, but this kind of analysis can be just plain fun.

Let me add that when I spoke to Bill on the phone to ask about this experience, he had just found a little clay owl he had made as a boy. This small owl figurine struck him as relevant to his UFO experiences. He told me that he felt a curiously strong connection to this little totem, and he now uses a photo of it as a sort of logo on his website.

That owls appear in dreams should be expected. Owls have such a rich role across the world's mythic traditions you could assume it would have an equally rich place within our subconscious. Interpreting an owl's meaning within a dream might be impossible, but when they do appear, the simplest message would be to *pay attention*, and this is the same advice when they appear in reality.

Chapter 21:

Highly Charged Moments

What follows are the opening lines of what might be the most important email I've ever received. The text is edited slightly to ensure the author's anonymity.

> I read your blog posting about owl experiences, for obvious reasons I've never shared this with ANYBODY.
>
> In 1978, after many years of crushing teenage depression, I finally decided I had no more reason to live and was going to commit suicide. I had planned on carbon monoxide poisoning from my car at an abandoned area a few miles outside my town. I got everything together, including a long hose and pillow to lay my head. I had made up my mind, I was really going to do it.

She drove down a lonely road at night toward the turn-off she had chosen for this final act. Wet slushy snow was falling, and her eyes were swollen from crying, so she was driving slowly.

> Suddenly a large snowy white owl appeared out of the darkness ahead, it was flying directly at me. I stopped and the owl came within a foot of my windshield and simply hovered there, staring me right in the eye. He just hovered like this for ten seconds or so, gently using his wings to stay aloft and steady. He was floating directly in front of my face, staring right at me. Then he flew off.
>
> I was stunned, confused and amazed... I took it as a sign to not go through with the suicide. After a good long cry, I turned around and went home.

She clearly felt the owl was sending the message to face her fears of growing up and moving on. She sensed she was being told; be patient,

292

life will get better. She told me, "I'm now a happy grandmother and, although life has been tough, I am still here. I honestly have to thank that owl."

My first question to her was if she'd ever had any UFO experiences; she replied, "no." She did say that she's had a life of psychic premonitions, mystical flying dreams, a sense of alienation from the rest of humanity, as well as empathetically feeling other people's emotions. When she was six, she saw Jesus (or what she perceived to be Jesus) in the sky. This sighting unleashed such powerful emotions that she was physically knocked unconscious.

Despite the lack of any UFOs, these are exactly the kind of things that an abductee would report. She's also dealt with lifelong clinical depression, one more thing commonly reported by abductees.

Obviously, owls can show up in people's lives without any relation to the UFO phenomenon. Yet they seem to be connected to extremely intense emotions and events. In many traditions, owls have an association to impending death, and much of this folklore can be dark and frightening. But this woman is very clear that an owl *saved her life*. Perhaps the owl sensed she was teetering on the precipice of death, and it made an appearance in the hopes of tipping her back towards the living.

This book has been a complex undertaking, and at times I've been awash in doubts. Whenever I get lost in this uncertainty, I come back to this woman's experience of a white owl that turned her around on the road to suicide. Her story gives me faith. Early on in this book, I said there are no one-offs, that every story here is part of a bigger pattern of accounts. This literal rescue from death is the exception, it stands alone in all the accounts I have collected.

The story above no longer stands alone. Since the initial publication of this book, I've received a nearly identical account from a young man planning to kill himself. He also saw an owl, recognized it as a message, and feels that it saved his life.

Like the woman who saw the owl on her way to commit suicide, I've also suffered from a lifetime of severe depression. As part of my own self-exploration, I've sat with many UFO abduction researchers and spoken in depth about my memories and experiences. I've made it a point to tell them about the ongoing challenges with my depressive mood. They all nod knowingly, obviously having heard the same thing from many others.

Clinical depression has close associations with the effects of buried trauma. Both Dr. John Mack and Budd Hopkins did a standard battery of psychological testing with the folks they've worked with—these would be people who claimed repeated abduction experiences. According to these very conservative psychological evaluations, these people were deemed stable and sane, but they did show symptoms of having experienced trauma.

Hallucinations, delusions, and dreams—as powerful as they might be—don't produce the same psychological indicators as trauma. These symptoms include hopelessness, anxiety, deep insecurities, low self-esteem, isolation, a disassociation from their own bodies, and difficulty with relationships. When the clinicians doing the testing found out the pool of people being tested were reporting something as unbelievable as UFO abduction, they were understandably cautious about the reality of these claims. Yet, they did point out that if this *were* the case, these would be exactly the symptoms they should expect if such a thing had actually been experienced.

In the cage

I had some back and forth emails with a guy who first knew me from my cartoon illustration work. He contacted me and said we shared some experiences. He told me of his having a traumatic emotional breakdown that completely rewired his brain. Here's a short excerpt of our correspondence (italics my own):

> This illness permanently altered my consciousness and opened me to all sorts of altered state type experiences like OBEs (out of body experiences), lucid dreams, abduction type events (being very cautious here) to name just a few. The first thing I did when I was well enough to return to some kind of work was volunteer at an owl sanctuary. My job was to clean out their enclosures, so I was right in there with them.

In many ways, his story parallels my own. I completely understand his need to be very cautious when trying to make sense of personal experiences that seem to imply "abduction type events." Something profound had changed him, and the first thing he did as his newer self was to volunteer to work directly with owls! That's the kind of thing that gets my attention. His emotional healing involved being *inside a cage* with owls.

When I asked him if he thought he was an abductee, he said no, but then went on to share some things an abductee might report, like an expanded consciousness. He too falls into the shadowy *maybe* category. If he's had potentially harrowing traumatic UFO abduction experiences in his life and these memories are somehow suppressed, then having an emotional breakdown is understandable. Obviously, these contact events can be mind-shattering. If an abductee tells me they've suffered from depression, panic attacks, or severe anxiety, I tend to trust their claims all the more.

His story parallels my own struggles with clinical depression. I truly don't know the source of this malady. It could be hereditary, seasonal, or that I'm more susceptible as a creative type. My own darkest days, quite literally a traumatic emotional breakdown, came just as I started compulsively reading UFO books. Curiously, this desperate time coincides exactly with the memory of seeing five gray beings out my bedroom window.

My first memories of what I would now call depression were in junior high school. This matches the timeline of my missing time experience in 1974. I have wondered how much to read into the timing of these events. It would be easy to connect the dots and say one thing caused the other, but I'm far too cautious to just blurt out *aliens made me depressed.*

Like my reader, I too entered the owl cage, immersing myself in their mythos to the point of obsession. Also like my reader, something died in my own breakdown and something else was reborn out of the ashes. It is this newer person who is writing this book on owls, something my previous self never could have done.

Summoned by royalty

A woman named Louise contacted me with a letter that began simply enough: "This is my owl story." A complex set of events were set in motion in the mid-1990s while looking out her window on a rainy day. She suddenly knew that she needed to take her dog for a walk. She lived along the coastline, and she felt a strong *knowing* that she should go to a jetty stretching far out into the ocean. This was one of the regular places to walk her dog, but it was unusual because she normally wouldn't consider going outside in such harsh weather.

Louise walked with her dog in the downpour as if it were perfectly normal. When she was about halfway out along the jetty, she again knew she should start walking back towards the land.

> When I turned around to head home, I suddenly saw a very large white owl standing at the edge of the pier just watching us, as if he were waiting for our return. Riker—my large German shepherd—instead of barking or pulling at his lead simply walked quietly beside me until we were a few feet away from this owl. He then just sat quietly by my side, as if he were in the presence of royalty. It was very strange, very surreal. We stayed that way for what I guess to be around ten minutes. Then the owl just up and flew away. I walked back to my car with the feeling that we had been royally summoned, and I had simply complied with the request.
>
> … I must say as well, that had I not had my dog with me, I might have been tempted to doubt my experience as it was so surreal. But to have Riker sense the majesty of this bird, it was overwhelmingly clear to me that even he had recognized that something special had just occurred.

Louise described the owl as white and the size of a large sitting shepherd. She has spent years trying to find any kind of owl that looks similar, but cannot. She has seen both snowy and barn owls (her favorite), so she would have recognized those. She is resolute that what she saw was definitely an owl, yet it was tall and slender with a regal look.

She is also clear that her dog wasn't acting normal. He is usually eager to run and chase birds, but she felt Riker acknowledged the power of that owl. There is an aspect of this story that plays out like nothing more than a screen memory, but the aura of significance is impossible to ignore.

In our correspondence, Louise told of a twenty-year chapter of her life that had been very active with both UFO sightings and abduction experiences. Like so many others, she also tells of having a lot of psychic events, including a time of automatic writing as a form of communication with another realm. At the time of this owl sighting, she was involved in the local UFO community with a primary focus of moving beyond the intense fear that these events generated.

Shortly after seeing that owl on the jetty, Louise experienced an unusual paralysis in her arm and was forced to go on disability. She was later told she had stage 4 cancer and given less than one year to live. "Two weeks before I was diagnosed, I had a very profound dream, which was the only thing I had to hold on to as I came very close to dying."

She was an angel in this dream, looking down at her family, "I can only describe it as the most all-encompassing feeling of love I have ever experienced. Suddenly I heard God's voice giving me a choice, to complete the process and become an angel, or to stay. However, if I stayed, there would be conditions." She interpreted the message that if she chose to stay, it meant a duty to help people.

Louise had aggressive radiation treatment and surgery that brought her right to death's door. She has since been cancer free for over 18 years.

I asked how she is doing as far as the oppressive fear relating to her abduction experiences. She answered, "How am I doing? One-hundred percent! At that time, I was afraid of the dark, afraid of what I couldn't control. Not any more."

There are a surprising number of accounts where people tell of miraculous healings under the aegis of these alien beings. Some abductees have experienced the complete end to a serious illness directly after a UFO encounter. I asked Louise if the owl on the jetty could have performed some sort of healing, that it might have helped save her. She replied, "No, but the owl experience was really the start of all the big and challenging chapters of my life. As I look back, it still feels as if I had been summoned by royalty, perhaps to wish me well on a most difficult journey ahead... The whole experience for me from start to present has been a very spiritual journey, challenging indeed, but profoundly spiritual above all else."

297

The owl can be seen as symbolic of something powerful, but also very difficult, the totem of the deepest inward journey.

Louise has not only survived a devastating cancer, but has also overcome her fear of the unknown. She feels that all these events are connected to her UFO experiences, but she doesn't know how. She stated that the white owl on that rainy day held court with her and her dog. She said, "I've seen owls before and since—I love seeing them—but this experience was being in the presence of something of power that I cannot explain."

Forgiveness and a winking owl

After a long winter in the cold valley I've called home, springtime means I can finally ride my bicycle to town again, and I try to do it daily. There is a bike path in front of my cabin and it leads right to the main street of my town. There's a bridge where the path crosses a creek, with a grove of cottonwoods along that waterway.

There is a huge nest up in one of those trees, and each spring for the past few years it has been home to a family of great horned owls. I started carrying binoculars on my rides to town. I would sit in the grass for a few minutes and focus on these amazing creatures. The very first day I peered through those binoculars, something funny happened. As I focused on the owl's face—*it winked at me!*

A few times I've seen two owls, but mostly you can only see one, with its cat-like head poking up above the big nest. I feel blessed to see something so beautiful.

In the early evening of April 30th, 2013, I was riding my bike back home from the little downtown. I had my iPod on shuffle and the sun was setting. As I approached the big owl's nest, one song faded off and I waited for the next one to start. Instead of music, I heard a familiar woman's voice.

"Hi subscribers, this is Anne Strieber..."

Anne is Whitley Strieber's wife, and she had been hosting a series of special audio shows called *The Contactee Interviews*, where she talked with close encounter witnesses. These podcasts are of special interest to me because Anne would dig so deeply into the very human side of the contact experience.

Her voice came on just as I was stopping my bike next to a gap in the trees. From that spot, the big nest lined up exactly with the setting sun, making for some dramatic backlighting. This was the only good spot to get a view on the bike path. It's a narrow opening along the scrubby bushes and aspens that allows a view of the nest. From this one place, I could see the silhouette of the owl's head and tufted ears. The way the sun was positioned, there was literally a halo around the owl. I was staring directly into a shimmering aurora with an owl at the center, and all the while listening to Anne's calm and soothing voice.

It took a moment to realized that *she was interviewing me!* What I was hearing was the very first in a series of audio interviews from January of 2010, and I was the very first guest.

I have a ton of stuff crammed onto my iPod, mostly music, but also a lot of podcasts. I'm pretty sure I've downloaded all of Anne's contactee episodes, and that my interview would pop up at this moment was beyond chance.

What I also realized was right at that moment Anne was having brain surgery to remove a meningioma tumor. Before heading to town on my bike, I had read this Facebook message from Whitley: "Anne is in surgery now. There are probably about nine or ten hours to go. It is a very meticulous, exacting surgery. Pray for my wonderful girl!"

So I saw an owl backlit by the setting sun while listening to Anne's voice introducing me, and this happened at the exact moment she was having a very serious operation on her brain. This was an impressive cluster of points all in alignment. I am pretty sure this was a female owl sitting on her eggs. So I was looking at an image of motherhood in this same straight line. Some of the mythology surrounding the owl is steeped in foreboding and death, but I felt none of that. Instead, the experience was delightful and inspiring.

I posted this story, what you've just read, on my blog in May of 2013. This would have been within a few days of the synchronous incident. What I didn't share online, I want to share here.

A little over a week before this event, Anne had interviewed Trish and Rob MacGregor about their book *Aliens in the Backyard*. During this audio interview, Anne's voice seemed awkward and faltering. At one point, she spoke about Budd Hopkins and how he would treat some of the women he was working with while they were under hypnosis. Anne said that he sexually assaulted some of them during these sessions.[74]

I did not believe what she said. To me, it sounded like bitter gossip. I had worked with Budd in 2007 and 2008, at a point when I was wrestling with my own experiences. He even performed a hypnotic regression with me, but nothing much new emerged. This took place near the end of Budd's life when he was frail and weak. He was enormously kind to me during our time together, and I felt he treated me with a lot of respect. Budd died in August 2011.

Anyone in the UFO community knows that Budd and Whitley had a very well publicized clash. This traces back to the late 1980s when both of them, each in their own way, were the public face of the UFO abduction phenomenon. I feel I know Budd, Whitley, and Anne, at least as acquaintances. Each of these dedicated people have been very supportive of me and my experiences.

But I truly didn't know what to think of Anne's comments about Budd during that interview. I was angry, mostly because I found Budd to be so understanding in my time of very real distress. Anne's quavering voice and unusual comments seemed so unlike her, and within weeks of this interview she had a seizure and was rushed to the hospital. Soon after, she had brain surgery. In hindsight, her odd behavior was quite probably a sign of something very dangerous happening in her brain.

Leading up to that spring evening along the bike path, I was angry and judgmental. That's how I felt in the moments before I looked up at that mother owl, backlit by the sun, and listening to Anne *talking to me* in her steady, thoughtful voice. Right at that moment I felt a beautiful spirit of forgiveness wash over me. Listening to Anne's voice and seeing that owl, it was no longer possible to feel any anger. Some hard part of my heart melted away. The change was powerful.

I got on my bike and rode home. I felt like I had shed something brittle, and was now a new person. Since that moment, I have tried hard to live up to the power of that beautiful lesson.

I told this story among a small group of experiencers and researchers. We were all spending the weekend together as a sort of personal retreat. Something odd happened as we sat at the dining room table after our first dinner together. These folks were asking about my owl research, and I could tell by their questions they didn't quite understand the depth of what I was finding. I shared this story, the one you've just read, in the hopes of articulating the emotional power of some of these experiences.

We were all sitting at the same dining room table the following night, and a woman named Rachael said, "I need to ask you about the story you told last night, about the owl and Anne Strieber. Did you notice the candle went out while you were talking?"

Another guest, Ryan, chimed in and said, "Yeah, I noticed that too."

One more guest, Jane, said she also saw it, and she was surprised because the room was so still at the moment the candle went out.

I had no idea what they were talking about. Rachael explained that when I got to the end of the story, the candle in the center of the table went out abruptly. I asked when it was, and she said, "It was kind of spooky. It was right when you spoke about letting go of anger and the feeling of forgiveness."

Then, just as she said those words—at that very moment—the candle went out again. We were all seated at the same dining room table, and the same candle went out precisely when she said *forgiveness*, just as it had done the night before as I spoke that same word.

The UFO enigma seems like it can get bogged down within its own weighty implications. There is so much that is complex and impenetrable, but this lovely event with a candle left all of us feeling deeply reassured. The message being delivered was gloriously simple, that of forgiveness.

During the final editing of this book project it was announced that Anne Strieber had died peacefully, with her husband Whitley by her side. Anne's last words were spoken to her son, she said, "I love you." Later, she may have whispered the word "joy."

Chapter 22:

Owls and the Unconscious

A UFO abductee was recorded talking about her experiences. This audio was then played in reverse with an attentive ear listening for anything recognizable emerging from the babble. Here is a tiny excerpt of what she said, first written as spoken forward, and then transcribed in reverse:

Forward: 'cause she remembers an orange light, right?

Reversal: Care. The owls knew it was their memory ship.

The snippet spoken forward is a question, and the reversal is an answer. There is a nonsensical quality to the answer, but at the same time there's a sneaky kind of wisdom. What seems telling is that an owl shows up.

Reverse speech analysis is a rather curious but simple investigative tool used by some of the more open-minded researchers as they attempt to look into the paranormal aspects of the UFO phenomenon. This technique involves using a recording of a person talking, and then playing that audio backwards. If you listen carefully you can pull out some odd gems from this gibberish, what can emerge are surprising little phrases, and sometimes these can be quite clear.

Abduction researchers Eve Lorgen and Patricia Mason, both experiencers themselves, have worked together using reverse speech analysis as a tool to examine the recorded voices of UFO abductees. They were trying to see if any clues would show up in these recorded testimonies.[75]

Lorgen saw a curious pattern in the reverse analysis of these abductees—there were repeated references to owls. Beyond just owls, Lorgen was impressed that metaphors and archetypes would show up so consistently in the reverse speech. The challenge is to figure out if these metaphoric clues could indicate if someone is telling the truth, or if they're communicating something they only think to be true, or the reversal might be evidence of some form of internal conflict.

Here's another example of a short bit of dialog, both forward and backward, from a UFO abductee describing an experience.

> **Forward:** Oh, that's interesting. Maybe he (the UFO investigator) was too embarrassed to have another woman (abductee) call or something…

> **Reversal:** God throw off to move in with the mystery of mysteries. Teach babies to set that up.

This reversal has the kind of absurd mystical grooviness that I just love. No easy way to interpret the deeper meaning, but it sure seems to be hinting at something. It feels like a line from a poem, where much is implied but in a roundabout way.

I've listened to a lot of these little snippets, and some of the audio is warbled and indistinct, and you need to try hard to pick out what might be a hidden message. Other times you can hear very distinct dialog popping out from the droning cloud of nonsense, and some of these insights in the excerpts can be really impressive.

Some of the proponents of reverse speech analysis will declare that what emerges from this analytical technique is a person's true unconscious thoughts. They'll argue that you can literally hear the deepest levels of the human mind as it reveals its unspoken secrets. That would be tricky to prove conclusively, but the fact remains that there are some remarkable examples of someone saying one thing in normal forward speech, and a direct contradiction shows up when it's reversed. Or, it's a metaphoric reflection, or a playful jab.

Advocates of this kind of analysis will declare that it might be the ultimate truth detector. Again, tricky to prove. What's more interesting to me are the poetic statements that sound like clues to the unconscious intention of the speaker. These can manifest like ironic Zen koans.

The definition of a koan is a puzzling, often paradoxical statement or question used in Zen Buddhism. It's meant as an aid to meditation, as a way to train the monks to abandon dependence on reason and to force them into gaining sudden intuitive enlightenment. This means absurdity is the path to spiritual awakening!

Played backwards, Barack Obama's campaign catchphrase, "Yes we can," comes out as, "Thank you Satan." You don't need to listen carefully to hear this, it comes across pretty darned clear. This heavy-handed example can be interpreted as nothing more than pure coincidence, yet some will see it as absolute proof that our president made a deal with the devil himself. The more challenging (and the more fun) way to look at this, is to try to unravel any metaphoric meaning. What mythic symbolism is trying to make itself known?

Australian born reverse speech expert David Oates was interviewed by Lorgen in 1998 for the British magazine *Alien Encounters*. Oates had recently had his own UFO sighting in Bonsall, California, and a reverse speech analysis was done using the recorded interview about his own experience. He described seeing an enormous craft from his home near the coastline.

> **Forward:** ...so I walked out of the house, I'll never forget this, it was the most incredible thing...
>
> **Reversal:** They pull you with Samson's soul. Have to recognize that it was so big.

Wow, the line "They pull you with Samson's soul," sounds like a poet trying to dazzle his reader with heavy-handed eloquence. Other mythic and archetypal words show up in reverse speech. Obama thanking Satan is a perfect example. Wolves, deer, gods, and goddesses also show up— and each bring their own symbolic power.

What follows is a woman abductee's description of how there might be some sort of deception, the UFO occupants seem to be distracting people from the truth.

Forward: Part of it is truth detracting, trying to get people away from…

Reversal: My fair wolf speaking up. He passed his truth to the girl.

Patricia Mason worked with an abductee, Mary (a pseudonym), and during their recorded talks Mary spoke about the eerie glow under ultraviolet light, or black light. The assumption is that the alien beings leave a residue on the things they touch. Under ultraviolet light, this residue can show up as a visible florescence on the skin of an abductee, or at the site of a contact event.

When Mary heard about the use of black lights in abduction research, she went into her son's room where he had a black light set up to shine on a poster. She looked at herself in a mirror with the black light and saw an orange-pink fluorescent substance on her face. Mary then bought a better black light and found the same fluorescence on her chest and lower torso. She collected samples and had them sent off for analysis, hoping for an explanation. She did this three separate times, but never got an answer.

In the first of the three examples below, Mary is talking about the glow of the black light, and wondering about who might be analyzing the samples.[76]

Forward: …under the black light.

Reversal: The owl called within it.

Mary also told of seeing orange balls of light in her home, and described how they were dancing near the ceiling above her bed.

Forward: … pretty lights …

Reversal: The owl lead her.

Mary spoke about memories that were retrieved during hypnosis. She describes seeing a gray alien close up and how it frightened her.

Forward: ... and having this face with these two eyes ...

Reversal: See owl. Wishes you could see it. Send me back a net.

This reversal seems to reply to the spoken words about two eyes, in essence answering that it's an owl. This plays into the screen memory aspect, where the experiencer thinks they are seeing an owl, but it's something else entirely.

None of the remaining reversals mention owls, but they do point to the overall weirdness tangled up in the UFO mystery. An abductee named Jody (a pseudonym) was trying to explain the weird mind games that are part of the contact experience, and how the aliens seemed to be interrogating her. They showed her a picture of her and her brother laughing. They didn't understand and asked, "Why is this funny?"

Forward: Because it is. Look at the picture. Because it is.

Reversal: Zeta took it. First get the people. Zeta took it.

Zeta is a term used by some abductees to describe the gray aliens with the big black eyes. This title assumes their origin is the star system Zeta Reticuli. Anne (a pseudonym) is an abductee who has devoted her life to researching UFO and paranormal phenomena. She states bluntly:

Forward: Well, I'm just obsessed. I don't even have a job now.

Reversal: White bars. They're making a mirror outside. It's in their aura.

Sometimes the curious implications of the reverse speech are obvious, and sometimes it's baffling, but there still seems to be a deeper meaning. There can be a playful aspect to these clues. Below are some examples, all taken from the recorded voices of UFO abductees.

Forward: I don't know, all I have is a weird dream memory and...

Reversal: They amend these dreams, if they make 'em, I'm learning.

Most abduction researchers will take dream imagery very seriously. As noted earlier in the chapter, buried experiences might be showing up in the form of a dream. Another thought is that the UFO occupants are co-opting dreams, stage managing our subconscious with specific narratives. It's as if they are bypassing our sentient mind with projected ideas that are meant to serve some hidden purpose.

Forward: I guess psychically, you know, the girl saw something like a reptilian (alien), psychically with the third eye, but I didn't see it and she saw it.

Reversal: In the darkness...we seem to help the aliens.

Forward: Yeah, cause I have, uh...

Reversal: Ride on the gray.

Forward: The truth is the truth. It needs to be there, you know.

Reversal: Why in the gray deep seed. They pierced us, they pierced us, hey.

In the three reversals above, we get the words *aliens* and *gray*, and these would seem to represent the same thing.

David Oates has a lot of experience using reverse speech with people who've had UFO abduction encounters. He is adamant that this could be a very important tool when working with abductees, declaring that these techniques could confirm the reality of the experiences. Quite literally, he sees this as a form of lie detector.

Oates says an "experienced analyst can determine whether someone's experience, say a UFO abduction experience, was real or a hallucination, or whether [what] they think happened was really some [other] issue they need to work through. You can tell by the type of language and terminology which events were real, or imagined, or a blatant lie." These are bold statements, and it would be tough to prove that these techniques are indisputably trustworthy. What interests me so much more is the poetic symbolism that can rise to the surface in the reversals.

Oates has looked into both the spiritual experience and its UFO connection by using reverse speech analysis. This includes his own sighting from his home in California. The UFO accounts he's researched all seem to have an underlying theme, and in every case there is an emphasis on the spiritual state of our planet. He is convinced that these UFO experiences are connected with the redemption of mankind. As Oates puts it:

> If there's one over all theme in Reverse Speech, it's that the human race is in a sick and sorry state spiritually. We are spiritually corrupt. And that as a race we are so far off track from where we should be on a spiritual path. And it is time for change... It is time to take the next evolutionary leap in order for us to move to the next stage of human history... And that is the overall message in reverse speech, and that is the overall message I'm getting in the whole UFO field as well.[77]

Whitley Strieber spoke with speech reversalist Wayne Nicholson for his radio show in 2008. A week before this interview, Wayne recorded Whitley in conversation and then searched through those tapes for any hidden messages. What the listener got to hear was a conversation where Wayne would play segments of Whitley talking, both forward and reversed, and then the two would discuss any meaning that might be emerging from the reversal. One of these caught my attention:

Forward: She says that it was me from the future.

Reversal: The screech from the thieves.

In 1998, Whitley had spent several hours with a very unusual man, and he was saying that his wife Anne felt that it was actually himself coming back from the future. Whitley has called this man the Master of the Key, and he devoted a whole book to their meeting, titled *The Key*. The core of the story is a dialog between Whitley and this unusual man, it reads like a carefully scripted stage play where the master delivers wisdom to the student.[78]

Wayne said that the screech is a reference to owls, which is a common screen memory, and Whitley quickly agreed, saying he felt the same thing. Then Wayne questioned who the "thieves" might be.

Whitley stated, "Oh I know who the thieves are, if anyone picks up my book *Majestic,* you'll find that the triad of three grays are called 'the three thieves,' there really was such a triad in my life called the three thieves. So, in my opinion, the screech from the thieves, that's the visitors speaking with me. So I think it's a confirming reversal, and I think Annie may have a point... (laughing) That's very fascinating and very illuminating, because if it's me from the future, I'm doin' okay!"[79]

While transcribing the dialog from the audio interview with Whitley and Wayne, what you've just read, I was wondering if I should point out that Whitley laughed as he spoke about his conclusion. I mulled it over for longer than I needed to, should I or shouldn't I? Then I thought sure, why not, I figured it would lighten up something that could be read as overly serious.

Right as I typed the word "laughing" in the paragraph above, I heard an audible ping from my computer telling me an email had arrived. The message was from Wayne Nicholson, the man doing the reverse speech analysis of Whitley. I had sent him a note late the previous night asking if he could answer some questions for this book. He replied right as I was transcribing his conversation.

So Whitley receives a message where owls and gray aliens are seen as one thing, and he feels this might confirm that his future self came back in time as a messenger to talk to his present self. All this gets confirmed (at least to me) by an email synchro-ping from the speech reversalist himself!

My reverse speech analysis

It was months later before I finally spoke with Wayne, and I was hoping to get a comment or two on his work doing this kind of analysis. One of the first questions I asked was about owls, and he said they certainly show up in people's readings, but so do a host of other archetypal animals and symbols. I was impressed at the thoughtful way he treated this very unique methodology. At the end of this first conversation he suggested I undergo a reverse speech session myself, and I was quick to agree.

We made a formal appointment to record my voice. He asked me questions, and simply encouraged me to talk. I spoke about this book and what it covers, focusing on my own challenges with these elusive issues, specifically the stuff with owls and UFOs.

A week later, after he had analyzed my speech, we had a follow-up talk. Shortly before our call, he sent me a list of 38 little quotes gleaned from my spoken words. Some of these were easy to dismiss as nothing at all, yet a few of them knocked my socks off with their clarity and power.

I had told Wayne about Anne Strieber and the winking owl; this story ends the previous chapter. I had been deeply conflicted about sharing that account. It seemed important, but it was so emotionally charged, and I was worried it might come across as petty. Anne had died just three days before my voice was recorded by Wayne, and I was concerned the way it was written might be seen as disrespectful. Here is what I said.

> **Forward:** I don't know if you knew this, but Whitley Strieber's wife Anne just died...
>
> **Reversal:** The observers see the wolf.

Wayne said that the word wolf shows up a lot in reverse speech, often as an inner protector, or a symbol for personal motivation. Also, wolves will sometimes show up as a screen memory for gray aliens. Whitley wrote the popular horror novel *The Wolfen,* and he feels the wolves in that book were a stand in for the grays. But who are the observers? Could they also be alien entities? There's a lot going on in this little phrase, making any meaning difficult to untangle.

One very personal way to read it would be that, "The observers (the aliens) see the wolf (my personal motivation)." This would directly answer my own unease about whether to include the difficult story of Anne and the winking owl in the book. Another interesting reversal emerged as I spoke about Anne.

> **Forward:** She had a seizure and that was the source of her brain malady…
>
> **Reverse:** You know I'm here.

I can read this only one way. As Wayne was recording my voice, the spirit of Anne had been right here in the room with me. Some of the other reversals seemed to be encouraging me to be bold in how I proceed forward with both the research and my own life. Here's an example.

> **Forward:** The intensity seems like it could be too much at times. So I'm wondering…
>
> **Reversal:** You're no mouse.

I was talking about being overwhelmed with the emotional intensity of these experiences. Saying I'm no mouse seems an obvious statement that I have what it takes to live up to these challenges, a call to be brave.

Wayne is a sympathetic therapist, and I was impressed at his cautious approach. Yet he is open to the deepest interpretations, where the subconscious seemed to impart profound philosophical messages. At the same time, he was content to see some of the reversals as just a playful nudging without getting stuck in the mystery.

During our phone conversation, Wayne politely asked if he could share some of his own experiences. I replied, "Of course," but wasn't sure what he wanted to tell me. It soon became clear that he wanted my insights as a UFO researcher. I listened closely as he shared several fascinating stories. None of his accounts had hovering flying saucers or skinny aliens stopping his car on a lonely road, instead they were of a much more subtle nature. What he told me put him in that foggy gray zone without any easy answers. Like so many others, I see Wayne as one more of the maybe people.

My voice played backwards hasn't given me any answers, yet it has offered up clues and confirmations to things that I either already knew or strongly suspected. I take these little tidbits less as evidence and more as a way to deepen my own search. This is reassurance that I am on the right path, even if I feel lost. I refuse to be content with the easy answers. Instead, I'm eager to dive down into the deepest waters.

There are two more speech reversals from my session with Wayne that I need to share. These are both deeply revealing, but cannot be understood until I recount the details of my confirmation event in the last act of this book.

Chapter 23:

Owls Communicate

Rebecca Hardcastle Wright, Ph.D., has had enough experiences through-out her life that she is well beyond having doubts of the reality of her own contact. She is forthright about what has happened, almost disarmingly so. In 2008 she authored the book *Exoconsciousness.* The title uses the Greek prefix *exo* meaning "outside" or "external" in relation to our human consciousness. She advocates a bridge-building between humanity and extraterrestrials. Along with all her other experiences, Rebecca had a very revealing owl event.

It happened on a sunny afternoon in a strip mall parking lot in the suburbs of Phoenix, Arizona. She'd just left a restaurant, and felt com-pelled to look at one of the tall industrial lights looming above her. It was as if her vision was literally pulled up, and she was surprised to see a massive owl looking down at her from the top of that pole.

Rebecca felt she was receiving a psychic communication from that owl, and the very clear message was, "You are not who you seem to be."

She also felt an all too familiar sensation, *knowing* she was going to have a contact experience that night—and she did.

When we spoke together, she described this owl in such an odd way that I had to ask if she thought it was a real owl. She said no, it wasn't real in the way we would understand it. She sensed it was some sort of a psychic projection. Even though she described this owl as large, it was still owl-sized, and in a place where an owl might sit. But the top of a light pole in a suburban parking lot is hardly where you would expect an alien. This is one of many examples of how hard it can be to truly know what might be a real owl, and what might be a screen image.

Rebecca told me she saw an unusual number of large owls during her years in Phoenix. She said, "They came to me, they hooted, they were even there during the day. I knew they were a screen. I felt the ET presence through them." She describes this as a time of awakening, and it's worth noting that, like the owl, the Phoenix is also a mythic bird—one that symbolizes rebirth.

What's also fascinating is that the owl *spoke* to Rebecca. That it happened telepathically is consistent with how nearly all communication with aliens is reported. This is most often described as mind to mind, but others will say it's something deeper, as if it's soul to soul.

I've heard a lot of stories where an owl does something that could be seen as a kind of roundabout communication, like crossing one's path or showing up at a prescient moment. These actions require the observer to interpret a deeper meaning. This could be an obvious message delivered symbolically, where the witness understands it right in the moment, or it might take some time to decipher its metaphoric meaning. More clear-cut is when an owl actually talks to the witness, but this is rare.

The owl is a messenger in both ancient folklore and present day experiences, and sometimes these communications unfold in very bizarre ways.

Two owl downloads

A woman named Jessica sent me an email describing a powerful owl experience. She first explained her feelings of *waking up* to her own spiritual truth, something that began a couple of years earlier. This was a time of a growing awareness and emerging clairvoyant abilities. Her past seemed peppered with the kind of events that might generate psychic powers. She also saw a very unusual triangle craft as a girl. This, and other life experiences, seem to imply some sort of UFO contact.

She wrote to me about one specific night. She was lying in bed and having lucid experiences in a near-dream state. Jessica explained (italics my own):

> In this state the physical body is asleep but the mind is fully awake and aware, almost as if it's a meeting place between our world and other worlds.

314

She then described something unusual that happened around 3:30 in the morning, a time noted with consistency for UFO contact. She had just moved around in her bed and, although sleepy, she was quite aware of being awake.

> I could see in my mind's eye, or what some have called the third eye, an owl land on a tree branch outside of the house. In the next moment a silver blue beam of light came from the sky and was given to the owl, the owl then turned his head and beamed the light into my third eye, my whole head was illuminated with this light. I knew without words, and without seeing any ETs, that this was extraterrestrial in nature. It was just a knowing that I received a download... I KNOW this was not a dream, I was fully aware that I was given a download.

When I asked her what she received in the download, her reply was exactly what I expected, "In all honesty, I don't know. I feel the answers may come when I am ready, or it may forever be an unspoken thing." She said it feels like a gift and that she would be guided to an answer.

Jessica sent me this account because she wanted to know if anyone else had similar experiences. My answer was a cautious, "Yes." Although the details of what happened to her stand alone, the vibe parallels a lot of other stories. Other accounts might not match exactly, but they feel alike in their tone, and this includes how the download gets explained.

The account that follows is eerily similar to Jessica's, and it's an incident where I was present.

My girlfriend Andrea came home on a winter's afternoon, but her normal parking spot was filled by another car, so she parked in a different place than usual, just a few yards away. She pulled in facing the forest, and looked up between the dense trees to see a barred owl on a branch. If she hadn't parked in that exact spot, she would've have seen the owl. She called me from her cell, telling me to come out quick to see the owl. I grabbed my camera, ran outside, and we both stood in the cold and watched this handsome bird. It obviously knew we were there, but seemed unfazed.

Barred owl seen in the Adirondack Mountains, winter 2015

Suddenly Andrea said, "Something's happening." She had locked eyes with the owl, and felt it was impossible to look away. As she stared, things began to change. She described a glowing magenta light, like an aura encompassing the owl's body. The space around the owl started to shift, as if the environment itself was somehow warping. There was a waviness, as if everything outside the center ceased to exist.

I was standing directly behind her this whole time, taking photos of the owl. I am tall enough to hold the camera right above her head as Andrea described what she was seeing. From my perspective, the whole thing lasted about a minute, but Andrea felt as if time had stopped. The owl was entirely motionless for the duration their eyes were locked.

Later she compared the visual imagery to those garish paintings from India, where a halo of swirling colors surrounds the head of a Hindu deity; only it was encircling the entire owl. All the pictures I took clearly show a plump barred owl perched on a branch, there was nothing unusual in any of the images.

We must have been out there watching that owl for over ten minutes. It never moved, except occasionally turning its head. At one point we looked at each other and said something like, pretty awesome, eh? When we looked back a second later, the owl was gone. We both said how disappointed we were that we hadn't see it fly away.

The following morning Andrea saw the owl again, it was sitting on the same branch. She called me and I hurried outside. Andrea was standing at the same spot in the driveway as the previous afternoon. Within a few seconds of me arriving we watched the owl gently drop from the branch and float off through the trees. We both felt the owl was letting us see it fly away, as if it had heard us lamenting that we had missed seeing that the night before.

Months later I asked her if she thought this owl sighting was some form of communication. She rolled her eyes in exasperation, "Like, *yeah!*" She went on to explain she had received a download. I asked her what she meant by download, and she said, almost word for word, what Jessica had answered to that same question. Andrea described the download as "a strong sense of *knowingness*—as if something was imparted—and this would reveal itself when the time is right."

I pressed her for more, and she replied, "I don't know, all I can say is that I was shaking the whole time we locked eyes, like an intense vibration was happening *within*."

The term *download* is woven into the lingo of the "love and light" side of the UFO continuum. It's usually the aliens, not the owls, that will impart these mysterious messages. The implication is that this data is somehow hidden or blocked from the experiencer, but remains stored on their hard drive. Pretty much every abductee I've ever talked with will say *I feel that I have a mission, but I don't know what it is.* Sometimes this sense of mission is so powerful that they'll succumb to bizarre obsessions (like writing a book on owls). It's as if all these people are anxiously waiting for some cosmic software update so they can finally run this secret program that has been pre-installed in their minds.

When Andrea first pulled into that parking spot and initially saw the owl, she was talking on the phone with a close friend. They were discussing chapter three of a book by Buddhist author Pema Chodron. Andrea realized she had that book on her shelf, but had never read it completely. The first thing she did when she got into the house was open to that chapter, aptly titled: *This Very Moment Is the Perfect Teacher.* She read on, and the message was exactly what she needed to hear in that moment. Also, leading up to this sighting, Andrea had been working with a local shaman who felt the owl was her spirit animal with the message to confront her fears.

317

On the night of June 2nd, 2015, Andrea and I were quietly sitting together by the fire in the living room. We were both reading, and there came a point when Andrea commented under her breath, "Oh wow." I asked what it was, and she said, "This is so weird, this is the same thing that happened to me and the owl."

The book was *Calling on Extraterrestrials*, written by UFO contactee Lisette Larkins. Andrea read some passages aloud, and it described the author's experience of locking eyes with a hawk and receiving a download. Although it wasn't an owl, she described something eerily similar to Andrea's experience. The book was focused on how to contact and communicate with extraterrestrials, but it also has many personal accounts from Lisette's life.

This story that Andrea read aloud was about the author's struggle with a difficult decision. Her mood was down, and each day while walking her dog she would pass a yellow pick-up truck with the license plate that read "moping," and every time she would chide herself that she had to stop moping. It was as if that truck was a stand-in for herself and her mood. There came a day when she was driving with her boyfriend and she saw a hawk on top of the cab of that same yellow pick-up. She ordered her boyfriend to stop the car. She told him, "I've got to get up close. It's got a message for me." Then she got out to get a better look. She slowly approached the bird until she was standing only two feet from it.

> To me, this was no ordinary hawk. As I continued to inch forward, I was able to look deeply into its eyes as I was just inches from its face. As I did so I became mesmerized by some inexplicable force. All activity around me blurred, and I knew without a doubt that I was connecting with extraterrestrial life... A message was transferred from the hawk's eyes to my own. My scalp felt as if it had been plugged into a generator.

Just like my experience with Andrea, Lisette's boyfriend was taking pictures as she stared into the eyes of the bird.

... To me, I was communicating with the higher realms, and those realms had sent me an enlightened being who had taken the form of a hawk.[80]

I searched online, found Lisette Larkins' contact info, and sent her an email that said, in essence, we gotta talk. It was earlier that same day I had Andrea read Jessica's owl download account, and she noted the obvious similarity. This was also the night of a full moon. One detail that seems striking, Andrea's middle name is *Lisette*. Another little detail, when I picked up Lisette's book to transcribe the excerpt above, the bookmark left by Andrea featured a photograph of a snowy owl.

A few weeks later, after some phone tag, I finally spoke with Lisette Larkins. When I described Andrea's owl experience, she thought that was odd because she saw an owl on the day she received my first email. She was out by her swimming pool when an owl landed on a flag pole in her yard. This was unusual because it was the middle of the day and there was a lot of commotion. Kids were yelling and splashing in the water, and her dog ran to the base of the flagpole and barked up at the owl. It just sat there, unperturbed by all the ruckus below.

Lisette was also struck by the eerie similarities between Andrea's download from an owl with her own experience with the hawk. When I asked her what she thought it might mean, she answered without skipping a beat. She said the owl's message was, "Don't forget what you came here to do." She went on to implore the importance of meeting your soul's goal in this lifetime. This advice came from someone who tells of direct ongoing communication with alien beings.

Anticipating contact in the forest

In late April of 2013, Charis Melina Brown excitedly called to tell me she had locked eyes with an owl, and it changed her life. A few days earlier, she had gone for a hike in a forested area near her home with the direct intention to have a shamanic experience in nature. As Charis walked along the path, she clearly felt that this would be the day she would actually see an alien in full daylight, and this created a very potent sense of fear and excitement. Until this point, her lifetime of contact experiences came in the form of dreams, meditations, and psychic visions—yet she'd never seen any kind of entity.

Charis is a self-proclaimed *starseed*, a term used to describe someone who has made some sort of soul agreement in their previous life to play an important role during their present incarnation here on Earth. Starseed also implies a heightened set of spiritual and metaphysical skills, like psychic abilities and intuitive powers. I've spent a lot of time with Charis and this description seems entirely accurate.

Charis described the lead-up to seeing that owl. She had been walking for a while, and then she felt directed to leave the path. She struggled through the tangle of underbrush and then felt steered to a rock, "A specific rock, not that one over there, or any other one, *this* rock. I was told to sit on it." She felt she was being instructed exactly where to sit. *Move a little this way, no too much, move back, now turn a little that way.*

It took her a while to realize that the exacting way she was positioned gave her a direct line of sight through a tunnel-like opening in the bushes in front of her. She was suddenly aware of a huge owl, staring directly at her with its intense yellow eyes. They were precisely lined up, not more than 50 feet away. If she had been sitting just an inch or two right or left, she wouldn't have seen it.

Charis felt an immediate connection, and she telepathically asked the owl, "Are you a faerie or an ET?"

It replied in a very exasperated tone, "Why can't I be both. *You're* both."

Charis tried to explain what happened next, but her description sounded so mystical that it was difficult for me to follow. It began with telepathic communication between her and the owl, and then it seemed to morph into a transcendent multi-dimensional distorting of realities.

Upon reflection, she thought that it might not have been an owl at all, but exactly what it said it was, some kind of alien-faerie hybrid. She feels that a lot of things we call faeries are simply ETs that have been here a lot longer than we have, and over the millennia, they've merged into the natural world. Charis clearly stated that she experienced a direct download with this owl, and it lasted almost four hours. She describes the emotional intensity of the experience as shock, happiness, joy, gratitude, and terror.

I was told a similar story by a man named John. He had a day off from work and was going for a hike alone in the woods. Like Charis, he had a strong feeling that he would have contact that day—literally, that he might meet an ET during the hike. While driving to the park he saw a bumper sticker that said *Maybe Today*. It was a beautiful day, and he planned to hike to the top of a mountain.

As he was walking along the trail he saw a huge owl sitting on a branch staring down at him. He was spellbound.

> I must have stood there having a staring contest with this owl for five minutes. Finally I realized that this owl was not going to fly away and I that I couldn't just stand there all afternoon. I slowly started walking. The owl never broke his stare, slowly turning his head as I walked. When I looked back, its head had turned a full 180 degrees and it was still staring at me.

Later, when John got to the top of the mountain, he saw a shining light on the other side of the valley. There were other people up there, and he heard one guy anxiously blurt out, "I don't know what that fuckin' light is." The light remained stationary the whole time he was on the summit, and it didn't look like any kind of ship. In retrospect, he truly doesn't know what he saw, but thinks it could have been some sort of ET or inter-dimensional craft.

During his hike, he saw both an owl and some sort of unidentified light, and neither flew off as he stared at them. The next morning, as John was meditating, an owl began hooting just outside his window. That owl was heard hooting every morning for the next few months.

So, both Charis and John went on a hike expecting to see an alien, but both saw an owl instead.

333 and orchestrated clues

The events surrounding direct contact can be tailored in deeply personal ways, playing out as a sort of made-to-order theatrical presentation. The key plot points show up at the perfect moment in the narrative, as if directed at the individual needs of the observer. I cannot say this happens with all abductees, but it sure feels like a majority.

The phenomenon seems fully capable of reading the minds of the witness, as well as peering off into the past and out into the future. The timeline of life seems to be set up with preordained events along this path, each one carefully positioned to influence the next, as if some outside intelligence has intervened for some unknown purpose.

When I ponder my own experiences in this framework, I see a kind of methodical odyssey. I have been given just the bare minimum of clues, sometimes separated by decades, and this has forced me into the role of the detective, albeit an obsessive and introspective one. All this plays out as a form of deeply personal communication. Many others have been confronted with this same kind of interaction, where enigmatic details match their own distinctive quirks and persona.

An event took place along a quiet stretch of road in Canada on a winter's evening in 2003. A woman named Kaye (a pseudonym) was driving home from work when she saw a triangle craft moving slowly towards her, it was still early enough to see clearly in the fading light of dusk.

She slowed to a crawl as this object passed directly over her car. She rolled down her window and looked straight up at the bottom of the craft. The shape was a perfect equilateral triangle, and the size struck her as oddly small, even though she estimates each edge of the craft to be about 100 feet.

Kaye said, "It was just barely over the trees. I could have thrown a rock up and hit it." She described a dark gray surface, with a white light in each of the corners. The radio was on with the volume low, but her sense was that the craft was totally silent. It gradually moved over her, and she kept driving.

Kaye said, "I was watching it closely. I wasn't scared in the least, but for some reason I thought it better not to stop." Understandably, the power of this close-up sighting impacted her greatly.[81]

For about a year leading up to this triangle sighting above her car, she had been noticing the number 333. This began with her waking from a deep sleep and rolling over to look directly at 3:33 on her digital clock. Then Kaye would see the same numbers on the clock at work, on the license plates of cars in front of her, the change from purchases, or the price of a coffee and breakfast muffin.

Confronting this number everywhere was unnerving, and after months of persistently seeing 333, Kaye mentioned it to one of her co-workers. She wondered if she had somehow reset her own internal clock to repeatedly wake her up at 3:33. After that conversation, she started seeing 111, 222, 444, and 555. She felt as if some hidden intelligence were toying with her.

When Kaye acknowledged to herself that somehow 333 seemed most important, she was again plagued by that number. She had the feeling that this was some sort of a clue, but couldn't figure out any meaning. Then, oddly, right after the triangle sighting on that winter's night, the frenetic appearance of the 333 diminished greatly.

Like so many people who have had these experiences, Kaye has a strong connection to the world of psychic phenomena. For years preceding the triangle sighting, she participated in a small group that engaged in deep trance channeling, and her role was the primary note-taker. She is also dedicated to the serious study of both astrology and astronomy.

As an astrologer, Kaye uses a reference book known as an *ephemeris*. This gives the daily positions of heavenly bodies. The sun, moon, and planets are each given a numerical value listed in degrees and minutes; these numbers are used for astrology readings.

Later that same year, while browsing her ephemeris, Kaye noticed something odd. For the entirety of 2003, the number 3:33 appeared one and only time for the Sun, the brightest and most important astrological luminary—*and this fell on the very day of her triangle sighting.*

This manifestation of that ever-present number had a heightened significance, but she was entirely baffled as to what it meant. She was trying to explain her quandary by showing a co-worker the 3:33 in her ephemeris. She told him that she knew it was somehow meant as a clue.

At the very moment she was expressing her frustration at being incapable of putting the puzzle pieces together, Kaye looked at an aquarium in the office. She was shocked to see that the little catfish *Draco* had been chewing on his favorite treat, an English cucumber. She said, "It was almost like a magnet drew my eyes to the cucumber!"

The fish had eaten out the middle of the cucumber slice, so there was now a perfectly formed hole in the precise shape of an equilateral triangle. Seeing this, she realized instantly how all the clues were related and couldn't believe that she had missed something so obvious.

Kaye had seen a *three* sided craft, with *three* lights, and *three* points on a day that resonated 333 in the book she used to access the deeper meaning of celestial alignments. The implication is that the pilots of that craft must have known full well her passion for astrology, and then orchestrated her sighting on that very day with the intention of her someday finding this strange clue in the puzzle of her own life. That this realization was triggered by a slice of cucumber makes it all the more bizarre. The implication is that these cryptic clues had been purposely placed in her path for her to *notice* and then to *solve*. They were meant for her and her alone.

Kaye said, "I find it more than mildly amusing at this point that some of the clues are so *out there*, yet so interwoven like some puzzle tapestry, that virtually every serendipitous and bizarre thing that happens to me seems to be somehow oddly connected."

The appearance of these orchestrated clues is a clue in itself. It all points to something purposely toying with UFO witnesses. There is a sense that we are rats in a carefully constructed maze, yet we are incapable of looking up to see the examiners peering down at us, let alone understanding their agenda. Why this is happening seems unknowable, but it is happening.

While there is no owl in this account, it does show up indirectly. The catfish shares its name with *Draco the Dragon*, a constellation that wraps itself around Polaris, the North Star. In Greek legend, Draco was a dragon killed by the goddess Minerva and thrown into the heavens where we still see it each night. Minerva, as we know, has a companion little owl.

Also of note, the little catfish was named after *Draco Malfoy* from the Harry Potter books. This Hogwarts student had a Eurasian eagle-owl deliver the mail for him. But, every character at the school had their own owl as messenger. So, if this is a clue, it's a subtle one.

One more thing, in the initial 2015 print version of this book, this sub-chapter, '333 and orchestrated clues', ended on page 333. That was a funny surprise to the publisher and me.

Channeling an owl

I spoke with a woman who is both a researcher as well as having had her own direct contact experiences. We talked together in the busy setting of a UFO conference, and I asked her for her impressions on the connection between seeing real owls and the UFO phenomenon.

She is very soft-spoken and answered thoughtfully, "I have one person I'm working with who has had a lot of owl experiences, and she feels they will arrive shortly before an abduction, or just after."

This was early in my owl research, and she gave me the one answer that had been in the back of my mind, but until that point I hadn't dared to consider. I replied, "Well, that means I'm totally screwed!"

She smiled and tried to reassure me, "Now don't worry. That's been *her* experience, it doesn't mean it's happening to you too."

This has been the core question at the forefront of all of this: *Is this happening to me?* Have all the owls I've been seeing been foreshadowing abduction events? The funny thing is—I've had that thought right in the moment while looking at real owls. I questioned if these owls were some kind of sign of impending UFO contact.

The woman I spoke with is Jacquelin Smith, and along with having UFO contact experiences, she is an author, psychic, and animal communicator. Her first book from 2005 was titled, plainly enough, *Animal Communication*. She published a second book in 2010 that features the back and forth channeled conversations she's had with a wide range of animals, including cats, dogs, butterflies, jellyfish, a giant tortoise, and what struck my interest, a barred owl. The book is titled *Star Origins And Wisdom Of Animals: Talks With Animal Souls*, and most of the transcribed conversations were not with the animals per se, but with their souls. Other conversations in the book were with star beings that were inhabiting the physical bodies of certain animals. These communications revealed the personality of the visiting spirit as well as the deeper aspects of the animal's soul.

Jacquelin wrote: "All of this could sound sci-fi, but I had so many outrageous synchronicities while writing this book, all I could do was laugh and keep writing."

I understood this at my core. She could be quoting me because I've been at the receiving end of some freaky intense synchronicities while writing *this* book. Something is at play, and I feel it's urging me to keep at it, no matter how far off the well-worn path these ideas lead me.

Jacquelin has always had psychic skills, an interest in metaphysics, and a deep connection with animals. When she was 27 years old, she was in a serious car accident and had a near-death experience. While she was on the other side, she was told to come back. After this life changing event, her psychic abilities blossomed, something that is commonly reported following such a profoundly transformative event.

After the accident, she felt a need to combine her psychic skills with her love of animals; she tested this in 1979.

> One of my first experiences was with a Zebra. I was at a zoo and asked a particular zebra to come and stand in front of me. Within a minute, the zebra walked from the far side of the exhibit and stood in front of me. Then I heard the zebra ask, "What do you want?" I was off and running into communicating with animals.

It was a telepathic conversation with an owl that drew me to Jacquelin's book. Her initial owl connection happened in the springtime, it unfolded on a path that she would walk daily. She would see a barred owl perched on the same branch every day. Mostly it ignored her, but there came a day when the owl looked directly into her eyes. She felt a wonderful disarming sensation zooming through her body as the owl scanned her with its big black eyes. She started a conversation, and what follows is an edited excerpt from her book:

> ***Jacquelin said:*** *Hello. I am happy to see that you are volunteering to speak with me.*

> **The owl replied:** Hello. You saw beyond what humans call owl. You saw the star being aspect of me...

326

Did you look through me?

When you looked into my eyes and I looked into yours, you felt my eyes penetrate through your bodies. I was scanning you. I was checking out your aura as well as your physical structure... For you, this was a close encounter with someone from outside earth's realm (smile). But remember you are not of this world either. I am from the third universe beyond the universe in which earth exists...

Why have you come to earth?

My soul agreed to be part of an experiment on earth...

Thank you. What's your mission while living as an owl?

Owls bridge the earth and sky. We are part of a much larger group of beings and our overseers who keep the inter-dimensional highways clear and open in order to be accessed and traveled by All.

Thank you. What other roles do owls play on earth?

We are helping to lift the veil of illusion on Earth so that all beings can awaken and remember the truth that all living forms are One... Everything is energy...

Thank you. What else would you like to say about the work owls do?

One owl can cover a great distance when helping to lift veils and shift inter-dimensional energies. Owls assist with creating intersections and countless inter-dimensional highways so connections are clear and energies are integrated. This is the Creator's plan. It is Earth's desire to be shifting into higher frequencies and this takes integration of all energies... All current creations are shifting into new creations, but then again, this is always taking place. What messages do you have for humans? What do owls

327

mirror to humans? We bring the messages of seeing the bigger picture while being able to focus on the details... If you chose to look at us as a mirror, we reflect to you the part of yourself that needs to remember to look at the bigger picture of your lives as well as goals and details...

What thought would you like to leave with me tonight?

Fly above the Earth, fly beyond the Milky Way, and experience the vastness of the creative All. Be wise and open your inner eyes. See all around you the wonders of the Creator. They are you.[82]

The voice of this owl has a similar tone to much of what gets shared throughout the contact literature, and it fits in neatly with what other sources have said. Many points are consistent with what's reported by UFO abductees; the mind scan, the telepathic communication, and the beings coming here from some higher dimension.

Other points are almost word for word what a UFO contactee might say about themselves; that some part of their own soul had made an agreement to come here from some far off galaxy to play an important role. This would imply a visiting spirit, or some deeper part of themselves, is inhabiting their body to perform this duty here on Earth.

This back and forth dialog also parallels a lot of other channeled information. One good example would be the book *Conversations with God* by Neale Donald Walsch (who also had a near-death experience). Reality gets described in a similar way across a wide spectrum of channelers. They'll say things like: all living forms are one, everything is energy, the creator is within all of us, and everything around us.

Like much of the larger pool of channeled material, some concepts are rather hard to follow, such as when the owl said, "I am from the third universe beyond the universe in which Earth exists." Again, this fits a pattern. I am not saying that I doubt Jacquelin's sincerity (I don't), but what I'm seeing is an almost unified message seeping in from beyond the veil. I say *almost* unified because certain aspects of it are slightly nuanced, the message seems tailored for each source, whether it's a UFO abductee, alien, owl, angel, or God.

I spoke with Jacquelin on the phone as part of this research, and there were a few things I wanted to ask that weren't in her book. One question was answered before I even asked, and what she said didn't surprise me. She told me she was working on a third book about her own direct contact experiences with Star Beings. She avoids the term UFO *abductee,* choosing instead the term *taken* as a way to describe her experiences. I very much understand her reluctance to limit herself with the heavily loaded word abduction.

Both her near-death and contact experiences could be seen as part of an initiation into the role of the shaman. I also asked Jacquelin what the word shaman meant to her, and she shied away from thinking of herself as a shaman, but she recognized her role as an animal communicator could easily be seen in that light by others.

Jacquelin's laundry list of experiences fits cleanly into what I have been finding with people who tell of alien contact. They'll recount psychic skills, a near-death experience, writing books about their experiences, and using synchronicity to direct their path. But more than any of those points, she radiates a powerful heartfelt sense of mission. She is profoundly sensitive and devoted to her role as an animal communicator. She sees the human connections with animals as part of our overall relationship to the natural world, and all of reality.

There was one question I needed to ask. This was my own selfish request, and it triggered a remarkable response.

> **Mike:** If you do see an owl anytime soon, and you can communicate, I would love for you to ask why are UFO abductees and contactees seeing owls more often than, let's say, Joe Normal?

> **Jacquelin:** There are beings here from other galaxies and it's their mission to communicate with, and to open humans, and that is part of what the owls are here for.

At this point she struggled to say something. She seemed to be concentrating and even whispered, "Words, words," under her breath, as if she were challenged by something so limiting. When she spoke again, it was halting and slow.

Jacquelin: They are souls who come from other galaxies, who have chosen to be in owl form. Part of their mission is to assist with opening humans to ET contact, so you could say that they're part of the team. If someone is taken onto a craft, the owls are like the predecessors for the experience with certain humans. It might be deer for some and it might be owls for others.

I'm trying to put this into words. So, aboard there can be grays, mantis beings and reptilians, you've heard about this right?

Mike: Oh yes.

Jacquelin: The owls are working with all of them as a team, the owls are the Earth connectors. This is what they are telling me, that they are part of the whole team, they are the initiators. The owls call the human's attention to them, they are putting out a certain frequency, and then that creates a certain energy field and that then allows for the frequency of the humans to be adjusted to then be taken aboard in a safe way. Human's need to be comfortable in that frequency, so that the person isn't just blown away. Now that does happen sometimes, but the owls are doing their best.

Yes, it can also be a screen memory, so there is not just one function. They have multiple functions for the image of the owl, and how humans think about owls. And another thing, they are saying that they are the initiators, but this is an initiation of going aboard a craft.

So I look at it in that sense, they are using the owl symbolically, but the owl is still the owl frequency, to mirror to us in an archetypal sense, because humans think of owls in a certain way, right? There is an archetypal image that is mirrored to the humans, this goes in on a subconscious level and connects with the human's genetic memory bank.

Because humans think with symbols, they are touching us on that level, and that goes back to the beginning of human kind, and how we see owls. Not only here, but in soul connections in other star systems.

Mike: Did this come from your own research, or were you channeling? I ask because you weren't talking in generalities, you were talking to me! Everything you just said reflects my direct experience.

Jacquelin: I'm channeling, right now, this was the owls speaking, they were channeling through me. This is what the owls wanted me to tell you, the group-owl, or however you can say that. For what it's worth, I'll just say they wanted to let you know that these concepts are important to relate to humans so they better understand.

What it does is to demystify it so the fear can dissolve, which I love. So, their intention is positive, I love this, this, [their intention is] to announce initiation, that's the word they're choosing. I have heard this word in some of my experiences on different starships, the ETs have used that word with me, saying that this was an initiation for your soul's evolution.

Mike: Those are very large grand concepts, and that's what I'm trying to do. I'm trying to take these simple stories quite literally, I mean, if someone sees an owl in the woods, I recognize that there are these big, powerful, grand things behind that.

This short channeled dialog between me and an owl, with Jacquelin as the medium, cleanly summed up the entirety of this book project. That the role of the owl would be to *announce initiation* is exactly what has played out in most of the experiences I've documented, especially my own.

I don't pretend to understand how channeling works. It could be that Jacquelin was using her psychic skills to tap into my mind, and she merely told me what I wanted to hear. This doesn't feel like some parlor trick where the charlatan deceives me. The concepts are too complex and too cleanly tailored to my own needs. Instead, it could be that the channeled voice of the owl was really my own higher self, using Jacquelin to bring forth the answers I required. I say this only because the voice of the owl delivered precisely the message I needed, both as an author and for my own personal journey.

331

But more than that, I was given clues that sent me into deeper terrain. The concept of *owls as an archetype* was something I hadn't ever heard or even considered. This avenue of thought came from the channeled words of an owl, spoken aloud by a UFO experiencer. Thanks to Jacquelin, archetypes got its own chapter in this book. And it was this one idea, more than anything else, that summed up the central question of my inquiry, *why owls?*

So much of what has been reported in this book feels like it's lit up with a golden glow, as if it's all cheery and wonderful. That certainly isn't the case, many of the people I have talked with have suffered terribly. These experiences, both with UFOs and owls, have created confusion and chaos in their lives. It's not all love and light.

Many experiencers are devastated by the out-and-out trauma that can come with these intrusions. The challenge for them is to integrate what has happened and live their lives. Some might see their experiences in a more positive light, often after years of deep inward contemplation. A lot of the stories I have collected reflect this perspective. Others see it as negative, and yet they still manage to integrate these bizarre experiences into their lives. No story is the same, and nobody reacts the same. I've heard people tell me of being swallowed up in ecstasy, and yet there is still a very frightening aspect to this mystery.

Ben is one of the experiencers in this book, and he's seen a lot of owl in highly charged moments. He sent me a quick note in an online chatbox, "I'm not a 'hippy dippy all is new age' type person, but my sense after living with this my whole life is that it isn't harmful, it only broadens your scope of reality. But it certainly is difficult."

His statement reflects what most of the people who've shared their experiences might say.

I know what I *want* this to be. I would love nothing more than to find conclusive proof that all of this is benevolent, a grand unfolding for the greater glory of humanity. Perhaps that's exactly what it is, but *wanting* that doesn't make it so. There are enough stories of trauma that the scales keep swaying, leaving me unable to decipher any agenda behind this mystery.

We are confronting something complex that shares its secrets at a great cost.

Chapter 24:

The Touch of an Owl's Wing

I gave my first public talk on owls at the annual International UFO Congress (IUFOC) in February of 2014. After stepping off the stage, I was mobbed with people eager to tell me their owl stories. I took the time to sit and listened to each of their experiences. These accounts were all fascinating, and each in their own way confirmed what I had already been finding.

A while later, just as I had the chance to catch my breath, a fellow stopped me in the hall and said he had an owl story he thought I should hear. This guy had a special glow about him, and I asked, "Where should we talk?" What then unfolded could be the single most powerful owl story I have ever heard.

Jonathan (a pseudonym) and I went to the bar. He ordered a beer and I ordered a glass of wine. He spoke with a quiet voice and began talking about a friend who had been reading a book on the ancient folklore of the Native Americans. The book is titled *The Seven Arrows*.[83]

Jonathan's friend was reading this book during his lunch break while working for a timber scouting crew in a remote mountainous area of the Northern Rockies. He was all alone and lying on his back in the sun when he got to the part where the author describes how your spirit animal will find you. He then set the book on his chest and drifted off to sleep.

He awoke to the foul smell of something right in close to his face, he realized it was a big animal trying to smell his breath. He froze with his eyes closed, all he could do was hold his breath and play dead. After a little while, the loud sniffing ended and he heard heavy footsteps moving away. When he got up the nerve to open his eyes, he saw a huge grizzly bear lumbering off into the forest.

This man still had the book on his chest, setting on his heart, and it was open to the page that described how to find your animal spirit guide.

Understandably, that man took the bear to be his animal spirit, and not long after he gave the book to Jonathan.

Jonathan was sitting at home, deeply immersed in the book when he heard a knock at the door. It was his former roommate, and he was there to get all of his things that had been stored in the garage for the last year. The catch was Jonathan needed to give him a ride, along with everything in storage, to his new home. He was eager to get all his old roommate's stuff out of the garage, so he agreed.

Jonathan was a little annoyed because he had just gotten to the part in the book he had been told about, the point where the author describes how your spirit animal will find you, so he carried the book to his van in the hopes of reading during any free moments. He set it on the dashboard, open to the same page his friend had been reading when the grizzly bear had smelled his breath.

It was a warm summer night and the window was open as Jonathan drove. The former roommate was next to him in the passenger seat, and his present roommate came along for the drive, she was sitting behind the driver's seat. They were traveling on a desolate stretch of highway in Montana. The road wound along the edge of a lake on their left side, and there was another car following close behind them.

As Jonathan drove, he noticed something lit up at the outer edge of his headlights. It was gliding towards him from the lake side of the road, and seemed like it was on a collision course for the van. He slowed down and realized it was an owl, and it flew directly into the beam of his lights. He feared hitting the owl, and at the same time he was worried that the car behind him would crash into him if he stopped. This owl eased up close along the open driver's side window. It was so close that the tip of its large wing lightly stroked the side of Jonathan's face.

I sat in the bar listening to Jonathan tell his story, and watched as he used his fingertips to lightly caress his left temple. He said, "It was so gentle. It felt as if I had just walked through a spider's web and my face tingled."

At this point, the car behind him was now right on his bumper, and its headlights lit up the side view mirror like a spotlight. Jonathan told me:

I saw a sight I will never forget. This owl's head was only inches from my side view mirror. His huge eyes looked directly into mine as I stared back into his. It was as if I was caught up in some sort of hypnotic trance and couldn't tear my eyes away from the owl in the mirror. I can't explain it but I was locked in that wise-eyed stare. He flew at the exact same speed I was driving for what seemed an eternity compressed into what I'm sure was just a few seconds. How I stayed on the road I do not know. Then we separated gracefully and he flew off into the darkness.

Then he reminded me that all this happened while the book about how to find your animal spirit was right in front of him on the dashboard. It was lying open on the same page, in the same copy, that it had been on when his friend was nose to nose with a grizzly bear.

There was a lull in the conversation as I tried to make sense of what I'd just heard. Then Jonathan went on to explain that he had surgery as a boy to remove what the doctors thought was a tumor. There was a mass growing inside his skull, and it was affecting the vision in his left eye. When it was removed, it proved to be something entirely different than cancer—it was a small undeveloped fetus. The doctors described "it" as a self-contained embryonic sack that had tapped into a blood supply deep within Jonathan's brain. Somehow, he had been conceived along with a twin, and he is convinced this growth in his skull would have been his sister. Her fetus was subsumed by his head while they were together in the womb.

Jonathan described how, as a young boy, he always had a helpful voice in his head. He described this as a form of psychic communication with the spirit of his unborn twin sister. It was an ever-present part of his life, but after the surgery and the removal of this fetus, the voice was silent. He told me, "That marked the end of my relationship with my sister, a sister no one but me knew existed."

Jonathan has endured hardships, especially as a young boy. He had a series of out of body experiences, these happened in hospitals while under

anesthesia during traumatic emergency procedures. He remembers floating up off the operating table and looking down at his own body. It was
during one of these events that he heard his sister telling him, *I can't die
until you die.* He feels she is connected to him on some deep soul level,
and he's since had a lifetime of profound psychic experiences. He feels
she is still playing a role and using his physical body.

Then he turned slightly and touched his finger to a spot alongside his
left eyebrow. He told me, "See this scar? This is where my twin sister was
removed." He paused, then said, "And this is right where the tip of that
owl's wing caressed my temple."

Jonathan then described the challenges he's had dealing with his psychic abilities, and how they all trace back to his unborn sister. He tried to
articulate his own profound sense of knowing, as well as the strange synchronicities that put him in the path of certain highly charged events,
many of which involved death.

When describing the role his sister has played, he used the term *psychopomp*. This is an ancient Greek word, literally meaning *guide of souls*.
A psychopomp is a spirit or deity with the responsibility of escorting
newly deceased souls to the afterlife, and they are meant to play their
guiding role without any judgment.

He then told me about a deep moral decision that had been thrust upon
him, and how this was tied into his sister's presence, and his own psychic
knowing. He felt a responsibility to speak out about what he knew concerning a person who had recently died. Earlier that day, he had followed
through with this decision, and he told certain people news they didn't
want to hear. Later that night, he looked out his front door to see an enormous UFO hovering directly over the house across the street. This sighting was seen by lots of other people in the area and was reported in the
local news.

This soft-spoken man with the owl as his spirit guide was playing the
role of *messenger*, delivering hidden knowledge about death. He did what
he felt was his responsibility, and saw a huge UFO as a reply.

About a month after we met, Jonathan shared a poem he had written. Here's an excerpt where he reflects on his unborn sister:

> She hung around a short while after the doctor had her removed.
> To say goodbye and tell me she loved me.
> I wanted to follow but couldn't, that path was barred.
> I vowed to kill myself so I wouldn't be left alone in my sad state
> but she knew things and warned me not to.
> For our fates are intertwined and one is not to take their own life
> in this world she said
> We would be together again in the end she told me as she could
> not truly die either til that time comes.
> Where she resides now is neither in the land of the living nor in the
> land of the dead but somewhere in between.

Jonathan later went on to tell me a little more about the night that owl touched his temple. He said that the woman in the back seat had a perfect view of that owl as it flew alongside his van, all lit up by the car behind them, and she couldn't quit talking about it for weeks. He told me:

> She said it was the most spectacular thing she had ever seen. For me it was even more than that, more than I would even be able to attempt explaining til many years later.
>
> The owl has supernatural connotations going back to the beginning of time throughout all cultures. It isn't just a Native American belief or myth. Something very deep is linked and that spirit takes no heed of race, color, creed, or religion. It's something else.
>
> I suspect many a personal journey that no one has ever heard of has been triggered and ordained by a visit from the owl. What it all means is hard to decipher. Understanding it may be on an individual basis only, but nonetheless, the depths of this have yet to be plumbed.

I have listened carefully to what must be, at this point, many hundreds of owl stories. Each one is sacred to me, but what Jonathan shared with me in that bar is perhaps the most sacred of all. In our follow up phone calls and emails, he took on the role of mentor. He was further down a similar path to my own, and he knew it.

I've spoken at length with Jonathan in person, but we've had only one phone conversation. Near the end of that emotional call, which lasted over two hours, there was a beeping on my phone. It was an incoming call from my friend Phil. After I said goodbye to Jonathan, I called Phil back. He was the bearer of tragic news—two of our closest friends and co-workers had died in an accident. Tears were shed as he told me what little he knew of their death. It was weeks later when I realized I had been talking with a man who feels an intimate connection to a *psychopomp* when Phil called me to share the tragic news. I am not sure how much I should read into this, but I can only hope there was a gentle deity escorting my friends to the afterlife.

This book is more than just a collection of odd owl stories, it's meant to be a reflection of a mystery, something vital within the human spirit. Gathering all these owl accounts has been an awakening for me, and I have become a disciple to *the story*. There is a deeper message folded into many of these personal narratives, a message that goes far beyond seeing an owl in the forest. It is my sincerest hope that some of these stories will someday be shared around the campfire, filling the listener with some elusive understanding, and perhaps a more heartfelt way to proceed forward with their own lives.

Chapter 25:

The Messengers

This book started with what seems like a simple story, I saw a bunch of owls in the mountains with a woman named Kristen. That account might be easy to dismiss compared to a lot of the other more dramatic accounts in this book, but its impact on my life has been profound. It happened in the autumn of 2006, and in the aftermath I was hit by a flood of both owl sightings and absurd coincidences. This torrent of synchro-weirdness forced me to look into my own UFO memories, and I teetered on the tightrope of denial for the next seven years. I was very aware *something* weird was manifesting in my life, but I was terrified by the intensity of the message.

I've seen a lot of owls since that initial event, often in highly charged moments. I could easily drone on and on with these personal experiences, and what I am sharing here in this chapter is just a mere taste of my owl sightings. Some stand out as more persuasive, and there is a fable-like flavor to much of what I've experienced. It would be completely correct to say that all these owls have changed the direction of my life.

In early September 2009, I was on a seven-day trip teaching light-weight camping skills in the mountains of Southern Montana. Our little expedition had eight members, and we were backpacking just outside the border of Yellowstone. There was a small pond near where our shelters were set up, but the water was green and stagnant, and the team was disappointed in its quality.

As twilight approached, a student named Peter and I collected all the empty water bottles from our teammates and left camp. We walked to a nearby spring a few minutes down the trail. It was a lovely chance to talk with Peter. We spoke about our lives, and the curious paranormal events that seemed to flavor both of our personal experiences. I was quite open and told him that my life had been plagued with unusual owl sightings. I tried to articulate my worries, that all the owls were somehow connected to UFOs.

We got back to camp with bottles full of cold clear water, and the first thing we did was lie down to watch the darkening sky. This was a little bit unusual, something I had never done before, but we both did it that evening. The scene was peaceful, both of us were on our backs, looking up from the edge of a small meadow surrounded by dense trees. Peter is a psychiatrist, and the conversation seemed to get deeper and deeper as the sky got darker and darker.

There was a crashing noise in the trees above us, and the sky was suddenly filled with five owls. Yes—*five owls!*

They seemed big, over a foot from beak to tail, probably short-eared owls. This flurry of owls darted and swooped just above us for about ten minutes, and we were both thunderstruck at the majesty of what we were seeing. Eventually they all flew off, and once they were gone I asked Peter what I was talking about the moment the owls appeared.

He said I was speaking about my mother.

I said, "Really?"

He said, "Yes, they appeared right when you mentioned your mother."

That night I had a dream my mother was crying, and the image of her face was terribly sad. The next day I called her using a cell phone from high on an alpine ridge top, the only spot we could get reception. I asked how she was doing and was relieved when she said she was fine. Two years earlier she had been diagnosed with Alzheimer's, and her life was now terribly confusing and stressful. I was worried, and it was nice to hear her voice.

A formal plea

A few weeks later, I was again camping out with a different set of students. On our final night at dusk, three owls flew around our camp and landed in the trees, watching us as we cooked dinner on our little camp stoves. This was a worrisome time—I was seeing so many owls and needed some way to filter out the ordinary ones from the more prescient ones. It was too much, and I was scared.

Early in October of 2009, I walked into the woods alone and made a formal pledge, literally stating out-loud that I would no longer pay attention to owls that were out at my periphery. I live in a place where it's pretty normal to see an owl off in the distance sitting in a tree or on some fence post, and those would no longer count. I declared to the universe that I would only pay attention if an owl *crossed my path*. From this point on, an owl would need to swoop down in front of me, as if it were demanding my attention. Almost immediately after this verbal proclamation, owls seemed to respond—they would appear in front of me in flight, cleanly bisecting my path.

The first overt owl "performance" happened just a few days after making my plea. I was riding my bike through my little home town at twilight. While gliding down the middle of the street, I noticed an owl perched on a telephone line off to my left. As I got closer it dropped down, flying slow and smooth, passing in front of me right at eye level. Then it gracefully floated up and landed in a pine tree on the other side of the street. I had a few more sightings like this over the rest of that month, where an owl would blatantly cross my path.

After that, there was pretty much nothing for almost a full year. I saw a few normal owls off on the side of the road while driving, but those didn't count. Their overt performances had eased off to zero.

In September 2010, I spent several nights in a row recording and editing an audio post about the month of October 2009. This was when I had made my pledge in the woods asking owls to cross my path. That month stands alone in my life for its overwhelming load of weirdness. I was getting hit with so many synchronicities that I feared for my sanity. Speaking into a microphone and recording this podcast was emotional and time-consuming. I would edit late into the night, awash in a sort of compulsion to get these experiences out.

Here's where it gets weird. One early evening while riding my bike from a friend's house to my home, and knowing full well that I was on my way to work on that heavy-handed podcast—an owl swooped down from a telephone pole and silently crossed my path right at eye level. It landed on a fence post on the other side of the lonely road. I was immediately aware this was somehow linked with the podcast.

Now, here's where it gets *really* weird. Two nights later I was again riding my bike at twilight, this time on a different road. And again, an owl swooped across my path right at eye level. Just like the previous sighting, I was on my way home to work on that heavy-handed podcast.

These two back-to-back path crossing events came after a year of almost zero owl sightings. My interpretation of these kinds of owl incidents has been either, *you're on the right path,* or *pay attention*. But after having two owls cross my path while on my way to edit that audio essay about synchronicities and paranormal experiences, I was imbued with an even deeper dedication to be as honest as possible.[84]

As I write out these events, I'm surprised at how many of these owl sightings involve me on my bicycle. I know I've said this already, but there is a paved bike path right in front of my house that goes straight into the center of town. Here is one more bicycle story.

It was late in the afternoon in mid-October 2010 when I looked out my window and saw a woman named Carol (a pseudonym). She was my girl-friend from exactly a decade earlier. She was now married, and she was with her three kids heading toward town on the bike path. Two of her children were on bikes, and she was pushing the youngest in a jogging stroller.

I was on my way out the door when I saw her, and I hopped on my bike and quickly caught up to her and her children. I rode slowly along-side Carol and we chatted. Her only daughter, about nine years old, was on a bike a little ways in front of us. At one point, her son said he had cold hands and she pulled out a pair of gloves for him. Right then, Carol and I both laughed, each of us realizing I had given her those gloves as a gift a decade earlier.

Without any prompting from me, she talked about all the animals we had seen together when we were dating. I told her that recently I'd been seeing a lot of owls. Less than two minutes later, I saw an owl fly across the bike path (yes, *across my path*) and land on a low branch in a tree about fifty yards ahead of us. I was the only one who saw it, and the way the bike path turned, I caught just the briefest glimpse.

This happened near a bridge in a small stretch of cottonwoods along the river. I whispered to the two children, neither of whom had seen it, that we needed to find the owl. We all crossed the bridge, set our bikes down and tip-toed along the path. It was only a few steps before we saw a handsome great horned owl on a low branch in a tree. This was an amazing sighting in the daylight, and I think this is as close as I've ever been to a perched owl. I'm not exaggerating, it was probably less than fifteen feet from where we stood on the bike path! It was a little over a foot tall, with those cat-like tufts that look like ears, and bright electric yellow eyes. It stared at us for about a minute, then casually flew off. It felt like it had been posing for us. Everything about the experience was beautiful.

After the owl flew away, the daughter started yelling to her mother, asking over and over, "Mom, do you love Mike? *Do you love Mike?*" This wasn't awkward at all—it was entirely endearing.

Carol never saw the owl, but her son and daughter were right up close to the tree where it had landed. All three showed up on the hiking trail the morning after my initial sighting of three owls with Kristen in 2006. I carried her boy, and the little girl held Kristen's hand four years earlier as we walked down the trail towards my car. I'll add that we all saw a big beautiful moose just off the path that morning.

I live near a non-profit raptor center. They take in injured, ill, and orphaned birds of prey in the hopes of returning them to the wild. I recently had the chance to speak with a doctor who was working with the veterinarians and naturalists at the center. I briefly told him about the experience with Kristen and seeing three owls on two separate occasions within a few days—the story that begins this book. I asked if he'd ever heard of anything like that, and he said no.

Then I told him another story of seeing five owls fly above me and my friend Peter while lying on our backs in a meadow as we talked about metaphysical issues. I asked if he had ever heard anything like that. Again, he said no. He hinted that such things simply don't happen. Then I told him another of my experiences, and another. He looked at me with concern. As I talked, I recognized he was getting uncomfortable. I shared more, and he began moving away from me. It was a curious feeling to see an owl expert look at me as if I were insane.

A lone owl and the full moon

> Last night I saw a lone owl, and the experience was
> absolutely magical. I was alone in the Tetons, and
> was sleeping out under the stars in one of the most
> beautiful meadows imaginable.

These are the opening lines of a blog post dated August 13th, 2011. I travel in the mountains with very little on my back. I had checked the weather before leaving home for a single night of camping, and the report promised a calm clear night—and that meant no tent and thus an even smaller pack. This was the night of the full moon, and I needed to be out there! That night I hiked right to the point where it was getting too dark to see. I simply set my pad down on the ground and climbed into my sleeping bag. There is nothing in the world I love more than sleeping out under the stars. The full moon was rising in the east, and I watched it creep its way up above the big peaks. I was awash in awe and amazement.

I spent the next half hour or so lying in my sleeping bag reading *The Handprint of Atlas* by an author with the pen name Sesh Heri. The book is about synchronicity, UFO contact, and the alignments of important land features. Much of the book is devoted to examining the alignment of global ley lines, both to significant sites on Earth, and points in the cosmos.

I was reading by headlamp, and was startled by a blurry swoosh right above my face. I looked up to see a huge bird land at the very top of a nearby dead tree. The moon was full so I could clearly see the silhouette of a huge owl. It didn't have the cat-like ear-tufts, so I'm guessing (by its size) that it was a great gray owl. I'll add that it looked way too big to be perched on such a spindly little branch.

I turned off my headlamp, and stayed still on my back. I watched the owl for maybe ten minutes, and it was looking right at me the entire time, its body hunched in a pose of scrutiny. Now here's the amazing part. From where I was lying on the ground, the tree with the owl was precisely back-lit by the full moon. The symmetry was perfect. From the owl's point of view, the shadow of the thin tree would have been directly across my face.

344

alignment of a full moon and an owl

I was seeing something spectacular. A huge owl had landed on *that* exact tree, when I was lying in *that* exact spot, and when the full moon was in *that* exact point in the sky—all while reading a book on mystical alignments. It felt crystal clear that something more was at play than just mere chance. I even did an illustration to define what I saw and posted it on my blog.

I asked a series of questions from my sleeping bag: What are you trying to tell me? Can you communicate with me? Why are all you owls showing up in my life? Is someone watching me through your eyes? If you want to tell me something, can you give me information through my dreams? All those questions were asked out loud, addressed to an owl as it stared down at me. Unfortunately, I didn't have any dreams that night, at least that I remember.

The owl scared me when it left. It gently dropped off the top of the tree and flew away from me, but in the dim light, it looked like it was zooming right at my face.

Earlier that evening, I saw something in a perfectly clear sky while hiking. The sun was setting behind me, and I was facing a bright light in the east. This was probably nothing more than an airplane reflecting the sun. It was moving north to south above the mountains, its speed and altitude seemed like a normal airplane, but it was brighter than anything I've ever seen in the sky. I remember thinking it looked like a flying mirror.

More about the short trip. I saw a black bear eating huckleberries while hiking into the mountains, and I saw a wolverine in the early morning sunshine on the way out. Both were a safe distance away, so there was nothing intimidating about either. Bears are rather common to see, but it's extremely rare to see a wolverine, so I felt perfectly blessed. Bear, owl, wolverine—a trio of powerful animal totems in less than 24 hours.

My confirmation event

To better understand this final story, or more correctly, this set of stories, I'll need to share a few things about myself. These are important points that'll give you a better idea of who I am. I have spent a lot of time doing professional outdoor wilderness work as well as my own ambitious personal travels, starting back in the late 1980s. I've taught camping and mountaineering in all seasons, including winter, spending up to a full month traveling in some of the most remote areas of North America. My classroom for over two decades has been the pristine mountains of the Rockies, Canada, and Alaska.

I feel very comfortable alone in the wilderness, and equally comfortable sleeping outside under the stars. I have excellent map skills, both using and creating maps. These are all things I dearly love, and each will play a part in this transformative experience.

I've been using the term *paradox syndrome to* describe some of the more complex stories. As noted earlier, these accounts play out as a tangle of messy threads with clues leading off in countless directions. This makes any easy interpretation impossible, but at the same time, for me it's a form of confirmation. I've come to trust these chaotic narratives, especially when an owl is involved.

This heightened complexity defines what I have come to call my *confirmation event.* The core of this experience took place in a cold, dusty corner of Southern Utah. Until that point, I'd never truly been able to say that I've had UFO contact. I certainly would not have described myself as an abductee, it wouldn't have felt honest. The problem was, at that point in my life, I'd already had enough unusual experiences that I knew with certainty that *something* was going on, but I fought any implication that I might be a UFO abductee. All that changed on the night of March 10th, 2013.

*   *   *

It happened while traveling back home to Idaho after an annual UFO conference in Arizona. I was driving north on Highway 89 through some of the most beautiful areas of Southern Utah. My plan was to find a secluded spot to pull off alongside the highway and sleep out under the stars. I've traveled a lot around the West and this kind of camping is normal for me. I do it partly to avoid paying for hotels, but more than that, it's something I dearly love.

I pulled into a nice spot around 9 p.m., right off Utah Highway 20 and just a few miles east of I-15. I got out of my car and walked around a little bit with a headlamp to stretch my legs. The area had low bushy junipers and these divided a series of beaten down roads and little turnouts. Plenty of people had been here before, and typical of this part of the West, there was some litter and evidence of campfires. This was a cold Sunday night, so I wasn't worried about anyone else pulling in. It was a perfect spot to sleep out. I set my thick sleeping pad down in the dirt right next to my little Subaru. Then I climbed into my big winter sleeping bag, put my head on my pillow, and it wasn't long before I drifted off to sleep.

At some point, probably around midnight, I woke up. Given the dry desert air and the cloudless night, the stars were spectacular. I was completely at peace as I looked up at the big, glorious sky. From where I was lying, I could look up at a ridge line of rounded peaks off to the south, and I noticed something odd. I saw what appeared to be a large round structure perched on a gentle saddle between two small hills. My first thought was that it was a big round house, it was low and wide with a row of lights or windows around its circumference. It seemed like the kind of

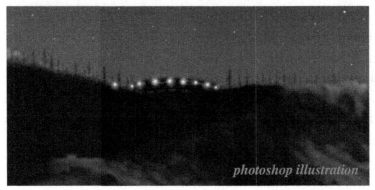

photoshop illustration

What I saw throughout the night from where I slept

fancy home you might see facing the ocean in Malibu, but it was way out of place in rural Utah.

While lying there, I thought to myself, *that looks just like a landed flying saucer.* I feel like my intuitive skills are pretty good, so if this really was a flying saucer, I would know it. I should've felt some sort of internal anxiety, but I didn't. The mood was calm and peaceful, so after a long while of staring up at that round structure, I rolled over and went back to sleep.

I woke up again a little later to the sound of a coyote howling somewhere right near my head. I scanned the sagebrush near where I was lying, but there was nothing to see. It was close enough that if I'd tossed a dog treat underhand from my sleeping bag, this coyote could've caught it in his mouth. I've spent half my life out West, and over those decades, I've slept out in a lot of places just like this, and I've heard a lot of coyotes. But I've never heard one that loud and that close—it was amazing and I felt blessed. I didn't do anything, I simply rolled over and went back to sleep.

I woke up a third time, and there was a light on the ground near me. It was on the other side of a clump of bushes, close to where I was lying. It didn't seem like a car headlight, and it didn't seem like a flashlight either, just a motionless white glow. I sat up in my sleeping bag to try and see what was on the other side of the bush. I even did the thing where you move your head back and forth in the hopes of getting some glimpse of what the light might be. Eventually, I shrugged it off and laid back down and looked up at the big round structure on the hilltop. I noticed one thing, there was now a single dot of light a little off to the side of the structure, and it hadn't been there before. My impression was that someone had turned on the lawn light in the yard of this enormous house. I was staring up at this round structure as I fell back to sleep.

It was still dark when I woke up the next morning. I felt rested and tossed all my sleeping gear in the back of the car and started the drive north to Idaho. Now here's something interesting, I don't actually remember looking up on the hillside that morning. I may have—I just don't remember. The drive was uneventful, but I had a nagging question in my mind that afternoon when I arrived back home to my cabin.

I got on my computer and used Google Maps to locate that big round building. I quickly found the exact location of my sleeping spot, but the weird thing is that I couldn't find anything on the satellite image that would match the circular building. I am very skilled with maps and interpreting topography, and I feel confident that I zeroed in on the precise spot where the big round structure should have been, but there was nothing, no roads or buildings, just an open meadow on a hilltop. It was 1.6 miles between where I slept and the site where the round structure should've been. This meant that the building would have been enormous.

So, I did exactly what I do in this kind of situation: I wrote a blog post about it. I shared the experience of seeing the round structure from my sleeping bag and then not being able to find any evidence of it on a satellite map. I even did an illustration of how that round structure looked from where I was lying. This essay was posted on March 12th, at 12:34 in the afternoon. I didn't notice the time count until days later, and that 1234 number sequence is a powerful clue.

A year later, I traveled back to this sleeping spot in southern Utah. I was desperately curious to know if there was, in fact, a huge round building perched on that hilltop. I found what I already knew in my heart—that there was nothing there, just an empty ridgeline dotted with small trees.

Back to the afternoon of March 12th. I was standing near my desk shortly after adding the post to my blog. Everything about the scene was perfectly ordinary, but I was suddenly hit with this odd sensation. The only way to describe it would be an instantaneous visual download—the term *psychic flash* feels very accurate. I clearly saw a map in my mind

Psychic flash seen in my mind's eye

with a straight yellow line running west to east with three distinct markers on it, and I knew this was the Four Corners area of southern Utah.

This vivid psychic download lasted barely a second, but the image was seared into my mind's eye. So I took one step over to my desk, sat down at the computer, and started creating a map. I knew exactly what the markers on each end of the yellow line were. The western marker was the event that had just happened on March 10th along Highway 20 in Utah. The eastern marker was the site of an event from May of 2010, right outside the town of Dolores Colorado. I'm in no way exaggerating—there was a sense of *absolute knowing* about these points. The two outside points were at each end of a 231 mile long straight line. Initially, I didn't know what the point in the middle might be.

*   *   *

The story of Byrd, like so many of the experiences in this book, plays out like its own novel. I was with my dear friend Natascha, and she had come from her home in Germany specifically to travel and camp with me around the Four Corners area of the desert southwest. Natascha and I had met at the 2008 Laughlin UFO conference. We became very close and planned this trip together. Like so many people in this book, I would have to put her in the maybe category. She's had a lot of very strange experiences, some of which seem to imply UFO contact.

It was during this road trip that we pulled into the town of Cortez Colorado after spending the day exploring the ancient cliff dwellings of Mesa Verde. My brakes were acting funny, so I took my car to an auto shop a few blocks off the main street. The mechanic brought it into the back and told us to wait. A little while later he came out, and while wiping his hands with a greasy rag, he said, "I can't let you leave town—*or you'll die.*"

I was obviously taken aback by his dramatic comment, but he carefully explained that the brakes were at the point of failing and it would've been dangerous for me to drive on the highway. So legally, he wasn't allowed to let me have the car. Then he added, "And it'll be five days before we can get the parts." So, Natascha and I found a cheap rental car, and our plan was to drive around for the next five days.

It was late in the afternoon by the time all this played out, and the hippy espresso girl at the local coffee shop pointed us to a nice place to camp out that night. We followed her directions out of Cortez, driving a few miles down the highway to the very small town of Dolores, Colorado. From there, we drove a forest service road out to a beautiful camping spot in the woods. We found a secluded site with an old fire ring and some broken beer bottles, perfect for our one-night camping needs.

We set up our tent, then headed back into Dolores and had pizza at a brewery just off the main street. During dinner, Natascha was quite emotional. She was feeling sad and didn't know why, crying off and on while we ate. After dinner, we went back to the campsite, climbed into our small tent, and quickly went to sleep. This is when things got strange.

I was suddenly jolted awake—Natascha was screaming. My instantaneous response was to bolt upright and scream with an intensity that would be hard to describe. I was screaming in fear, sure enough, but it was also a primal outburst of defense. We were both in the throes of something powerful, and I don't know if it's possible to accurately explain the ferocity of this sensation. Natascha and I both tell the story the same way—we awoke into a place of overwhelming terror.

I've spent years of my life sleeping out in tents, and it's an environment I'm very comfortable in, but this was different. If a grizzly bear had ripped through the tent and put its jaws around my throat, I would not have been as scared as I was in that moment. I have *never in my life been* frightened in a way that would come close to that moment. I've since described it as *synthetic fear*, this is the only way to articulate the absolute irrational intensity. It felt as if my very soul was at the precipice of being extinguished.

I switched on my headlamp, held it in my hand, and asked Natascha what happened. She couldn't answer, she was paralyzed in terror. I actually had the wherewithal to say, "Tell me the first thing that comes to your mind. Don't think, just tell me what happened."

She said almost nothing, only whispering, "I saw a face."

This primal fear lasted for maybe ten minutes, and then suddenly both of us were asleep. It seems like we went from a panicky adrenaline freak-out to total unconsciousness in the snap of a finger.

May 13th 2010, near Dolores Colorado

The next thing I remember was floating.

I felt the very tangible elevator-up sensation while rising off the sleeping pad, a feeling that was eerily familiar. As I floated upwards, I saw a big glowing mandala figure to my left, situated in a very specific point near the door of the tent. It was a simple circle about the size of a large pizza pan, with a lone dot in its center. This image was strangely flat, as if it was void of any dimensionality. Right in that moment, I was reminded of a blurry cataract image that had appeared in my right eye over a year before—more on that shortly.

I continued floating up and passed directly through the top of the tent. It was almost like I faded through it, like a lap-dissolve in a movie, and I was now in a strange white realm. As I floated, I was repeating to myself, *"I need to remember this. I need to remember this. I need to remember this…"* I have no memory of being on board any kind of craft, just this totality of white light. There was nothing but an unending whiteness.

At some point my repeating chant changed to, *"Am I on a table? Am I on a table? Am I on a table?"* I have absolutely no sense of being on any table, but those were the words in my head. I didn't understand where I was. All I can say is there was a mysterious realm with a uniform white glow around me. Was I on my back, or was I upright? Was this a dream, or was this really happening?

The next thing I remember was hearing Natascha, in her German accent, saying, "Mike, you're floating!" And then—whoosh—I was back in the tent. I didn't wake up, and I'm quite certain Natascha never said I was floating, but that's how it plays out in my mind. Unlike the initial jolt of fear in the tent, this vivid sensation of floating up into the white realm was curiously void of any emotion, it felt neither good nor bad.

The next morning was sunny, the birds were chirping, and things seemed perfectly normal. We talked about that paralyzing fear while still in our sleeping bags. At that point, I hadn't told her anything about floating up into a white realm. I simply asked Natascha, "Last night all you said was 'I saw a face.' Please, what did you see?" She replied, "I don't know. I can't describe it." I pressed her, and she said, "I saw the face right there." And she pointed to the exact spot where I had seen the glowing mandala.

I asked what it looked like, and she said, "I can't say, but the only thing that seems to match is that drawing you did, of the thing in your eye, the face in the circle from your blog."

Again, I hadn't shared anything, but she pointed to the spot where I'd seen the floating mandala, and she described it the exact same way I had—as *the image in my eye.*

This requires that I fill the reader in on another strange story. During the summer of 2008, I began noticing that lights at night looked different. Things like streetlights and the full moon had a shimmering halo around them, something I had never seen before. Later an optometrist diagnosed me with a small cataract on the lens of my right eye.

It was over a year later, in October 2009, while lying on my back in a park in Pasadena, I saw something bewildering—something only I could see. It was a lovely afternoon, the sun was shining, and my face was pointed upwards. I squinted, and then opened my eyes just enough to let a tiny amount of sunlight filter in through my eyelashes. I was seeing a psychedelic lens flare in my vision while in this relaxed state of concentration.

image within my eye

pencil sketch   how it appeard in my eye

Because of the cataracts in my right eye, I was seeing these slightly distorted halo type blooms as I squinted at the sun. Rather than a true circle of light, they appeared as doughnut or mandala shaped. I had noticed this effect a few times in the previous year. But that afternoon, in the sunshine in that park I saw, quite clearly, *the image of a little face* in the center of this shimmering optical effect. I could distinctly focus on it. There was a vivid rainbow of colors all warped around this perfectly-defined little face. It was distinctly skull-like, and at the same time, it had that big-eyed alien look. But more than anything, *it looked like me!* Bald,

with big eyes, and sideburns too. This felt like a weirdly personal caricature.

The little face was flawlessly symmetrical, and it was framed in bright
swirling halos. The body appeared to be seated in the lotus position, so it
had the feel of a Hindu deity in one of those garish paintings.

About a week later, I drew an image while lying on my living room
floor with a clipboard and a pencil. I faced into the sun as it shone through
a window while squinting my eyes, and again I saw the little face. It felt
important to draw this vivid image, like I desperately needed to share
what only I could see. This, like most of my odd experiences, became a
blog post.

It was this image, the drawing of the little face, that both Natascha and
I felt we had seen in the tent that night.

Back to that morning with Natascha outside Dolores. When I got out
of the tent, I walked around hoping to find some clue that might help
explain what had happened the night before. I was looking for a burn mark
on the ground where a flying saucer had landed. I didn't find one.

There are some other odd details with this story. Later that day when
I took my shirt off, I had a long scratch that started at my left shoulder
and went down to my belly button. This didn't make any sense, because
I certainly would've remembered getting a scratch like this. When I first
looked, there wasn't anything that unusual about it. It looked like a thin
little scratch, like maybe a single cat claw, or a rose thorn had run across
my skin. But when you looked at it closely, it wasn't a scratch at all. It
was a row of tiny, raised, fluid-filled blisters, all bunched together. They
were so small that you couldn't see them unless you really looked. It was
painless and washed off in the shower a few days later.

After the scratch was gone, both Natascha and I sort of exclaimed,
"We should have taken a picture!" We both think of ourselves as UFO
investigators, but it never occurred to either of us to take a photograph.
We were on vacation, and we were taking pictures of every cactus and
sunset, but we never pulled out a camera to document this very unusual
scratch.

We took down the tent, packed up, and drove to the little coffee shop on the main street of Cortez. I made a phone call to Miriam Delicado, a friend who's had her own profound set of UFO contact experiences. She has spent a lot of time down in the Four Corners area, so I was hoping she could help us. So I asked, "Listen, we're stuck for five days. What do we do?"

She didn't hesitate. "Here's what you need to do. Drive down to the Navajo Reservation in Arizona and visit Canyon De Chelly." Then she told me how to find a Navajo friend of hers who would lead a traditional sweat lodge ceremony.

Both Natascha and I were excited about this plan, and for the next few hours we drove south through native lands in our rent-a-car. Canyon De Chelly is one of the most beautiful and magical places on earth, and we spent the afternoon exploring the towering corridors of red rock with a Navajo guide. The next morning, we took part in a sweat lodge lead by a local man with strong connections to the land. It took place on a sandy plateau near the rim of the canyon.

I was naively unaware of what I was getting myself into, it felt like I was proceeding without intention. It was more like I was being pulled toward that sweat lodge, rather than actively seeking it. The lodge itself was a low domed tent-like structure made from arched metal rebar and covered in old blankets, and there was a fire pit alongside for heating the rocks that would be used in the ceremony. When I entered the lodge, I wore a bathing suit, and my bare chest displayed that long red scratch. There were eight of us in the dark cramped shelter, with a pit in the center for the hot rocks.

The Navajo who led the ceremony spent the hours talking, chanting, singing, and drumming. It was mystical and playful all at the same time. I felt rooted in my own world, and simultaneously connected to something beautiful and ancient. The overriding theme was to surrender to the heat.

There were four separate sessions within the dark little lodge, each one getting progressively hotter. The final session was insanely hot, and everyone inside needed to lie down to breathe the cooler air near the dirt floor. I tried to fully surrender, not only to the heat, but to the entire ceremony. This was a hauntingly beautiful experience for both Natascha and myself.

That was a long set of stories to describe an experience that began with someone telling me, "You can't leave town or you'll die," and ended with a shamanic ceremony of death and rebirth.

*   *   *

The events from May of 2010 and Dolores Colorado define the eastern point on the map I saw in my mind's eye during a psychic flash. Curiously, Natascha had studied past life regression hypnosis with the late UFO researcher Dolores Cannon. I can't help see the coincidence of the name *Dolores C* in connection to these events.

Using Google Maps, I zoomed in and placed a marker exactly where our tent had been set up the night Natascha and I woke in terror. Then I connected it to my sleeping site below the round structure on the hilltop. You can take any two points on a map and make a nice straight line between them, that's easy. There's always going to be a perfectly straight line between two points, but the map I saw had three points. What I had to figure out was: what's that third point in the middle?

After thinking for a while, I realized something happened, again with Natascha while we slept out under the stars, this time in March of 2011. It was along the gloriously scenic Burr Trail Road just east of the very small town of Boulder, Utah. Natascha had crossed the ocean to attend the annual UFO conference in the outskirts of Phoenix, and she added about a week to the end of her trip so we could drive around the desert again, like our previous adventures a year earlier. As we had done many times before, our plan was to sleep under the stars during the drive home to my house in Idaho after the conference. We found a sandy parking area tucked behind some scrubby trees about 150 yards off the Burr Trail Road—a perfect spot to sleep out.

When we climbed into our sleeping bags, I was tired and needed to sleep after our long day of driving, but Natascha was jet-lagged and restless. At some point in the night, she woke me up and said, "Mike, I can't sleep, I need to do something."

I said, "I'm sorry, I'm tired. Maybe take a walk. It's a beautiful night, don't worry, it's totally safe out here."

She said okay, and headed out to the road and started walking east. It was a perfectly calm night, and the sky was gleaming with a trillion stars in a way that can only happen in the desert. While she was walking, I was in my sleeping bag, drifting in and out of sleep. At the same time, I was listening to the hooting of a great horned owl, somewhere in the bushes very close to me. I could hear it, but I didn't understand why I couldn't see it. The hooting rang out loud and bold. Hearing this owl was absolutely magical, I truly loved it.

I can't help but recognize how similar this was to the howling coyote that was so close to me as I slept out along Highway 20 in March of 2013.

A little while later, Natascha woke me up saying, "Mike, we gotta leave!"

She explained that when she left me lying there, she was nervous but excited to walk alone on such an amazing night. She didn't need a flashlight, the glorious starlight was enough. Everything seemed so beautiful, and she felt like all her senses were heightened, as if there was a buzz in the air—she actually said she felt like she was *sparkling*.

Then, off to the side of the road, she saw a light. At first, she thought it was someone with a very bright flashlight, but it was moving too smoothly and too low, gliding down near the sagebrush. After a moment of watching, she realized it was a glowing orb of light, maybe two feet wide. She watched in amazement until it flashed brightly, like it exploded, and then it was gone. Now she was scared, and she ran back to where I was sleeping.

Exact sleeping spot, March 2nd 2011

After she woke me and said that we needed to leave, we hastily tossed everything in the car and started driving. It was probably close to four in the morning when we left our camping spot.

I used Google Maps and placed a little marker right where I had been sleeping along the Burr Trail Road. What I'm going to describe next changed everything for me.

Everything.

I clicked my mouse and brought up the yellow line that I had already created on the map. I was stunned to see that thin yellow line *exactly* bisect the spot where I had been lying while listening to that great horned owl. These three locations are exactly positioned along a 231-mile-long perfectly straight line.

If I had tried to align points like this in the era before computer-assisted mapping, I would've needed to draw a line on a paper map with a pencil and a ruler. Even if I had a really big map and a really sharp pencil, that line might be a mile wide. I can now make the line one pixel thick, zoom in on satellite imagery, and see this razor-thin line crossing precisely over where I'd been lying in the sand.

Before clicking that yellow line, my life had been swallowed up in questioning and yearning. I had been denying all the UFO events in my

coyote   orb   shaman

life. I knew *something* had been happening, but I couldn't admit what it obviously implied. Then one mouse-click brought up a thin yellow line, and it changed everything, including me. I saw three events along a straight line in a psychic flash, and these points screamed at me with spiritual meaning—the one on the west had a coyote, the one in the middle had an owl, and the one on the east had a shamanic ceremony.

Whatever is going on—this big totality of weirdness—has presented itself in a way that was distinctly and powerfully designed for me. Creating maps is what I do, I love making maps. Sleeping out under the stars is what I do, and I love it. I recognize the symbolic power of these three mystical elements along that line, *including an owl right in the center*. It feels like these experiences had been precisely tailored to the workings of my consciousness.

I cannot state this strongly enough, I was given a set of clues that only I could solve. This complex set of events, this *paradox syndrome*, was carefully orchestrated for me, and me alone.

I had spent years with an endless tape loop grinding away in my head, it was repeating *these things are impossible*. Yet I knew something had invaded my life, but I didn't understand what it was, or why it was happening. I was stuck in the feeling of *not knowing*.

But seeing that line on the map made it impossible to cling to that former identity of not knowing. I now *know*. I am directly intertwined with the UFO reality.

I hate the term "abductee" and all its baggage. That title is way too simplistic, but that's the term we're stuck with, and I use it grudgingly to define what's been going on in my life. That said, I am convinced that at the source of this mystery, there is something far more complex and far more bizarre than we dare imagine. The inadequate words abductee, experiencer, and contactee all seem flat in the face of this sweeping puzzle.

But the knowing remains.

The echoing clues

I call what happened on the night of March 10th, 2013, my confirmation event. It confirmed that something real is interacting with me and my life. It wasn't a singular incident, there was a great deal more, and it all emerged in connection to that one night under the stars. Here are a few more puzzle pieces that hammered home the power of this sweeping experience.

All three events took place on the new moon.

Two out of three of these events happened with my friend Natascha. I was alone on the night along Utah Highway 20 when I saw the big round structure up on the hillside. That happened on the night of March 10th, and *this is Natascha's birthday*.

I also heard a coyote that night. As I said before, this wasn't some distant yapping off in the sagebrush. It was so loud I can't understand why I didn't see it. In the Native American lore of the desert southwest, the coyote is considered the archetypal trickster. This means a playful character that defies normal conventions. They are rule breakers, jesters, and fools—playing tricks on both humans and gods. Historian Byrd Gibbens wrote:

> Many native traditions held clowns and tricksters as essential to any contact with the sacred... Humans had to have tricksters within the most sacred ceremonies for fear that they forget the sacred comes through upset, reversal, surprise. The trickster in most native traditions is essential to creation, to birth.[85]

Christopher O'Brien authored a book titled, *Stalking the Trickster*. He argued that the idea of the trickster might be the one overriding concept for the entirety of the UFO phenomenon. I contacted him, told him about my coyote experience, and asked what he thought it might mean. He listed a few ideas, but the first was that the coyote might indicate the end of a cycle in my life. This certainly rings true, especially in hindsight. A part of me died that night, and something new was re-born. If this howling coyote was playing a role, it might be the court jester heralding the arrival of my new life.

Two out of three of these events involved my friend Lucretia Heart, and both times she had an urgent need to call me in the middle of the night. She woke up twice with a profound sense of concern and was compelled to dial my number. She called my home phone in a panic on the same night I remember floating in the tent. I didn't get the call because I was traveling, and she didn't have my cell number. Three years later, she got up, once again well after midnight, with the intention of calling me. This was the same night I saw the big round structure on that hilltop in Utah. She said she was "freaking out" but never dialed the phone. Instead, she drank a glass of wine in the hopes of quelling her jangled nerves.

We've talked on the phone a lot over the years, but never at night. Lucretia described the need to call me so late as something decidedly unusual. She feels strongly there must have been some sort of telepathic link between us that created such a powerful compulsion. I agree.

I should repeat that Lucretia is very much a UFO experiencer, and a few of her owl stories are in this book. She also has a distinct memory of seeing something eerily similar to the big round structure I saw from my sleeping bag. Her experience tool place in the late autumn of 2006, seven years before my sighting. It happened at her home in Ohio while she was up late, unable to sleep. She looked out her window and saw a huge round "building" ringed with lights. It was positioned on a nearby hilltop. Like me, she thought it was a giant house, and didn't understand why she'd never noticed it before. Maybe the forest around her home had hidden it, and now that the leaves had fallen she finally had a clear view.

She saw it several times throughout that night, each time she passed that window. She went to bed thinking it must have been a big vacation home that was rarely used. The following morning she looked up and there was nothing there.

Hemi-sync vision

I will very occasionally meditate, and sometimes I'll listen to a guided meditation on my iPod. I like a series of audio tracks from Robert Monroe, the author of *Journeys Out of the Body* (1971), a first-person account of out of body travel.

He started a research facility, The Monroe Institute, with the mission of exploring human consciousness. He also pioneered a meditation technique using recorded audio called hemispheric synchronization. The process requires headphones, with a slightly different tone for each ear. To the listener, this sounds like nothing more than a calm humming. Monroe felt this system synchronizes the two hemispheres of one's brain, and there's evidence that this can help beginners more quickly achieve a state of deep meditation. These same sounds have the potential to evoke an altered state of consciousness.

There I was, alone in my living room, sitting on my little home-made meditation stool. My eyes were closed as I listened to Robert Monroe's voice describe some simple focusing techniques with the humming hemi-sync audio in the background. This would have been the fall of 2014.

I was calm and focused on his narration, and at some point he said, "Here is a simple way to remember any part of your life experience… Close your physical eyes and touch the fingers of your right hand gently to the center of your forehead. When you do this, *you will recall and remember immediately*, that which you consciously desire to remember…"[86]

Everything was so peaceful that I didn't think much about what he was saying, so there were no expectations when I touched my forehead. The instant my fingertips made contact, I saw myself lying on the ground in my sleeping bag surrounded by five or six spindly aliens. This image was in my mind's eye for barely a second, but it was unmistakably vivid, and

A clear momentary vision during meditation, 2014

I knew what I was seeing. It was a single snap-shot from the night of March 10th, 2013.

I wasn't at all surprised to see this, it felt like I'd been offered a gentle clue from some higher part of myself. The beings in the vision seemed to be wearing something tight-fitting and white, and they were taller than what would be the typical gray aliens. I was motionless in my sleeping bag at their feet. This scene in the Utah desert was presented without any fear or anxiety—as if to reassure me.

Curiously, these Robert Monroe audio files were sent to me from Derek, the fellow who's account opened the "maybe" people sub-chapter. His story was of seeing both an owl and UFO while camping out in the desert.

The momentary vision was clear, it was me on the ground surrounded by aliens. I recognize how seductive it would be to surrender to this image, to see it as a literal truth. Coming to terms with that mental snap-shot has been tricky, it might be my own mind deluding me, yet it might be exactly what happened.

He knows to surrender

During my reverse speech session with analyst Wayne Nicholson, I spoke about the power of all the events clustered around that night under the stars in Utah. He recorded my voice during our conversation, and here's a short excerpt from what I said.

> **Forward:** My confirmation event was lining that stuff up on the map...
>
> **Reversal:** Many owls.

Wow. It doesn't get any plainer than that. My confirmation event wasn't just one thing, it was many events lining up, going way beyond what happened in the Utah desert. The simple explanation would be that my confirmation event was "many owls" all lined up, all of them hitting me over the head with a reverberating smack.

In the earlier chapter on reverse speech there were a lot of examples of owls showing up in the context of an abductee's spoken words. Within some of these reversals the owls seem to play out as a synonym for the aliens themselves. So this might also mean *many aliens*.

During that same session, I talked specifically about the night of March 10th, 2013.

> **Forward:** I was in Utah and it was a cold night and I had a big sleeping bag and slept out under the stars...
>
> **Reversal:** He knows to surrender.

Again, this one is crystal clear. When I sleep outside, I will very often make a plea to the universe. I will state out loud that, "I am open and receptive to whatever you have to offer." Asking the universe is a little less churchy than asking God, but it's essentially the same thing. I am asking for a message. I don't do this every time I sleep outside, but I do it a lot, and I'll often get remarkable things showing up either in my dreams or within hours of waking. I don't remember if I actually made any formal plea that night, but I've done it enough over the years that lying on the ground under the stars has, for me, become an act of surrendering. This isn't something vague and fluffy, when I sleep outside I fully *surrender* to the stars above. I mean that sincerely.

How do we know these UFO contact experiences are real? When abduction researcher Mary Rodwell was asked that question, she replied that the people who've had these contact experiences will *change*. That is the evidence.

She said, "You don't change after a hallucination. You don't change after fantasies. But you do change after an experience, and every single person changes after these experiences. They change in a multitude of ways in terms of their understanding of their own spirituality and consciousness."[87]

A heap of orchestrated clues were set in my path, some were fleeting, like momentary images in my mind, while others were palpable and real. These events, and all the owls, carried an ominous weight that couldn't be denied. I have been confronted with a conflict, what Dr. John Mack called a *reified metaphor,* something that is presenting itself as both real and symbolic, and there is an anxious tension in this contradiction.

The sound of that unseen yapping coyote was vividly real—*more real than real*—and at the same time it was something mythical. It was an animal totem screaming for my attention, howling at the stars to make itself known. That scrappy little trickster, quite literally, *woke me up*. I've come to see the entirety of these experiences as both real and unreal. It's as if reality itself is acting as a metaphor, and it's happening for some profound reason. I think the reason is to wake me up, to make certain my eyes are open.

I'll also say that all these experiences, or maybe the intelligence behind them, have conspired to make me write this book. That's a bold thing to say, but that's how it feels. I have tried to let go and allow the deeper story to emerge. Like sleeping under the stars on a desert night, this book has been an act of surrendering.

Conclusion

The owl of Minerva only takes flight as the
dusk begins to fall.

—G.W.F. Hegel, *Philosophy of Right* (1820)

This quote from the German philosopher Hegel implies that it's only possible to understand an epoch, or even your own life, as it comes to an end. Without the clarity of hindsight, it would be impossible to know the full philosophical meaning of a story. This book has been my own story, my struggle to come to terms with my own experiences. It's my own epoch, and as it comes to its end I would love to offer up some tidy conclusion about owls and UFOs, but I'm just as baffled as I was at the onset of this project. I have been confronted by a genuine mystery, one that cannot be easily solved like a murder in the last pages of a detective novel. Instead, the owl and its relation to UFOs, begs for exploration, because no real explanation is possible.

After all this exploration, all I've come away with is that owls are playing some role, seemingly the same as they did for our ancient ancestors, a blurry overlapping of messenger, archetype, and alarm clock. If the owls are delivering messages, what I'm hearing is wake up, pay attention, and look within. The same could be said for UFOs.

The chapter on owls in dreams opened with a statement from pulp sci-fi publisher Ray Palmer, he said that flying saucers intrude into our lives "to make us think." I would amend that to say they intrude into our lives to make us think *deeply*. The same could be said for owls.

Trying to rein in these ideas about owls has confounded me. It feels like nothing was meant to be solved. Instead, it was all thrown in my face so I would chew on it until my rational mind cracked, with the ultimate outcome of seeing reality in an entirely new way. And with that, I might act in a new way too—and hopefully a better way.

Throughout these pages I have repeatedly asked, "Why owls?" The question is simple, the answer is not.

Before those owls flew above Kristen and me, I was in denial about all the UFO stuff that had happened in my life. Those owls at sunset didn't grant me enlightenment or anything so grand; instead, they initiated a process of crumbling. Some brittle part of me started falling away and something new has been trying to emerge.

All my life I'd been instructed to believe that reality is one way, it was well-defined and orderly, but that definition no longer fits. There is a loneliness that comes with seeing the world so fundamentally different, and what unfolded was a deep inward turn. I wallowed in my dark night of the soul, desperately clinging to something I knew was disintegrating. It was scary, and I tried my damnedest to deny what had happened. This book has been a sort of memoir of the challenges along that path. I'm still not washed clean of that old self—it's there all the time. I still bristle at the term UFO abductee, but I recognize it's the only vocabulary word that fits. Although imperfect, I accept it as describing who I am.

I have changed. I now see magic in the world around me. It's woven into the fabric of everything. This might seem naive, but I see owls, UFOs, and synchronicity as an expression of this magic, all blurring together and playing a singular role. These are deeply challenging ideas, but they are also seductive, and they've been tugging at my soul.

No matter how highly evolved we want to see ourselves, we're still just primitive people walking down the path at twilight. However, I sense there is a magical essence that wants to communicate with us as we move forward. If we are even a little bit aware, we'll find clues manifesting in the mist. These messengers are always there, either whispering or screaming, but they are truly there. For reasons I don't pretend to understand,

369

I've been bumping into owls along this path, and these owls are proof of magic.

I am different now. It was not seeing the aliens in my backyard, or the missing time, or seeing UFOs—these things didn't change me—it was the owls that pushed me off the cliff. It was the owls that forced me to look into my own experiences.

The challenge is, do I have the bravery not only to hear that message, but to truly live it.

About the author

Mike Clelland's 2015 book, *The Messengers*, was met with high praise. The focus of this work was been the mysterious connection between owls, synchronicities and UFO abduction. It was his firsthand experiences with these elusive events that have been the foundation for his research.

His long running website, *Hidden Experience*, explores alien contact and how it overlaps with a long list of other strange phenomena. It also features extended audio interviews with visionaries and experts examining the complexities of the overall UFO experience.

Mike is also considered an expert in the skills of ultralight backpacking, and is the author and illustrator of a series of instructional books on advanced outdoor techniques. He has worked as an outdoor educator in some of the most beautiful and remote areas of North America.

Other books by Mike Clelland

Stories from The Messengers

A companion to the groundbreaking ideas that began with *The Messengers*, and a further exploration into the connection, both symbolic and literal, between owls and UFOs. Each chapter tells a deeply personal story where these mysterious experiences are explored in depth. The ancient mythology of the owl is repeating itself within the modern UFO report. What plays out is a journey of transformation, with an owl at the heart of each story.

Hidden Experience

> "I wrote about the most difficult time of my life as it was happening, and posted it on a blog. I'd been confronted with a chain of strange events that seemed impossible to understand. I tried to dismiss what was happening, but all the clues pointed to one thing, and I was forced to ask myself, *Am I a UFO abductee?*"

Those are the opening lines from this first person memoir. This is a collection of the most vital posts from the popular blog *Hidden Experience*. It's a roller coaster journey of doubts and fears as I wrestle with UFOs, missing time, synchronicities and owls. The story that unfolds is scary, mysterious, disturbing—and at times funny. It's an insight into the strange challenges of otherworldly contact. Confronting the darkest unknowns ultimately lead to an awakening of consciousness.

Both of the works above are available as audiobooks, read by Mike.

Ultralight Backpackin' Tips

A backpacking instructional with cartoons! This humorous book carefully explains advanced techniques to reduce your pack weight, without sacrificing safety or comfort. This is the ultimate guide for traveling ultralight in the wilderness.

About the updated 2020 edition

This book was an obsession poured onto the page. Its creation wasn't a conscious decision, it was more like being pulled downstream. I'd been writing a lot on my blog about owls and UFOs, and those posts were all-consuming. That chapter of my life was a blur of listening to people and trying to document their experiences, as well as my own. I never said, "I will write a book," it was more that I woke up one morning and said, "Oh, I guess I'm writing a book."

Once started, I gave myself over completely, and before this book was finished, I knew there would be a second. That companion book, *Stories from The Messengers*, came out in 2017. After that came *Hidden Experience* in 2019. These follow-up books were more formal in their creation, and I learned a lot about writing in the process.

In early 2020 I began working with Michael Hacker, the voice artist who read *The Messengers* as an audiobook. This meant going back through the initial manuscript and finding the points where it addresses "the reader" and changing those to "the listener." During this review, I'd catch an awkward phrase, clean it up, and keep looking. At some point, I started at the beginning and scrutinized every sentence. When done, I started again with a more determined eye.

I've had experiences with owls that've played out like dreams, and I'm not alone. I'm now friends with a lot of the people in this book, and their experiences have continued. Some of these new developments are in this second edition, but otherwise it's essentially the same book that was published in 2015.

The text has been streamlined, some points have been clarified, and a few stories have been told more completely. I feel strongly it's now a better read.

I am astonished at the power of the experiences told within these pages. It has been an honor to give life to so many amazing stories. I am enormously proud of this book.

—Mike Clelland, September 2020

Index

Endnotes

1 Dolores Cannon, *The Custodians*, page 40-42. Ozark Mountain Publishers, 1999.

2 Strieber, Whitley, *Communion. A True Story*. p. 21, 103. Avon Books, paperback edition. Wilson & Neff, Inc., 1987

3 Interview with abduction researcher John Carpenter, time count 1:34:30, *The Paracast*, Jan 17, 2010, http://www.theparacast.com/podcast/now-playing-january-17-2009-john-carpenter/ Additional information via personal email correspondence with John Carpenter, June 2015.

4 Lucretia Heart, blog post title: *Talking Deer, Daytime Alien/Owl, & Love Letters: Summer of 1989,* https://spirals-end.livejournal.com/46181.html

5 Saebels, Corina, *The Collectors,* Trafford Publishing, 2007, p. 115.

6 Slattery, Peter Maxwell. *Operation Starseed*, Lulu.com (2013)

7 A more detailed account of Alan's story is featured in: *Stories From The Messengers* (2017)

8 Alan Caviness, *The Owl and the Deer Incident,* http://www.cavinessreport.com/CD1.html Also; *The Allen Jay Incident,* http://www.cavinessreport.com/ED4.html

9 *"How the Owl Tracks Its Prey: Experiments with trained barn owls reveal how their acute sense of hearing enables them to catch prey in the dark,"* Author: Masakazu Konishi. Source: American Scientist, Vol. 61, No. 4 (July-August 1973), pp. 414-424.

10 Randles, Jenny. *UFO Reality: A Critical Look at the Physical Evidence.* 1983. Randles, Jenny, "View from Britain," MUFON UFO Journal, June 2004, pp. 18-19.

11 Blog posting, *Looking out my window at night*, March 19th 2009, http://hiddenexperience.blogspot.com/2009/03/looking-out-my-window-at-night.html

12 A more detailed account of Heather's story is featured in: *Stories From The Messengers* (2017)

13 Most folks who study the UFO abduction experience haven't noticed any pattern of owls beyond the screen memory aspect. This anecdotal survey of abduction researchers feels accurate. I have asked all of these people the same questions either in person or on the phone, and the general response was the same. Jerome Clarke and John Carpenter were asked over email.

14 Mack, John E., M.D. *Passport to the Cosmos* (White Crow Books; Commemorative edition 2010). Original copyright 1999. Two separate passages were used to express Dr. Mack's concept of a reified metaphor: "I have used the term reified metaphor to capture the idea that these words may express both a literal or instrumental meaning and a metaphor or symbolic idea." (p. 70), "The report of this encounter of Dave's contains several examples of the paradoxical phenomenon I have called reified metaphor. On one hand, the experience is vividly and undeniably real for him, while at the same time it is deeply metaphoric or archetypal, including representations of death, birth, rebirth transcendence and enlightenment." (p. 162).

15 Hamilton, Bonnie Jean. *Invitation To The Self: Journey With The Star People* (lulu.com, 2011).

16 Austin, Tracie. *Alien Encounters in the Western United States* (Shiffer Publishing, Ltd. 2012), p. 39.

17 Håkan Blomqvist's blog, *Owls and UFOs*, 2013, https://ufoarchives.blogspot.com/2013/07/owls-and-ufos.html

18 Billy Meier (born February 3, 1937) is a controversial figure in the community of UFO researchers. Over the decades, this Swiss farmer has taken hundreds of photographs of alleged UFOs. These highly controversial pictures show flying saucers hovering above alpine meadows in Switzerland. The crafts themselves look somewhat goofy, ornamented with shiny metal spheres and corrugated trim. Many appear to be merely models suspended on wires. Meier reports regular contacts with human looking extraterrestrials called the Plejaren, and they gave him permission to photograph and film their "beamships" so that he could offer the world evidence for their existence. Meier's outlandish claims are

both believed and disputed by UFO skeptics and enthusiasts. That said, sometimes witness descriptions within UFOs reports match the Meier photos.

19 BBC article about owl imprint on window, 2011, https://www.bbc.com/news/uk-england-cumbria-14111152

20 Graham-Barber, Linda. *Say Boo!* (Scholastic Press, 1998).

21 Prescott, Gregg, M.S. Editor, *Edgar Cayce 11:11 and Synchronicity*, https://in5d.com/edgar-cayce-1111-and-synchronicity/

22 From a 2011 audio interview with Jeffrey Kripal, http://hiddenexperience.blog-spot.com/2011/11/audio-conversation-with-jeff-kripal.html

23 Surprise, Dr. Kirby. *Synchronicity*, 2012, Career Press p. 255

24 Surprise, Dr. Kirby. *Synchronicity*, 2012, Career Press, p. 47.

25 MacGregor, Rob and Trish. *The Synchronicity Highway,* Crossroad Press, 2013.

26 Chris Holly's site and her posting on owls, http://endlessjrny.blog-spot.com/2013/06/owls-and-odd-events.html

27 A longer more detailed telling of Stacey & Marla's story is featured in: *Stories From The Messengers* (2017).

28 Home, Shonagh. *Love and Spirit Medicine*, Turning Stone Press, 2013.

29 The quotes from Bert are from a 2013 audio interview, http://hiddenexperi-ence.blogspot.com/2013/11/bert-janssen-and-heather-clewett.html

30 A longer more detailed account of Bert & Heather's experiences is featured in: *Stories From The Messengers* (2017)

31 Text references two newsletters from reseacher Nancy Talbot. These are both from 2014, and detail the experiences of Robbert van den Broeke.

32 Campbell, Joseph and Moyers, Bill. *The Power of Myth*, (Anchor 1991).

33 *Grimm's Fairy Tales*, 1812 edition, by Jacob Ludwig Grimm and Wilhelm Carl Grimm. (Barnes & Noble Books, 1993). pp. 122-123

34 Morris, Desmond. *Owls*. (Reaktion Books, 2009), p. 56.

35 Long, Kim. *Owls: A Wildlife Handbook* (Johnson Printing, 1998).

36 Weston, Paul. *Aleister Crowley and the Aeon of Horus* (Avalonian Aeon Publications; 2009)

37 Hieronimus, Dr. Bob, from a personal email, Dec. 2014. Excerpt: The owl is both a symbol of life and death. What is death. One dies in the physical world and reenters the spiritual dimension. One then leaves the spiritual dimension and returns to the physical and the cycle continues. Death is not the end of anything, but reentering other dimensions. You don't say how far back you are taking your research, but if you are basing it on the Greco-Roman patriarchal stories written by Homer and Hesiod, then you are missing 90% of the iceberg under the surface. These are not ancient sources when it comes to the owl symbolism, which goes back at least as far as 30,000 B.C.

38 Jef Harvey, from an audio interview with Mel Fabergas, *Veritas Radio,* posted April 12, 2013. Minimal editing for clarity.

39 Jim Sparks discusses his Alien Abduction Experiences, MUFON 2007, https://www.YouTube.com/watch?v=WveMU0XUd9c&feature=youtu.be&t=1m3s

40 Midgley, Mary. *Owl of Minerva: A Memoir* (Routledge; New edition, 2005) p. xi.

41 *Orcas circle ferry transporting tribal artifacts to Bainbridge Island*, The Associated Press, https://www.seattletimes.com/seattle-news/orcas-circle-ferry-transporting-tribal-artifacts-to-bainbridge-island/ - Also, some of the ideas in this chapter came from a comment posted on my blog by "tiny junco" from 2013.

42 Campbell, Joseph and Moyers, Bill. *The Power of Myth*. (Anchor, 1991), p. 206.

43 Isley, Niara Teresa, *Facing the Shadow, Embracing the Light: A Journey of Spirit Retrieval and Awakening* (CreateSpace, 2013)

44 Graham, Robbie. *Silver Screen Saucers: Sorting Fact from Fantasy in Hollywood's UFO Movies* (White Crow Books, 2015).

45 Vallee, Jacques. *Passport to Magonia: From Folklore to Flying Saucers* (Henry Regnery Company, 1969), and subsequent editions.

46 Weston, Paul. *Avalonian Aeon*. (Avalonian Aeon, 2010).

47 Randles, Jenny. *Beyond Explanation: The Paranormal Experiences of Famous People* (Salem House Publishers,1986).

48 Sitting at Tolkien's Table, https://runesoup.com/2013/09/sitting-at-tolkiens-table-a-middle-earth-guide-to-life/

49 This book was first published in 2015, and the statement that the "US government has a strict policy of denial " about UFOs is no longer accurate. *The New York Times* ran a series of articles beginning on December 16, 2017 where Navy sources spoke on the record that they had witnessed unidentified craft. There was also an admission of a pentagon program studying the subject. This reporting shied away from any mention of abduction or anything paranormal, focusing instead on testimony from pilots and radar operators. These articles have changed the way UFOs have been treated in main stream news.

50 Hanson, Mike. *Bohemian Grove: Cult of Conspiracy* (River Crest Publishing, 2012).

51 Zimmermann, Linda. *In the Night Sky* (Eagle Press, 2013). 57% Kindle version.

52 I don't have a recording of Budd saying that in his kitchen, but I feel I'm paraphrasing him pretty closely. When I heard him say it, it had the feel of something he had said before, like I wasn't the first person in his kitchen to hear those comments.

53 YouTube video, *Experiencers John E Mack*, 13:25 time count, https://www.YouTube.com/watch?v=LFSxjBY9bPl

54 Keel, John A. *The Complete Guide to Mysterious Beings*, p. 262-263. (Tor Books, 2002). First published as *Strange Creatures from Time and Space*, 1970 by Fawcett Publications.

55 Gerhard, Ken. *Encounters with Flying Humanoids* (Llewellyn, 2013), p. 65

56 Nick Redfern wrote a two part article on the Owlman for the *Mysterious Universe* website. Part one, http://mysteriousuniverse.org/2015/02/red-eyed-owlman-or-black-eyed-alien/. Part two, http://mysteriousuniverse.org/2015/02/the-owl-ufo-connection-continues/

57 Tucker, Lindy. *Beeping UFOs,* http://www.beepingufos.com/sounds/

58 Tucker, Lindy. "Tracing Sound to UFO Encounters," *MUFON UFO Journal*, #318, October 1994. p. 3-7.

59 The strange life of Kenneth Arnold is featured in a full chapter of: *Stories From The Messengers* (2017)

60 Audio interview with David Weatherly, 2012, http://hiddenexperience.blog-spot.com/2012/07/audio-conversation-with-david-weatherly.html

61 Campbell, Joseph and Moyers, Bill. *The Power of Myth* (Anchor, 1991) p. 107.

62 Grof, Stanislav. *The Cosmic Game: Explorations of the Frontiers of Human Consciousness* (State University of New York Press, 1998), p. 96.

63 Phone conversation by author with Sequoia Trueblood, March 4, 2015. Mack, John. Audio interview with Whitley Strieber, Dreamland Nov. 14th 1999. Subscribers only. Edited slightly for clarity.

64 Laufer, Berthold. *Origins of the Word Shaman*, American Anthropologist 19, (1917): p. 326-7. Sarangerel. *Chosen by the Spirits: Following Your Shamanic Calling,* (Destiny Books, 2001).

65 A more detailed account of Adrianne's story is featured in: *Stories From The Messengers* (2017)

66 The name *Lauren* traces back to the laurel tree, and the Latin meaning for laurel is "seer of second sight" or "gift of prophecy."

67 Strieber, Whitley. *Solving the Communion Enigma: What is to come* (Tarcher, 2012).

68 Peter and Elizabeth Fenwick. *The Art Of Dying* (Bloomsbury Academic, 2008).

69 Fenwick, Peter, *"Experiences surrounding near-death and dying"* YouTube video, 1:22:00 time count, https://www.YouTube.com/watch?v=rlXK68tMm7Y

70 A more complete account of Gypsy Woman's experiences is featured in: *Stories From The Messengers* (2017)

71 Lonn Friend podcast Energize, episode 35: https://www.stitcher.com/podcast/energize-the-lonn-friend-podcast/e/30784457

72 Quoted from Fred Nadis, *The Man From Mars, Ray Palmer's Amazing Pulp Journey* (Penguin Books, 2013). The full quote, from 1976, one year before Palmer's death, was: "It is still true, as I predicted in 1947, that no flying saucer has ever been 'captured' or even

'proved.' They are as real as Shaver's caves, and just as 'psychic.' They are unknown, the hidden world, that all of us at one time or another are aware exists, and which intrudes on our lives to make us think."

73 As an aside, it's worth explaining why the 1990s was a busy time for some abductees. The late 1980s saw the publication of Whitley Strieber's *Communion* and Budd Hopkins *Intruders*, both from 1987. In the follow-up to these two books, there was a flood of other books and tabloid television documentaries. By the early 1990s, the public awareness of the UFO abduction phenomenon had gone from virtually zero to commonplace. This societal recognition paralleled what seems to have been a high point on the bell curve of abduction activity. I've spoken to a lot of people with these experiences, and they'll say something to the effect of: I was getting taken a few times a week in the 80s and 90s, but it has tapered off since then. This doesn't mean the abduction events have stopped—they still seem to be happening—but the experiences have changed. One thought is that these are just aliens visiting Earth to gather data on humans. They are following a defined program of some sort. This would mean that there is a beginning, middle, and end to their agenda. Some reports imply that the UFO occupants are here to collect human genetics and create a psychically advanced hybrid race of new humans. Both men and women tell of sexual and reproductive procedures at the hands of their alien abductors. At some later time, these people are shown partially human children while aboard a craft. This might account for the busy time reported by abductees all across the globe. The aliens had a strict timetable and job to perform. If this was happening in the 80s and 90s, there should now be a new breed of young adults out there on a mothership for some unknown purpose. Perhaps to come down to earth in the event of some global upheaval, then they can play their role in helping humanity survive dire events. There is no way to know what it all might mean, but these avenues of speculation are commonplace within the UFO research community.

74 Dreamland audio interview hosted by Anne Strieber, 2013, interview with Rob and Trish MacGregor on their book *Aliens in the Backyard*. https://www.unknowncountry.com/dreamland/syncrhonicity-close-encounters-and-the-fear-factor/ Also, blog post titled: *Owls and Anne Strieber:* http://hiddenexperience.blogspot.com/2013/05/owls-and-anne-strieber.html

75 Eve Lorgen, *"Owl Synchronicities, UFO Experiencers and Reverse Speech Analysis,"* Posted on Sept. 15, 2013, https://evelorgen.com/wp/articles/miscellaneous/owl-synchronicities-ufo-experiencers-and-reverse-speech-analysis/

76 Audio clips and analysis from Patricia Mason, 1998. *UFO Experiencer Reversals,* http://members.tripod.com/~Patricia_Mason/ufo.html

Interview with David Oates, by Deborah L. Lindemann, C.H.T., 1998, http://reversespeech.com/2012/07/reverse-speechanalysis-interview-with-david-john-oates/

78 Strieber, Whitley, *The Key: A True Encounter* (Tarcher; Reprint edition 2011).

79 Whitley Strieber Speech Reversals with Wayne Nicholson, archived interview dated December 6, 2008, https://www.unknowncountry.com/subscriber-specials/whitley-strieber-speech-reversals/

80 Larkins, Lisette. *Calling on Extraterrestrials,* (Hampton Roads, 2003) p. 199-200.

81 NUFORC (National UFO Reporting Center) links, http://nuforc.org/webreports/027/S27412.html (and) http://www.nuforc.org/CBIndex.htm

82 Smith, Jacquelin. *Star Origins And Wisdom Of Animals: Talks With Animal Souls* (AuthorHouse, 2010).

83 Hyemeyohsts Storm. *The Seven Arrows* (Ballantine Books 1972).

84 Audio podcast describing the events of October of 2009: http://hiddenexperience.blogspot.com/2010/09/october-2009-audio.html - This is also covered in the book Hidden Experience (2019).

85 Gibbens, Byrd, quoted in *Napalm and Silly Putty* by George Carlin (Hachette Books, 2001).

86 Blog post with audio: http://hiddenexperience.blogspot.com/2015/07/hemi-sync-vision-with-audio.html

87 *Skeptiko* podcast with Alex Tsakiris interviewing Mary Rodwell, episode 233. http://www.skeptiko.com/233-mary-rodwell-extrodinary-human-experieences-matter/

If you have ever had any odd experiences with owls, please feel free to contact me. I've been documenting and archiving these accounts, and can insure anonymity to anyone who shares their story. People all over the world are having remarkable experiences with these beautiful creatures. It's a mystery that may never be solved, yet there is an unmistakable power within each story.

There is contact infomation listed at both *mikeclelland.com* and *hiddenexperience.blogspot.com*

Sincerely,
Mike Clelland

Made in the USA
Monee, IL
23 October 2021